CONTEMPORARY IRISH SOCIAL POLICY

BY THE SAME EDITORS

IRISH SOCIAL POLICY IN CONTEXT

edited by
Gabriel Kiely, Anne O'Donnell,
Patricia Kennedy and Suzanne Quin

Irish Social Policy in Context traces the historical development of Irish social policy and discusses major influences – such as the European Union – on policy formation. Ireland is presented in a comparative context and as an example of the mixed economy of welfare. The policy-making process is analysed, and the financing and evaluation of social policy measures are clearly and fully explained. Separate chapters are devoted to the treatment of women, the concept of citizenship, the rise in the significance of partnerships, the place of the family, the understanding and measurement of poverty and the role of consumer participation.

Intended especially as a textbook for students of social policy, it is also a basic reference book for anyone wishing to gain an understanding of the historical background to social policy making in Ireland. *Irish Social Policy in Context* is a companion volume to *Contemporary Irish Social Policy*.

July 1999 ISBN 1 900621 25 8

Contemporary Irish Social Policy

edited by

Suzanne Quin
Patricia Kennedy
Anne O'Donnell
Gabriel Kiely

University College Dublin Press
Preas Choláiste Ollscoile Bhaile Átha Cliath

First published 1999 by University College Dublin Press,
Newman House, 86 St Stephen's Green, Dublin 2, Ireland

© The editors and contributors 1999
ISBN 1 900621 24 X

Cataloguing in Publication data available from the British Library

Typset in Bantry, Ireland, in 11/12½ Bembo and Gill Sans by Elaine Shiels
Index by John Loftus
Printed in Ireland by Colour Books, Dublin

Contents

This book is dedicated to the memory
of Linda Marie Kiely

Preface

This book is designed primarily as a textbook on Irish Social Policy but also will be of interest to a much wider readership. While being a companion volume to *Irish Social Policy in Context* by the same editors, it is also a stand-alone book providing the reader with a comprehensive review of the range of social policy provision in Ireland. Therefore, in addition to being a textbook, it is also a basic reference book for anyone wishing to gain an understanding of the extent to which social policy impacts on the lives of so many people in Ireland today.

In planning the contents, the editors sought to ensure that the major areas of Social Policy provision, those of education, income maintenance, employment, housing and health, were included. With regard to the delivery of Irish Social Policy, the editors elected to have the area of personal social services addressed within the appropriate chapters relating to different categories of consumers of services including children, people with disabilities, older people, Travellers and the growing population of refugees and asylum seekers in Ireland. Also incorporated were key areas of policy development such as youth policy, the criminal justice system and the field of drugs policy.

Each chapter, therefore, is complete in itself, providing both description and analysis of current policy, an overview of its historical development, and discussion of current and future issues in the field. In addition to a bibliography, each chapter has a short list of recommended readings indicating key texts in the subject. Also included at the end of the chapter is a table of the main policy developments to facilitate understanding of the sequence and timing of change in each field.

The authors of each of the chapters were selected according to their expertise in the specific area. Care was taken to provide a cross-section of writers in the field of social policy to include academics, researchers and managers of services in both the public and voluntary sectors. An examination of the biographical details of the authors shows them to be well qualified in a variety of respects for the task they have undertaken. One interesting aspect of this is that each of the authors currently engaged in academic research and teaching has also had direct work experience in their field of social policy.

Suzanne Quin
Patricia Kennedy
Anne O'Donnell
Gabriel Kiely
Dublin, January 1999

I
Introduction:
Social Policy and Social
Change in Ireland

This is a particularly appropriate time for new texts in Irish Social Policy for a variety of reasons, not least of which is the coming to the end of a century and moving into the new millennium. This has coincided with a time of sweeping social and economic changes in Irish society. The enormity of these changes is evident from their diverse impact on the many aspects of social policy covered in the companion volume *Irish Social Policy in Context*.

One of the most obvious of these changes has been the unprecedented economic growth which has been labelled the 'Celtic Tiger'. Contrast this with the tone of a text such as this had it been published a decade ago when the overriding themes would be of debt, cutbacks, spiralling unemployment and pressures on social welfare provision. The current climate of remarkable growth which is predicted to continue into the new century provides a unique opportunity for the creation and development of social policies which contribute to the quality of life of all citizens and ensure that each sector of society benefits. That this will not happen automatically is evident. Fitzgerald in her chapter quotes the view of Lemass that a rising tide will raise all boats, an assumption still found today, although now increasingly challenged by policy makers. That this is not so is graphically illustrated in Fitzgerald's chapter in relation to the long-term unemployed, Silke's concerning those on the lower and lowest end of the housing market and Crowley's in relation to the Travelling community. The last named provides a particular graphic illustration of deprivation in the midst of relative plenty and evidence that changes in policy can only be effective when matched by adequate resources. That this small section of Irish society remains so under-resourced can now be accounted for only by lack of will rather than funds.

The extent of change in the Irish economy has resulted in not just an inflow of returned migrants but also the new phenomenon of other EU nationals coming in response to the availability of employment (Fitzgerald). They are one element of the shift from a monocultural to a multicultural society in Ireland. Clearly not all who come to settle here have the same range of skills and choices. Moran's chapter on social policy and refugees examines the needs of those who have experienced trauma and displacement, and the challenges for traditional policies to be responsive to a new set of needs.

The change from a monocultural to a multicultural society creates both opportunities and challenges for all aspects of policy provision. The need to provide a service for consumers with differing cultural practices, traditions and religious beliefs is in marked contrast to the assumptions of sameness which have been a feature of service delivery in Ireland. Moreover, this change coincides with the declining power, influence and service capacity of the Roman Catholic Church which, up to recently, has played a major role directly and indirectly in many areas of social policy in Ireland but particularly in the fields of educational provision (see Clancy), health care (see Quin) and youth policy (see Kennedy).

The declining role of the Roman Catholic Church, both as a conservative, traditionalist force and as a provider and innovator of services, is but one further aspect of change in Irish society which influences social policy. Along with its fellow EU member states, there are social changes such as the increasing proportion of lone parent families who are disproportionately represented in statistics pertaining to poverty and welfare dependency (see Mills). While low in comparison with other EU countries, the proportion of married women in the workforce is increasing (Fitzgerald), which has implications for the provision of family care for children (see Richardson), those with physical dependency arising from disability or those with serious learning disability (see Quin and Redmond) or older people in need of care (see O'Loughlin). This raises issues for a policy of community-based care which is built on the assumption of availability and willingness on the part of one section of society to forego gainful employment in order to provide largely unsupported care.

This assumed altruism is a good example of how social policies can be based on principles, expectations and assumptions about what is appropriate and desirable. In some areas of policy there seems to be wide acceptance of what are desirable goals and acceptable means. Silke's chapter on housing policy illustrates this in relation to home ownership. He demonstrates the extent to which pursuance of this policy has resulted in significant attainment of the desired goal but at a high cost to consumers in a time of rapidly increasing house prices in relation to earnings and costs to the exchequer in subsidies given and income foregone. The greatest costs, however, are borne by those unable to enter the housing market on account of inadequate means. Unlike other EU countries, Silke shows that in Ireland local authority housing and much of the private rented market provide only for residual need rather than offering viable alternatives and choices. Another example of accepted 'givens' is the continued public/private mix in the provision of education (see Clancy) and health services (see Quin).

The impact of changing demography is of significance for the provision and development of different areas of Irish social policy in the coming decades. Clancy refers to the decline in numbers of participants in primary and secondary levels of education as providing the opportunity to improve teacher/pupil ratios and to develop second-chance education to a much greater extent than is available presently. As in other EU countries, older people constitute a growing sector of the population, albeit to a lesser extent than in some member states such as Germany and France. The large proportion of single older people, along with the disproportional increase in those described as older elderly, is likely to place increasing demands on health and, more particularly, on personal social services for this group as described by O'Loughlin. At the other end of the age spectrum, the needs of the young, in particular children at risk of abuse or neglect (see Richardson), and young people, especially those in deprived urban areas (see Kennedy), are evident. The costs of not recognising and responding to such needs are high, primarily for the individual concerned and also for society as a whole as discussed by Cotter in his chapter in relation to criminal behaviour and its consequences and Loughran's chapter in respect of drug abuse.

It is the very interrelationship between different aspects of social policy which makes a multidimensional approach to the solution of social problems so important. Examples of the connection between different areas identified in this text are the relationship between early school leaving (Clancy) and the subsequent risk of long-term unemployment (Fitzgerald). Another is the effect of homelessness or of poor-quality housing (Silke) linked to poverty (Mills) and the likelihood of poor health (Quin).

Changes in legislation can be both a cause and a consequence of service development. Richardson demonstrates the impact of childcare legislation on the provision of childcare services. In addition to national legislation, of great consequence also has been the impact of EU directives and the provision of EU funding in social services (see in particular the chapters by Crowley on Travellers and Moran on refugees).

Changes in thinking and attitudes can lead to a redefinition of a social issue and its solution on the part of those concerned. This is evident in the chapter by Quin and Redmond in relation to disability. There can be no doubt that the media now play a significant role in the definition of social problems and the attention given to any one of them at a given time. In relation to childcare, Richardson, for example, shows the impact of child abuse scandals and the resulting impetus for change in this area.

Readers who are interested in pursuing the contextual influences which have impacted on the development of the many areas of social policy contained in this book are referred to its companion text *Irish Social Policy in Context*. The factors which have shaped current policy, the impact of the EU on policy development, the changing social climate and the growing participation of service consumers are considered at length in that volume. Taken separately and together, these two new texts offer the reader a reference point for understanding current Irish social policy, the elements which have forged its creation and development, and the challenges facing it in the early decades of the twenty-first century.

2
Income Maintenance

Frank Mills

INTRODUCTION

This chapter traces the historical development of income maintenance services in Ireland and examines some of the factors that influenced this development. The distinctive features of the Irish system are outlined and the growth in expenditure and the reasons for this growth are explored. The criteria for evaluating the system employed by the Commission on Social Welfare are examined. Some current problems with the system are outlined. These include problems of take-up, unemployment traps and poverty traps. The factors contributing to unemployment and poverty traps are described and recent changes introduced to tackle these problems are enumerated. Finally, a radical alternative to the present system, i.e. a Basic Income System, is described and evaluated.

HISTORICAL BACKGROUND

Until the middle of the nineteenth century, no state income maintenance system existed in Ireland. Under the Brehon Law, local rulers provided hospitaller facilities for the sick and homeless. However, with the coming of Christianity and the subsequent development of a network of monasteries, a system of care for the destitute, sick and homeless was provided throughout the country. Following the Reformation this system was no longer available, and over the following centuries a combination of plantations and penal laws resulted by the second quarter of the nineteenth century in a population that was dispossessed, poverty-stricken and with no recourse to relief other than begging and charity.

In England the Poor Relief Act of 1601 was introduced to deal with the problem of pauperism and begging. However, its provisions did not apply to Ireland. This Act allowed for the provision of work, the establishment of workhouses and the levying of local rates to pay for these provisions. In the eighteenth century a small number of workhouses were established in Ireland – Dublin (1703), Cork (1735) and Belfast (1774). Under the legislation, beggars and vagrants were rounded up and effectively forced to work within the workhouses. In Dublin and Cork these workhouses also catered for abandoned children.

In England throughout most of the eighteenth century and the earlier part of the nineteenth century, relief was provided in the main outside the workhouse. However, the Act of 1834 changed this and provided that relief would be provided only within the workhouses; it also introduced the infamous 'workhouse test'. This stipulated that the condition of inmates should be less tolerable than that of the lowest labourer outside. The provisions of this Act were applied to Ireland under the Poor Relief (Ireland) Act 1838. However, there was a problem with enforcing the workhouse test in Ireland, where the lowest labourers were themselves below subsistence level.

The Irish were unwilling inmates of the workhouse, that is, until the failure of the potato crop in 1846 and the ensuing famine. The workhouses were overwhelmed with the numbers seeking entry, forcing the government of the day to introduce the Poor Relief (Ireland) Act 1847. This introduced for the first time in Ireland the concept of outdoor relief, albeit in a very limited form.

THE DEVELOPMENT OF INCOME
MAINTENANCE SERVICES IN IRELAND

The form of outdoor relief introduced under the 1847 Act remained the only form of state income maintenance until the Workmen's Compensation Act of 1897, which required employers to pay compensation where an accident at work led to the injury or death of an employee. The Old Age Pension Act, 1908, introduced a strictly means-tested pension for people over seventy years old. The concept of social insurance was introduced with the National Insurance Act, 1911. This provided for the payment of Unemployment Benefit and Sickness Benefit to insured persons. However, it was not until 1933 that the means-tested Unemployment Assistance was introduced.

Statutory provision for blind persons was introduced in 1920, but provisions for widows and orphans did not come into effect until 1935. While these and other categories were awaiting designated state schemes, claimants had recourse only to the provisions of the Poor Law, which had been renamed Home Assistance in 1923. Children's Allowances were introduced in 1944 for families with three or more children. The war years also saw the introduction of the Cheap Fuel and the Cheap Footwear schemes.

There were no developments of income maintenance schemes during the 1950s. However the 1960s saw the introduction of the Contributory Old Age Pension (1961), and Occupational Injuries Benefit (1966), Free Travel and Free Electricity (1967). In the 1970s a wide range of new schemes were introduced: Retirement Pension, Invalidity Pension and Deserted Wife's Allowance (1970); Deserted Wife's Benefit and Unmarried Mother's Allowance (1973); Prisoner's Wife's Allowance, Single Woman's Allowance and Pay-related Benefit (1974) and, most significantly, the Supplementary Welfare Allowance Act (1977), which, in the words of the late Frank Cluskey, removed 'the last vestiges of the Poor Law'.

The 1980s saw the introduction of the National Fuel Scheme (1980), Family Income Supplement (1984) and Lone Parent's Allowance (1989). The 1990s commenced with the introduction of the Carer's Allowance and the Back to School Clothing Scheme (1990), followed by Survivor's Pension, Health and Safety Benefit and Adoptive Benefit (1994), Disability Allowance (1996) and the One Parent Family Allowance (1997).

While all of the above schemes are under the control of the Minister for Social, Community and Family Affairs, it is important to note that over the years a number of income maintenance schemes were introduced by the Department of Health. These included the Infectious Diseases Maintenance Allowance (1947), the Disabled Person's Maintenance Allowance (1954) and the Domiciliary Care Allowance (1973). The Supplementary Welfare Allowance Scheme is unusual in that it is funded by and comes under the control of the Department of Social, Community and Family Affairs, yet it is administered by the health boards, which come under the control of the Department of Health.

Factors Influencing the Development of Income Maintenance

At the outset it must be said that income maintenance services in Ireland developed in a fairly ad hoc and piecemeal manner. There is no evidence of any coherent plan or consistent ideology underlying their development. However, at various stages a number of factors can be seen to have influenced the type and the timing of income maintenance schemes. Indeed, as Cousins (1995: 10) points out, it could be argued that 'the social welfare system is a reflection of the economic, political, ideological and cultural structures and conflicts in Irish society'.

The UK Influence

Clearly, in the period prior to independence, developments in Ireland
followed on from developments in the UK, albeit with a time lag.
However, the introduction of workmen's compensation, old-age pensions
and national insurance coincided with their introduction in the UK,
with the notable exception that medical care was not covered by
national insurance in Ireland. Ireland did not adopt the Beveridge model
of the welfare state introduced in the UK in 1948. Indeed, for several
decades following, it lagged far behind income maintenance services in
the UK. Ireland did not, however, experience the retrenchment of services
that occurred in the UK in the 1980s. In many cases schemes were
introduced in Ireland after they had been tried and tested in the UK. A
recent example would be Family Income Supplement.

During the early decades of the welfare state, commentators
frequently pointed out the meagreness of the income maintenance provisions in Ireland compared with their more generous counterparts in
the UK. In the 1990s, it is arguable that the situation has reversed in that
many mainstream schemes in Ireland are now more generous that their
UK equivalents.

Economic Developments

The economic state of the country at any point in time had an important
influence on income maintenance services. In times of economic depression expenditure on income maintenance tended to rise, owing to
increased levels of unemployment, and at the same time developments
came to a standstill. A good example is the 1950s where, at a time of
economic depression, no developments took place. However, in the
economic boom of the sixties and early seventies a lot of important
developments were introduced. The late 1970s and 1980s saw rapid
increases in expenditure on income maintenance, mainly due to the
dramatic increase in unemployment. This in turn led to attempts to
control, and in some cases cut, income maintenance services.

Role of the Catholic Church

While the Catholic Church has played a major role in many aspects of
social policy in Ireland, notably in the areas of health and education, its
role in income maintenance is less clear-cut. In 1911, when social
insurance was being introduced, the Catholic Church and the medical
profession both opposed the extension of social insurance to cover
medical costs. However, in 1945, the bishop of Clonfert, Dr Dignam,

was ahead of the government of the day when he published a paper calling for the increased coverage and expansion of social insurance. In more recent times the Conference of Religious of Ireland (CORI) has played a major role in providing a critique of the existing social welfare system and in suggesting radical alternatives.

In the early part of the century the Catholic Church, based on the principle of subsidiarity, would have been opposed to excessive intervention by the state in the area of income maintenance. However, the state at that time was not in a position, for economic reasons, to provide improved services. It is interesting that in recent years the Catholic Church has been calling for increased action by the state to combat poverty and social exclusion.

Special Interest Groups

Special interest groups have always played a role in lobbying for change in the income maintenance system. The First Commission on the Status of Women, which reported in 1972, led to the development of a number of income maintenance schemes targeted specifically at women. The trade union movement through its involvement in national agreements has been an important voice in calling for and securing improvements in income maintenance schemes. In more recent times, community and voluntary groups and groups representing the socially excluded have played an important role and have been given a voice in the development of services through involvement in the National Economic and Social Forum (NESF).

Role of the European Union (EU)

The EU directive on the equal treatment of men and women in matters of social security was a very important development for income maintenance services in Ireland. Prior to the implementation of the Directive, married women received lower rates of social welfare payments and in some instances were paid for a shorter period than men. Likewise, in most cases married women were excluded from claiming unemployment assistance. The Government did not introduce the requisite legislation to give effect to the Directive until two years after the operative date leading to successful claims for arrears by the women affected. Also, it changed the means test in relation to unemployment assistance to ensure that households were no better off if the wife claimed unemployment assistance or remained as a dependant of her husband.

DISTINCTIVE FEATURES OF THE IRISH
INCOME MAINTENANCE SYSTEM

Contingency-Based

Entitlement to income maintenance is based on the contingency experienced by a claimant (e.g. unemployment, old age, illness). The one
exception is the Supplementary Welfare Allowance Scheme, which is
based on need. The contingency can determine not only the category
of payment but also the amount of payment. Thus, two households of
similar size and similar need may receive different amounts of income
maintenance depending on the category of payment they receive. While
efforts have been made in recent years to equalize the rates of payment
between the different categories, the difference between the lowest rate
of payment for a single person (Supplementary Welfare Allowance) and
the highest rate payable to that person (Contributory Old Age Pension)
is 21% (June 1998 rates).

Social Insurance Payments

Payments based on contributions to the Social Insurance Fund by both
employees and employers are an important feature of the Irish income
maintenance system. Deductions are a percentage of pay up to a ceiling,
hence the term pay–related social insurance (PRSI). The policy over the
years has been to increase the number of people paying PRSI and thus
increase the number of people in receipt of social insurance payments. In
general, claimants must have paid a defined number of contributions in
order to qualify for payment. If they meet this condition, the prescribed
rate of payment is made irrespective of any other income the claimant or
their adult dependant may have. Some social insurance schemes are of a
fixed duration (e.g. unemployment benefit is payable for a period of 15
months). Over the years, the contributions made into the Fund have
been insufficient to cover payments made and the shortfall has been met
out of general taxation. However, recently, due to the increased level of
employment in the country, the Fund has shown a surplus.

Social Assistance Payments

The essential difference between social insurance and social assistance
payments is that in the case of the latter a means test is applied to
determine eligibility. There are different means tests for different schemes.
This can lead to a situation whereby a person recently unemployed could
find themselves applying within the space of a week for unemployment

assistance, Supplementary Welfare Allowance, a medical card, Back-to-School clothing scheme, and undergoing a separate means test for each scheme. The main items taken into account in a means test are cash income, the value of investments, the income of a spouse or cohabitee and, in some instances, the value accruing from the enjoyment of free board and lodgings. The manner in which these factors are taken into account varies between the schemes. The situation is extremely complex and can at times lead to perverse results, for example, applying a value to free board and lodgings to a single person living at home can result in the person being asked to leave. This person is then paid their full entitlement and in addition if they move into private rented accommodation they may qualify for a rent allowance. The eventual cost to the state will be greater than if they had paid the full entitlement to the person while they were residing at home. There is a compelling case for rationalizing the means tests, thus ensuring that at any point in time a person who undergoes the test can have their entitlement to all social assistance payments decided at the one time.

Cash vs Kind

The majority of income maintenance payments are in cash rather than in kind. However over the years a number of payments were made in kind. The Cheap Footwear Scheme and the Cheap Fuel Scheme are examples where goods or vouchers were supplied to claimants. Other examples of payments in kind are free electricity, free travel and free telephone rental. It was also the practice over the years under the Home Assistance Scheme and more recently the Supplementary Welfare Allowance scheme to provide applicants for exceptional needs payments with goods rather than cash. In many instances it has been argued that the provision of goods or vouchers is demeaning and paternalistic. Thus, payments under the national fuel scheme and the Back-to-School clothing scheme are now made by cash and likewise most payments under the supplementary allowance scheme are made by way of cash payment.

Entitlement vs Discretion

Virtually all the main income maintenance schemes are entitlement based, that is they are prescribed by rules and regulations governing entitlement and if an individual fulfils the conditions for entitlement they receive the payment. If they fail to meet the conditions they receive no payment, subject to a right to appeal the decision. In effect the administrator has virtually no discretion in the matter. This system has the merit of being transparent and impartial. However, it can lead to situations in which an individual is disallowed on a minor technicality.

The Supplementary Welfare Allowance scheme by contrast has large elements of discretion, especially in relation to exceptional need payments, which are one-off payments designed to meet unplanned need. In this scheme the sole criterion for eligibility is need. The scheme recognizes that no two individuals' needs are ever totally identical, and allows payments to be tailored to suit the individual circumstances. The downside of this is that the impression can be given that decisions are arbitrary and are based on the particular prejudices of the administrator. The fact that internal guidelines were not published added to this impression. This situation was rectified in October 1998 when the Freedom of Information legislation was applied to the scheme. It is clearly not possible for entitlement-based schemes to anticipate and cater for all the possible current or future needs of individuals. A scheme with large elements of discretion is therefore an important safety net for all the schemes of income maintenance.

EXPENDITURE

The total expenditure of the Department of Social, Community and Family Affairs in 1997 was £4,524m. The following table shows the expenditure over the ten-year period to 1996.

Table 1. Social Welfare Expenditure 1987–1996

Year	Total Exp. (£m)	Index of Exp.	Consumer Price Index	As % of net Govt. Exp.	As % of GNP
1987	2,593	100.0	100.0	32.3	13.7
1988	2,614	100.8	102.1	32.7	13.0
1989	2,663	102.7	106.3	33.1	12.0
1990	2,809	108.3	109.9	33.3	11.6
1991	3,092	119.2	113.3	34.1	12.1
1992	3,532	136.2	116.8	36.0	13.1
1993	3,628	139.9	118.5	34.5	12.6
1994	3,761	145.0	121.3	33.7	12.0
1995	4,199	161.9	124.2	34.9	12.4
1996	4,377	168.8	126.5	34.5	12.0

Source: Statistical Information on Social Welfare Services (1996). Department of Social Welfare.

It is clear from the above table that expenditure on social welfare is continuously rising with a 68% increase in expenditure between 1987 and 1996. This level of increase was mirrored in previous decades. There are a number of factors contributing to the increase in expenditure:

- There have been increases in the numbers applying for and qualifying for the various schemes, e.g. the increase in the number claiming unemployment payments.

- There have been increases in the real level of payment. From the table above it can be seen that social welfare payments increased at two and a half times the rate of the consumer price index.

- There have been increases in the number of schemes, e.g. Carer's Allowance was introduced in 1990.

- There have been changes in eligibility conditions of existing schemes allowing more people to qualify, e.g. in 1989 male lone parents were allowed to claim the Lone Parent's Allowance.

The continuous increase in expenditure has led to the belief that social welfare payments are absorbing a disproportionate and increasing slice of national income. However, the table above shows that as a percentage of current government spending and as a percentage of GNP, expenditure on social welfare has remained fairly constant over the ten-year period, and actually fell between 1992 and 1994. Indeed, the current high growth rates, coupled with increasing employment, are likely to see that ratio fall even further in the period from 1996 to the end of the century. It is also interesting to note that in the period 1987–90, expenditure on social welfare increased at a slower rate than the consumer price index, indicating a fall in the real level of payment during that period.

COMMISSION ON SOCIAL WELFARE

As mentioned earlier the system of income maintenance in Ireland had developed in a piecemeal and ad hoc manner since the mid-nineteenth century. By the early 1980s it was clear that a review was badly needed. In 1983 the Minister for Social Welfare established the Commission on Social Welfare. The brief of the Commission was to review and report on the entire social welfare system and related social services. The Commission reported in 1986 with 65 major recommendations. Most importantly, the Commission listed five principles that should both guide the operation of the system and be used in its evaluation. These are discussed below.

Adequacy

Payments should prevent poverty and be adequate in relation to prevailing living standards. The Commission adopted a relative definition
of poverty (i.e. people are poor when they are excluded from ordinary
living patterns, customs and activities). In addressing adequacy, differences
in family size have to be taken into account with appropriate payments
for adult dependants and children. There should also be in place a
method of altering the amount of payments in line with evolving prices
and incomes.

The Commission found that there were no links in the existing
structure to any standard of adequacy, that different categories received
different levels of payment and that adult dependants and child dependants
were treated differently under the schemes. Indeed, it found that there
were 36 different child dependant rates in the system. It recommended
a standard basic rate of payment be made to all recipients which in
1985 figures was in the order of £50–£60 per week. This would be
£70.10–£84.10 per week in 1998 figures. In 1998 all social welfare
payments had reached the lower figure, with the exception of Supplementary Welfare Allowance and short-term Unemployment Assistance.
However, none had reached the higher figure.

Redistribution

The Commission noted that social welfare payments are an important
part of the redistributive process. However, they cannot be considered in
isolation from the tax system that finances them. They concluded that
in terms of redistributing resources from the better off to the less well
off, the social welfare system was more effective than the tax system.

Comprehensiveness

The Commission pointed out that in assessing how comprehensive the
social welfare system is in its coverage, an important dimension is the
extent to which individuals are covered, as of right, to benefits under
social insurance. There is a perceived stigma attached to applying for
social assistance schemes, due to the means test, and this may deter some
people from applying. Also, because schemes are categorical in nature,
people who do not fit into one of the defined categories are excluded
and must rely on Supplementary Welfare Allowance, which is the lowest
rate of payment in the system. Comprehensiveness also implies that the
process of application and the method of delivery of services should
respect the dignity of the individual.

Consistency

It is important that the system be internally consistent and also consistent with other aspects of social policy. The Commission found large levels of inconsistency between levels of payments for different categories and also between the various means tests applied to social assistance payments. It also found inconsistencies between social welfare and other Government agencies (e.g. between social welfare recipients residing in private rented accommodation who are receiving a rent allowance and people with similar incomes and family size residing in local authority accommodation).

Simplicity

The Commission found a system that was extremely and unnecessarily complex, with a plethora of different schemes covering different contingencies, a range of means tests and a large variation in the manner in which applications were processed and decisions made. This complexity made it very difficult for applicants to understand their entitlements, resulting in low take-up or unnecessary appeals and also greatly added to the cost of administering the system.

SOME CURRENT ISSUES

Take-up of Benefits

Very little research has taken place in Ireland to indicate the level of take-up of various income maintenance schemes. However, two surveys conducted in Dublin in recent years produced some interesting results. The first was conducted by Free Legal Advice Centres (FLAC) in a housing suburb in west Dublin (Cousins and Charleton, 1991). The second was conducted by the Dublin Inner City Partnership (DICP) amongst inner city communities (DICP, 1994). Both surveys showed remarkable similarities.

FLAC interviewed 103 households, of whom 85% were not claiming their full entitlement, and DICP interviewed 101 households, of whom 87% were not claiming full entitlements. FLAC identified 305 possible claims of which 42% referred to the exceptional needs provisions of Supplementary Welfare Allowance. A claim was made by applicants in respect of just 32% of these claims. At the conclusion of the survey 44% were successful in their claim, 27% were refused and 29% were still pending a decision.

DICP identified 211 possible claims of which 49% referred to the exceptional need provision of Supplementary Welfare Allowance. In this survey a claim was made in respect of two thirds of the claims. At the conclusion of the survey 38% were successful in their claim, 41% were refused and 21% were still pending a decision.

The surveys indicate the importance of information in relation to benefit take-up. However, there are clearly other factors operating given the number who still did not apply after they had been given information about their possible entitlements. The following emerged as the main reasons why people did not apply:

• Lack of information as to what is required in relation to particular applications e.g. what back-up documentation is required.

• Fear of bureaucracy generally. The complexity of the system and the form–filling.

• The stigma attached to the means test.

• The costs associated with applying, relative to the actual benefit.

• Specifically in relation to Supplementary Welfare Allowance, the queues, the discretionary nature of the scheme, the lack of trust in the appeals system.

Unemployment Traps

This term refers to the situation whereby, due to the combined impact of the tax and social welfare system, an unemployed person may find that accepting paid employment produces little or no increase in net disposable income. As a result, it is argued that some unemployed people have no incentive to move into employment.

The relative severity, though not the actual extent of unemployment traps, is measured by means of replacement ratios, i.e. the ratio of income when unemployed to the net income if employed. These show, for given levels of gross earnings, the disposable income of an unemployed person in relation to the disposable income gained from employment. They take into account cash and non-cash benefits and costs associated with the withdrawal of medical cards, rent allowance reductions, travel costs etc.

Unemployment traps tend to increase at a time when social welfare rates are rising faster than increases in general wage rates and when there is a high tax burden on the low paid. The following table shows the real changes in the value of both net income for a married couple with two children on the average industrial wage, and unemployment assistance for the same family size, over an eighteen-year period:

Table 2. Index of Growth in Net Income and Unemployment Assistance 1977–94.

Year	Net Income	Unemployment Assistance
1977	100	100
1978	110	101
1979	121	101
1980	113	111
1981	106	111
1982	101	116
1983	97	116
1984	98	121
1985	100	123
1986	102	122
1987	104	120
1988	106	128
1989	108	133
1990	109	139
1991	110	143
1992	112	145
1993	114	147
1994	118	148

Source: Report of the Working Group on the Integration of the Tax and Social Welfare Systems, 1996.

As can be seen from Table 2, in the period 1977–80 wages grew at a faster rate in real terms than unemployment assistance. However, from the mid-1980s onwards the increase in unemployment assistance greatly outpaced wages. This was due to an explicit decision to target extra increases at the long-term unemployed and the high tax rates faced by people on relatively low incomes. It must also be borne in mind that in 1977 unemployment assistance was starting from a very low base.

Table 3 shows the replacement ratios for the same hypothetical family, consisting of a couple with two children. In the case of the unemployed person it takes into account the value of the medical card, free fuel allowance, differential rent, back-to-school clothing allowance. In the case of the employed person it takes into account tax and PRSI and it assumes take-up of Family Income Supplement. This is a social welfare payment made to people in employment §with dependent children. The amount paid depends on family size and level of earnings.

Table 3. Replacement Ratios: Couple with Two Children

Gross Earnings (£)	Net Weekly Wage (£)	Replacement Ratio %
5,000	142	88
6,000	147	85
7,000	153	82
8,000	152	83
9,000	151	83
10.000	147	85
11,000	149	84
12,000	158	79
13,000	166	75
14,000	176	71
15,000	187	67

Source: Report of the Expert Working Group on the Integration of the Tax and Social Welfare Systems, 1996.

The table shows that this family faces high replacement ratios at low wage rates. Clearly, there is not a huge incentive to take up employment at wages up to £11,000 gross. However, as the wage approaches the average industrial wage of approx. £15,000, the incentives increase. The bigger the family size, the higher the replacement ratios (as social welfare payments increase with family size) and therefore, the greater the disincentive. In this context it must be borne in mind that large families constitute a small proportion of the unemployed with single people comprising 62% of the live register. Also, employment has many positive psychological impacts and people may seek employment even if the monetary gain is slight.

Poverty Traps

The poverty trap refers to the position of people in employment, on particular incomes, who are faced with a reduction in net income as their gross income increases. This arises because as income increases taxation comes into play and means-tested benefits (such as Family Income Supplement) decrease or are withdrawn. Table 3, above, gives a good illustration of the poverty trap. Between a gross income of £7,000 and £11,000, net income decreases so that the person on £11,000 is actually worse off than the person on £7,000.

FACTORS CONTRIBUTING TO UNEMPLOYMENT AND POVERTY TRAPS

In 1996 the Report of the Expert Working Group on the Integration of the Tax and Social Welfare Systems outlined a number of factors which at that stage were contributing to unemployment and poverty traps. These included the following:

Adult Dependant Allowances

This is an additional allowance paid to a social welfare recipient who has a spouse/partner. It is valued at approximately 60% of the basic rate. No allowance is made for an adult dependant in respect of people in employment. It thus adds to the unemployment trap. However, it also creates a severe poverty trap if the adult dependant has earnings. If the earnings are less than £60 the full social welfare rate for that family is paid. However, once the earnings go over £60 all of the adult dependant allowance and half of the child dependant allowances are lost.

Child Dependant Allowances

These are paid to social welfare recipients at the rate of £13.20 per week (1998 figures) for each dependant child. Clearly, these increase the unemployment trap for large families.

Family Income Supplement

This was introduced to combat the unemployment trap by compensating people with children who lose their child dependant allowances on taking up employment. However, since its inception it has had a low take-up and was calculated on gross income. Perversely, it also contributes to the poverty trap as it has a sharp withdrawal rate when income increases.

Rent and Mortgage Supplements

Under the Supplementary Welfare Allowance Scheme people on social welfare payments can receive assistance with their rent (if in private rented accommodation) or their mortgage. The amounts payable can go from £35 per week for a single person to over £100 per week for families. The allowance is not payable to people in full-time employment (defined as more than 30 hours per week). It can therefore contribute greatly to the unemployment trap. Likewise, it can act as a disincentive to spouses/partners taking up part-time work as there is a pound for pound clawback in place.

Medical Cards

Due to the fairly severe means test attaching to medical cards, people in employment on relatively low incomes can be disqualified from entitlement. Clearly, the extent to which this would act as a disincentive depends on the value one places on the card. Families with children are likely to value this more than single people.

Tax Rates and Tax Bands

Tax rates, tax bands and tax exemptions are very important in relation to poverty traps. People enter the tax system on relatively low incomes and single people can start paying the top rate of tax at an income well below the average industrial wage.

RECENT CHANGES AIMED AT REDUCING
UNEMPLOYMENT AND POVERTY TRAPS

In each of the three years 1996–98 explicit measures were introduced to deal with unemployment and poverty traps. The principal measures are:

- If the earnings of an adult dependant go over £60 the recipient of the social welfare payment does not immediately lose the adult dependant rate. It is now phased out between earnings of £60 and £90 and withdrawn completely when earnings exceed £90.

- Child dependant allowances have not increased since 1994. Increases in respect of children have been concentrated on Child Benefit, which benefits equally those in work and those out of work. The child dependant allowances can be retained for a period of three months after obtaining employment. At this stage Family Income Supplement becomes payable (see below).

- The most important change in relation to Family Income Supplement is that it is now assessed on net income. Also, the number of hours worked per week to qualify has been reduced to 19, and it is now paid after three months of employment, instead of six.

- Medical cards can be retained for a period of three years after obtaining employment.

- The standard rate of tax has been reduced from 27% to 24%. However, the tax band for the lower rate has only increased by 12% in the period 1995–98, which means that people still enter the higher rate at low incomes. However, the PRSI-free allowance has risen from £50 to £100 in the same period. Also the rate of PRSI has reduced from 5.5% to 4.5% for most employees.

- Long-term unemployed people who go back to work after April 1998 will get a special tax-free allowance spread over three years. In year one it will be £3,000 plus £1,000 for each child. In year two it will be two-thirds of the year one amount, and in year three it will be one-third of the year one amount.

- The Back-to-Work Allowance scheme was introduced in 1993. It applies to long-term unemployed people or lone parents who take up paid employment or who become self employed. In general, it applies only to newly created jobs. In the first year of employment people can retain 75% of their social welfare payment. This reduces to 50% in the second year and 25% in the third year, after which it ceases. For self-employed people the allowance extends over four years with 100% of the social welfare payment being retained in the first year. When the scheme was introduced relatively few places were available. The number of available places has increased to 27,000 in 1998.

- People availing of the Back-to-Work scheme can retain their rent or mortgage allowances for two years after obtaining employment.

INCREMENTAL CHANGE vs RADICAL REFORM

In many ways the changes to the system in recent years have had little real impact. They have impacted slightly on unemployment and poverty traps but hardly at all on take-up problems. It could be argued they have shifted the timing of the traps rather than eliminating them. Thus, after three years when the medical card is withdrawn and after two years when the rent/mortgage is withdrawn the poverty trap will reassert itself. Likewise, the withdrawal, as income increases, of the now more generous Family Income Supplement will lead to a further poverty trap. Reducing unemployment traps may in the short term reduce disincentives and encourage people to take up employment. However, people will then face sharp poverty traps after a few years of employment. The government of the day may then be forced to either extend the ameliorating measures or introduce some other cushion, thus complicating the system even further.

All this raises the question of whether incremental reform will ever really tackle the fundamental problems and has led some commentators to suggest a more radical approach. One such approach, known as the Basic Income Approach, has gained currency in recent times in Ireland and is considered below.

Basic Income

A Basic Income can take several forms. However, each type of Basic Income system has the following characteristics:

- Every individual (man, woman and child) would receive an income from the state.
- The Basic Income would not be taxed.
- All other income over and above the Basic Income would be subject to a standard rate of tax.
- The Basic Income would replace the entire social welfare system.
- It would be paid automatically to every citizen without the need to apply.
- There would be no means test or work test attached to it, thus reducing stigma.
- It would treat men and women equally – the concept of adult dependency would be abolished.
- It would be age-related with children receiving a lesser amount than adults.
- It would be administered by a single agency.

The advantages of such a scheme can be summarized as follows:

- It eliminates unemployment traps and poverty traps. There would be no withdrawal of benefit as people move from unemployment to employment or as income increases.
- It provides a comprehensive and automatic safety net. There is no stigma attached as people are paid automatically.
- It would provide an independent income for all, including those who do not participate in the labour force, such as people who work in the home.
- It would be simple to administer with no need for form-filling, means-testing etc. It could be paid automatically into a person's bank account.

In 1994 the Economic and Social Research Institute (ESRI) published an analysis of the various Basic Income options (Callan et al., 1994). The biggest drawback it identified was the high tax rate required to finance such a scheme. They estimated that a tax rate of 69% would be necessary if everyone was to get a Basic Income that was not less than the current rate of unemployment assistance. For many people this made the concept politically unacceptable.

In the same year, Sean Ward (1994) put forward a proposal that could be achieved at a tax rate of 50%. However, this involved giving people in the age group 21–64 a Basic Income less than the current lowest social welfare payment. This age group constituted over half the population of the country. It also envisaged giving everyone under the age of 21 an income of £20 per week. The problem with this proposal is that virtually everyone between the age of 18 and 64, who was not in employment, would require a top-up. This would require them to be subject to a means test thus creating a new layer of bureaucracy and adding to the problems of stigma and low take-up.

Since 1994, however, there have been significant changes in the Irish economy. Growth has remained at an exceptionally high level and is forecast to remain so over the coming years; unemployment has decreased and the numbers at work have greatly increased thus increasing tax buoyancy.

This changed environment has led Clark and Healy (1997) to revisit the debate. They suggest that a basic income scheme which would give everyone over the age of 21 a Basic Income of at least £70 per week (1997 figures) could be achieved with a tax rate of 48%. The amount payable to each age group is shown in Table 4. The proposal envisaged the establishment of a Social Solidarity Fund, which would be a replacement for and an enhancement of the existing Supplementary Welfare Allowance Scheme. This would provide a top-up to those requiring it. Employers would pay a Social Responsibility Tax instead of PRSI at a reduced rate of 8%. The disadvantage of this proposal is that it still leaves people in the age group 18–20 requiring a means test to determine if they require a top-up.

Certainly, the proposal by Clark and Healy indicates that in a buoyant economy it is possible to introduce a Basic Income for all without penal tax rates. However, it is important to note that a Basic Income in its

Table 4. Basic Income Rates

Age	£ per week
80+	82
65–79	77
21–64	70
20	45
19	35
18	25
0–17	21

Source: Clark and Healy (1997)

complete form has not been introduced in any other country. There are still a number of questions that need to be addressed:

• What happens if the economy takes a downturn in future years? Will tax rates have to be increased to the levels suggested by the ESRI in 1994 or will the Basic Income rates have to be reduced?

• How are Basic Income rates to be adjusted each year? Will it be in line with inflation or at a higher level? Indeed, could the Basic Income itself fuel inflation?

• What effect will it have on the labour market? Will more people seek employment? Will people opt out of the labour market in favour of home duties or study? Will some people be content to enjoy the basic income rather than seek employment?

• What will be the impact on wages? Will employers take the Basic Income into account and seek to reduce wages?

• Could we have an influx of immigrants seeking to enjoy the Basic Income?

• How will we make the transition from the present system to the Basic Income system?

It is interesting to note that the Department of the Taoiseach is currently sponsoring a study on the viability of introducing a Basic Income System in Ireland. The purpose of the study is to consider and evaluate the economic, social, budgetary and administrative impact of the introduction of a Basic Income System.

CONCLUSION

The present system of income maintenance may have served us well over the years. But we must ask if the system is appropriate to the changed environment in which Ireland finds itself today – where the nature of work is changing and being redefined, where the concept of the welfare state is being questioned and new models sought, where the economy is experiencing exceptional growth, but where arguably the fruits of that growth are not shared equally by all the citizens.

Judged by the principles set down by the Commission on Social Welfare the present system is found wanting. The payments are barely adequate, it is extremely complex, it lacks consistency and comprehensiveness. In its interaction with the tax system the welfare system creates unemployment and poverty traps. The complexity of the system and the means–testing acts as a deterrent to people.

It is therefore timely that the Government is prepared to examine radical alternatives to the present tax and welfare systems. The present system has to some extent created a dependency culture. It would be more appropriate to move in the direction of a participative culture in which people are facilitated to participate fully as citizens in society.

TABLE OF POLICY DEVELOPMENTS

19th century	Workhouses established
1838	Poor Relief (Ireland) Act
1847	Workmen's Compensation Act
1908	Old Age Pensions Act
1911	National Insurance Act
1920	Provision for Blind Persons introduced
1923	Poor Law renamed Housing Assistance
1933	Unemployment Assistance introduced
1935	Provision for Widows and Orphans
1944	Children's Allowances introduced
1947	Infectious Diseases Maintenance Allowance
1954	Disabled Person's Maintenance Allowance
1961	Contributory Old Age Pension introduced
1966	Occupational Injuries Benefit
1967	Free travel and electricity introduced
1970	Retirement Pension, Invalidity Pension and Deserted Wife's Allowance
1973	Deserted Wife's Benefit and Unmarried Mother's Allowance
1974	Prisoner's Wife's Allowance, Single Woman's Allowance and Pay-Related Benefit
1977	Supplementary Welfare Allowance Act
1980	National Fuel Scheme
1981	Maternity Benefit introduced
1984	Family Income Supplement
1989	Lone Parents Allowance
1990	Carer's Allowance and Back to School Clothing Scheme
1994	Survivor's Pension, Health and Safety Benefit and Adoptive Benefit
1996	Disability Allowance
1997	One Parent Family Allowance

RECOMMENDED READING

Clark, C. and J. Healy (1997) *Pathways to a Basic Income*. Dublin: Conference of Religious of Ireland.

Commission on Social Welfare (1986) *Report of the Commission on Social Welfare*. Dublin: Stationery Office.

Expert Group on the Integration of the Tax and Social Welfare System (1996) *Report of the Expert Group on the Integration of the Tax and Social Welfare System*. Dublin: Stationery Office.

REFERENCES

Callan,T., C. O'Donoghue and C. O'Neill (1994) *Analysis of Basic Income Schemes for Ireland*. Dublin: Economic and Social Research Institute.

Clark, C.M.A. and J. Healy (1997) *Pathways to a Basic Income*. Dublin: Conference of Religious of Ireland.

Combat Poverty Agency (1988) *Poverty and the Social Welfare System in Ireland*. Dublin: Combat Poverty Agency.

Commission on Social Welfare (1986) *Report of the Commission on Social Welfare*. Dublin: Stationery Office.

Conference of Religious of Ireland (1994) *Towards an Adequate Income for all*. Dublin: Conference of Religious of Ireland.

Conference of Religious of Ireland (1995) *An Adequate Income Guarantee for All*. Dublin: Conference of Religious of Ireland.

Conference of Religious of Ireland (1996) *Progress, Values and Social Policy*. Dublin: Conference of Religious of Ireland.

Conference of Religious of Ireland (1997) *Planning for Progress – Socio-Economic Review*. Dublin: Conference of Religious of Ireland.

Cousins, M. (1995) *The Irish Social Welfare System: Law and Social Policy*. Dublin: Round Hall Press.

Cousins, M. and B. Charleton (1991) *Benefit Take-up*. Dublin: Free Legal Advice Centres.

Curry, J. (1998) *The Irish Social Services* (3rd ed.). Dublin: IPA.

Department of Social Welfare (1996) *Statistical Information on Social Welfare Services*. Dublin: Stationery Office.

DICP (1994) *Benefit Take-up: Campaign Report*. Dublin: Dublin Inner City Partnerships.

Expert Group on the Integration of the Tax and Social Welfare System (1996) *Report of the Expert Group on the Integration of the Tax and Social Welfare System*. Dublin: Stationery Office.

Healy, J. and B. Reynolds (1998) *Surfing the Income Net*. Dublin: Conference of Religious of Ireland.

Hills, J. (1997) *The Future of Welfare*. Cork: Joseph Rowntree Foundation.

Ireland (1997) *Sharing in Progress – National Anti-Poverty Strategy*. Dublin: Stationery Office.

O'Connor, J. (1995) *The Workhouses of Ireland*. Dublin: Anvil Books.

Ward, S. (1994) 'A Basic Income System for Ireland', in *Towards an Adequate Income for All*. Dublin: Conference of Religious of Ireland.

3

Improving Health Care: Health Policy in Ireland

Suzanne Quin

In total, almost seven per cent of current government expenditure in Ireland is spent on public health care. Coupled with private spending in this area, the total amounts to almost one-tenth of Gross Domestic Product (Department of Health Information, 1997). This does not even take account of ongoing capital expenditure on building new hospitals such as Tallaght and updating facilities that rapidly become outdated in size and design. Health is one area of government spending which impinges on the vast majority of the population. It is certainly an area of public provision which excites a great deal of attention and is one of the few which generates public protest when cutbacks are proposed or are introduced such as the reduction in hospital beds in the latter part of the 1980s (Curry, 1998).

There is a long tradition of providing health care in Ireland. In the Brehon Laws there is reference to the proper conditions for a hospital which, in many respects, would be in keeping with good medical care as we know it today. These stated that the hospital 'should be free from dirt, have four doors that the sick man may be seen from every side and there should be a stream of water running through the middle of the floor' (Robins, 1960: 145). The monasteries of mediaeval Ireland offered refuge and care to the sick and dying. Later the Poor Law system developed institutionally based care for the indigent sick along with other categories of those without the most basic resources. There also grew the system of voluntary hospital care arising from the individual and group efforts of various philanthropists who established institutions such as the Adelaide and Meath Hospitals in Dublin. After Catholic Emancipation, the Roman Catholic Church also began to set up hospitals for those too poor to pay for any medical care such as the Mater Misericordiae and St Vincent's Hospital in Dublin (Robins, 1960). Apart from such institutions, there was no attempt to provide generalized coverage in the form of a general hospital system (Hensey, 1972:47). The Medical Charities Act 1851 required the Poor Law Commissioners to provide dispensaries and appoint medical officers. The geographical boundaries of the dispensary system remained until the Health Act 1970.

The perceived responsibility of the state to provide health care for the population as a whole is very much a twentieth-century characteristic. Barrington (1987) points out that, at the beginning of the 1900s, government responsibility was limited to controlling outbreaks of serious epidemics and providing the poorest people with the most basic general practitioner and infirmary services which originated from the Poor Law. By 1970, the government had accepted responsibility for providing a high standard of health care for all the population at no cost or at a very subsidized cost to the recipient of services. By 1991, entitlement to free public hospital care was a basic right of everyone (1991 Health (Amendment) Act).

There are many factors which influence the provision of health care in a country. These include the prevailing disease patterns, the demographic profile and the way in which the health services are structured and funded. It is the unique blend of these features in tandem with historical, cultural and ideological influences, economic conditions, contemporary knowledge about health and disease and the relative power positions of the various protagonists involved in providing health care which have determined the shape and thrust of current services in Ireland.

CHANGING DISEASE PATTERNS

At the beginning of the twentieth century, the most common causes of disease and death in Ireland were infectious diseases arising from poverty, malnutrition, poor and unsanitary housing conditions, lack of clean water and ignorance about the mechanisms by which disease will spread. In many respects, the conditions then are similar to the ones facing many in the so-called third world countries where famine and disease are constant twin hazards. By the end of this century, Ireland's disease patterns (morbidity) and death statistics (mortality) now mirror those of other relatively affluent countries. In terms of maternal mortality, Ireland has achieved an average of less than two per 100,000 live births per year. This is far lower than the World Health Organization target of less than 15 per 100,000 for every country by the year 2000. However, in other respects health statistics show that Ireland has somewhere to go yet in furthering the nation's health.

In regard to lowering premature mortality (death before 65 years), for example, Ireland trails behind other EU Member States. When one looks at the causes of death in this category, it can be seen that many of these deaths are regarded as potentially preventable, since strokes, heart disease and many forms of cancer are linked to a greater or lesser extent with aspects of lifestyle such as diet, smoking, lack of exercise, alcohol consumption and stress – the hazards of affluence. A target of current health policy, therefore, is to reduce the numbers who die before the age of 65 to the level of or, better still, lower than, the EU average (Department of Health, 1994). There has been recognition for some time that this involves strategies other than just the provision of curative services. The Department of Health Report (*Health: Wider Dimensions*, 1986), following the World Health Organization's document (*Health for All by the Year 2000*), emphasized the need for health promotion programmes to reduce levels of morbidity and early mortality by giving people the knowledge and sense of responsibility to maximize their health potential for as long as possible. This approach was further endorsed in the Health Strategy Document (*Shaping a Healthier Future*, 1994) which emphasized the importance of health gain (improvements in health status) and social gain (quality of life changes resulting from improved health status). In 1995 the Department of Health issued its proposals for improving the health promotion aspect of health services in *Making a Healthier Choice the Easier Choice,* which established goals and targets for a national strategy for health promotion.

Demographic Characteristics

Ireland's demographic profile is changing in the same way as in other countries in the EU and this has implications for health care demands and provision. However, the link between demographic change and resulting adjustments in health services is not always as direct and immediate as might be expected. Falling birth rates, for example, do not necessarily mean the automatic closure of maternity hospitals or wards, as other factors also influence such provision such as the geographical spread of facilities, public pressure, tradition and employment. Nevertheless, the proportion of those aged over 65 years in the population is considered to have particular implications for health care services. While the proportion of those over 65 relative to others in Ireland is increasing, it is not as high as most other European countries. Estimates of the proportional size of this group by the year 2011 vary from 11.4% to 12.5% of the population (Fahey, 1995). A particularly large increase is anticipated in the over-80 year old group which is predicted to increase by two-thirds during this time. Moreover, it is calculated that almost half of those over 70 will be living alone. A particular feature of Ireland's population is the large number of those over 65 who have never married and therefore have no spouse or children to provide care if needed. Statistically, those over 65 have greater need for health services than others. This is particularly true for the 'older elderly', those aged over 75 years. Those over 65 make more than twice the number of visits to their GP compared to average for the population as a whole and, when admitted to hospital, they spend a longer time on average as in-patients (Department of Health Statistics, 1993). Increasing frailty and poor health generates the need for community-based services which are provided by health services – such as public health nurses, physiotherapy, occupational therapy, home help, meals-on-wheels and day care. Some of these are provided directly by the health services and others are provided by voluntary organizations subvented by public funding. Deficits in the availability of primary care such as these are likely to lead to increased demand for the more expensive secondary (acute hospital) and tertiary (long-term care) services.

ELIGIBILITY FOR HEALTH SERVICES

Entitlement to publicly funded health services is determined by a person's income from whatever sources. All Irish residents belong either to Category 1 or Category 2 eligibility. Those in Category 1 hold what is known as a medical card. This is subject to a means test, the amount allowed being reviewed on a yearly basis. In circumstances where the need for medical services may be greater than the average, those whose income exceeds the guidelines may be given a medical card if they are considered to be unable to provide necessary medical services for themselves and their family (Department of Health, 1994: 3)

The decision to grant or withhold a medical card is at the discretion of the health board (or health authority as they are to be renamed according to the *Health Strategy Document* 1994). The most recently published Department of Health Statistics indicate that around 36% of the population hold medical cards. Within this overall percentage, the statistics reveal considerable variations (up to 20%) between the eight health boards/authorities. Whether these variations are entirely due to income differences is subject to question. An indication that eligibility criteria between different areas may be less than perfect is contained in the Department of Health's Strategy Document (1994) commitment to the ongoing review of medical card eligibility procedures so that 'whatever improvements are necessary in the interests of equity' (1994: 36) can be made. Equity is of particular importance given the range of medical care to which the holder is entitled. This includes free general practitioner service with a choice of doctor, provided the practitioner is listed to take medical card patients and has not exceeded the maximum number of such patients he/she is allowed. Prescribed medicines and drugs are also available free of charge. The holder is also entitled to free dental, ophthalmic and aural services and appliances, although actual provision in these areas is limited in reality. All public hospital out-patient and in-patient services in a public ward, including consultant services, are free of charge.

Category 2 comprises the rest of the population who, on grounds of income, are not entitled to medical cards. Category 2, therefore, is just over 64% of the population. This group shares with Category 1 entitlement to public hospital out-patient and in-patient services in a public ward, including free consultant services in both instances. Category 2 patients, however, must pay for every visit to their general practitioner. They are also liable for a nominal charge per day for all public hospital accommodation up to a maximum in any twelve-month period for all public in-patient treatment. These charges do not apply to maternity services, services for prescribed infectious diseases, children referred from school health assessment and health clinics or children who are receiving treatment for certain conditions such as cystic fibrosis. In addition, there is a fee for use of a hospital's accident and emergency department without a referral note from a general practitioner, a charge which can be waived in situations of hardship.

Drugs and medicines are available free of charge to any person suffering from certain conditions, that is those drugs necessary for the treatment and control of their specific illness. These are: learning disability; mental illness (for those under 16); phenylketonuria; cystic fibrosis; spina bifida; hydrocephalus; diabetes mellitus; diabetes insipidus; haemophilia; cerebral palsy; epilepsy; multiple sclerosis; muscular dystrophies; Parkinson's disease and acute leukaemia. Those eligible are given a Long-Term Illness Book which lists the drugs and medicines for the treatment of that condition which they are entitled to get free of charge.

Aside from those conditions listed above, individuals in Category 2 must pay for all prescription costs. However, a drug refund scheme operates whereby any cumulative expenditure by a person and/or that person's dependants which exceeds the limit in a specified three-month period is refunded. In addition, there is a drug cost subsidization scheme available to those who do not hold a medical card or a Long-Term Illness Book, but are certified as having a long-term medical condition requiring regular, ongoing medical and drug prescriptions. In these circumstances, the person makes direct payment to their pharmacist which covers all prescriptions relating to the condition for that period.

As Curry (1998) points out, it has never been government policy to aim to provide a free health care service for all the population. The aim has been to ensure that no one goes without appropriate and necessary care for themselves or their dependants on account of lack of means. This was first explicitly stated in the 1966 White Paper, *The Health Services and Their Future Development*, and has formed the basis for developments in health entitlement to date. While entitlement to public hospital care has been extended to all, those without medical cards must pay for their general practitioner services, prescriptions and hospital charges as described above. The Report of the Commission on Health Funding (1989) did not favour the provision of free primary care (i.e., general practitioner) to all even though an argument could be made that it would encourage those whose incomes exceeds the medical card guidelines to seek care at an early stage of their illness, hence reducing demand for the more expensive and invasive secondary services provided by acute hospitals.

FINANCING HEALTH CARE

Barrington describes Irish health services as an 'extraordinary symbiosis of public and private medicine' (1987: 285). Indeed, Ireland can be truly described as having a public/private mix of health care in terms of both funding and delivery. By public is meant those services which are financed and/or delivered by public funds, while private services have been defined by Tussing (1985: 81) as 'that part in which fees or charges are imposed and where patients may not avail of the services unless they pay for them.' The Report of the Commission on Health Funding (1989) emphasizes that the distinction between public and private applies both to funding and delivery systems in that public funding can be compatible with private delivery systems, and vice versa. Nolan (1991: 19) argues that a four-fold classification system is necessary in order to separate out the different strands of the public/private interweave. These are:

(*a*)   services which are publicly financed and delivered such as hospital services for those with a medical card;

(*b*)   services which are publicly financed and privately delivered such as GP services for those with a medical card;

(*c*)   services which are privately financed and publicly delivered such as the element of direct payment for public acute hospital facilities for those in Category 2;

(*d*)   services which are privately financed and privately delivered such as GP services for Category 2 patients and use of private hospital services.

The *Report of the Commission on Health Funding* (1989) considered that there was a consensus among the population as a whole that health needs were matters of priority and public justice. It did not regard the public/private mix in provision as being incompatible with these. This view was endorsed by the Strategy Document (1994) which cited the public/private mix as being a compatible arrangement which it regarded as one of the strengths of the Irish health services. This fits with O'Shea's (1992: 238) view that 'private practice has been quite deliberately retained and encouraged at all levels in the medical services – primary care, secondary care and tertiary care'. It can be argued that such a policy which enables those who can afford it to access alternative paths to what they see as being a more comprehensive, superior quality and faster service is hard to justify on grounds of social justice. Tormey (1992: 381) argues that 'fundamental change bringing real equity in access to services will only come when there is the political will to change the state's well-entrenched policy direction. There is little cause to believe that such change is likely'.

Payment for private services is largely through the insurance mechanism. Until recently, the Voluntary Health Insurance Board (VHI) held a monopoly position in providing health insurance. VHI was established in 1957, at a time when approximately 15% of the population were not covered for acute public hospital care. It was required to provide cover at what is termed 'community rating' which is a standard charge for all members regardless of age and health status. At the outset, therefore, it was created to cater for the relatively affluent minority who were, at the time, excluded from access to public provision. However, in reality, far more joined than needed cover for basic care and, when entitlement to public hospital care was extended to the whole population in 1991 it had little effect on VHI membership. In a study of VHI membership, Nolan (1991: 132) estimated that, in 1989, 34% of the population had VHI cover. Furthermore, he found that, even when premiums were increased substantially, it had little effect on the membership size. Clearly, those who take out cover must consider it worth the costs incurred. Nolan found that the most important reasons identified by members were the sense of security engendered as well as speed of access and perceived quality of care (1991: 154). A further incentive was the tax relief on premia which was of greatest advantage to those in the highest tax bands. The Report of the Commission on Health Funding (1989) recommended that this tax relief should be eliminated on the grounds that those who opted for cover for private care should not be subsidized by tax remits. However, this recommendation was only taken in part when the tax relief was reduced to the standard rate only in 1994. The Third Directive on Non-Life Insurance for the European Union resulted in the VHI losing its monopoly position and, since The Health Insurance Act, 1994, any company is entitled to offer cover for medical care provided it operates the community rating system. So far, the major alternative to the VHI has been Bupa, a company which had been offering health insurance in Britain for many years before entering the Irish market.

Health care can be funded using one or more of three basic mechanisms: general taxation, social insurance or private insurance schemes. Most countries have one predominant means which is supplemented by one or both of the other two. The main determining factor is the historical development of health cover that can vary from country to country. In Germany, for example, health care schemes developed from employment-related benefits; the National Health Service in the UK is primarily funded by general taxation, while the US is based on private insurance with a state funded system for those who cannot cover themselves on account of age or low income. Ireland's public system is paid for through general taxation. There is some cover via social insurance and the private system and aspects of the public system are funded through private insurance for those who can afford to pay.

The amount spent on health care is determined by a number of factors such as the relative wealth of a country, the amount paid in taxes, the value placed on health care services vis à vis competing demands from other welfare sectors, the age and health status of the population and the way in which health care is funded. Given the demands that an ageing population will make on health care, as discussed earlier, it might reasonably be assumed that, the larger the proportion of those over 65 in a population, the more will be spent on health care. Fahey (1995), in a comparison of spending across countries, argued that this factor can be overridden by a more important one – that of the relative wealth of the country. He found that the higher the Gross Domestic Product, the greater the proportion of overall spending devoted to health care. However, this does not necessarily mean that the more that is spent on health care, the better the quality and cover for health care. Depending on the funding mechanisms used and the system of delivery of health care, a country may get relatively good or poor value for the amount spent.

Within overall spending, a further concern is the amount that is apportioned to the different sectors of health care. Since the costs of health care are constantly rising, and potential demand is virtually limitless, difficult decisions must be made about the allocation of funds for prevention, cure and ongoing care. Within these categories, also, there will be competition for scarce resources and choices may revolve around the conflicting demands for development of services which pertain to life-threatening conditions vis à vis those which are not life-saving but life-enhancing, such as the expansion of organ replacement procedures or increasing the number of hip replacement operations. At present, just over one-half of total state spending on health goes on the acute hospital sector. This is not unusual in comparison to other EU countries where the labour intensive and high-tech facilities of this sector consume a similar proportion of spending, and there is no indication that the needs of this sector will diminish. While much attention has been given to the importance of health promotion and illness prevention, spending in this area has not matched aspirations. Spending on community-based services accounts for just 16% of total expenditure. Curry (1998:131–2) comments that 'despite the increased emphasis on the value and importance of community care and some rationalization of hospital services, this pattern of expenditure has not altered significantly over the past two decades'. The large proportion of overall spending which is taken up by the acute hospital sector has made this area a particular target for cost containment. As Wiley and Fetter (1990) point out, it is not just the number of patients but rather 'the type and mix of patients which will have the greatest influence on service delivery and resource needs at hospital level' (1990: xii–xiii). A mechanism for containing costs utilized by Wiley and Fetter is the application of Diagnostic Related Groups (DRGs). This system, originating in the US, relates predetermined rates of payment to a classi-fication of diagnosis. Payment is made per hospital stay. Linking payment to diagnosis in this way gives the payer and the payee a means of predicting and controlling costs and expenditure.

One aspect of the acute hospital which has changed radically in recent years is the average length of stay per patient. Changes in treatment processes arising from increased knowledge and treatment options as well as alterations in funding hospital care, have all contributed to this phenomenon. Increasing numbers of patients are being treated as day cases. In 1994, Department of Health figures put the total number at just over 193,000; by 1996 this figure had risen to over 200,000. Attendance for day cases is at a prearranged time for a planned procedure following from an out-patient visit. The Audit Commission (1995: 298) in Britain identified three main factors which have influenced the growth in day surgery:

(a) changes in clinical practice which have contributed to the decline in the number of days a patient will spend in hospital;

(b) technological developments which have radically changed a range of procedures on account of less invasive techniques and improved analgesic/anaesthetic drugs;

(c) financial pressures resulting in a reduction of in-patient beds.

Writing in the context of the United States, Duffy and Farley (1995: 675) describe the shift to day care as being 'swift and far-reaching'. They comment that 'many interventions that could have been performed for years safely and effectively on an out-patient basis remained in-patient procedures. It was not until new reimbursement policies encouraged treatment in out-patient settings that a significant shift occurred' (1995: 675–6). In Ireland, overnight admission to hospital for those with private insurance was, in the past, encouraged by the policy of VHI of not paying for other than in-patient treatment for its members; while in the public sector, there was pressure to maintain full usage of existing hospital beds even at a time when, by the standards of other European countries, such beds were over-supplied relative to the size and demographic profile of the population.

Financial considerations, therefore, would seem to play a significant role in the direction and speed of change in the functioning of the acute hospital sector. The cost-saving potential of increased day care include a reduction of staff needed for overnight and weekend shifts, patient 'hotel' costs are reduced substantially and through put can be maximized. In this instance, financial expediency may not clash with good patient care. There is plenty of evidence that day admission may be both appropriate and in line with most patients' wishes concerning the nature of their hospital care. Kelly (1994), in a study of day case patients in Ulster, found that compliance among patients of post-discharge instructions was good and that the patients reported little post-operative pain, but many did report various side-effects. In Kelly's study, few had recourse to their GP immediately following discharge. However, there is conflicting evidence as to whether or not the advent of day surgery has increased the demand for GP services in the immediate aftermath of discharge which is likely to involve evening or night-time calls. This illustrates that a change in policy in one aspect of health care may have implications for another.

STRUCTURES FOR PROVIDING HEALTH CARE

Given the escalating costs of providing health services, it is not surprising that attention has increasingly focused on value for money. An important aspect of this is to ensure that structures for providing services are as efficient and cost-effective as possible. This was emphasized in the *Health Strategy Document* (1994) which regarded the framework for service provision as one of three dimensions needing reorientation. The three dimensions of health care identified in the Strategy were:

(*a*) the services which were to become more focused on improvements in health status and quality of life as well as placing emphasis on providing care at the level of intervention most appropriate and cost effective;

(b) the framework within which services are provided is to be altered. This framework refers to the organizational and management structures of health care. The adjustments are to create greater accountability and decision-making capacity at local and regional level to take account of local conditions and needs;

(c) the participants – which encompassed both the service providers and, most importantly, the service users. The shift in focus is to ensure that the needs and rights of patients are central in the planning and delivery of health services.

The Strategy Document acknowledged the importance of restructuring the framework to take cognizance of the changing demands of health care into the new millennium. The last major change had taken place over twenty years before, following the 1970 Health Act. This had created a structure of eight regional health boards with responsibility for the provision of services in their area within the budget allocated to each by the Department of Health. The health boards differed substantially from each other both in terms of size of population and the geographical area. In terms of population size, by far the largest was the Eastern Health Board, which, encompassing the counties of Dublin, Kildare and Wicklow, covered approximately one-third of the total population of the country. The management structures of the health boards when they were established followed the recommendations of the McKinsey Report (1968). Services provided by each board were divided into three areas: general hospital care, special hospital care and community care. Each had a programme manager who reported to the Chief Executive Officer, who had responsibility for the implementation of policy decisions made by the board. The board in each instance was made up of a majority of elected representatives from local corporations/councils, professionals involved in the provision of health care, and some nominees of the Minister for Health.

While each health board was given responsibility for general hospitals, this only referred to the hospitals directly run by the board and did not include the acute voluntary hospitals within the geographical area which continued to receive direct funding from the Department of Health. Over time, this emerged as one of a number of structural difficulties which hindered efficiency and effectiveness of service delivery. The community care structure, as conceived, did not develop to its full potential as the range and numbers of professionals providing community-based services were insufficient to meet existing and emerging needs.

The fact that the GP service remains outside the system meant that a pivotal primary care service operated independently from other primary care services. Voluntary organizations which were engaged in the provision of services similar or ancillary to those required of a board could be funded by a grant under Section 65 of the Health Act 1953, but there was no built-in mechanism of accountability for funding given or received. The division into three programmes (some of the boards only operated two in effect, on account of the limited number of hospitals in the area under their jurisdiction) led to problems of continuity of care for patients across programmes, because of separate funding and management structures. Moreover, there were tensions between the individual health boards and the Department of Health around issues of funding and accountability.

Problems relating to the control of expenditure and provision of services in all areas of the publicly provided health services intensified in the economic recession of the mid to late 1980s. The Department of Health Document, *Health: The Wider Dimensions* (1986), questioned the necessity of having eight health boards in a population of just over three million. It suggested that health boards should be renamed to take cognizance of their wider brief which encompassed welfare as well as health. While it did not suggest a particular title, it could be inferred that the title of Health and Social Services Boards such as existed in Northern Ireland might be suitable. The Strategy Document 1994 took a different line in both respects. It maintained, and indeed extended, the pivotal role of health boards, to be renamed health authorities, in the provision of health care, and created a three-fold geographical division within the Eastern Health Board (Eastern Health Authority) in recognition of the particular difficulties relating to its size of population. The Task Force on the Eastern Region Health Authority Interim Report (1997) was concerned with detailed proposals for the more effective operation of its resources and services. The remit of the newly named health authorities was extended in that, from henceforth, the Department of Health (now renamed the Department of Health and Children) would play no role in direct service provision. In future, the voluntary hospitals, while maintaining autonomy in their management, will form part of the health authorities' continuum of health care services. In the Eastern Region Health Authority, each acute hospital will have a clearly defined catchment area as envisaged by the Dublin Hospitals Initiative Group 1990. This Authority has now created five programmes of service provision which are: Community Services; Acute Hospital Services and the Elderly; Services for Persons with Disabilities; Mental Health, Addiction and Social Development; and Children and Families.

Women's Health Care in Ireland

In recent years there has been growing recognition of the particular health care needs of women in Ireland. Prior to this, women's health care was subsumed within the general health care system which was not sufficiently responsive to them. The discussion document, *Developing a Policy for Women's Health* (1995) was designed to redress this imbalance by creating a consultative process for the development of a women-friendly service. The document covered a range of areas pertaining to women's health including childbirth, menstruation, gynaecological services, breast and cancer screening and family planning. It also addressed the area of women's participation in the formulation and management of health services as well as identifying women who were particularly disadvantaged in terms of health needs and/or access to an appropriate range of health services. It divided the services under consideration into sections whose titles indicated a very traditional approach to women and health care. For example, under the heading 'Health Issues which Predominantly Affect Women' were included family planning, genetic counselling and supporting carers. The document saw the objectives of a women's health policy to be the identification, planning and promotion of a health policy which ensured that the services provided were appropriate and accessible based on consultation and participation. This approach very much reflected the Strategy Document's (1994) approach to greater consumer participation in the planning and delivery of health services generally.

Taking Irish women's health in the EU context, the statistics reported showed that, while there had been much improvement since the middle of the century, women in Ireland have a lower life expectancy and a higher premature mortality rate than average. Of particular concern is the health of Traveller women who have a life expectancy of twelve years less than average, reflecting a lifestyle and service response that grossly neglects their needs (Department of Health, 1997). Indeed, the Discussion Document (1995) did acknowledge the context in which some specific aspects of women's ill health arose, such as the health implications of domestic violence and the socioeconomic factors underlying their mental health profile, particularly in relation to gender differences between men and women in the incidence of depression (see Quin, 1995; Cleary, 1997 for further discussion of this). Following the publication of the document, there was consultation with women in different parts of the country to incorporate their views. This process did at least represent an institutionalized attempt to garner the views of consumers. The resultant *A Plan for Women's Health* (1997) aimed to incorporate these views and included in its plans a mechanism to institutionalize the process of consultation on an ongoing basis in the creation of a permanent Women's Health Council, as well as the establishment of advisory committees in each health authority area. Considering it was based on consultation, the new document did not differ greatly in approach from its original. Two important inclusions were a focus on the need for services which were experienced as more accessible and user friendly and the desirability of including alternative treatments and approaches including the availability of counselling in non-medical settings. The importance of greater accessibility and targeting at those at greatest risk/ need was amply demonstrated in Wiley and Merriman's (1996) study of women's needs in relation to the reproductive sphere. Two particularly interesting findings were indications that Irish women across geographical and socio-economic boundaries 'may be less traditional than is assumed' and, less surprisingly, that the extent of knowledge about health enhancing practices was less than desirable, most particularly amongst those with low levels of educational attainment. This latter finding indicated the need for health promotion strategies which take account of socioeconomic differentials within Irish society.

Socioeconomic Inequalities in Health Care

There is evidence of strong links between health status and socio-economic differentials. As living standards improved during the latter half of this century, and with them increased access to health services for all, it was assumed that health differentials arising from differences in socioeconomic status would disappear. However, the publication of the Black Report in Britain (Report of the Working Group on Inequalities in Health, 1980) indicated that this was not so. This report found that, in spite of overall improvements in health status in the population, health differentials between the higher and lower socioeconomic strata had, in fact, increased during the period 1930 to 1970. The Report cited the multicausal nature of health inequalities of which material conditions were the main factors. A subsequent report by Whitehead (1982) confirmed these findings and demonstrated that, in the following decade from 1970 to 1980, little had changed in this respect. Relatively little research has been carried out in Ireland on this subject. What has been done indicates that there is no room for complacency (see Nolan, 1989; Cook, 1990; Nolan, 1992; Wiley and Merriman, 1996). Research on varying aspects of health internationally indicates the powerful effects of socio-economic differentials and 'data specific to the Irish situation, although not extensive, is convincing and consistent with international findings' (Collins and Shelley, 1997: 88). The findings that poorer people, on average, live shorter lives and are subject to more ill-health at an earlier age than their richer counterparts leads to what Nolan (1989: 2) describes as 'a double injustice – life is short where quality is poor'. The transgenerational nature of the inequalities is reflected in the lower birth weight, smaller stature and poorer nutritional status on average of those who are poor. As Blaxter (1989: 219) points out, 'variation in health is part of the human condition, and the degree or nature of variation which is unacceptable has political and historical dimensions'. The definition of health inequality is ultimately an ideological one concerning qualitative judgements about what is acceptable, preventable and just. It also requires a broad perspective on the concept of health that encompasses inequalities in life chances and in service provision both within and outside the health sphere into, for example, education, housing and income maintenance.

CHALLENGES FOR THE FUTURE

There is no indication that health care will be perceived as any less important in the future. The potential for new demands on health services is great and, as Tormey predicts, 'demands on health services will continue to outstrip supply' (1992: 381). There is certainly no sign of reduced spending and it is likely that the coming decades will be characterized by ongoing preoccupation with ever rising costs and demands. Evans (1996) argues that demands on health services inevitably increase more rapidly than resources are allocated. Further, he argues that from a resource perspective, some developments in treatments will result in increased demand in the future. He cites the example of the treatment of renal failure with dialysis and its impact on the demand for health care. A few decades ago, a person with renal failure would make but brief demands on the acute sector as terminal care would be the only requirement. Advances in treatment have extended this condition to a chronic one needing ongoing intervention. This example can be applied to other conditions which have become chronic such as AIDS. Indeed, he suggests, the very success of health services in contributing to the overall health status of the population has resulted in increased numbers living longer and thereby utilizing more health care services.

Caplan (1995: 110) argues that recent medical advances are of the order to challenge 'thinking on living, dying and being human'. These include hitherto uncharted areas such as therapy in the womb, genetic manipulation, construction of artificial organs and innovative techniques for improving or restoring organ functioning. Such developments present formidable challenges for health care in the coming decades of the twenty-first century. The capacity to genetically map predisposition to health risks offers scope for preventative measures which could change the relative position of preventative vis à vis curative practice. The repercussions of genetic adaptation have the potential to change the health profile and status of future generations.

Optimists would suggest that the development in treatments such as genetic manipulation and treatment in the womb may lessen the costs of health care for future generations. Certainly, it would be a great deal more economic to correct a genetic disorder such as spina bifida in vitro than to provide health care services for the same individual during the course of their lifetime. However, such potential savings are in the future and pessimists would counter with the point that the alleviation of one set of health problems is likely to be replaced by others, especially related to advanced ageing and continuing 'affluent' disease patterns.

In the foreseeable future, therefore, concern with spending on health services is likely to intensify, particularly if another period of economic recession should occur. If past patterns are repeated, actual spending will continue to rise even if the proportion of total expenditure is curtailed. Regardless of the economic conditions which prevail, the debate about fair allocation of resources to different sectors and needs will, if anything, intensify. As discussed earlier, one reason is the projected increase of the proportion of elderly people within the population, especially those over 75 years. However, Fahey (1995) cautions against making the assumption that increased numbers of those over 65 in future decades will automatically create increased demand in the same ratio as at present. He argues that, in the future, there may be a need to redefine 'old age' to take account of improved health status. It may be that, by the year 2020, old age may be defined in terms of seventy-five or eighty, rather than sixty-five as at present. However, it is still likely that the older person will make disproportionate demands on health care. How society will respond to this will depend upon many factors, not least, the values and ideology pertaining to ageing (See chapter 10, pp. 221–42).

An issue which has provoked considerable attention in recent times has been concern about individual control over the nature and timing of death and, in particular, questions about the validity or otherwise of voluntary euthanasia. Concern about the process of dying is likely to increase rather than diminish. Avoidance of the prospect of one's own death in Western society, it can be argued, has been facilitated by the removal and sanitization of death in a hospital setting. However, 'the image of another person dying in a tangle of tubes all over his body, breathing artificially, is beginning to break through taboos to galvanize a sensibility that has long been paralysed' (Aires, 1987: 593).

Advanced directives, also called living wills, are becoming increasingly utilized to ensure that, should a person be incapacitated to the extent that they are not able to express preferences regarding the giving or withholding of treatment, their wishes in this respect are recorded. As Cusack (1997: 161) points out, the legal standing of an advanced directive is not clear in Ireland although 'the right of a patient to refuse treatment itself is beyond doubt'. An advanced directive can only record a person's wishes regarding the provision or non-provision of what is termed medical interventions, it cannot require that the medical personnel take any steps to hasten death by active or passive means. What constitutes treatment in this context has been the subject of medical and legal debate, particularly in relation to patients who are in what is termed a persistent vegetative state and thus unable to either continue living unaided or be able to express any wish regarding their care. In the case of Anthony Bland, a soccer fan injured beyond recovery when crushed, the British House of Lords in 1993 held that artificial feeding could be stopped as it constituted treatment (Walton, 1995). A similar case in Ireland in 1995 of a women, who had been living for 23 years in a near persistent vegetative state, resulted in a judgement by the High Court, which was upheld by the Supreme Court, that artificial feeding could be lawfully discontinued. This judgement was made without precedent and there is an absence of guidelines in this area in Ireland (Cusack, 1997).

McDonnell (1997) argues that the reluctance of the state to become involved in the debate surrounding the repercussions of contentious issues such as the right to die and the anomalies relating to the practice of new reproductive technology has left a vacuum whereby the implied responsibility and power of decision is often left to individual medical practitioners acting within the self-regulatory sphere of medicine. The Netherlands is the only European country where euthanasia is openly practised. While any measure to hasten death is still technically a crime in that country, courts have set explicit conditions in which it may be excused. Writing about the United States, Markson (1997) quotes unofficial estimates that between one and fifteen per cent of deaths per year are physician-aided ones which are 'typically recorded officially as cardiac arrest' (1997: 86).

As stated above, the public/private mix of health care has been enshrined in the Strategy document (1994) as a desirable and permanent feature of our health care system. Thus, inequality of access is inbuilt within Irish health services so that those with resources have choice and speed of access to a wider range of health care than others. There is evidence that private health care is an increasing feature of health care provision in many countries (Puntes-Markides, 1992). Private health care has been traditionally endorsed by the Catholic Church in Ireland, both in its support for the principle of subsidiarity and by its provision of actual facilities such as the private hospitals run by religious orders. It has been strongly supported by the medical profession with GPs acting as private entrepreneurs, while many hospital consultants apparently have no difficulty reconciling the fact that they are among the highest paid public employees and, at the same time, can and do reap the considerable benefits of private practice in the same field. It is not simply the issue of 'double-jobbing' which is in question. Consultants interviewed in the study by Brown and Chadwick (1997: 203) claimed that most consultants worked more than the requisite hours in their public capacity. The more important issue is that, by engaging in extensive private practice, they are witnessing and contributing to an unequal system endorsed by the state which condones preferential treatment to those who can afford it. Good health and fast access to high quality care when needed are commodities which are equally precious to all. However, in a variety of respects, they are not equally distributed across the population and the existence of a private health care sector, supported by tax relief on premia, serves to institutionalize and perpetuate socioeconomic inequalities. Together and separately the Catholic Church and the medical profession have acted as a conservative force in Irish health care long after the controversies surrounding the proposals for a comprehensive health care scheme for mothers and children (Whyte, 1980). The profit motive which governs, at least in part, all private provision is hard to reconcile with best possible standard of care and the existence of a two-tier system is surely irreconcilable with the stated desire to provide the highest possible standard of care for all. In view of the advancing knowledge in the area of genetics discussed above, there is real danger that, in future, particularly given the private availability of health care, there will be differences in genetic endowment created which could result in health inequalities unprecedented in the history of health care.

TABLE OF POLICY DEVELOPMENTS

1838   Poor Law (Ireland) Act – first provision of state health services, infirmaries provided in association with workhouses

1851   Unions divided into dispensary districts, physicians attached to each district to provide free service to the poor

1872   Poor Law Commissioners abolished, replaced by Irish Local Government Board

1924   Department of Local Government and Health established

1947   Department of Health established when functions of above were divided into Health, Social Welfare and Local Government

1953   Health Act extended entitlement for health care. Maternity and Infant Care Scheme established

1957   Voluntary Health Insurance Act

1960   Local Authorities responsible for the provision of services reduced to 27

1966   White Paper on the future of the health services

1970   Health Act established eight regional health boards

1986   Publication of *Health – The Wider Dimensions*

1989   Report of the Commission on Health Funding

1990   Dublin Hospital Initiative Group, proposed organizational structures for the Dublin area

1991   Entitlement to free public hospital care extended to all under the Health (Amendment) Act

1994   Department of Health Strategy Document

1994   Health Insurance Act ended monopoly position of VHI

1995   Publication of Health Promotion Strategy

1997   Publication of Plan for Women's Health

1998   Department of Health renamed the Department of Health and Children

RECOMMENDED READING

Barrington, R. (1987) *Health, Medicine and Politics in Ireland 1900–1970*. Dublin: Institute of Public Administration.

Cleary A. and M.P. Treacy (eds) (1997) *The Sociology of Health and Illness in Ireland*. Dublin: University College Dublin Press.

Curry, J. (1998) *Irish Social Services*. Dublin: Institute of Public Administration. Chapter 5.

O'Donovan, O. (1997) 'Equity, Quality and Accountability: Guiding Principles for Health Policy in Ireland', pp. 79–92 in M. Ferguson (ed.), *Social Policy: Course Reader*. Cork: Centre for Adult and Continuing Education, UCC.

Robins, J. (ed.) (1997) *Reflections on Health, Commemorating Fifty Years of the Department of Health, 1947–1997*. Dublin: Department of Health.

REFERENCES

Aires, P. (1987) *The Hour of our Death*. London: Peregrine Books.

Audit Commission (1995) 'A Short Cut to Better Services: Day Surgery in England and Wales', pp. 298–309 in B. Davey, A. Gray. and C. Seale (eds), *Health and Disease: A Reader*. Milton Keynes: Open University Press.

Barrington, R. (1987) *Health, Medicine and Politics in Ireland 1900–1970*. Dublin: Institute of Public Administration.

Blaxter, M. (1989), 'A Comparison of Measures of Inequality in Morbidity', pp. 199–227 in J. Fox (ed.), *Health Inequalities in European Countries*. Aldershot: Gower.

Brown, P. and G. Chadwick (1997) 'Management and the Health Professional', pp. 189–209 in J. Robins (ed.), *Reflections on Health, Commemorating Fifty Years of The Department of Health 1947–1997*. Dublin: Department of Health.

Caplan, A. (1995) 'An Improved Future?', *Scientific American*, September 1995: 110–11.

Cleary, A. (1997) 'Gender Differences in Mental Health in Ireland', pp. 193–207 in A. Cleary and M.P. Treacy (eds), *The Sociology of Health and Illness in Ireland*. Dublin: University College Dublin Press.

Collins, C. and E. Shelley (1997) 'Social Class Differences in Lifestyle and Health Characteristics in Ireland', pp. 87–98 in A. Cleary and M.P. Treacy (eds), *The Sociology of Health and Illness in Ireland*. Dublin: University College Dublin Press.

Cook, G. (1990) 'Health and Social Inequalities in Ireland', *Social Science and Medicine*. 31 (3): 285–90.

Curry, J. (1998) *Irish Social Services*. Dublin: Institute of Public Administration.

Cusack, D. (1997) 'Medico-Legal and Ethical Issues', pp. 159–73 in *Reflections on Health, Commemorating Fifty Years of The Department of Health 1947–1997*. Dublin: Department of Health.

Department of Health (1966) *White Paper: The Health Services and Their Future Development*. Dublin: Stationery Office.

Department of Health (1986) *Health – The Wider Dimensions*. Dublin: Stationery Office.

Department of Health (1993) Statistics. Dublin: Stationery Office.

Department of Health (1994) *Shaping a Healthier Future. A Strategy for Effective Care in the 1990s*. Dublin: Stationery Office.

Department of Health (1995) *Developing a Policy for Women's Health*. Dublin: Stationery Office.

Department of Health (1995) *A Health Promotion Strategy: Making the Healthier Choice the Easier Choice*. Dublin: Stationery Office.

Department of Health (1997) *A Plan for Women's Health*. Dublin: Stationery Office.

Duffy, S.Q. and D.E. Farley (1995) 'Patterns of Decline Among Inpatient Procedures', *Public Health Reports*, 110: 674–81.

Evans, D. (1996) 'The Limits of Health Care', pp. 159–73 in D. Greaves and H. Upton (eds), *Philosophical Problems in Health Care*. Aldershot: Avebury.

Fahey, T. (1995) *Health and Care Implications of Population Ageing in Ireland 1991–2011*. Dublin: National Council for the Elderly.

Hensey, B. (1972) *The Health Services of Ireland*. Dublin: Institute of Public Administration.

Kelly, M.C. (1994) 'Patients' Perception of Day Case Surgery', *The Ulster Medical Journal*, 63(1): 27–31.

McDonnell, O. (1997) 'Contesting Concepts of Care: The Case of the Home Help Service in Ireland', pp. 69–84 in A. Cleary and M.P. Treacy (eds), *The Sociology of Health and Illness in Ireland*. Dublin: University College Dublin Press.

McKinsey & Co. Management Consultants (1968) *Towards Better Health Care – Management in the Health Board*.

Markson, E. (1997) 'Moral Dilemmas', pp. 83–7 in C.L. Weiner and A. Strauss (eds), *Where Medicine Fails*. London: Transaction Publishers.

Nolan, B. (1989) *Socio-Economic Mortality Differentials in Ireland*, ESRI Working Paper No 13. Dublin: Economic and Social Research Institute.

Nolan, B. (1991) *The Utilisation and Financing of Health Services in Ireland*. Dublin: Economic and Social Research Institute.

Nolan, B. (1992) *Perinatal Mortality and Low Birth Weight by Age, Parity and Socio-Economic Basis*, ESRI Working Paper No 37. Dublin: Economic and Social Research Institute.

O'Shea, D. (1992) 'Customer Care in the Public Sector', *Administration*, 40 (3): 234–47.

Puntes-Markides (1992) 'Women and Access to Health Care', *Social Science and Medicine*, 35:620–5.

Quin, S. (1995) 'Family, Women and Health', pp. 175–84 in I. Colgan McCarthy (ed.), *Irish Family Studies: Selected Papers*. Dublin: Family Studies Centre UCD.

Report of the Commission on Health Funding (1989). Dublin: Stationery Office.

Report of the Dublin Hospital Initiative Group (1990). Dublin: Department of Health.

Report of the Working Group on Inequalities in Health. (1980) The Black Report. UK: DHSS.

Robins, J.A. (1960) 'The Irish Hospital: An Outline of its Origins and Development', *Administration*, 8 (2): 145–65.

Robins, J. (ed.) (1997) *Reflections on Health, Commemorating Fifty Years of the Department of Health, 1947–1997*. Dublin: Department of Health.

Task Force on the Eastern Region Authority Interim Report (1997). Dublin: Stationery Office.

Tormey, W.P. (1992) 'Two-speed Public and Private Medical Practice in the Republic of Ireland', *Administration*, 40 (4): 371–81.

Tussing, A D. (1985) *Irish Medical Care Resources: An Economic Analysis*, ESRI Paper No 126. Dublin: Economic and Social Research Institute.

Walton, Lord (1995) 'Dilemmas of Life and Death: Part One', *Journal of the Royal Society of Medicine*, 88: 311–15.

Whitehead, M. (1992) *The Health Divide: Inequalities in Health*. London: Penguin.

Whyte, J. (1980) *Church and State in Modern Ireland, 1923–1979*. Dublin: Gill & Macmillan.

Wiley, M. and R.B. Fetter (1990) *Measuring Activity and Costs in Irish Hospitals, A Study of Hospital Case Mix*, ESRI General Research Series No.147. Dublin: Economic and Social Research Institute.

Wiley, M. and B. Merriman (1996) *Women and Health Care in Ireland*. Dublin: Oak Tree Press.

World Health Organization. *Health for All by the Year 2000*.

4

Housing Policy

David Silke[1]

INTRODUCTION

Shelter is considered one of the most basic of human needs and yet it does not seem to receive very much attention from Irish social policy analysts. Housing policy, however, is linked to many other areas of social policy. Studies have, for example, examined the link between poor housing conditions and ill health. The link between housing and employment can be seen at a very basic level by the practical difficulties of sustaining oneself within the work environment while experiencing homelessness. Links have also been drawn between employment and address, or location, which has a strong link to housing tenure in the Irish situation due to the high degree of geographical segregation of tenures. Policy reviews have examined the interaction of the social welfare system's support of housing costs and financial incentives to take up work (Expert Working Group on the Integration of the Tax and Social Welfare Systems, 1996). Local studies have also identified the impact that the lack of suitable study space can have on a child's performance within the education system, and by association their employment opportunities in later life. Similar links can be traced between housing and the availability of and access to social services. For older people, for example, unsuitable housing can lead to early or avoidable entry to institutional care if problems are not dealt with expeditiously.

It is for this reason that housing is considered as one of the five principal areas of study in social policy. In this chapter, students are offered an analysis of Irish housing policy. The chapter begins by outlining current provision and current policy. To understand the context from which current policy has developed, the historical origins of policy are reviewed. Current policies are then evaluated. The chapter concludes by highlighting some potential challenges for the future. Those who are very new to the study of Irish housing policy may find it useful to read Curry (1998) for more contextual information.

DEFINITION AND SCOPE OF IRISH HOUSING POLICY

Housing policy is of relevance to all residents in the country. Housing policy is 'any deliberate course of action which is designed to effect housing conditions' (Blackwell, 1988: 75). This is a very broad definition and gives some idea of the wide scope of policy actions in this area. It includes for instance support for owner-occupation and the private rented sectors through tax relief; direct provision of accommodation by local authorities; support for those who cannot afford their accommodation through the social welfare system; and support of the voluntary housing sector.

Blackwell (1988) outlines various reasons why governments intervene in housing markets. These include: a wish to make housing markets work more efficiently (i.e. to correct poor information or to help people secure mortgages); supporting the building industry and related employment in order to achieve minimum housing standards; promoting either private or social ownership as something desirable in its own right; the wish to achieve a different distribution of income than that which would be the outcome of housing market forces; and in particular to help lower income households with their housing costs.

Government intervention can take a number of different forms. The main ones are: regulation (e.g. ensuring minimum building standards are achieved); direct provision (e.g. through local authorities); the provision of information (to customers and providers); subsidies and tax levies (e.g. tax relief on mortgages, urban renewal); transfer payments (e.g. towards the cost of rented accommodation or grants for home improvement); and the direct provision of loan finance for housing on the part of State agencies (National Economic and Social Council, 1988: 141)

Housing Legislation

There is a great deal of legislation that has relevance to housing policy. What follows should not be considered as in any way comprehensive, but should be seen as an indication of the level of state intervention in the provision of housing. The Housing Act of 1966 is the principal enabling act covering local authority accommodation and includes sections on: financial provisions; provision and management of dwellings; over-crowding of unfit housing; land acquisition for housing and other uses; local authority housing policy adoption; land/house sales; and assistance to persons wishing to house themselves.

The Family Home Protection Act 1976 protects the family home from sale without spousal consent. The Housing Act 1988 is important in that Section 9 of the Act requires housing authorities to undertake periodic assessments of housing need. Section 2 of the Act is also important in that it defines the circumstances in which a local authority may assess a person as homeless. The Act gave additional powers to local authorities to meet the housing needs of homeless persons.

The Housing (Miscellaneous Provisions) Act 1992 provides safeguards for tenants in regards to rent books, standards of accommodation and notice to quit and also requires landlords to register a house let for rent with the housing authority.

The 1997 Housing (Miscellaneous Provisions) Act introduced special measures to deal with 'antisocial behaviour'. The core aim of the legislation was to enable local authorities to evict individuals from their accommodation if they were engaged in such behaviour (mainly drug-dealing). Some concern was raised about this legislation before it was passed as it defined the term 'anti-social behaviour' very loosely; it applied to local authorities only, and those evicted could be refused rent allowance from their health board, which could increase homelessness (Kelly, 1997).

It is too early to comment on how well the 1997 legislation is working out in practice. However, it should provide a good case-study for social policy analysts on the possible role and the effectiveness (or otherwise) of legislation of this nature to try to tackle very complex social problems such as drug abuse. It may also, unfortunately, provide lessons of the unintended consequences of policies if the legislation is used to evict tenants who may be 'unpopular' in estates, for example those with mental health problems or refugees, but who may not necessarily be engaged in antisocial behaviour.

Tenure Types

In 1991 there were 1,006,506 permanent housing units (including conventional houses, flats and temporary dwellings) in the state, in which there were 1,019,723 private households (defined as a group of persons living together and sharing a common budget) (Central Statistics Office, 1991). A little under one-third (30 per cent) of private dwellings are located in County Dublin.

Table 1 shows the distribution of dwellings by tenure in Ireland, 1946–91. The table shows the decline in the share of tenure occupied by the private-rented sector during the last fifty years and the growth of owner-occupation as the dominant tenure. The share of dwellings under the social housing category (local authority and voluntary sector) has declined steadily since 1961.

Table 1. Dwellings by Type of Tenure Types in Ireland, 1946–1991 (%)

Tenure	1946	1961	1971	1981	1991
Owner-occupied	52.6	59.8	68.8	74.4	79.3
Social housing	–	18.4	15.5	12.5	9.7
Private rented	42.7	17.2	13.3	10.1	8.0

Source: Census of Population 1981, 1991.

Fahey and Watson (1995: 20–1) noted that home-ownership has been promoted as the main tenure in Ireland in a number of different ways. First, home ownership is generously subsidized through tax relief for mortgage interest payments, grants to first-time buyers, waiving stamp duty on purchases of new homes, the non-taxation of imputed income from owner-occupied housing, and the exemption of homes from capital gains tax. Second, the sale of local authority housing to sitting tenants at discount prices has meant that social housing has been used primarily as a route to home ownership for low income households and only in a secondary way as an alternative to home ownership for that sector. Since Independence, local authorities have built about 300,000 dwellings; however less than one-third are still under local authority ownership. Finally, the lack of support, until recently, of the private rented sector has meant that it has traditionally been unable to compete with private ownership.

The dominance of one tenure type in the Irish situation may have unintended consequences for those who are not in that tenure. It can lead to segregation and marginalization of certain sectors of the community, or it can mean that some tenures are seen as 'temporary' or 'transitory', a means to an end of reaching owner-occupation, rather than as a legitimate, long-term tenure choice. This can mean that some tenures, such as the private-rented sector, lack adequate regulation, management and planning, while others, such as the voluntary, non-profit sector receive less financial aid then others. The stress on the importance of home-ownership has had the effect of reducing the importance attached to considerations of equity in housing policy. The two largest supports, for example, given to those buying their own home are not targeted at those with low incomes (first-time buyers grants and mortgage interest relief). (See Fahey and Watson, 1995: 21–3).

Some initiatives have been introduced that are targeted at those who are non-owner-occupiers. One example is that voluntary organizations are eligible for capital assistance to assist with the capital funding of housing projects for those with special housing needs, including older people, homeless people and those with a disability. The scheme does not, however, help with the maintenance and repair of property. A second example is that tax relief is available at the standard rate for those in the private rented sector. Another limitation is that, by definition, the scheme only applies to tenants who pay tax (which excludes many students, for instance). However, concern has been expressed regarding the imbalance in housing subsidization (National Economic and Social Council, 1993).

Quality of Accommodation

A central issue in housing policy is the quality of accommodation. This concept is often measured in terms of household facilities such as running water, flush toilet, age of dwelling and overcrowding. Census data shows a continuing improvement in the quality of Irish dwellings and the National Economic and Social Council (NESC) assess that, in general, Irish housing policy has been successful in enabling most Irish people to live in reasonable accommodation (NESC, 1993: 449). A survey of the housing stock was undertaken in 1990 (Finn, 1992). The national survey, which involved a survey of over 20,000 housing units, found that 5.5% of housing units were unfit for habitation. A variation by region was found, with 2.1% of those in the East unfit compared to 17.7% of those in the North-West region. The two main reasons for unfitness were inadequate water and sanitation facilities (49.3% of cases) and poor resistance to moisture (23% of cases). Approximately three-quarters of unfit dwellings were found in rural areas and almost half of all unfit housing units were occupied by a person living alone. While no age of resident breakdown was reported in the survey, other research would suggest that a high proportion of unfit dwellings are occupied by older people living alone or with another older person (Fahey and Murray, 1994).

Another important feature of accommodation quality – one that has received less attention – is the quality of the social and physical surrounds of households. Fahey (1998) argues that households, particularly in urban settings, draw significantly from their social and physical surrounds and that these characteristics can have an impact on their social integration and social exclusion. These environmental factors can heighten the stigma attached to certain areas and he argues that greater attention should be paid to how social exclusion operates and how its effects might be overcome.

Under the 1988 Housing Act, local authorities are obliged to assess the extent of need for local authority accommodation. Four assessments of housing need have been undertaken since 1988, and the results are presented in Table 2.

Table 2. Assessment of Housing Need 1989–96

Category *Households*	Year				Change 1989–96 %
	1989	1991	1993	1996	
Unable to afford existing accommodation	2,809	4,075	6,432	7,659	172.7
In overcrowded dwellings	4,621	5,896	7075	5,912	27.9
In unfit dwellings	4,324	4,590	5122	4,799	11.0
Involuntarily sharing accommodation	2,000	2,432	3,345	3,120	56.0
Elderly	2,349	2,379	2,191	2,140	-8.9
In need of housing on medical/compassionate grounds	1,187	1,331	1,861	1,762	48.4
Homeless	987	1,507	1,452	979	-.01
Travellers	834	748	884	749	-10.1
Disabled	108	180	194	241	123.1
Young person leaving institutional care or without family accommodation	—	104	68	66	—
In institutional care	156	—	—	—	—
Total	19,376	23,242	28,624	27,427	41.5

Source: Housing Statistics Bulletin: Department of the Environment and Local Government.

Table 2 shows, in general, an upward trend in housing need as defined by the survey between 1989 and 1996. The most dramatic increase has been in the number of households unable to afford their accommodation. In some instances, such as unfit dwellings or the elderly, need has tended to remain fairly stable.

The 1996 survey counted over 27,000 households as being in housing need, or less than three per cent of all households. Lone parent households accounted for 41 per cent of the net need and over two-thirds (69 per cent) of these households include one child. Over a quarter (27 per cent) of households assessed in need were single person households and less than one in ten (8 per cent) were two adults and no children households. This type of information is very important if social policy analysts are to consider how best 'housing need' should be met. However, as discussed below, planners need to be aware of the limitations of the information collected, especially if not all 'housing needs' are included in the survey.

Homelessness

Numbers in relation to the homeless category deserve separate comment. One of the problems here is how to define and measure homelessness. The 1988 Housing Act provides a definition of homeless. It can be interpreted narrowly as, for example, those sleeping rough or in night shelters, or more generally as all those on the housing list (Fahey and Watson, 1995: 102). The measurement of homeless can also take two forms. The stock measurement, used in the assessment, counts the number homeless at a particular point in time. The alternative measure is to count the flow of those who experience homelessness over a period of time. The stock measure is useful to get a measure of the problem while a flow measure is more useful at understanding the duration of homelessness people experience and also the dynamics of the problem (see Fahey and Watson, 1995: 99–121).

It is interesting to note that in the 1996 assessment over one-third of county council and borough corporations and over two-thirds of urban districts recorded no homeless persons in their area. The 1996 assessment also included an assessment of the number of homeless persons including those not seeking local authority accommodation. This assessment identified 2,501 homeless persons, of whom 983 were living in hostels, 811 had no accommodation they could reasonably occupy or remain in occupation of, and 707 were living in health board accommodation because they had no other accommodation. Criticisms of the measure of homelessness used are well documented (O'Sullivan, 1996 – see also for a detailed discussion of homelessness and social policy) and it has been suggested by others that the real level of homelessness could be closer to 5,000 persons (Daly, 1994).

Particular groups may be more prone to homelessness then others. Lennon (1998) identified people with mental health problems, young people under 18 years of age, families, people with substance addictions, young single people and older single men as being particularly at risk. Research carried out by the Gay and Lesbian Equality Network and Nexus (1995: 67) found that almost one-third (32 per cent) of lesbians and gay men interviewed said that they had left home at one time or another with no certainty as to where they were going to live next. The proportion almost doubled (to 62 per cent) for those who were considered to be living in poverty. O'Sullivan (1998) has also drawn attention to the problem of child homelessness in Ireland. Following a review of current services in the Dublin region, Lennon (1998) proposed that a more integrated and coordinated service for homeless people was required, possibly in the form of a 'one-stop centre'.

Housing Need

Fahey and Watson (1995) carried out an analysis of the 1993 assessment of housing need and concluded that the concept of housing need underlying the assessment did not refer in a comprehensive way to all types of housing deficiency in the population, but only to that which could be addressed by traditional local authority housing. This resulted in the exclusion of certain categories of households from the statistics, such as those in receipt of Supplementary Welfare Allowance rent supplement, some members of the Travelling community, and the homeless for whom local authority housing was not considered the appropriate solution. This was partly the result of the terms of the 1988 Act, which required local authorities to count and classify those who were likely to require accommodation from local authorities. Fahey and Watson (1998) concluded that what was needed was a more comprehensive assessment of all types of housing deficiency in the population, along with a classification of those deficiencies on the basis of the remedies which are most appropriate to deal with them. Following this research, changes were made to the collection of information in the 1996 survey. At a more general level, however, this case provides a very useful and practical example of the application of the concept of need to an area of social policy and its implications, in terms of how and who defines need and also in terms of how different needs are legitimized and responded to.

Housing Completions

Moving on from the concept of housing need, it is also important to examine trends in the number of house completions over time. Table 3 illustrates the general slowdown in the number of house completions during the mid-to-late 1980s, with local authority completions slowing down in particular. This general decline in completions was attributed to a downturn in the economy, an increase in emigration, a reduction in local authority waiting lists and a general policy across Europe to reduce expenditure on public housing (NESC, 1993: 452). During the mid-to-late 1990s, house completions recovered to the levels experienced in the early 1980s, although local authority completions have not recovered to the same extent. This is interesting since waiting lists for local authority accommodation have increased (NESC, 1993: 452). State spending on Supplementary Welfare Allowance Rent Supplement – to support low income households in the private-rented sector – has also increased dramatically (Review Group on the Role of Supplementary Welfare Allowance in Relation to Housing, 1995).

Table 3. Housing Completions 1981–97

Year	Private Houses	Local authority	Voluntary	Total
1981	23,236	5,681	n/a	28,917
1983	19,948	6,190	n/a	26,138
1985	17,425	6,523	n/a	23,948
1987	15,376	3,074	n/a	18,450
1989	17,300	768	n/a	18,068
1991	18,472	1,180	n/a	19,652
1993	19,301	1,200	890	21,391
1995	26,604	2,960	1,011	30,575
1997	35,454	2,632	756	38,842

Source: *Housing Statistical Bulletin* (various years) Dublin: Department of the Environment and Local Government.

CURRENT IRISH HOUSING POLICY

The Department of the Environment and Local Government takes the lead for policy responsibility in this area. The overall aim of housing policy, as defined by the Department, is 'to enable every household to have available an affordable dwelling of good quality, suited to its needs, in a good environment, and, as far as possible, at the tenure of choice' (Department of the Environment, 1995: 4; Department of the Environment and Local Government 1998: 30–1). Statements such as this require some unpacking. What is an affordable dwelling? Who defines and regulates quality? How best might needs be met? What is a good environment? How important is tenure choice?

The policy document, from which this statement is quoted, goes on to assert that owner-occupation 'of course, remains the preference for the vast majority of the population' (Department of the Environment, 1995: 4). Certainly a review of housing statistics (see Table 1, p. 52) indicates that owner-occupation (or private ownership, outright or with a mortgage) is the dominant tenure (the right by which people occupy their homes) in the Irish situation. It is important, however, to consider the relative weight of push and pull factors in the current balance of tenure options. Push factors in this case could be the type of accommodation and location people want or expect to live in and can afford to pay for. Examples of pull factors are government tax incentives, the supply of accommodation becoming available and the subsequent tenure options available to people.

Local authorities are responsible for the operation and management of public housing policy. The functions of local authorities include: the assessment of housing need and the enforcement of minimum standards; the provision of housing for those unable to house themselves, and of assistance (e.g. loans) for other persons; providing or reconstructing houses; and administering loans from the Housing Finance Agency. Traditionally, the Irish system of government has been very centralized and so local government is not considered very powerful. This state of affairs is now undergoing a radical review, within the general policy context of the consideration of greater devolution of power to local areas. There is an expectation that, in time, local authorities will take on more responsibility, with housing identified as an area in which local authorities could play a greater role (Devolution Commission, 1996).

Current housing policy is underpinned by seven specific objectives:

- to promote home ownership;

- to promote a thriving more diverse and well managed rented sector, both public and private;

- to ensure that households, who are not in a position to provide housing from their own resources, have suitable accommodation available to then at an affordable price;

- to promote the conservation and improvement of public and private housing;

- to reduce the extent and effects of social segregation in housing;

- to enable a prompt and adequate response to the accommodation needs of homeless people;

- to enable the provision of suitable housing and halting sites for Travellers.

(Department of the Environment, 1995)

The clear articulation of these policy objectives is commendable. It is less clear, however, how the contradictory nature of these objectives is to be addressed. For example, is the promotion of home ownership consistent with the promotion of the public and private rented sectors? In the context of limited resources, which of the seven objectives should be prioritized? What type of evaluation indicators can be used to measure the effectiveness and efficiency of these objectives?

Two other key state organizations in ensuring that people have adequate accommodation are the Department of Social, Community and Family Affairs, which funds the Supplementary Welfare Allowance rent and mortgage supplement scheme and the eight regional health boards which undertake the payment assessments.

HISTORICAL ORIGINS OF IRISH HOUSING POLICY

From the seventeenth century, Irish land was acquired by the British aristocracy so that in 1800, when the Act of Union with Britain was passed, the ownership and control of Ireland was in the hands of largely Protestant British landlords. By 1800, in contrast to the Irish hinterland, Dublin had grown into a powerful and elegant Georgian city, encompassing the original Viking port and the medieval city. Dublin had become Britain's second city, with over 100,000 inhabitants. By the beginning of the nineteenth century, Ireland's population had reached eight million people, and was to peak in 1841 at 8,175,124.

Following the Act of Union with Britain in 1800, much of Dublin's aristocracy left Ireland for a more prosperous England, while retaining ownership of the land. Belfast developed rapidly in the nineteenth century as an industrial centre while Dublin declined rapidly to an impoverished outpost. (Power (1997: 312–14) provides a useful short overview of this history in the context of housing policy.)

In 1841 the census included for the first time an assessment of housing quality. Four categories were used. The lowest, category four, comprised houses built of mud or perishable material, having only one room and window; the third category could vary from one to four rooms and windows; category two was the equivalent of a good farm house; and the top category included anything better than the preceding. The results show that in 1841 of a total of 1,328,839 houses: 37 per cent were of category four quality; 40 per cent were category three; 20 per cent in category two and the remaining three per cent were category one. By the turn of the century the total number of houses recorded had been reduced to 858,158. The number of category four houses had been reduced considerably to only 1.5 per cent of the total, category three houses had reduced to 29 per cent, category two houses had increased dramatically to 61 per cent and the top category houses had increased to 9 per cent (see, for discussion, Matheson, 1903).

The reduction in the level of poor quality accommodation was related to desolation caused by the famine, with one million people dying and a similar figure emigrating during this period, many from the poorer housing. The Dwellings for Labouring Classes (Ireland) Acts, 1860, enabled landlords to obtain loans for the provision of cottages (see Curry, 1998: 49–50). Government loans were also provided under the Labourers' Housing Act of 1883 and 1885 for the building of labourer cottages. The scheme was not very successful as the initiative for building the cottage rested with the Local Board of Guardians (the predecessors of local authorities), which were heavily representative of the farming community. The farmers were hostile to the scheme because of the possible impact it would have on increasing rates (Daly, 1981: 33). This provides an interesting example of the influence of vested interests in the effective (or otherwise) implementation of housing policy.

Kaim-Caudle (1967: 79) recounts that 'housing standards in Ireland in the first decade of this century were notoriously poor. The Dublin tenements were among the worst in Europe and many rural dwellings were not much better than hovels'. During the latter half of the nineteenth century, an expanding population living in urban tenement accommodation led to terrible slum conditions. The census of 1901 provides depressing reading on this topic. It included a special set of questions on tenements of less than five rooms. It found that three-quarters of families in the country occupied such tenements. 79,149 tenements of one room only were identified and of these 20,994 had one occupant only; 41,918 had two to four occupants; 13,351 had five to seven occupants; 2,886 had eight or more occupants. In total, 101,845 people occupied these rooms or 2.3 per cent of the total population of the country (Matheson, 1903: 205–6). Those who are interested in the social history of tenement life may find Kearns (1994) of particular value in his account of tenement life in Dublin during this period.

The Housing Inquiry in 1914, established after the Church Street Tenement disaster the previous year in which three adults and four children were killed, publicly exposed for the first time the extent of urban deprivation. The report also drew links between poor housing and ill-health and recommended the provision of self-contained dwellings of sufficient size to avoid overcrowding and the separation of the sexes (Powell, 1992: 123–7).

The Free State therefore inherited a poor housing stock in 1922 and set about trying to tackle the problem by introducing the 'Million Pound Scheme'. The scheme empowered local authorities to raise half a million pounds through the rating system and loans matched by £1 million from central government. It enabled 2,000 houses to be built. The 1924

Housing Act provided financial assistance to those erecting or remodelling homes. However, the scale of the problem was immense – a survey of housing needs in municipal areas in 1919 found that over 40,000 new houses were needed.

By the 1930s the housing issue had developed into a housing crisis. When Fianna Fáil took office in 1932, they established a Housing Board and increased spending. The scale of the problem was such, however, that a survey in 1938 discovered that 60 per cent of Dublin's tenements and cottages, which provided housing for 65,000 people, were unfit for human habitation. Nevertheless, this was a very productive era in public housing construction, and one which has been linked to Fíanna Fáil's interest in the three goals of encouraging the building industry, providing employment and winning votes (see Powell, 1992: 215–20). Building was to be dramatically reduced during the Second World War and following the War a White Paper on housing, published in 1948, estimated that a further 61,000 new dwellings were required, 38 per cent (or 23,500) in Dublin, another 35 per cent (21,000) in other urban centres and the remaining 27 per cent (16,500) in the countryside (Curry, 1998: 51). This is, perhaps, a good example of the way in which social policy needs are very difficult to satisfy. It also reflects the way in which need seems to outstrip delivery on an ongoing basis.

Construction of housing picked up again after the War, encouraged by government grant aid to private dwellings and particularly those building dwellings for their own occupation. In the late 1950s a downward trend was again evident, spurred on by an impression that the housing problem had been solved through the successful building programme and increased emigration. Demographic change and economic growth in the 1960s increased the demand for housing, particularly in urban centres. During the 1960s housing completions increased steadily and continued to climb into the early 1970s, reaching a peak of almost 27,000 in 1975. Completion rates remained high for the next ten years and then began to decline in the late 1980s. Throughout this period, however, housing policy remained high on the political agenda. In 1977, Fianna Fáil promised to abolish domestic rates and to introduce a £1,000 first-time buyers grant – both of which were enacted. The first-time buyers grant was doubled in 1985 and now stands at £3,000. In 1985, the Fine Gael–Labour government introduced a £5,000 home-improvement grant for houses constructed prior to 1946, which proved very popular.

A £5,000 surrender grant was also introduced in October 1984 to local authority tenants, with at least three years satisfactory tenancy, who wanted to buy a home of their own. The first corporation sale scheme was introduced in 1968, which facilitated the sale of corporation houses at a discount price (to a maximum of 30 per cent). The surrender grant, however, was different in that it allowed tenants to choose the area in which they wanted to live. While this increased tenant choice, it also had some unintended consequences, particularly for those living in disadvantaged areas. Research carried out in Dublin by a voluntary organization (Threshold, 1987) found that the scheme was mainly taken up by people who were in employment and could afford to buy a house. This often meant that they moved from their own area, and those who remained were mainly unemployed. Income levels in these areas then dropped and services deteriorated. Houses that were left behind often remained vacant for some time and were vandalized. These areas then became stigmatized, which provided additional motivation for people to leave and made vacant property hard to let. The impact of the scheme was highly localized with about two-thirds of the total applications in the Dublin Corporation area confined to three housing sub-areas – Darndale, Ballymun and Tallaght (Threshold, 1987). This policy is also of interest to social policy students as it offers an opportunity to reflect on the concept of choice, and particularly how extending one person's choice can restrict another's.

This short account of Irish housing policy is interesting in the way in which it shows how it has been seen as natural for the state to intervene in this area, and to encourage and support the development of home ownership as the preferred tenure. It has occurred both through direct subsidies for those entering the market and by selling local authority housing to tenants. It has weakened the development of alternative tenures, such as the private rented sector or local authority housing, which have been treated more as a temporary staging post on the way to home ownership rather than as valid tenures in their own right. Readers might find it useful to compare the acceptance of state intervention in the area of housing policy to the opposition to intervention in other areas of social policy, the Mother and Child Scheme in the area of health policy being a good example.

Those interested in a more detailed account of the history of housing policy in Ireland should refer to Meghen (1963), and a good overview of this area is also provided by Curry (1998).

Principal Actors Involved in Policy Development in Irish Housing Policy

As housing issues are of central important to all residents, there is a large number of different organizations and bodies active in this area. As outlined above, the main government bodies with policy responsibility in this area are the Departments of the Environment and Local Government and the Department of Social, Community and Family Affairs. Local authorities and health boards are key statutory agencies in this field. The Homeless Initiative, under the joint direction of the Eastern Health Board and Dublin Corporation, was established in 1996 to ensure that services for homeless people become more effective, particularly by improving planning, coordination and delivery. State-sponsored bodies with an interest in the area of housing policy include: An Bord Pleanála (responsible for dealing with planning appeals), the National Economic and Social Council (NESC) (comments periodically on Irish housing policy), and the Rent Tribunal.

The Construction Industry Federation is the management association for the construction industry, and among other activities represents the industry to government. The Irish Business and Employers Confederation (IBEC) and the Irish Small and Medium Enterprises (ISME) represent different aspects of the building industry. Banks and building societies would also be expected to keep an active watching brief on housing policy as it is of central importance to their mortgage and lending business. Private landlords are represented by two main organizations: the National Association of Professional Landlords and the Irish Property Owners Association.

Key voluntary agencies in this area are Focus Ireland, the Simon Community, Respond!, Threshold, the Irish Council for Social Housing, the National Campaign for the Homeless and St Pancras Housing Association. Many of these organizations undertake research and policy work in the area of housing policy and have library facilities open to the public which can be the source of very useful and otherwise difficult-to-find information. The Institute of Public Administration, which has a specialized Housing Unit, is another good source of information on housing policy.

Energy Action provides a draft-proofing service for elderly and needy people and the service is carried out by people who are long-term unemployed. Examples of other voluntary agencies who would not have a key role to play in the development of policy, but would have an important housing component to their work, are Alone (who have publicized the poor living conditions of some older people in Dublin) and the Society of St Vincent de Paul.

EVALUATION OF CURRENT IRISH HOUSING POLICY

Two main measures are traditionally used to assess housing policy: efficiency and equity (see Baker and O'Brien, 1997; Blackwell, 1988). Efficiency refers to the extent to which policy leads to the optimal amount of housing services; equity means the degree to which similar cases are treated in the same way. Equity can be further sub-divided into vertical and horizontal equity. Horizontal equity or equal treatment of equals means the extent to which those in a similar situation (such as a particular income group) are treated in the same way. Vertical equity refers to the way in which people with different incomes are treated. Treatment is considered progressive if those with lowest incomes benefit most, regressive if those with higher incomes benefit most, and proportional if net benefits are the same ratio of income throughout the range of income (Blackwell, 1988: 143).

The Expert Working Group on the Integration of Tax and Social Welfare (1996: 113–22) assessed government housing subsidies. The efficiency of subsidies was questioned on the grounds that subsidization of housing was likely to lead to increased house prices and with some of the benefit going to existing homeowners and owners of land. The overall system was also criticized on the grounds of vertical equity as mortgage interest relief was likely to benefit those with higher incomes, who are more likely to be able to take out higher mortgages.

The Expert Working Group also questioned the current system on the grounds of horizontal equity, particular for those on low incomes. Two main sources of assistance with housing costs for those on low income are the differential rent scheme operated by local authorities and the SWA rent and mortgage supplements. Under the differential rent scheme, tenants' rent is calculated on the basis of housing composition and income. This calculation is not standardized from one local authority to another, so horizontal equity between local authority tenants in different local authority areas cannot be assured. Those with low incomes in the private rented sector can apply for SWA rent supplement, operated by the Health Boards for the Department of Social, Community and Family Affairs. Again differences in entitlement are evident between Health Boards. There is also a difference between the differential rent and SWA schemes, so that people with equivalent circumstances may receive different levels of assistance depending on the scheme for which they are eligible and the area in which they live.

A third horizontal inequity exists between those in low-paid full-time work living in the private rented sector, who do not qualify for SWA rent supplement, and those categories who do qualify for a supplement. The Expert Working Group gave particular attention to the employment and poverty traps created by the scheme, which can lead to a disincentive for people either to take up work or to increase the amount of employment they undertake. The Group recommended the introduction of a more unified housing policy, and suggested that unemployed people should be able to retain their rent supplement for a period of time after they take up low paid employment, thereby easing the transition to work. Similar strategies have been pursued in relation to the retention of medical cards for those who take up employment. The Working Group's recommendation has not, however, been acted upon to date.

One of the problems with current policy is the fragmented nature of the system and its subsequent inability to respond to emerging issues in a strategic way. One example of this is the rising cost of SWA Rent and Mortgage supplements. These are paid to those in need of assistance with the cost of their accommodation, but who are not in full-time education or employment or engaged in a trade dispute. The cost of rent and mortgage supplements has increased from £7 million in 1989 to over £90 million (estimated) in 1998, but with little check on this growth. The scheme is funded by the Department of Social, Community and Family Affairs and administered by the health boards, who report to the Department of Health and Children. Meanwhile the Department of the Environment and Local Government and the local authorities have responsibility for overall housing policy and its implementation (see Review Group on the Role of Supplementary Welfare Allowance in Relation to Housing, 1995). Recommendations to curb spending in this area suggest the exclusion from entitlement of those under 25 years of age with no dependants, an increase in the minimum rent paid by recipients and a reduction in the maximum level of rent acceptable by the health boards (Review Group on the Role of Supplementary Welfare Allowance in Relation to Housing, 1995: 44–5). A more strategic approach, however, might consider how best to meet the long-term housing needs of those in low-income households.

A recent development in the housing sector is a rapid increase in house prices, particularly in the Dublin region. Bacon (1998) was commissioned by the Government to examine this price increase. He concluded that price increases were due to a number of factors including: sustained and rapid economic growth; rising levels of disposable income per capita; increasing employment and net migration into Dublin; falling interest rates and changes in social patterns resulting in diminishing household size and increased demand and increased investment demand for residential property; and encouraged by tax incentives for investors. While housing completions have increased in the last number of years, demand has out-stripped supply both in the owner-occupation and private-rented sectors, pushing up prices in both areas.

Bacon (1998) recommended major changes in housing policy, including: increasing the supply of land for building; a reduction in stamp duty for secondhand houses; repeal of 'Section 23' tax relief for investment in private rented accommodation; the introduction of stamp duty for purchases of new houses by non-occupants; moves to make the shared-ownership scheme more attractive; and the introduction of 35-year mortgages. Each of these moves can be analysed from a social policy perspective. Space does not permit a detailed treatment here, although a number of preliminary points can be made.

A first point to make is that while Bacon (1998) relates house price increases to socio-economic causes, they are not considered as central to the solution. An example might be that a more even spread of employment opportunities around the country would reduce the pull to Dublin. Concern has also been raised about the possible impact these changes will have on the private-rented sector, with increased rents predicted. Recommendations to expand access to the shared-ownership scheme, where low-income purchasers can become owner-occupiers in partnership with their local authority, were made without a thorough evaluation of the scheme, or reflection on problems in relation to debt (Threshold, 1997: 30-1). The introduction of 35-year mortgages, while resulting in lower monthly payments, would substantially increase the total repayments on a mortgage.

This scenario offers an interesting case study to students of social policy in how social problems get defined and acted upon. In contrast to the recent British situation where owner-occupation was considered a social problem because of negative equity trapping would-be sellers, in the Irish situation it is because of extreme positive equity, excluding would-be first-time buyers. In Ireland, the perceived importance of people having the chance to become owner-occupiers has helped to make the issue one for swift government action. Murphy (1998) has drawn attention to the speed of this response in contrast to the slower response to issues of pertinence to those in the private-rented sector – particularly those concerning the enforcement of legislation – which have received much less attention.

CHALLENGES FOR THE FUTURE

Perhaps one of the greatest challenges facing housing policy in Ireland is segregation. Research indicates the highly segregated nature of current provision and the consequent role which housing can play in the social exclusion of low-income households (Nolan et al., 1998; Fahey, 1998). Marginalized groups, such as members of the Travelling community, also suffer from this segregation (Task Force on the Travelling Community, 1995). Local authorities have a central role to play here, but it may take some time from them to build up the necessary capacity to address these very complex problems. Efforts to introduce more devolved housing management, through estate management for instance, have begun in Ireland, but could be further enhanced (Power, 1997). Local partnerships involved in local development are also taking an increased role in this area and may prove more successful. There is also a vital role for central government, in terms of policy development and enactment to develop a greater genuine choice of tenure. A substantial challenge will be the changing of public perceptions about mixed tenure, particularly changing the NIMBY (not in my back yard) stance which many more affluent areas adopt to the development of local authority accommodation, particularly for the Travelling community. A related challenge is to improve the living environment of the most marginalized housing estates, in consultation with local communities. Preservation of the rural landscape and consideration of the role of housing in shaping the social environment, particularly in coastal regions with high levels of holiday home construction, also requires serious consideration.

Affordability is a second challenge. Concern about the sharp increase in house prices in the owner-occupied sector has been discussed above. Substantial price increases, however, have also been evident in the private-rented sector (Downey, 1998). Some commentators have argued in the media that if these trends were to continue, housing inflation might call the collective pay agreement into question. It might also have a very immediate impact on those who are trying to access accommodation, particularly low cost accommodation, such as students. Research has also raised concern about the levels of housing debt, particularly for low income households (Threshold, 1997).

One possible policy development which could help to reduce housing segregation and increase the supply of low cost accommodation would be the encouragement of partnership relationships between the voluntary, statutory and private sectors. Housing policy also needs to be considered as a more integral element of social policy, with links to education, health, environmental and employment polices, for instance. The development of integrated local action plans under the urban renewal scheme is one example of how this is already happening. However, the value of this practice needs to be evaluated, documented and lessons transferred to other areas. On a more general level, the lack of hard data of relevance to the development of policy in this area must be addressed.

Finally, the suitability of the housing stock may become an increasing issue for the future. If the number of older people living in Ireland increases in line with projections, there may be some issues concerning the suitability of the current housing stock, and a need to introduce additional measures in relation to house maintenance, repair and adaptation for this age group (Silke, 1994).

IRISH HOUSING POLICY

TABLE OF RECENT IMPORTANT DATES

1966   Housing Act 1966 introduced – this is the main enabling
        act regarding local authority housing

1976   Family Home Protection Act, 1976, introduced

1984   £5,000 Surrender Grant introduced (ended in 1987)
        Capital Assistance Scheme introduced for non-profit and
        voluntary housing

1988   Housing Act 1988 introduced

1989   First assessment of housing need carried out.
        Local authority completions reach an all-time low of 768

1991   *A Plan for Social Housing* published by the Department of
        the Environment
        Shared Ownership Scheme introduced
        Second assessment of housing need carried out

1993   Third assessment of housing need carried out

1995   *Social Housing – The Way Ahead* published by the
        Department of the Environment
        Publication of the Report of the Review Group on the
        Role of Supplementary Welfare Allowance in Relation to
        Housing
        Tax Relief on Private Rent extended to all tenants in the
        Budget – a more limited scheme had already existed for
        those aged over 55.

1996   Homeless Initiatives established in Dublin
        Fourth assessment of housing need carried out
        Publication of the Report of the Expert Working Group
        on the Integration of Tax and Social Welfare Systems

1997   Anti-social legislation introduced

1998   Publication of Bacon Report *An Economic Assessment of
        Recent House Prices*
        Publication by the Department of the Environment and
        Local Government of its *Statement of Strategy 1998–2001*

NOTES

1 David Silke is a research officer with the Combat Poverty Agency. The views expressed are those of the author and are not necessarily those of the Combat Poverty Agency.

RECOMMENDED READING

Those who are new to the study of housing policy will find the housing chapter in Curry (1998) and also the chapter by O'Connell (1994) and Meghen (1963) very useful. Those interested in government statements of housing policy should read *Social Housing – The Way Ahead* (1995) and *A Plan for Social Housing* (1991), both by the Department of the Environment. The Department also publish a Housing Statistics Bulletin, on a quarterly and annual basis. Those particularly interested in housing issues for low-income group are referred to work by Fahey and Watson (1995): *An Analysis of Social Housing Need*, and Fahey in Healy and Reynolds (1998). The Report of the Review Group on the Role of Supplementary Welfare Allowance in Relation to Housing (1995) is also relevant in this context. Works by Anne Power *Estates on the Edge* (1997) and *Hovels to High Rise* (1993) provide useful international comparisons of local authority housing policy and practice. Those interested in reading more about owner-occupation should consult Bacon's (1998) report, *An Economic Assessment of Recent House Price Developments* and also Threshold's (1997) report on housing debt, *As Safe As Houses?* O'Sullivan (1996) provides a useful overview of issues relevant to homeless in Ireland. The Report of the Task Force on the Travelling Community (1995) has a section on housing policy. The Department of the Environment and Local Government's web page can be found at http://www.environ.ie, and includes a section on housing policy.

REFERENCES

Bacon, P. in association with F. MacCabe and A. Murphy (1998) *An Economic Assessment of Recent House Price Developments*. Dublin: Stationery Office.

Baker, T. J. and L. M. O'Brien (1997) *The Irish Housing System: A Critical Overview*. Dublin: Economic and Social Research Institute.

Blackwell, J. (1988) *Towards an Efficient and Effective Housing Policy: Special Issue', Administration*, 36 (4).

Central Statistics Office (1997) *Census 1991*, vol. 10: Housing. Dublin: Stationery Office.

Curry, J. (1998) *Irish Social Services* (3rd ed.). Dublin: Institute of Public Administration.

Daly, M. (1981) *Social and Economic History of Ireland since 1800*. Dublin: The Education Company.

Daly, M. (1994) *The Right to a Home, The Right to a Future: Third Report of the European Observatory on Homelessness, 1994*. European Commission and FEANTSA (European Federation of National Organisations Working with the Homeless).

Department of the Environment (1991) *Plan for Social Housing*. Dublin: Stationery Office.

Department of the Environment (1995) *Social Housing – the Way Ahead.* Dublin: Stationery Office.

Department of the Environment and Local Government (1998) *Statement of Strategy 1998–2001.* Dublin: Stationery Office.

Department of the Environment and Local Government (1997) *Annual Housing Statistics Bulletin 1997.* Dublin: Stationery Office.

Devolution Commission (1996) *Interim Report.* Dublin: Stationery Office.

Downey, D. (1998) *New Realities in Irish Housing: A Study of Housing Affordability and the Economy.* Dublin: Consultancy and Research Unit for the Built Environment, Dublin Institute of Technology.

Expert Working Group on the Integration of Tax and Social Welfare. (1996) *Report of the Expert Working Group on the Integration of the Tax and Social Welfare Systems.* Dublin: Stationery Office.

Fahey, T. (1998) 'Housing and Social Exclusion', pp. 411-29 in Healy, S. and B. Reynolds (eds), *Social Policy in Ireland: Principles, Practice and Problems.* Dublin: Oak Tree Press.

Fahey, T. and P. Murray (1994) *Health and Autonomy among the Over-65s in Ireland.* National Council for the Elderly (Report Number 39). Dublin: National Council for the Elderly.

Fahey, T. and D. Watson (1995) *An Analysis of Social Housing Need.* (General Research Series Paper Number 168) Dublin: Economic and Social Research Institute.

Finn, M. (1992) *Survey of Housing Stock 1990.* Dublin: Environmental Research Unit. Department of the Environment.

Gay and Lesbian Equality Network and Nexus Research Cooperative (1995) *Poverty: Lesbians and Gay Men: The Economic and Social Effects of Discrimination.* Dublin: Combat Poverty Agency.

Kaim-Caudle, P. (1967) *Social Policy in the Irish Republic.* London: Routledge & Kegan Paul.

Kearns, K. (1994) *Dublin Tenement Life: An Oral History.* Dublin: Gill & Macmillan.

Kelly, C. (1997) 'Eviction Plans for Drug Pushers are Flawed', *Poverty Today,* 35 (April).

Lennon L. (1998) *Under One Roof? A Report on the Future Options for the Organisation of Homeless Services in Dublin.* Dublin: The Homeless Initiative.

Matheson, R. (1903) 'Housing of the People of Ireland during 1841–1901', *Journal of the Statistical and Social Inquiry Society of Ireland,* XI (LXXXIII) November.

Meghen, P.J. (1963) *Housing in Ireland.* Dublin: Institute of Public Administration.

Murphy, K. (1998) 'Soaring Prices Only Part of Wider Housing Crisis', *Poverty Today,* 40 (June/July).

National Economic and Social Council (1988) *A Review of Housing Policy.* (Report Number 87). Dublin: National Economic and Social Council.

National Economic and Social Council (1993) *A Strategy for Competitiveness, Growth and Employment.* (Report Number 96) Dublin: National Economic and Social Council.

Nolan, B., C.T. Whelan and J. Williams (1998) *Where are Poor Households Found? The Spatial Distribution of Poverty and Deprivation in Ireland.* Dublin: Oak Tree Press.

O'Connell, C. (1994) 'Housing in the Republic of Ireland: A Review of Trends and Recent Policy Measures', *Administration*, 42 (2).

O'Sullivan, E. (1996) *Homelessness and Social Policy in the Republic of Ireland.* Department of Social Studies Occasional Paper Number 5. Dublin: University of Dublin, Trinity College.

O'Sullivan E. (1998) 'Homeless Children – Ireland's Failed Response', *Simon Community Newsletter.* No. 246, June 1998. Dublin: Simon Community.

Powell, W.F. (1992) *The Politics of Irish Social Policy 1600-1990.* New York: The Edwin Mellon Press.

Power, A. (1993) *Hovels to High Rise: State Housing in Europe since 1850.* London: Routledge.

Power, A. (1997) *Estates on the Edge: The Social Construction of Mass Housing in Northern Europe.* London: Macmillan.

Review Group on the Role of Supplementary Welfare Allowance in Relation to Housing. (1995) *Report to the Minister for Social Welfare.* Dublin: Stationery Office.

Silke, D. (1994) *The Altadore Research Project: Older People's Attitudes to the Accommodation.* Dublin: Trinity College and Dublin Central Mission.

Task Force on the Travelling Community. (1995) *Report of the Task Force on the Travelling Community.* Dublin: Stationery Office.

Threshold (1987) *Policy Consequences – A Study of the £5,000 Surrender Grant in the Dublin Housing Area.* Dublin: Threshold.

Threshold (1997) *As Safe as Houses? The Nature, Extent and Experience of Debt in the Irish Housing System.* Dublin: Threshold.

5
Education Policy

Patrick Clancy

INTRODUCTION

The 1990s have been a period of intense debate, analysis and policy
development in Irish education. While it is somewhat arbitrary to
identify a starting point for the recent flurry of activity in policy analysis
and development, the 1991 OECD, *Review of National Policies for
Education: Ireland*, report appears to have served as somewhat of a catalyst.
Although the explicit remit of this report was to deal with teacher supply
and training, it was the comments on the organization of education and
the perception of the weak administrative and policy making capacity of
the system which attracted most attention. These issues were to figure
prominently in the 1992 Green Paper, *Education for a Changing World,*
the publication of which initiated an unprecedented consultation process.
About 1000 written submissions were made in response to the Green
Paper and the national debate on education culminated in a high profile
National Education Convention where 42 interest groups and organizations were involved in public discussion on key issues of educational
policy in Ireland. The Report by the Convention Secretariat (1994)
formed a major input to the 1995 White Paper, *Charting our Education
Future*. The consultative process was further extended during 1994 by
position papers and roundtable discussions on local education structures
and school governance. A range of further policy documents were
published in recent years. These included: the Report of the Steering
Committee on the Future Development of Higher Education (1995)
and the Interim Report of its Technical Working Group (1995) which
was available prior to the publication of the White Paper; the Report of
the Special Education Review Committee (1993); the NESC (1993)
report on Education and Training Policies for Economic and Social
Development; and a report on Educational Disadvantage (Kellaghan
et al., 1995).

This intense debate has paralleled continuing rapid increases in enrolment in post-compulsory education. The centrality of education in Irish public policy reflects a continuing belief in the relevance of education for economic development and societal transformation. This policy orientation has had continuing public support since the 1960s when the state-led project of modernization first signalled a commitment to a restructured, diversified and greatly expanded educational system. This continuing affirmation contrasts with considerable oscillation in support in many other countries, ranging from periods of unbridled confidence (OECD, 1965) to profound pessimism (Murphy, 1993) about the potential of education to contribute to economic and social development.

The massive expansion in enrolments provides an indicator of the importance of education in Irish life. In 1995–96 a total of 962,250 students (27 per cent of the total population) were receiving full-time education. The distribution of these students, by sector, is shown in Table 1, which also shows the pattern of growth since 1965–66. The most spectacular growth has occurred in the third level sector with an almost five-fold increase over the thirty-year period. Second level enrolments have also grown dramatically, by a factor of about 2.6. Currently about 84% of the age cohort complete second-level education and about 50% of the age cohort go on to full-time higher education. The growth in enrolment is matched by a corresponding increase in the financial contribution made by the state to education. Government expenditure on education has grown from 3.7% of GNP in 1966, to 5.9% in 1996. Over this thirty-year period expenditure per student (in constant 1996 prices) had grown by 252% at first level, 167% at second level and 73% at third level to reach £1498, £2269 and £4097, respectively, in 1995–96.

Table 1. Enrolment in Full-time Education by Sector, 1965–66 and 1995–96

Level	1965–66	1995–96
Primary	504,865	485,983
Second Level	142,983	373,665
Third Level	20,698	102,662
Total	668,546	944,686

In prioritizing public expenditure on education in the late 1990s Irish policy is supported by the current consensus in most Western countries. This is especially evident in OECD publications, but also finds expression in the EU *White Paper on Education and Training* (1996). Two principal substantive concerns underpin this consensus. The first and dominant concern is the relationship between education and the labour market and focuses on education's contribution to economic growth and competitiveness. A second concern centres on considerations for equity, social justice and the needs of the disadvantaged. The pursuit of these twin economic and social objectives have legitimated the expansion of educational provision. These are not, of course, the only objectives of educational policy. The 1995 White Paper (1995: 10) sets out the principles which should underpin the formulation and evaluation of educational policy and practice – principally, the promotion of quality, equality, pluralism, partnership and accountability. More specifically, it sets out the following statement of educational aims:

- to foster an understanding and critical appreciation of the values – moral, spiritual, religious, social and cultural – which have been distinctive in shaping Irish society and which have been traditionally accorded respect in society

- to nurture a sense of personal identity, self-esteem and awareness of one's particular abilities, aptitudes and limitations, combined with a respect for the rights and beliefs of others

- to promote quality and equality for all, including those who are disadvantaged, through economic, social, physical and mental factors, in the development of their full educational potential

- to develop intellectual skills combined with a spirit of inquiry and the capacity to analyse issues critically and constructively

- to develop expressive, creative and artistic abilities to the individual's full capacity

- to foster a spirit of self-reliance, innovation, initiative and imagination

- to promote physical and emotional health and well-being

- to provide students with the necessary education and training to support the country's economic development and to enable them to make their particular contribution to society in an effective way

- to create tolerant, caring and politically aware members of society

- to ensure that Ireland's young people acquire a keen awareness of their national and European heritage and identity, coupled with a global awareness and a respect and care for the environment.

This statement of educational aims, which gives recognition to personal development and cultural objectives, seeks to go beyond the narrow concern with economic and social objectives which are frequently and sometimes exclusively invoked in educational debate. Many commentators have identified the marginalization of personal development and cultural objectives as a major weakness of contemporary educational policy in western countries (Bailey, 1984). In the Irish context, O'Sullivan (1992) has examined how the OECD report, *Investment in Education* (1965), may have been a modernizing force in changing the paradigm governing Irish education policy, in particular replacing the personal development with the human capital paradigm as the institutional rationale for education.

Following a prolonged period of consultation, the 1995 White Paper set out the future direction of educational policy. The most recent period could be characterized as the 'implementation phase', although this has inevitably been affected by a change in government in 1997. An important feature of the implementation phase is the enactment of legislation, a very scarce phenomenon in Irish education. This legislation is designed to underpin significant structural transformations in the educational system. The Universities Act was passed in 1997 and an Education Bill was introduced by the outgoing Rainbow Coalition government. This Bill was not enacted prior to the change in government and a new Bill, Education (No. 2) Bill, 1997, was being debated in the Oireachtas at the time of writing.

To date the main focus of educational policy has been on the formal system at first, second and third level. By comparison, pre-school education and adult and continuing education have received little attention, although there is some evidence that this may change. In Spring 1998, a National Forum on early childhood education was held and a report from the Forum Secretariat is in preparation. A Green Paper on Adult Education is being drafted. Pending policy developments in these areas these issues will not be examined in any detail in this paper. In addition, the limitations of a single paper demand further selectivity. For example, our consideration of disadvantage is limited to socio-economic disadvantage – gender issues, children with special needs and children of the Travelling Community are not considered. Other important topics not examined include: in-school management, curriculum reform at first and junior cycle level, assessment, the inspectorate and the school psychological service.

Following this introductory section the rest of the paper is divided into four sections. The next section reviews the historical origins of policy. This is followed by an analysis of the role of the partners in education. Current policy concerns are addressed in the next section while the final section looks to challenges for the future.

HISTORICAL ORIGINS OF POLICY

Before examining current policy developments it is appropriate to look at the historical evolution of educational policy. This brief venture into history is necessary since the nature of some of the key issues in contemporary policy is a direct legacy of historical experience.

The Irish educational tradition is a long one which dates back to the pre-Christian Bardic schools. After the introduction of Christianity, a thriving system of monastic schools was developed which, during Christianity's darkest days on the continent of Europe, led to the designation of Ireland as 'the island of saints and scholars'. From the time of Henry VIII there followed a long darker period during which the monastic schools were suppressed and 'thus began a definite English state policy in Irish education, namely, the Anglicization of the Irish people and the suppression of Catholic ideals in education' (Council of Education, 1954: 12). During the Penal Laws, which forbade any Catholic acting as a schoolteacher, recourse was made to the 'Hedge Schools' which were so named because they were often conducted in the open air under the protective cover of hedges. These schools were funded by students' contributions. This independent tradition persisted, even after the Penal Laws were ended, with Irish Catholics being distrustful of the educational initiatives of the State and the various charitable trusts and foundations and proselytizing agencies. In the early 1890s a number of religious orders, devoted specially to education, were founded. These included the Presentation Sisters in 1800, the Christian Brothers in 1802 and the Sisters of Mercy in 1828.

The system of National Schools, which in essence has survived to date, had its origin in the letter of the Chief Secretary, Lord Stanley, in 1831. Stanley made it clear that the state's role was that of assisting local initiatives on the basis of local schools adhering to the rules and regulations of the newly appointed Commissioners of National Education. While the national school system was intended to be non-denominational, this was resisted by the churches, especially the Presbyterians and Catholics. This opposition was ultimately successful and by 1870 the Powis Commission accepted that the attempt to establish a non-denominational system had failed and declared the system to be *de facto* a denominational one. It is of interest to note that the establishment of a national system of education in Ireland predated its establishment in England and Scotland. While there are several possible reasons for this, including the fact that, as a crown colony, Ireland was well used to state intervention and that 'the Irish peasantry showed a striking desire for their children to be schooled' (Akenson, 1970: 17), it is likely that the main motivating factor was the government expectation that the schools could serve politicizing goals, cultivating attitudes of political loyalty and cultural assimilation (Coolahan, 1981: 4).

The centrepiece of the national school system was the managerial system whereby state aid was disbursed by the Board of National Education to schools established and managed locally. The system was an aided one. State aid was contingent on a local contribution towards the cost of building and maintenance. In addition a site, approved by the commissioners, was to be provided and the school was to be vested in trustees approved by the Board. The system evolved into one of denominational management under parish priests or Protestant clergymen. State control was exercised via control of curriculum and textbooks and via an examination system whereby, for a long time, teachers' salaries were in part determined by pupils' results on examinations conducted by the Board's inspectors. After some time it was determined that schools operated by Catholic religious orders would be eligible for state aid, just as any other school, so long as the rules set down by the Board were complied with. However, the Irish Christian Brothers, after initially attaching some schools to the Board, withdrew them and operated their schools independently of the Board until 1925, after political independence.

The evolution of state aid to secondary education follows broadly the pattern established by the national school system. The Intermediate Education Act of 1878 established an Intermediate Education Board to distribute state funds on the basis of written examinations. However, in this case the level of funding was small and the operation of these schools required students to pay fees and/or personal sacrifices were made by members of religious orders. During the nineteenth century, secondary education was primarily a middle-class aspiration. An 1871 census listed a total of 186 schools which catered for about 21,000 students.

While the present system of vocational education dates from 1930, its antecedents go back to 1898 when the Local Government (Ireland) Act empowered local authorities to levy rates for the purpose of technical education. In the following year the Department of Agriculture and Technical Instruction for Ireland was established. The result was a system in which local committees, under the local rating authorities, planned and built schools called Technical Schools. At the time of transition to the Irish Free State some 65 schools existed. About two-thirds of the costs of these schools were borne by the state, with some 27 per cent coming from local rates and about six per cent from student fees.

Ireland's oldest university, the University of Dublin (Trinity College), received its royal charter in 1592. While some Catholic students were admitted to Trinity in the early years the operation of religious tests in the seventeenth and eighteenth centuries meant that only members of the Established Church could avail themselves of university education in Ireland. The first concession to allow higher education for Catholics was the granting of direct funding for the establishment in 1795 of a Catholic college at Maynooth. This college was founded to educate Catholic priests, the view being that it was preferable to provide this education at home rather than risk Irish students being 'exposed' to revolutionary thought and fervour which was sweeping Continental Europe in the wake of the French revolution. The problem still remained of providing university education for lay Catholics, as the atmosphere and control of Trinity College remained essentially Protestant. During the course of the nineteenth century several attempts were made to provide a form of university education which would be acceptable to Catholics. Three Queen's colleges at Belfast, Cork, and Galway were opened in 1849, with the Queen's University established as the examining and degree-awarding body for the colleges. The Queen's University was replaced by the Royal University of Ireland in 1879. This was purely an examining body and students attending the Queen's colleges as well as other students could enter for its degrees. The Catholic University was established in 1854, with John Henry Newman as its first rector. While Newman's stewardship was short-lived, the Catholic University, as well as a number of other institutions, evolved to become University College, Dublin. Finally, the university question was resolved in 1908 with the passing of the Irish Universities Act. A federal university, the National University of Ireland, was formed, with three constituent colleges: the former Queen's colleges at Cork and Galway, and University College Dublin. The other Queen's College, Belfast, became Queen's University of Belfast and the University of Dublin continued its existence unaffected. Until recent decades higher education in Ireland was almost synonymous with university education. The only other significant elements were the Training Colleges (now called Colleges of Education) and a small technological sector, mainly composed of the Colleges of Technology under the control of the City of Dublin Vocational Education Committee.

PARTNERS IN EDUCATION

The education system is constituted from a large number of interest groups, referred to collectively as partners in education. The White Paper (1995: 213) differentiates between those involved in the policy-formulation process and the delivery and practice of education in a direct and continuous way, and those with a more broadly based interest and involvement arising from their participation in the social, economic and political fabric of our society. In their strategy document, the Department of Education (1996) gives a figure of 120 groups whom it has identified as having an active interest in the educational service, while a total of 42 groups were given invitations to participate in the National Education Convention. In practice, of course, a much smaller number of groups can be identified as key players in the policy process.

Churches and the State

Perhaps the most distinctive feature of the Irish education system is the level of church involvement and control. Church control of education is rooted in the ownership and management of schools. After independence in 1922, the new state institutionalized the denominational school system which it inherited. Successive ministers of education adopted the view that the role of the state in education was a subsidiary one of aiding agencies such as the churches in the provision of educational facilities. The classic expression of this position is outlined in Minister for Education, Richard Mulcahy's speech to Dáil Éireann in 1956:

> Deputy Moylan has asked me to philosophise, to give my views on educational technique or educational practice. I do not regard that as my function in the Department of Education in the circumstances of the educational set-up in this country. You have your teachers, your managers and your Churches and I regard the position as Minister in the Department of Education as a kind of dungaree man, the plumber who will make the satisfactory communications and streamline the forces and potentialities of educational workers and educational management in this country. He will take the knock out of the pipes and will link up everything. (Dáil Debates, 159: 1494)

Currently about 98 per cent of children of primary-school going age (4–12) attend state-supported national schools, although the term 'national' is somewhat misleading since the schools are not owned by the state. Almost all of these schools are denominational, with 93 per cent under the patronage of the Catholic Church. At second level, about 60 per cent of students attend secondary schools, 89 per cent of which are owned and controlled by Catholic religious communities; the remainder are divided between those which belong to other religious denominations, and those which are either privately or corporately owned by lay Catholics. The churches are also involved, in partnership with vocational education committees, in the management and control of Comprehensive and Community Schools which educate about 14 per cent of students in this sector. While the churches have no formal involvement in the control of vocational schools, which are publicly owned, it is of interest that in some of the newly established vocational schools, called Community Colleges, the VECs have been prepared to enter into agreements with religious authorities in relation to agreed places on boards of management. Thus, the primary sector and the major part of the second level sector consist of privately owned state-aided schools, with the state now paying over 80 per cent of capital costs of buildings and facilities and over 90 per cent of current expenditure.

The issue of governance has come to occupy centre-stage in the recent policy debates. Part of this concern arises from demands for more democratic participation by parents and teachers in the management of schools. The debate also reflects an attempt to redefine the appropriate role of the state and of denominational authorities in the control of education. The demands for greater democratization represent a challenge to the traditional managerial system. Traditionally the patron (usually the bishop of the diocese) appointed the manager who administered the school in accordance with the regulations laid down by the Department of Education. Typically the manager was the parish priest or, in the case of the schools operated by religious congregations, the superior of the religious community. More recently (from 1975 in the case of primary schools and 1985 in the case of secondary schools) the single manager has been replaced by a board of management. This change has not signifi-cantly altered the power structure, since the patron's nominees constitute a majority of the board. The other members are elected parents and teacher representatives.

In responding to these demands for greater democratization and to the continuing insistence by the patrons and trustees on their need to appoint majorities on the boards so as to safeguard the ethos of their schools, the Secretariat of the National Education Convention suggested that both concerns might be accommodated by a clearer specification of the functions of patronage and management. It was suggested that the interests of patrons and trustees could be safeguarded by the drawing-up of agreed Deeds of Trust and Articles of Management, within the ambit of which a board of management could operate and departures from which could lead to its being called to account. In this context it was suggested that boards could be equally representative of patrons, teachers and parents (Report on the National Education Convention, 1994: 29). Agreement was finally reached on the composition of boards of manage-ment for National Schools in 1997, after several years of negotiations. The boards will be made up of two direct nominees of the patron; two parents of children enrolled in the school elected by the general body of parents; two teachers, one the principal and one elected by the teaching staff; and two extra members proposed by these nominees. The patron shall appoint one of the members so appointed as Chairperson of the Board of Management. The final element of the agreement included a model deed of trust, which provides a legal basis for guaranteeing the specific ethos of each school. No agreement has yet been reached on the composition of boards of management for second-level schools.

The controversy surrounding the constitution and rules of procedure of boards of management brings into sharp relief the respective role of the partners in education. Some of the legal and constitutional issues which arise are discussed in an incisive final chapter of the White Paper (1995: 214) which sought to prepare the ground for the drafting of the Education Bill. Here it is argued that:

> . . . legislation must have regard to the constitutional rights and duties of parents and of the state; property rights and the rights of religious denominations to manage their own affairs; the legal principles of estoppel,[1] legitimate expectation and proportionality as well as equality principles and the interests of the common good. Any provisions must reflect a careful balancing of the many legitimate rights and interests in education – rights and interests which at times may be in conflict with one another – so that the exercise of rights by one of the partners in education does not unreasonably delimit the exercise of their rights by any other.

The difficulty in reaching a 'harmonious interpretation' in respect of conflicting rights is illustrated by the different positions taken, in respect of boards of management, by Minister Bhreathnach and Minister Martin in the preparation of their respective Education Bills. Education Bill 1997, presented by Niamh Bhreathnach, upheld the right of the Minister for Education to require all recognized schools to establish boards of management appointed by the patron and composed as determined by ministerial order. However, it acknowledged that before making an order the minister must seek agreement with the patron, national association of parents, and unions and associations representing teachers. The Bill provided for the fact that if agreement cannot be reached then the Minister may make an order which shall be subject to ratification by the Houses of the Oireachtas. Notwithstanding this provision, the proposed sanction in respect of a failure to establish a board was limited. The Bill specified that where a school does not have, or ceases to have, a board of management constituted in accordance with the Act, public funding to the school and the number of teachers paid from public funds will be fixed at the level obtaining at the time of the passing of the Act or the date on which the school ceases to have a board of management.

In the debate on the Education Bill, prior to the 1997 General Election, spokespersons for both Fianna Fáil and the Progressive

Democrats argued that the Education Bill, as tabled, was unconstitutional in view of the excessive powers appropriated by the Minister for Education. Thus, it was no surprise that when Micheál Martin introduced his new bill, Education (No. 2) Bill, 1997, these provisions were changed. The new Bill proposes that 'it shall be the duty of a patron . . . to appoint where practicable a board of management the composition of which is agreed . . .'. There is no provision for sanctions where a board is not established. It is clear that in this Bill the state has settled for a less-controlling position vis-à-vis the churches.

The successful reassertion by the churches of their rights in education does not, of course, represent an overwhelming constraint on the powers of the state to act by virtue of its role as promoter and guardian of the common good. It is also clear that the scale of state intervention has increased dramatically since the 1960s, making redundant the image of the dungaree man. The OECD examiners, (1991: 37–8), while being intrigued by the degree of private (church) control, recognized that there is not a private monopoly and that the state exercises a much tighter control than appears at first sight. The state's prerogative gains particular legitimacy in view of the fact that it provides most of the funding for education. It pays teachers' salaries, determines teacher qualifications and pupil/teacher ratios; it controls curriculum and employs inspectors to monitor standards; it has *de facto* control of building policy and establishes rules for the management and maintenance of schools (p. 37).

While most of the state's power is exercised directly by the Department of Education and Science (formerly Department of Education), representing a high level of administrative centralization, a number of its functions have been allocated to specialist agencies which operate under its aegis. These include the National Council for Curriculum and Assessment (NCCA), the National Council for Educational Awards (NCEA), the National Council for Vocational Awards (NCVA) and the Higher Education Authority (HEA). The most recent such body to be established is TEASTAS, the National Certification Authority.

Apart from the Department of Education and Science and its associated national agencies, public control of education is also reflected in the operation of the Vocational Education Committees. The VECs are largely controlled by members of the local authorities – at least five and not more than eight of their fourteen member committee must be members of the local rating authority. The remaining members are selected from employers, trade unions or individuals with a special interest or expertise in education. The VECs represent a unique element in the Irish educational structure, being non-denominational, regionally based and publicly controlled. Currently vocational schools cater for some

26 per cent of second-level students and also provide continuing technical and vocational education, as well as a range of adult and community education and out-of-school services. At the time of their establishment, vocational schools were not intended to compete with existing denominational schools in the provision of 'general education'. Since the 1960s successive attempts have been made to end the essentially binary system which differentiated between Secondary/academic and Vocational/technical schools. The system remains, however, highly differentiated in terms of social selectivity, prestige and academic emphasis (Clancy, 1995a: 490). Vocational schools still cater disproportionately for students from working-class backgrounds and appear to have a higher incidence of social problems among pupils (Hannan et al., 1996: 82–3).

This commitment to meeting the needs of the disadvantaged has been identified as one of the perceived strengths of the VECs, in a study by two Scottish researchers (Brown and Fairley, 1993). Other perceived strengths include the contribution to providing vocational education, being innovative and flexible in their response to change, providing a coordinating and supportive function for local schools in their area, and facilitating links between local schools and the local labour market and economy. A principal criticism identified was the so-called 'politicization' of the VECs, especially in relation to the appointment of teachers and principals. While the VECs represent an extension of public control in education, their concern for survival, as a distinctive entity in a system which is predominantly privately owned, means that their interests are not synonymous with that of central government. In commenting on the mediating powers of the VECs, Lynch (1989) suggests that while their democratic representativeness serves to legitimate the functioning of the educational system it is the case that, like all local authorities, the VECs are dominated by middle-class personnel who are unlikely to seek to seriously challenge the status quo.

Teachers

While the churches and the state appear to have dominated some aspect of policy making it is also necessary to reckon with the powerful role of teachers as an interest group. The power of the teacher unions was identified by the OECD examiners, who noted 'the very active and well-organised professional teacher associations with their formidable negotiating skills' (OECD, 1991). Teachers are represented by four unions representing the different sectors. The Irish National Teachers Organisation (INTO) represents teachers in national schools, the Association of Secondary Teachers of Ireland (ASTI) represents teachers in secondary schools, while the Teachers Union of Ireland (TUI) represents teachers in vocational schools and lecturers in the third-level technological sector. Teachers in comprehensive and community schools are represented by either the ASTI or the TUI, the choice being largely determined by the former sector to which they belonged prior to school amalgamation. The fourth, and very much the smallest, union is the Irish Federation of University Teachers (IFUT) which represents university staff.[2]

Burke (1992) has pointed to the dilemma which confronts professionals in bureaucratic organizations who are torn between maintaining their professionalism and at the same time striving for working conditions which befit their status and responsibility. The latter orientation forces them into a trade union model of organization which has been especially significant in Ireland. The main teacher unions are among the most powerful white-collar unions in the country. Their influence is reflected in their establishment of direct negotiation rights with government (Lynch, 1989) and in their representation on statutory and investigative bodies on various aspect of Irish education. Barry (1989) has detailed this growing influence in respect of one union (the ASTI), while Burke (1992) has described the overall trend as involving a change from a position of inadequate representation on bodies such as the Council of Education in the 1950s to the current situation, in which teacher unions (and other special interest groups such as managerial bodies) enjoy a virtual veto on the formulation of educational policy. One of the implications of involvement in statutory bodies such as the NCCA and investigative bodies such as the Primary Education Review Body is that it serves to prevent certain issues getting on the policy agenda and circumscribes the range of solutions which are considered. A further increment in the power of the main teacher unions is their growing influence within the Irish Congress of Trade Unions in helping to set the agenda of the various national understandings negotiated since the late-1980s. This influence reflects a dual agenda. At one level it supports a number of initiatives designed to tackle the problem of disadvantage in Irish education. At another level many of the initiatives which have been negotiated, such as improved staffing levels, are also designed to improve the working conditions of teachers. While on occasions there may be a happy coincidence between both objectives, sometimes the latter consideration may dictate the choice of measure adopted. For example, an increase in staffing levels can be used to achieve an across-the-board reduction in pupil-teacher ratios or the extra personnel can be exclusively targeted to schools in disadvantaged areas. The options represent a choice between the pursuit of trade union interests versus the pursuit of an equality agenda.

A highly significant development for teachers, which offers the potential to enhance their professional status, is represented by the decision to establish a Teaching Council which will act as a professional regulatory body. Following the report of a technical working group in 1998, the Minister for Education promised that he will introduce legislation to establish the Council which will entitle teachers to appropriate regulation of their own affairs. It is envisaged that the Teaching Council will take over a range of functions now performed by the Department of Education and Science, including the registration of teachers. It will advise the government on the induction of newly qualified teachers and devise a framework for in-service training. It will draw up codes of professional practice and conduct and will have powers to investigate and adjudicate on complaints that teachers have failed to meet professional standards and to take disciplinary action in cases of serious misconduct. The establishment of a Teaching Council has been a long-standing demand of the INTO and the ASTI for many years, although the TUI has always had reservations about the idea.

Parents

While students are the principal clients of the education system, with the exception of third-level students who have their own representative organization (the Union of Students in Ireland), they have not been seen as an organized interest group. However, the Education (No 2) Bill 1997 (Section 27) does give students some consultative rights in schools. Boards of management are required to facilitate the involvement of students in the operation of the school 'having regard to the age and experience of the students' and, in the case of post-primary schools, they are obliged to encourage the establishment by students of a student council. In addition, in the case of a student who has reached the age of eighteen, a right of appeal to the board of management is given in respect of a decision of a teacher or other member of staff of a school. In practice, parents who are secondary clients of the educational system are expected to act in respect of the interests of their school-going children. However, as an interest group, parents as a collectivity have only recently become accepted as a part of the policy community in education.

The limited level and recency of involvement of parents in education policy making and administration represent something of an anomaly given the fact that the Constitution acknowledges that the primary and natural educator of the child is the family, and that Article 42.1 states that it is the inalienable right and duty of parents to provide, in accordance with their means, for the religious and moral, intellectual, physical and social education of their children. For a long time the representatives of the churches, acting as patrons and managers, saw themselves as representing the interests of parents. More recently, with more educated parents desiring a more active involvement in their children's education, the older model of patron 'acting on behalf of such people is coming under challenge' (Report on the National Education Convention, 1994: 25). A difficulty remaining arises from the heterogeneous nature of the parent body and the problem of securing spokespersons who are truly representative. It has long being established that middle-class parents take a more active interest in their children's education and, while we lack research evidence on the characteristics of those involved on parents' councils, it would appear that the great majority of activists are from middle-class backgrounds. Parent input into decision making at national level is via the National Parents Council (NPC) which has separate primary and post-primary tiers. The NPC-Primary has a branch in every county and currently has over 1,000 parents associations affiliated while the NPC Post-Primary is composed of delegates elected from the six national bodies representing second-level parents' associations. The Education (No. 2) Bill marks an important milestone for the NPC in that it formalizes its inclusion within the policy community. The Bill stipulates that the exercise of discretion by the Minister in a whole range of areas requires prior consultation with national associations of parents, as well as with the other partners.

CURRENT POLICY CONCERNS

Creation of New Legislative and Administrative Framework

Much of the recent intense activity in education policy which culminated in the White Paper (1995) and the two Education Bills has centred on the need to establish an appropriate legislative and administrative framework for the educational system. The absence of an appropriate legislative framework for primary and most of second level education and the unease of relying on administrative circular as the main regulatory and administrative instrument has been the subject of frequent comment, more recently by the influential Report of the Constitution Review Group (1996). A key objective of the Education Bill is to provide, on a legislative basis, for the respective roles and functions of all of the partners in the educational system. In introducing the Bill in the Dáil, Minister Martin stressed that it sought to promote and give statutory recognition to the principle of partnership as a principle which underpins the operation of the system. The role of the respective partners has been described in the previous section of the chapter, thus, this section will confine itself to describing some of the debate surrounding the reform of the administrative system. However, before doing so it is appropriate to set out some of the main parameters of the Education (No. 2) Bill. The main provisions of the Bill provide for: the recognition of schools for the purpose of funding by public funds; the establishment of the inspectorate on a statutory basis; the establishment of boards of management of schools; the establishment and role of parents associations; the functions of principals and teachers; appeals by students and their parents; the making of regulations by the minister; the establishment of the National Council for Curriculum and Assessment; and regulation of the state examination system.

The publication of the OECD (1991) report, which was highly critical of the weakness of the policy, decision-making and planning system in Irish education, initiated a major debate on the administrative system. The report noted that the Department of Education functioned like a classic, highly centralized bureaucracy and suggested that if it was to concentrate on the strategic policy making role it would be necessary to shed much of the routine administrative responsibility. Such a change, the report argued, would require an administrative layer interposed between it and individual schools. While the then Minister for Education, Mary O'Rourke, did not accept the need for a local or regional administrative system, much of the discussion following the publication of the Green Paper seemed to reflect a growing consensus that it was appropriate to transfer substantial coordination and support service functions to regional boards. This rationale was outlined in the White Paper, and the establishment of ten Education Boards was a central feature of the Education Bill 1997 introduced by Minister Niamh Bhreathnach, which, as we have already noted, was not enacted prior to the General Election. The rationale for the establishment of the Education Boards as set out in the White Paper (1995: 165) includes:

- a need for greater awareness of and sensitivity to the needs of local and regional communities in order to improve the quality, equality, efficiency, relevance and flexibility of delivery of all educational services
- the value of further involvement and empowerment of local and regional communities, in addition to their current and continuing involvement at school level
- the desirability of releasing the Department of Education from much of its current involvement in the detailed delivery of services to schools, in order to allow it to concentrate on the development and monitoring of the education system at national level

- a realization that the demands of educational provision cannot, in many instances, be met at the level of the individual school.

The proposal to establish a regional structure of administration was opposed by Fianna Fáil and the Progressive Democrats while in opposition, thus it came as no surprise that it did not feature in the new Education (No. 2) Bill 1997. In introducing his Education Bill, Minister Martin rejected the many 'inflated claims' which had been made in respect of the potential of regional education boards, arguing that their establishment 'would have involved a massive extension of state control and would have increased greatly the level of bureaucracy'. In addition, he argued that it had been estimated in 1995 that they would have cost about £40 million annually and that this cost would not have been justified, his preference being to use scarce resources where they most needed, in the classroom (Dáil Debates, 5 February 1998: 1287–8).

Part of the difficulty with the proposal for the establishment of regional education councils made by the Rainbow Coalition government, and which was mediated via a special Roundtable Discussion on a Position Paper issued by the Minister (Coolahan and McGuinness, 1994), was the problem of integrating within a single council a system of primary and post-primary privately owned schools with the VEC structure which was already regionalized and in public control. A decision to subsume the VECs within the regional councils in the interests of avoiding duplication of regional structures seemed to be unacceptable both to the VECs and to the patrons and managers of private schools. The latter feared that a regional council which owned some of the schools within its jurisdiction might not be impartial or be seen to be impartial in its allocation of resources and services, while the former had a vested interest in their own survival. The final proposals did not envisage the abolition of the VECs or their incorporation within the regional councils, although a limited rationalization was effected by the decision to amalgamate five town VECs – Bray, Drogheda, Sligo, Tralee and Wexford – with their respective county VECs.

The decision to abandon the attempts to establish regional education boards makes it difficult for the Department of Education to achieve the kind of administrative devolution which it seemed to endorse, to enable it to concentrate on its more strategic planning and policy-formation role. An inevitable outcome may be that it will have to set up more specialist agencies to carry out certain functions. A recent example, which predates the failure of the regionalization proposals, is the Commission on School Accommodation which was set up to plan, in an ordered way, for future school provision. It consists of a steering group representative of the partners in education and technical working groups which report to the steering group.

Increasing Participation and Programme Diversification

Turning to substantive policy developments, the most emphatic trend, as suggested in the introduction, has been the increase in participation rates in the post-compulsory years. This trend is driven both by labour market and equality considerations and is also associated with curriculum reform and programme diversification, especially at senior cycle level, and by attempts to develop a coordinated certification framework. Much of the impetus behind the increasing participation rates arises from repeated research findings on the relationship between level of education and employment levels. High levels of unemployment are disproportionately concentrated among those who leave school with no qualifications. The recent and unprecedented upsurge in job creation (Sweeney, 1998) is associated with a demand for highly skilled workers; those with minimal qualifications are not in demand. In this context the number-one policy priority is to eliminate the problem of early school-leaving and to increase to 90 per cent by the end of the decade the numbers staying on to take the Leaving Certificate. However, the success of the policy of increased participation rates has greatly increased the diversity, ability and aspirations of students in secondary education posing an ever-increasing challenge to provide an appropriate and beneficial education for all. A feature of second-level education has been the dominance of the traditional academic curriculum. The NESC (1993) study pointed to the low percentage of students enrolled on vocational programmes by comparison with other European countries, while the influential *Report of the Industrial Policy Review Group* (Culliton, 1992) argued that the inadequate provision for vocational education at second level demonstrated that the educational system is not attuned to the economic needs of society. It called for the development of a separate vocational stream at second level to rival the existing dominant academic stream. Also relevant are the findings of an ESRI study of school leavers' levels of satisfaction with their education, which reveal low levels of satisfaction among those whose experience was confined to the ordinary (lower) level academic Leaving Certificate programme (Hannan and Shortall, 1991).

A major restructuring of the senior cycle involving four main elements is in progress. This involves the availability of the transition year programme for all second-level schools; the revision of syllabuses for the established Leaving Certificate programme; the development of the

Leaving Certificate Vocational programme; and the introduction of a new Leaving Certificate Applied programme.

The transition year, which is an optional year between the Junior Certificate and senior cycle, was first introduced in the mid-1970s, but was available only in a limited number of second-level schools. While it remains an optional programme, since 1994 all schools are free to offer the programme and by 1996–97, some 24,000 students in over 500 schools were taking the programme. The transition year programme is interdisciplinary and student-centred, emphasizing interpersonal and experiential learning and practical skills which are difficult to accommodate in the pressurized Leaving Certificate cycle.

The introduction of the Leaving Certificate Applied (LCA) represents the most radical restructuring at senior-cycle level. This programme, which was first introduced in 57 schools in 1995, differs fundamentally from the conventional Leaving Certificate and replaces the experimental Senior Certificate and the Vocational Preparation and Training (VPT 1) programmes. The new LCA programme is built around three main strands: vocational preparation, which includes work experience, enterprise education, and oral and written communication skills; vocational education which is concerned with the acquisition of knowledge and skills in vocational specialisms such as horticulture and tourism; and general education which involves arts, civic, social and economic education and languages. It is envisaged that students on the LCA will spend a minimum of 55 per cent of their time on vocational preparation and vocational education, compared to a minimum of 30 per cent on general education. The LCA is designed as a separate and distinct form of Leaving Certificate, a vocationally oriented stream which will provide for the needs of those students for whom the traditional Leaving Certificate was deemed inappropriate. Notwithstanding the reservations of many educationalists, whose concerns were reflected in the Green Paper (1992) proposals which sought to avoid completely separate tracking, the introduction of the LCA has reinstated the dual system in second-level education (albeit now at senior cycle in contrast to the junior cycle differentiation which prevailed from the 1930s to the late 1960s). While students who complete this programme will not gain direct entry to third level, they will be able to proceed to Post Leaving Certificate programmes.

A second and less radical alternative to the traditional Leaving Certificate, the Leaving Certificate Vocational programme, has been available in schools since 1989. It was originally devised as a subset of the Leaving Certificate course with an emphasis on a limited number of technical subjects. It has now been developed and restructured and, following piloting in September 1994, was made available nationwide in 1996. In its restructured form it involves five subjects from the existing Leaving Certificate programme, including two subjects chosen from a set of vocational subjects, a recognized course in a modern European language and three mandatory link modules (enterprise education, preparation for work, and work experience). It is estimated that in 1996–97 over 11,000 students took the LCVP while 4500 students took the LCA programme. It is projected that by 1999 one Leaving Certificate student in three will take either the LCA or the LCVA programme.

Tackling Disadvantage

The drive to eliminate the problem of early school-leaving and to greatly increase overall qualification and skill levels of school-leavers is an intrinsic part of the strategy of tackling the problem of disadvantage. And in spite of considerable progress in recent years the best estimates for 1995 suggest that about 5000 students each year leave school without any qualification and that a further 8000 leave before taking the Leaving Certificate. These differential qualifications of school-leavers are directly related to parents' social backgrounds. In an analysis of three cohorts of school-leavers in the early 1990s it was revealed that while 22 per cent of school-leavers had left without completing the Leaving Certificate, this was the case with some 47 per cent of the children of unskilled manual backgrounds compared with less than three per cent of those with parents from higher professional backgrounds. Furthermore, for those who did persevere to Leaving Certificate, the levels of attainment were strongly related to social background, with higher levels of attainment for those from higher socio-economic groups. Finally, for those school-leavers who attained a Leaving Certificate, the percentage going on to third-level education varied by socio-economic group and level of attainment in the Leaving Certificate. The socio-economic group disparities in percentages making this latter transition was especially marked for those with low levels of attainment. In contrast, the class differentials in making this transition were very modest for those with a high level of attainment in the Leaving Certificate (Clancy, 1995b: Technical Working Group, 1995).

Policies to counter disadvantage in education have evolved over time. Initial effects were concerned to eliminate barriers to access. Thus, there was a concern with increasing the provision of places, and initiatives such as 'free' post-primary education and a school transport system were introduced. However, as in other countries, research demonstrated that equality of access does not guarantee equality of participation, much less equality of performance. More recently, many policy initiatives are characterized by the acceptance of the need to provide additional resources to students who experience difficulty in adapting to and who make poor progress at school. These initiatives have been the subject of examination in a variety of recent publications (NESC, 1993; *Report on the National Education Convention*, 1994; Kellaghan et al., 1995).

Most policy analysts have come to accept that the earlier one intervenes in tackling disadvantage the better the results. Following this logic and following the example of the innovative Rutland Street project which, since 1969, has served a severely disadvantaged area in Dublin's north inner city, the government in 1994 introduced its pilot pre-school intervention programme, Early Start, in designated disadvantaged areas. The curriculum in the pre-school makes language and literacy a priority and parental involvement is a key objective, striving to create a shared exchange of expertise between staff and parents. By 1996, Early Start operated in 40 locations. At primary level a range of initiatives are in place. These include the provision of remedial teachers, the designation of disadvantaged areas which qualify schools for additional capitation grants and some concessionary teaching posts, the home-school-community liaison programme, and most recently the Breaking the Cycle initiative. Under this latter scheme, which represents the most extensive form of affirmative action, a number of selected primary schools in urban and rural areas have been targeted for an intensive package of additional supports including additional staffing and reduced class sizes in large urban schools, special additional funding for materials and equipment and a special programme of in-career development. The urban dimension of this programme involves 33 large schools from Dublin, Cork and Limerick, while the rural dimension involves 118 small schools grouped into 25 rural clusters. As an example of the special targeting, in the urban schools chosen, all infants, first and second classes will have a maximum of 15 pupils.

An important dimension of the intervention in schools in disadvantaged areas is the involvement of parents. This policy is reflected in the development of the Home-School-Community-Liaison (HSCL) scheme which was initiated in 55 primary schools in 1990. The scheme allows schools to appoint a teacher as coordinator with the full-time task of developing relationships between schools, homes and communities and represents an acknowledgement of the role of the family and community as agents of learning and development. The number of primary schools included in the HSCL scheme had increased to 134 in 1994–95, while provision was made for an additional 49 schools to join the scheme in 1995–96.

Many of the interventions at post-primary level parallel those found at primary level. Thus, there is provision for remedial teachers and Home-School-Community-Liaison teachers. A Scheme of Assistance to Schools in Designated Areas of Disadvantage has operated since 1990–91. By 1994–95, 22.5% of post-primary schools, catering for some 24% of the post-primary population, were in the scheme (Kellaghan et al., 1995). Many of the curriculum initiatives at second level are at least partially designed to assist the disadvantaged. As discussed above, most of the recent activity has taken place at senior cycle level, although the revamped junior cycle was introduced in 1989. A recent initiative was the introduction of the Junior Certificate Elementary programme which commenced in September 1996 in up to 45 schools. It is intended that the number of schools will increase to 80 on a phased basis. This programme has been introduced to cater for a small number of students who have repeatedly experienced failure during their school career, who may have serious difficulties with basic skills of literacy and numeracy and who may be at risk of leaving school before taking the Junior Certificate examination.

While the emphasis in present policy is to reduce the incidence of early school leaving, the level of earlier failure has left a large minority of older age groups who are poorly equipped to take advantage of the new employment opportunities in the economy. A number of post-school programmes are in operation. Youthreach, a programme for unemployed early school leavers aged 15–18 with no formal educational qualifications, was first introduced in 1989. In recent years this target group has been seen as a policy priority and the programme has been extended. In 1998 about 4000 were on the Youthreach programme. A second scheme, the Vocational Training Opportunities Scheme (VTOS) catering for adults over the age of 21 and who were unemployed for at least six months (12 months in the original scheme), was also introduced in 1989. In 1996 some 5000 VTOS places were provided. The scheme provides an opportunity for participants to update their general education while retaining their Social Welfare entitlements. The most extensive provision for second-chance education is through the Adult Literacy and Community Education (ALCE) scheme. This scheme, which originated in 1983, is administered by the VECs and aims to provide basic literacy courses and community education in disadvantaged areas. The need for much greater provision of basic adult education has been documented in a disturbing recent report, which reveals that 25 per cent of the Irish adult population are operating at the minimum level of literacy and that, with the exception of Poland, the Irish sample are significantly less literate than eight other comparator countries (Morgan et al., 1997).

Inequalities in participation in higher education, which were first examined in *Investment in Education* (OECD, 1965), have been well documented by the present author in a series of studies (Clancy, 1982; 1988; 1995c). While it is widely accepted that these inequalities represent merely the end of a cumulative process which first manifests itself early in the educational career, and that early intervention represents the best policy option, it has also been accepted that third-level institutions have some responsibility for helping to redress the inequalities. Two pioneering schemes which have been in operation since 1990 have attracted a good deal of attention. The Ballymun Initiative for Third Level Education (BITE) and the Limerick Community-Based Educational Initiative (LCBEI) focus on post-primary schools in disadvantaged areas close to Dublin City University and the University of Limerick. These interventions, which are designed to counter early drop-out from post-primary school, include supervized evening study facilities, supplementary tuition by university students, summer schools to familiarize second level students with third-level courses, briefing sessions for parents, and financial assistance for some students from the age of 15. More recently many other colleges have introduced broadly similar programmes, while the White Paper states that all third-level colleges will be encouraged to develop links with second-level schools building upon existing good practice. The Universities Act 1997 places an obligation on all colleges to put in place arrangements which facilitate an increase in participation of students from disadvantaged backgrounds. The strongest form of affirmative action recommended to date is that of the Steering Committee on the Future Development of Higher Education (1995) which suggests that a pool of reserved places for students from disadvantaged backgrounds for which there would be alternative entry requirements with, where appropriate, success in a special access programme a prerequisite for a place. This pool of reserved places would represent about two per cent of total entrants in each institution.

The concern for under-represented minority groups extends beyond that of social disadvantage to include those with disabilities. Both the White Paper and the report of the Steering Committee on the Future Development of Higher Education address the question of special support measures which seek to improve access and participation for students with disabilities, while this issue has been examined in detail by the Committee on Access and Participation of Students with Disabilities (1995). The Steering Committee sets as a 'modest target' doubling by the year 2000 the current annual intake of about 150 students with disabilities. A special fund, £105,000 in 1996, has been established by the Minister for Education to assist students with physical disabilities.

Further Education Sector

Efforts to strengthen the vocational element of the senior cycle curriculum are complemented by developments in certification and the evolution of a further education sector. The latter development stems largely from the provision of Post Leaving Certificate (PLC) courses. These courses seek to provide vocational training to enhance students' employment prospects. The emphasis in these programmes is on technical knowledge – the development of vocational skills needed for a particular discipline; work experience – including on-the-job training, where feasible; and personal development – fostering interpersonal skills, computer familiarization, adaptability and initiative etc. The number of students on PLC courses has increased very rapidly to almost 18,000 in 1995.

A feature of the evolution of PLC programmes is the *ad hoc* and relatively unstructured nature of the development. This was most evident in respect of certification arrangements. While all students received a certificate of participation from the Department of Education, a range of other external bodies were sometimes involved in certification. These included the Business and Technology Education Council (BTEC), City and Guilds of London, Royal Society of Arts and the Marketing Institute of Ireland. In 1991 a National Council for Vocational Awards (NCVA) was established for the certification and assessment of vocational and training programmes provided outside the third-level system. In addition to the PLC courses, programmes within the remit of the NCVA include the Youthreach Foundation Year, the Vocational Training Opportunity Scheme (VTOS), and Programmes in Travellers' Training Workshops. The NCVA will also be involved with Teagasc and Coillte in course certification of areas such as horticulture and afforestation and, as required by the Department of Education, in the certification of some vocational training modules within senior cycle programmes.

An important first step for the NCVA was the development of a framework of vocational qualifications at three levels for programmes within its remit. This is within the overall context of a five-level framework of vocational qualifications in line with EU practice. While much of its early work was at Level 2, involving PLC courses, it has also developed a Foundation Certificate aimed at trainees who have no formal educational qualification and a range of Level 1 awards which can be offered as a progression option from foundation training. While it is envisaged that the NCVA may offer some Level 3 awards for more advanced PLC courses, most Level 3 awards are being certified by the National Council for Educational Awards, whose National Certificate belongs to this level. The need to develop articulation between the

NCEA and the NCVA, together with the need to coordinate all further education and training, underlined the government decision to establish TEASTAS, the Irish National Certificate Board. TEASTAS will be the authority with full responsibility for development, implementation, regulation, and supervision of all non-university third-level and all further and continuation education and training programmes.

Higher Education

Rising participation rates have had their most dramatic impact on the higher education sector. Higher education issues have been the focus of policy analysis, not just in the 1995 White Paper, but were also the subject of specialist analysis by the Steering Committee on the Future Development of Higher Education (1995) and in the report of its Technical Working Group (1995). Notwithstanding the demographic decline which will begin to impact on the size of the school leaving age cohort in 1999, continued expansion is projected for the higher education sector. The continued expansion is driven by labour market considerations and more recently by projected skills shortages in selected areas. In 1997 an additional investment package of £200 million was announced to strengthen the technological sector while more recently an additional 6000 places were announced for 1998–99. An important basis for continued expansion, in the considerations of the Steering Committee, was the need to provide enhanced opportunities for mature students who have been very poorly represented. Its projections provide for an increase in the percentage of mature students among full-time entrants, to rise from less than four per cent in 1994 to about 15 per cent in 2010 (Steering Committee, 1995).

Growth in higher education has been accompanied by diversification, evolving into an essentially binary system, following the establishment of the Regional Technical Colleges in the early 1970s (Clancy, 1993). While there is some evidence internationally for binary systems to evolve into more unified systems (Scott, 1995), both the White Paper and the Steering Committee Report strongly endorse the binary system. The White Paper argues that because of the multiple purposes of higher education there was a need to have a diversity of institutions, with distinctive aims and objectives. It specifically affirmed the remit of the RTCs with their primary focus on sub-degree programmes and only a limited level of degree provision. The Steering Committee targets the RTC/DIT sector for two-thirds of the recommended increase in admissions, although it recommends that the proportion of students graduating from the RTCs with degrees should rise to 20 per cent, from the current level of 16 per cent. The process of 'academic drift' has been observed in many countries and is also evident in Ireland. The former National Institutes of Higher Education (NIHEs) have become universities (University of Limerick and Dublin City University), the former Colleges of Education have all become affiliated with universities, and the Dublin Institute of Technology has been given degree-granting power and is seeking to become designated as a university. The future status of the RTCs has become a matter of great controversy since the initial decision to 'upgrade' Waterford RTC to Institute of Technology status. This decision was made to legitimate the provision of a greater concentration on degree level courses there to cater for the under-provision in the South East region. The decision evoked a storm of protests from staff and local communities in the other RTCs, who interpreted the 'sponsorship' of one college as an effective downgrading of status for all of the others. All former RTCs have now been given a change of title, to Institute of Technology, and while it is envisaged that some of these will have the power to validate their own qualification, a proposed National Institute of Technology, incorporating the existing NCEA, will validate the courses offered in the others.

A further development which may ultimately have implications for the future of the binary system is the decision by government to extend gradually the remit of the Higher Education Authority until it has executive responsibility for all of the higher education sector. To date, the executive responsibility of the HEA has been mainly confined to the university sector, leaving the newest and most rapidly growing RTC/DIT sector, which caters for 37 per cent of full-time students and 51 per cent of entrants, to be administered directed by the Department of Education. Most of the Colleges of Education have now been brought within the scope of the HEA and it is envisaged that the DIT and then the RTCs will follow, to create a unified administrative structure. The incorporation of all of these colleges within the scope of the HEA may be viewed as a growth in autonomy for this sector and as such might be interpreted as a counter-trend to the apparent contraction in the autonomy of the universities. One interpretation of the partial trend towards 'self-regulation' is that when government is satisfied that it has achieved satisfactory *product control* (as in the case of the vocationally oriented RTC/DIT sector), it may be willing to grant greater *process control* to these colleges (Clancy, 1991).

An important development for the universities has been the passing of the Universities Act, 1997. This Act sought to restructure the National University of Ireland, introduce new governing structures at college level and set out a revised statutory framework governing the interaction between the colleges and government, providing for autonomy and accountability. It was in respect of the latter element that the Universities Bill, in its original version, faced concerted opposition especially from spokespersons from the universities who argued that it represented an unwarranted intrusion by the state on university autonomy. In the course of its passage through the Oireachtas, the Bill was amended very substantially largely to the satisfaction of the academic community (*IFUT News*, 1997).

Over the past few years there have been considerable developments in student support systems. Until recently financial support for students in higher education came via three separate schemes. Both the Higher Education Grant Scheme and the Vocational Education Scholarship Scheme were means-tested and were targeted mainly at students in the university and technological sectors, respectively. More recently the European Social Fund came to be the main source of financial support for certificate and diploma students in the RTC/DIT sector. Initially neither the tuition or maintenance element of this scheme were means-tested, but in 1992 the maintenance element of the ESF grant was means-tested. The assessment of eligibility for all means-tested third-level student support has long been a matter of controversy, arising from a widespread perception that the system discriminated against the PAYE sector. This was the subject of a report by the Advisory Committee on Third Level Student Support which reported in 1993 – the report was published in 1995. The main recommendation of this committee was for the introduction of a capital test as well as an income test to determine eligibility for all means-tested student support. The committee also recommended that the grant in respect of the tuition element for ESF-funded courses be means-tested, subject to a review of the effect of means-testing the maintenance element.

These recommendations have not been accepted. Instead, in 1995 the Government announced its intention to abolish all undergraduate fees from 1996–97 (these fees were halved in 1995–96). This decision was taken in tandem with a decision to abolish tax relief on covenants which had been increasingly used by high and medium-income families as a way of subsidizing third-level education. An important rationale for the abolition of tuition fees was that it would 'remove important financial and psychological barriers to participation at third level' (White Paper, 1995: 101). The decision to abolish tuition fees applies only to full-time undergraduate courses in publicly funded colleges. However, subsequent decisions taken include the granting of tax relief on tuition fees paid by part-time students and for NCEA-validated courses taken in private colleges. In addition, the government decided that students attending full-time higher education courses in overseas colleges would, from 1996, be eligible for a maintenance grant, subject to the normal means-test requirement.

While the populist decision to abolish undergraduate fees did neutralize the controversy surrounding the equity of the means test, it has attracted a good deal of criticism. Many have questioned the wisdom of substituting public expenditure on higher education for existing private expenditure by families who are well-positioned to meet current fee levels (Clancy, 1995c: 166). Furthermore, while it was widely accepted that the existing means test excluded some families who required support, this could have been rectified by an increase in the income threshold governing eligibility. Perhaps the strongest claim for additional state support for higher education is that made for an increase in the level of the maintenance grant for students from disadvantaged backgrounds. The report of the Technical Working Group (1995: 127) identified this as the number-one priority in any revamping of the student support system.

Because of differential class participation rates, one effect of the decision to abolish undergraduate fees is that it will further increase the already disproportionate (Callan, 1992) amount of state support going to middle-class families. Furthermore, because of the very substantial private rates of return to expenditure on higher education (Callan and Harmon, 1997), it seems reasonable that those who stand to benefit, and who can afford it, should pay some contribution to the cost of their higher education. One of the 'unintended consequences' of the abolition of undergraduate university fees is that is has altered the 'pricing structure' of different forms of higher education. Previously all certificate and diploma courses in the RTC/DIT sector were exempt from tuition fees for all students irrespective of means and this may have stimulated demand for these courses, especially from those who would not meet the means-test requirement. The effect of the elimination of university fees is to make university courses relatively more attractive since they are no longer less favourably priced. Thus it is no surprise that client demand has been influenced – the points requirement for very many degree courses increased in 1997, while an increasing number of certificate-level courses were admitting all qualified candidates, in spite of the apparent skills shortage at technician level.

FACING THE FUTURE

The substantial achievements in educational policy over recent decades are matched by the myriad challenges for the future. Many of these challenges facing educational systems in the future are outlined in a recent report by an EU Study Group on Education and Training (1997) which identified three major imperatives that Europe's education and training systems must take into account: (i) the need to strengthen European competitiveness in economic, technological, innovatory scientific and organizational terms, (ii) the need to appreciate the difficulties of the current situation, and (iii) the need to respect the basic principles of education, whose aims go far beyond a purely utilitarian perspective. While this report gives consideration to the problems of developing personal autonomy, citizenship and social cohesion, inevitably much of the focus is on the problem of reinforcing European competitiveness within the world system. This will remain a central concern of Irish national policy where much of the success of the Irish economy in the last decade has been attributed to the quality of the educated workforce. The IDA has identified this as one of the key factors which is influencing multi-national investment in Ireland (Sweeney, 1998). The recent success gives no grounds for complacency since with the weakened power of the nation state vis-à-vis economic policy, more and more countries have come to realize that the development of human capital is the main weapon available to individuals and governments in the fight for economic prosperity (Brown and Lauder, 1996). Since increasingly the competitive advantage of nations is being redefined in terms of the quality of national education and training systems, the struggle to enhance the operation of educational systems will be an ongoing battle.

Public policy will have to focus on eliminating existing system weaknesses. Firstly, the concern with the problem of unqualified school leavers will call for even more targeted attention. And even if this problem can be eliminated in relation to the present school-going cohort, there remains a large deficit with older cohorts, many of whom have experienced long-term unemployment because their low level of education and skills leaves them ill-equipped to compete for jobs in the present economic environment. The educational needs of adults, whether this is for basic literacy or numeracy skills or for professional recurrent education, are poorly catered for. Future policy will have to see a shift in the balance of attention, investment and organization between initial and continuing education, with an increased importance being attached to the latter. A particular difficulty which faces many types of adult and continuing education, including part-time higher education, arises from inadequate funding. In many cases part-time courses will only be provided where they are self-financing and consequently tend to command relatively high fees for which the student grant system does not apply. The failure to apply the free-fees initiative to part-time courses seems short-sighted because of their potential to provide second-chance education for mature students, for whom the part-time route is frequently the only viable option.

A further element which requires attention is the provision of an adequate infrastructure to support the research function of higher education. In a comparative assessment of Irish research, the CIRCA (1996) report noted that the public funding of higher education research in Ireland is among the worst in the OECD. The problem has also been addressed in the report of the STIAC Advisory Council (1995) and in the White Paper on Science, Technology and Innovation (1996). In addition, numerous calls have been made for the establishment of separate national research councils for the natural sciences and for the humanities and social sciences. In this context it is appropriate to endorse Coolahan's (1997: 207) remarks that there is no lack of analysis, diagnosis and prescription; what is required is 'the political, public and collegiate will to give the research issue the priority which is required'.

While most of the challenges for the future will call for additional resources, the demographic decline offers some scope for curtailing spending. The most recent pupil projections suggest that over the next twenty years primary school enrolment may decline by 25 per cent and second-level enrolments by about 20 per cent. And while third-level enrolments are projected to continue growing by about 16 per cent over the next decade, this compares with enrolment growth of 86 per cent in the past decade, and there is unlikely to be any further growth in the following decade. There has been much talk about how best to utilize the 'demographic dividend'. A principal target must be to improve primary school provision. Comparative OECD data reveal that while, in 1994, expenditure per student on third-level education was about average for member countries of the OECD, expenditure on secondary education was about 78 per cent of the average and expenditure on primary education in Ireland was only 63 per cent of the average for these countries. However, to reallocate existing levels of expenditure in order to improve provision for the smaller cohort of students is not a straightforward process. It will involve school closures and amalgamations to achieve the optimum use of resources. An additional difficulty arises because of a growing demand for a wider choice of schools. Thus, while the national need is for fewer schools there is an increasing demand for gaelscoileanna and multidenominational schools. The Commission of School Accommodation Needs is currently addressing these difficult issues.

In looking to the future, a further important consideration arises in respect of the implications of the sharp decline in religious vocations. Some of these implications are explored in a reflection paper published by CORI (1997). It is clear that current levels of involvement cannot be maintained, taking account of the decline in personnel. For example, by 1995–96, less than six per cent of teachers (753) in voluntary secondary schools were members of religious orders, compared with one-third (2300) in 1969–70. In addition, of the religious working in secondary schools, about 40 per cent are within ten years of compulsory retirement, whereas less than five per cent are aged under 35. The challenge extends beyond the issue of the religious congregations providing teachers, as the report argues that religious congregations will find it increasingly difficult to find the personnel and resources necessary to discharge their responsibilities as trustees of schools.

In the final analysis, perhaps the most generic challenge facing the educational system concerns the system's administrative capacity to provide for both strategic planning and policy implementation in a constantly changing environment. In this context the problems posed for the Irish system are in some ways the opposite to those posed in many other countries where, over the past decade or more, the ideological climate has questioned the efficiency of democratically elected and publicly controlled education systems and championed the virtues of privately owned market-led providers (Chubb and Moe, 1988). In contrast, invoking the distinction made by Evans et al. (1985) between state autonomy and state capacity, one of the critiques of Irish public policy (including education policy) is that notwithstanding the more active role of the state in establishing policies and providing resources for social change, it did not establish effective control over the institutions that would use the resources and implement the policies (Breen et al., 1990). More recently, Lynch (1998) has provided an example of one aspect of this dilemma when she points to the difficulty of dealing with the problems of inequality in a system which is privately owned. She argues that one of the indirect effects of the principle of subsidiarity in education, and the voluntarism flowing from it, is the development of significant differences in the quality and range of resources and facilities across schools (Lynch, 1998: 335). The challenge of achieving a correct balance between maximizing individual freedom and institutional autonomy, on the one hand, and simultaneously catering for the common good, will remain a touchstone by which the educational system will be evaluated as we approach the new millennium.

CHRONOLOGY OF DEVELOPMENTS IN IRISH EDUCATIONAL POLICY

1591   University of Dublin (Trinity College) founded
1795   Foundation of Maynooth College
1831   Establishment of National School System
1850   Queen's University established
1864   The Catholic University formally opened
1899   Agricultural and Technical Instruction Act
1879   The Royal University set up
1908   The Irish Universities Act
1924   Department of Education set up
1930   Vocational Education Act
1954   Report of Council of Education on Function and
        Curriculum of the Primary School
1962   Report of Council of Education on Curriculum of
        Secondary Schools
1965   Investment in Education Report
1967   Introduction of 'Free Education' Scheme and School
        Transport Scheme
        Report of Commission on Higher Education
        Report on Regional Technical Colleges
1968   Higher Education Authority set up on ad hoc basis
        (statutorily in 1971)
1970   National Institute of Higher Education, Limerick receives
        first students
        Establishment of first Regional Technical Colleges
1971   New Curriculum for National Schools
1972   National Council for Educational Awards established on ad
        hoc basis (statutorily in 1979)
1976   Establishment of Central Applications' Office
1980   White Paper on Educational Development
1987   Establishment of National Council for Curriculum and
        Assessment
1989   Introduction of new Junior Certificate Programme
        Introduction of Youthreach
        Introduction of Vocational Training Opportunities
        Scheme
1990   Introduction of Home School Community Liaison
        Scheme
1991   Establishment of National Council for Vocational Awards

1992	Report of the Industrial Policy Review Group (Culliton Report)
1992	Green Paper: Education for a Changing World
1993	Report of the Special Education Review Committee
1993	National Education Convention
1994	Introduction of Early Start Programme
1995	Introduction of Leaving Certificate Applied Programme
	Report of the Steering Committee on the Future Development of Higher Education
	White Paper on Education: Charting our Education Future
	Establishment of TEASTAS, as interim authority
1997	Universities Act

NOTES

1 Estoppel arises when a person makes a promise or a representation as to intention to another, on which that other person acts. The representor is bound by that representation or promise.

2 A minority of university staff are represented by SIPTU (Services Industrial Professional Technical Union), while the Teachers Union of Ireland represents teaching staff in the RTC/DIT sector.

RECOMMENDED READING

Coolahan, J. (1981) *Irish Education: Its History and Structure*. Dublin: Institute of Public Administration.

Drudy, S. and K. Lynch, (1993) *Schools and Society in Ireland*. Dublin: Gill & Macmillan.

Mulcahy, D.G. and D. O'Sullivan, (1989) *Irish Educational Policy: Process and Substance*. Dublin: Institute of Public Administration.

O'Buachalla, S. (1988) *Education Policy in Twentieth Century Ireland*. Dublin: Wolfhound Press.

Report on the National Educational Convention (1994) Dublin: The Convention Secretariat.

Steering Committee on the Future Development of Higher Education (1995) *Report*. Dublin: Higher Education Authority.

White Paper (1995) *Charting our Education Future: White Paper on Education*. Dublin: Stationery Office.

REFERENCES

Advisory Committee on Third Level Student Support (1993) *Third-Level Student Support*. Dublin: Stationery Office.

Akenson, D.H. (1970) *The Irish Educational Experiment*. London: Routledge & Kegan Paul.

Bailey, D. (1984) 'The Challenge of Economic Utility', in J. Ahier, B. Cosin and M. Holes (eds), *Beyond the Present and the Particular*. London: Routledge & Kegan Paul.

Barry, D. (1989) 'The Involvement and Impact of a Professional Interest Group', in D.G. Malachy and D. O'Sullivan (eds), *Irish Educational Policy: Process and Substance*. Dublin: Institute of Public Administration.

Breen, R, D.F. Hannan, D.B. Rottman and C.T. Whelan (1990) *Understanding Contemporary Ireland*. Dublin: Gill & Macmillan.

Brown, A. and J. Fairley (1993) *Restructuring Education in Ireland*. Dublin: Irish Vocational Education Association.

Brown, P. and H. Lauder (1996) 'Education, Globalisation and Economic Development', *Journal of Educational Policy*, 11: 1–24.

Burke, A. (1992) 'Teaching: Retrospect and Prospect', *Oideas, 39*.

Callan, T. (1992) *Who Benefits from Public Expenditure in Education?* ESRI Working Paper, No. 32.

Callan, T. and C.P. Harmon, (1997) *The Economic Returns to Education in Ireland*, Working Paper 97/23. Dublin: UCD Centre for Economic Research.

Chubb, J.E. and T.M. Moe (1988) 'Politics, Markets and the Organisation of Schools', *American Political Science Review*, 82: 1065–87.

CIRCA Group Europe (1996) *A Comparative Assessment of the Organisation, Management and Funding of University Research in Ireland*. Dublin: Higher Education Authority.

Clancy, P. (1982) *Participation in Higher Education*. Dublin: Higher Education Authority.

Clancy, P. (1988) *Who Goes to College?* Dublin: Higher Education Authority.

Clancy, P. (1991) 'Numerical Expansion and Contracting Autonomy in Irish Higher Education', *Higher Education Policy*, 4 (1): 30–6.

Clancy, P. (1993) 'Goal Enlargement and Diversification: The Evolution of the Binary System in Ireland', in C. Gellert (ed.), *Higher Education in Europe*. London: Jessica Kingsley.

Clancy, P. (1995a) 'Education in the Republic of Ireland: The Project of Modernity?', in P. Clancy, S. Drudy, K. Lynch and L. O'Dowd (eds), *Irish Society: Sociological Perspectives*. Dublin: Institute of Public Administration.

Clancy, P. (1995b) 'Access Courses as an Aid to Addressing Socio-Economic Disparities in Higher Education', in *Access Courses for Higher Education: Proceedings of Conference at Mary Immaculate College, Limerick*. Dublin: Higher Education Authority.

Clancy, P. (1995c) *Access to College: Patterns of Continuity and Change*. Dublin: Higher Education Authority.

Committee on Access and Participation of Students with Disabilities (1995). Dublin: Higher Education Authority.

Coolahan, J. (1981) *Irish Education: Its History and Structure*. Dublin: Institute of Public Administration.

Coolahan, J. (1997) 'Third-Level Education in Ireland: Change and Development', in F. Ó Muircheartaigh (ed.), *Ireland in the Coming Times: Essays to Celebrate T.K. Whitaker's 80 Years*. Dublin: Institute of Public Administration.

Coolahan, J. and McGuinness, S. (1994) *Report on the Roundtable Discussions in Dublin Castle on the Minister for Education's Position Paper 'Regional Education Councils'*. Dublin: Department of Education.

CORI (1997) *Religious Congregations in Irish Education: A Role for the Future?* Dublin: Conference of Religious of Ireland.

Council of Education (1954) *Report of Council of Education on Function and Curriculum of the Primary School*. Dublin: Stationery office.

Culliton Report (1992) *A Time for Change: Industrial Policy in the 1990s*. Dublin: Stationery Office.

Department of Education (1996) *Implementing the Agenda for Change*. Dublin: Stationery Office.

EU White Paper on Education and Training (1996) *Teaching and Learning: Towards the Learning Society*. Brussels, European Commission.

EU Study Group on Education and Training (1997) *Accomplishing Europe through Education and Training*. Brussels: European Commission.

Evans, P. B., D. Rueschemeyer, and T. Skocpol (1985) 'On the Road Towards a More Adequate Understanding of the State', in P. B. Evans, D. Rueschemeyer and T. Skocpol (eds), *Bringing the State Back In*. Cambridge: Cambridge University Press.

Green Paper (1992) *Education for a Changing World, Government Green Paper*. Dublin: Stationery Office.

Hannan, D. and Shortall, S. (1991) *The Quality of Their Education*. Dublin: Economic and Social Research Institute.

Hannan, D.F., E. Smyth, J. McCullagh, R. O'Leary and D. McMahon (1996) *Coeducation and Gender Equality*. Dublin: Oak Tree Press.

IFUT News (1997) Vol. XXIV. Dublin: Irish Federation of University Teachers.

Kellaghan, T., S. Weir, S. Ó hUallacháin, and M. Morgan (1995) *Educational Disadvantage in Ireland*. Dublin: Combat Poverty Agency.

Lynch, K. (1989) *The Hidden Curriculum*. London: Falmer.

Lynch, K. (1998) 'The Status of Children and Young Persons: Educational and Related Issues', in S. Healy and B. Reynolds (eds), *Social Policy in Ireland: Principles, Practice and Problems*. Dublin: Oak Tree Press.

Morgan, M., B. Hickey, T. Kellaghan (1997) *International Adult Literacy Survey: Results for Ireland*. Dublin: Stationery Office.

Murphy, J. (1993) 'A Degree of Waste: the economic benefits of educational expansion', *Oxford Review of Education,* 19 (1).

NESC (1993) *Education and Training Policies for Social and Economic Development*. Dublin: NESC.

OECD (1965) *Policy Conference on Economic Growth and Investment in Education*. Paris: OECD.

OECD (1991) *Reviews of National Policies for Education: Ireland*. Paris: OECD.

O'Sullivan, D. (1992) 'Cultural Strangers and Educational Change: The OECD Report Investment in Education and Irish Educational Policy', *Journal of Educational Policy,* 7: 445–69.

Report of the Constitutional Review Group (1996) Dublin: Stationery Office.

Report on the National Education Convention (1994) Dublin: The Convention Secretariat.

Report of the Special Education Review Committee (1993) Dublin: Stationery Office.

STIAC (Science, Technology and Innovation Advisory Council) (1995) *Making Knowledge Work for Us.* Dublin: The Stationery Office.

Scott, P. (1995) *The Meanings of Mass Higher Education.* Buckingham: The Open University.

Steering Committee on the Future Development of Higher Education (1995) *Report.* Dublin: Higher Education Authority.

Sweeney, P. (1998) *The Celtic Tiger: Ireland's Economic Miracle Explained.* Dublin: Oak Tree Press.

Technical Working Group (1995) *Interim Report of the Steering Committee's Technical Working Group.* Dublin: Higher Education Authority.

White Paper (1995) *Charting Our Education Future: White Paper on Education.* Dublin: Stationery Office.

White Paper on Science, Technology and Innovation (1996). Dublin: Stationery Office.

6

Unemployment

Eithne Fitzgerald

INTRODUCTION

For decades, Ireland's problems of unemployment and emigration have been seen as primarily the outcome of economic underdevelopment. Public policy in relation to unemployment focused on raising economic growth, job creation and improving competitiveness in line with Lemass's dictum that the rising tide would lift all boats.

The emergence of high levels of long-term unemployment in the 1980s and 1990s, and in particular the persistence of high levels of unemployment during the unprecedented economic boom of the mid-1990s, led to an increasing focus on long-term unemployment, and the realization that economic success alone will not eliminate it. The policy emphasis is moving from purely economic solutions to social policies which address the wider context of disadvantage associated with persistent unemployment. Two key elements in securing this policy shift were the establishment under the Programme for Economic and Social Progress (PESP) in 1991 of twelve Area Based Partnerships with a specific remit to pilot new approaches to long-term unemployment and the National Economic and Social Forum's seminal 1994 report *Ending Long-term Unemployment.*

Ireland's economic lift-off in the 1990s has produced a rapid rise in employment on a scale never before seen in the Irish economy. From 1994 – when jobs-growth began to accelerate – to 1997, the increase in the numbers at work was just under 200,000. This is twice the total employment growth of the previous twenty years.

Increasing numbers of young people coming out of education, increasing participation by women, and a ready supply of returning emigrants have given employers up to the late 1990s a plentiful supply of potential workers, leaving unemployed people, in particular the long-term unemployed, at the back of the jobs queue. This rapid increase in job numbers has not, therefore, led to reductions in unemployment on a corresponding scale. About two-thirds of the extra jobs have gone to an expanding labour force, while under a third have resulted in falling unemployment. Unemployment has thus remained stubbornly high in the face of sustained economic expansion and indeed concern at the end of the century about emerging labour shortages.

The unemployed are not a random sample of the working-age population. Three-quarters of adults have never experienced unemployment, while four per cent of adults have experienced almost half the total years of unemployment in the population (Nolan et al., 1994). The risk of unemployment, and particularly long-term unemployment, is very closely related to poor or no educational qualifications. Three-quarters of the long-term unemployed have no Leaving Certificate, and half of them left school without a Junior/Intermediate or Group Certificate (Labour Force Survey, 1996). Early school leaving and unemployment among young people are strongly associated with parental unemployment, perpetuating a cycle of unemployment (Hannan and Ó Riain, 1983)

While unemployment is not confined to the large urban centres, in those centres, there is significant clustering of unemployment in particular neighbourhoods characterized by multiple deprivation and lack of amenities (Dublin County Council, 1987). Eighty per cent of tenants renting from a local authority are on a welfare payment, and in only a third of local authority homes is there any household member in a job (1994–95 *Household Budget Survey*). Unemployment blackspots may suffer a pervasive loss of heart and of hope. Without specific action, these communities are likely to experience little of the general rise in prosperity in good economic times.

Prolonged unemployment is corrosive of individual self-esteem, and unemployed people are five times more likely to reach clinical levels of psychological distress than those in employment (Whelan et al., 1991). People who have had years of job refusals may withdraw from the labour force altogether and say they no longer want work. There is a clear continuum between long-term unemployment and withdrawal from the labour force.

Unemployment represents a waste of the talent and potential of individuals. It imposes severe costs on society. Direct financial costs include social welfare provision (over £1bn in 1996), the loss of potential output, income, and tax revenue. There are social costs of neighbourhood blight, vandalism, crime, and drug abuse whose roots lie in social alienation and high unemployment. Unemployment is a prime cause of poverty. Over half of all households headed by an unemployed person are in poverty, and account for a third of all living in poverty (Callan et al., 1996a).

The growth of unemployment may have its roots in failures in economic policy. But success in eliminating unemployment requires programmes that address the legacy of long-term unemployment on individuals and communities, that address labour market disadvantage arising from poor skills or incomplete education, and that offer a bridge back to the world of work for those who have been excluded.

ECONOMIC EXPLANATIONS OF UNEMPLOYMENT

Unemployment arises from a mismatch between the supply of labour and the demand for labour. There are different economic theories and explanations for why such a mismatch persists, each with different economic prescriptions for reducing unemployment. The demand for labour depends on the level of economic activity in the economy, the skill levels of the workforce, and the cost of employing workers. It is a derived demand – employers employ workers for what they can produce. If wage costs rise or the price of equipment falls, employers may switch to more capital-intensive production, substituting machines for labour, and employing fewer workers for any given level of output. An economy which taxes labour and subsidizes capital investment encourages firms to switch from more labour-intensive production.

Employers are interested in the gross cost of hiring workers, including wages, pension contributions, and employer's PRSI. Workers are interested in the net take home pay from the job. The gap between what it costs to hire a worker, and what the worker receives is called the 'tax wedge'. Growth in the tax wedge usually leads to higher unemployment.

It pays an employer to take on workers up to the point where the marginal revenue product of labour – the value of the output of the last worker taken on – exactly equals the wage rate. If an additional worker's contribution to output is higher than the wages paid, it pays to expand the workforce. If the worker's addition to output is worth less than the pay rate, the worker is likely to be laid off, and employment will fall. Thus, if a minimum wage is set which is above the value to the employer of having the worker on the payroll, the result may be that low-produc-tivity workers are laid off or more skilled workers hired in their place.

Labour Supply

Economic theory suggests that labour supply is primarily determined by real wage levels. At higher wages, more people are attracted into the job market. Higher wages may encourage the existing workforce to work longer hours, but may also allow workers to trade off extra income for more time off once they have reached a target income level. Demographic factors have played a particularly important role in Ireland's labour supply, as shown later.

Frictional Unemployment

The job market is not static – there are new job openings and redundancies occurring all the time as some products, service or firms prosper and others go into decline. Even in a well-functioning job market there will always be some unemployment – frictional unemployment – with people between jobs. The level of frictional unemployment reflects the time it takes for employers to match workers to vacancies, and for workers to find a vacancy that suits them. An economy with no frictional unemployment would probably mean a lot of square pegs in round holes, and significant numbers of people working in jobs which do not make best use of their talents.

Classic Economic Theory

In normal markets for goods and services, the price is set by the inter-action of demand and supply and the market tends towards an equilibrium price which balances supply and demand. In the labour market, the price of labour is the wage rate. Classical economic theory suggests that in the long run wage rates will fall to equate the supply and demand for jobs, and virtually eliminate unemployment.

This theory holds that unemployment is primarily due to an imbalance between the supply of labour at the going wage, and the demand for labour at that wage. If unemployed people were willing to work for less than the going wage rate, that would put a downward pressure on wage rates and that in turn would increase the demand for labour and help clear the jobs market.

Flexible wage rates, the theory goes, should prevent the emergence of mass unemployment by allowing wages to fall to market-clearing levels. The demand from unemployed people for work creates this down-ward pressure on wages. Minimum wage laws, trade union power, or the existence of a social welfare safety net may prevent wages from falling to market clearing levels, and give rise to unemployment. Classical economists argue there would be no involuntary unemployment if wages were allowed to find the proper levels.

Keynesian Theory – Unemployment and Slumps

The emergence of mass unemployment during the Great Depression after the 1929 crash led to a questioning of classic economic theory and its prescription of further wage cuts during a slump. Keynes, in his 1936 book *The General Theory of Employment, Interest and Money*, argued that in the short run, wages and the price level are not flexible, and that automatic mechanisms to clear the job market may take a very long time to take effect. In the meantime a shortfall in spending power in the economy can lead to mass unemployment. Keynes argued that, in the short run, the level of output and employment in the economy depends on the level of spending, or aggregate demand. He saw the main cause of unemployment in the short run as being in the goods market, not the labour market. Cutting wages in a depression would lead to a fall in consumer spending and exacerbate the slump.

In a closed economy running below full capacity, injecting extra spending power into the economy would have a multiplier effect in increasing demand for goods and services and getting people back to work. Overall spending in the economy could be raised by directly raising government spending, or by raising consumer or investment spending through expanded credit or lower interest rates. If the economy is already running at capacity, an extra spending injection would simply raise inflation. Social welfare systems act as automatic stabilizers adding extra government spending in a downturn, and leading to falling government spending in an upturn.

In a very open economy like the Irish one, however, a spending injection leads to a significant increase in imports, and has little or no multiplier effect in the domestic economy. Attempts in the late 1970s to inflate the Irish economy through expanded public spending brought no lasting increase in employment; in fact the resulting problems created for the public finances, and the corrective measures on the tax side to bring the finances under control, contributed to the steady growth in unemployment during the 1980s.

The post-war Western world was characterized by steady growth and low unemployment, and a belief that unemployment could be minimized through appropriate Keynesian demand management policies. The oil price shocks of 1973–74 and 1979 led to the emergence of simultaneous high unemployment and inflation, which has left a legacy in Europe of high unemployment. The popularity of Keynesian policies waned, and a new emphasis on tackling underlying structural causes of unemployment has characterized reports like the OECD *Jobs Study* (1994).

Structural or 'Natural' Unemployment

Modern macroeconomics does not assume that the labour market clears automatically although it may over the long run. Structural features of the economy such as the degree of monopoly and excess mark-up, the tax wedge (the gap between an employer's labour costs and what a worker takes home), the efficiency of the process of matching unemployed workers to vacancies, and the extent to which the level of unemployment in fact exerts any influence on wage levels set an underlying structural or 'natural' rate of unemployment. If unemployment is above its underlying structural rate, active demand management policies, or monetary policies which lower interest rates or increase credit, can be effective in raising output and jobs and in recovering from a cyclical downturn or short-term fluctuation. If unemployment is already at its underlying structural rate, then any attempts to lower unemployment through expanding spending or monetary policy simply lead to extra inflation, and the economy reverts to its underlying unemployment rate, but with higher inflation. This is why the 'natural' rate of unemployment is also called the non-accelerating inflation rate of unemployment or NAIRU. The evidence suggests that following the oil price shocks, Europe's underlying structural unemployment rate or NAIRU has risen (OECD, 1994). Reducing structural unemployment involves addressing underlying structural issues.

One explanation for increasing levels of structural unemployment is *hysteresis* or the theory that today's unemployment rate depends not only on other economic factors, but on last year's unemployment rate – that economies do not respond symmetrically to economic shocks, but that jobs lost in an economic downturn are not all regained in an economic upturn. The adjustment mechanisms in the economy become more sluggish, and wage rates become less likely to adjust downwards in response to growing unemployment. This may be due to *efficiency wages* – it is worth an employer's while to pay more to hold the loyalty commitment and skills of the existing work force than the wage for which those outside the factory gate are prepared to work.

High unemployment means many people living on low welfare payments for prolonged periods. This increases the pressure to raise welfare rates relative to other incomes, in turn making low-paid jobs less attractive to unemployed workers. As unemployment remains high for a period, some workers lose heart and drift out of the active work force, and employers use age or length of unemployment as a proxy for regarding someone as unemployable. Long-term unemployment becomes a condition from which it is harder and harder to escape. And the rising burden of paying for unemployment and the lower tax revenues puts pressure on tax rates and the tax wedge, making it less attractive for employers to take on workers.

Unemployment and the Irish Job Market

Heavy emigration took the brunt of Ireland's job shortage for most of the period since independence, and up to 1980 recorded unemployment remained relatively low. From 1980 onwards, Ireland's unemployment rate began to rise rapidly. Studies suggest that almost half the rise was due to domestic policy factors such as the rise in the tax wedge and in replacement rates, a third to a quarter due to external factors, such as the world recession and the shortage of job opportunities in the UK, with demographic factors such as the growing number of school leavers playing a smaller role (Barry and Bradley, 1991; Browne and McGettigan, 1993). Unemployment in Ireland grew steadily during the 1980s, dipped in the latter half of the decade, and peaked in 1993. At its peak, in 1993, unemployment measured by Principal Economic Status (PES) was 2.5 times the level of 91,000 in 1980. Since then the numbers of persons unemployed have shown a steady fall, as the economic boom of the 1990s took effect. However, even after sustained jobs growth, PES unemployment in 1998 was still 50% higher than in 1980 (Labour Force Surveys). The numbers signing on the Live Register grew significantly faster (due partly to changes in entitlements and classification) and peaked at 295,000 in 1993.

Irish Labour Flows

The level of unemployment is the outcome of a series of flows – changes in the numbers of people coming on to the job market, new job creation and job losses, and exits from the job market for retirement or other reasons. The net change in unemployment is usually small relative to the size of the gross flows. During 1997, on average the monthly change in the numbers signing on the Live Register averaged 2,000, while about 26,000 people a month signed on with a new claim, and 28,000 a month signed off.

The number of people who are unemployed depends on the match between the demand for labour or supply of jobs, and the supply of potential workers. The supply of labour reflects demographic change, labour force participation, and migration flows.

- **Migration** For most of our economic history since independence, poor job performance was reflected more in high emigration figures than in unemployment at home. More recently, the healthy jobs market from the mid-1990s has resulted in net immigration

- **Natural increase in labour supply** The numbers of young people coming on to the job market from the baby boom of the 1970s has averaged about 25,000 more than the numbers retiring, who came from a generation depleted by emigration

- **Increased participation of women** In the twenty years to 1997, the number of men at work grew by 5%, but the number of women at work grew by 71%, mainly due to sharply increased participation by married women in the workforce. The labour force participation rate of married women aged 25–34 went from 17% to 58% over that period, and for women aged 35–44, from 14% to 47%.

- **Early retirement and drift out of the labour force by older men** There has been a significant drop in the labour force participation of men over 55, due to earlier retirement, and a drift out of the labour force of the older age group following redundancy. In the twenty years to 1997, the labour force participation of men aged 55–59 dropped from 87% to 75%, and for men aged 60–64, from 76% to 54%.

- **Later age of first job** As more students complete a Leaving Certificate and go on to third level education, the numbers in work in their late teens and early twenties have dropped sharply. In 1997 only 23% of boys and 15% of girls aged 15–19 were in work or on the job market.

Box 1
Measuring Unemployment

There is no single agreed measure of unemployment. Alternative ways of measuring unemployment are discussed in detail in NESF (1997b). Economic definitions of unemployment concentrate on those who are actively seeking work, while the social and financial problems of unemployment apply equally to the economically inactive as to those out of work who are in the active job market.

There are three principal sets of data on unemployment. The Labour Force Survey/ Quarterly National Household Survey has two alternative measures:

ILO measure – the most commonly used international measure, based on active job search. Published since 1983

PES measure – based on people's own assessment of their principal economic status. Data available for census years: 1977–9, and 1983 onward.

The monthly Live Register is a count of social welfare claimants, and is affected by administrative change in the welfare system as well as underlying changes in unemployment. These figures exclude unemployed people claiming other benefits (lone parents, disability) and those unemployed women whose partner's income puts them over the means test for payment. They also include about 30,000 part-time workers. Following a special survey of Live Register claimants by the CSO in 1996, as part of the Labour Force Survey, where 44% of those surveyed did not classify themselves as unemployed, and 21% had jobs, serious doubts have been cast on the reliability of the Live Register figures as an accurate measure of unemployment, in the sense of the job market. Some of the sharp fall in Live Register numbers since the survey's publication may reflect more the tightening of welfare administration than underlying improvement in job chances.

The following table shows the three measures for April 1997

	Men	Women	Total
ILO unemployed	97,000	62,000	159,000
PES unemployed	131,000	48,000	179,000
Live Register	159,000	97,000	257,000

The number who were classified as unemployed on both the PES and ILO measures was 122,000, the main reason for difference being people classed as unemployed on one measure who were classed as economically inactive on the other.

Unemployment and Gender

While participation rates for men and women in the workforce are very different, overall unemployment rates for men and women, as measured by the ILO active job search criterion, are very similar.

Table 1. Participation and Unemployment Rates for Men and Women, ILO Basis

| | Participation Rates | | Unemployment Rates | |
	M	F	M	F
1994	68.0	39.0	14.7	14.8
1995	68.0	39.7	12.1	12.2
1996	68.1	41.4	11.9	11.9
1997	67.8	42.0	10.4	10.3

Source: Labour Force Surveys

While more men describe themselves as unemployed than are actively looking for work, for women it is the other way round – fewer women who are in active job search describe themselves as unemployed, and many describe their principal economic status as being on home duties.

Figures on unemployment for women derived from social welfare claim statistics are very much distorted by administrative rules around women's entitlement to claim unemployment payments. Historically, the rules for social welfare entitlement concealed the true level of unemployment among women. When unemployment assistance was introduced in 1933, women both married and single were not in general eligible – their place was assumed to be in the home.

Formal equal treatment in the social welfare code for men and women was only achieved in 1986 following implementation of the 1978 EU Directive to that effect. While men and women in principle can now qualify on equal terms for unemployment benefit or assistance, the reality is that unemployed women who are living with a husband or partner are far less likely to qualify for unemployment assistance, because the means test assessment includes their partner's income. If the partner is himself unemployed, there is little financial incentive for the woman to sign on, because the total unemployment assistance paid to the couple is the same whether one claims or both claim. Lone parents seeking work receive more money on Lone Parent Allowance, and would not be included in social welfare unemployment statistics. As an indirect result, unemployed women were underrepresented on programmes like

Community Employment where entitlement to participate was based on the Live Register; the inclusion of lone parents since 1996 as eligible has been the main factor in increasing women's participation on that programme.

Administrative changes have tended to increase the number of women on the Live Register in recent years. The extension of the duration of unemployment benefit from 12 months to 15 months for married women, following the Equal Treatment Directive, increased the numbers of women claiming. Part-time workers are now eligible to claim unemployment payments for the periods they are not in work; these are mainly women. The Live Register figures include people signing on for credits (who are almost all women) who receive no cash payment.

Table 2. Unemployment among Men and Women Live Register, Principal Economic Status and ILO Measures

	'000s						
	Men				Women		
Year	LR	PES	ILO		LR	PES	ILO
1988	171.8	169.6	141.5		69.9	49.0	75.8
1989	162.6	157.3	129.3		70.5	44.9	68.0
1990	150.5	138.1	110.7		70.5	40.8	63.8
1991	168.4	155.9	125.3		79.6	52.8	72.5
1992	188.4	163.7	133.6		92.5	55.4	75.5
1993	195.3	170.2	138.3		99.3	59.7	81.4
1994	187.5	162.5	130.9		97.0	55.9	78.6
1995	179.2	142.7	109.1		96.8	47.9	66.2
1996	179.3	137.7	109.1		102.0	52.2	68.4
1997	159.4	130.6	94.5		97.4	48.3	62.0

Sources: Labour Force Survey, Live Register

The proportion of women who are long-term unemployed (ILO) is lower than that for men, and women form about a third of the long-term unemployed, as shown in the Table 3. The fact that fewer women can draw long-term unemployment assistance because of their partner's income may be one factor, another may be that women whose sense of personal identity may be less caught up with being the family breadwinner may have fewer fears than long-term unemployed men about re-entering a world of employment that has offered repeated rejection. Employers may feel less negatively about women whom they perceive as having been on home duties while out of work than someone they perceive as having been simply unemployed. The fact that women on average work for lower pay may also make them more employable.

Table 3. Long-term Unemployment, Men and Women

	Men		Women	
	Total ltu,'000s	% who are ltu	Total ltu, 000s	% who are ltu
1994	85.4	65%	42.9	54%
1995	70.2	64%	33.1	49%
1996	69.2	63%	34.0	49%
1997	58.8	61%	27.5	44%

Source: Labour Force Surveys

Emigration and Unemployment

From the early-nineteenth century, Ireland's job market was a very open one, with high emigration rather than the level of unemployment at home the principal response to shortage of work opportunities. Net emigration peaked in the 1956–61 period where it averaged 42,000 a year – equivalent to 70% of those born twenty years earlier. The boom conditions of the mid-1990s has resulted in net inward migration. In 1997 44,000 people came to live in Ireland, while 29,000 emigrated, resulting in net inward migration of 15,000 (*Labour Force Survey*).

Emigration is particularly sensitive to conditions in the United Kingdom, our nearest and most important destination job market. Honohan (1992) found that net migration from Ireland occurred when Irish unemployment rates went 4% above the corresponding UK rates. Besides better job openings abroad, other factors which can influence the balance between emigrating or being unemployed at home are relative living standards at home and away including housing costs, relative earnings, and relative levels of welfare payments. Adding net migration and unemployment figures together might give a truer historical picture of the shortfall on the Irish jobs market.

With a substantial pool of Irish emigrants living abroad, an upturn in the job market at home attracts a strong return inflow. Together with the steady increase in women's participation, and the flow of people leaving the education system they offer employers a ready source of potential recruits which lessens the impact of net job creation on the unemployment numbers. Other EU citizens have also been coming to Ireland in increasing numbers to take up job opportunities. About two per cent of those aged 15 or over have been born outside Ireland or the UK. Over 15,000 EU citizens, two-thirds of them from the UK, came to live in Ireland in 1998 (*Quarterly National Household Survey*, 1998).

Unemployment and Non-employment

Labour market conditions and people's assessment of the chances of getting work can affect whether people classify themselves as unemployed or economically inactive, and the extent to which they are interested in taking a job or are actively looking for work. Unemployment and non-employment (particularly for men who rarely withdraw from the work force to engage in home duties) form a continuum rather than two clearly distinct sub categories. Discouraged workers (those no longer looking for work but who would accept a job if it came along) and the 'inactive unemployed' experience similar problems of low income and disadvantage to those who are in the active job market, and most are dependent on a social welfare income. Murphy and Walsh argue that '. . . their inactivity might be regarded as an extension of the problem of unemployment' (NESF, 1997b: 125). They show (1996; NESF, 1997b) for men of working age (20–59) that long-term unemployment, giving up active job search, and withdrawal from the labour force into the inactive category are all associated with similar factors:

- poor educational qualifications,
- living in local authority housing especially in larger cities
- in the older age groups
- sharing a household with other unemployed or economically inactive
- being single *or* having a large family

For women also, factors such as poor education, local authority housing, and sharing a home with other unemployed or economically inactive adults are associated with low participation in the work force and higher unemployment.

Significant numbers are involved. In 1996, a quarter of men on the Live Register would be classified as 'inactive' by the International Labour Organisation criterion, and conversely a quarter of those who are described as ILO inactive are on the Live Register. 1993 figures show that among ILO inactive men aged 20–59, relatively few (14%) were inactive for specific reasons of ill health, disability, home duties etc; two thirds had given up job search because they were no longer interested in work. A further 10% have given up job search but would accept work. (NESF, 1997a: Table II.2)

Improvements in the economic situation and the job market generally are likely to have limited impact on people who have given up active job search or have effectively withdrawn from the job market. Active social policies which counter labour market disadvantage, which rebuild confidence, which tackle real and perceived obstacles to participation in the world of work, and which rebuild the broken links back to the world of work are required.

Labour Supply and Incomes

The number of people in the active job market is affected by net income from work, which in turn reflects both prevailing wage rates and the level of taxation on income. At higher take-home pay rates, more people come into the active job market. For low-paid jobs in particular, the supply of labour is affected when people see themselves as little better off than on welfare.

The *reservation wage* is a term for the minimum wage below which someone will not take a job. Classical economic theory argues that unemployment payments keep wages too high to allow the labour market to clear, because workers will not work unless they get a reasonable margin over what they would have earned on the dole.

The Welfare System and Replacement Rates

The replacement rate is defined as the ratio between what someone receives on the dole and what they would earn if in a job. Since the unemployed are disproportionately drawn from those with poor education or skills, the income they are likely to command in the open market will be lower than average industrial earnings. Callan et al. (1996b) found unemployed people on average could expect to earn two-thirds of average earnings if in work. This study also found that about 30% of the unemployed (and 16% of current employees) had a replacement rate above 70%. Ireland's welfare rates for unemployment benefit and assistance grew rapidly following the Commission on Social Welfare's (1986) recommendations on a minimum adequate welfare income, narrowing the gap between incomes on welfare and incomes in work.

Ireland's welfare system contains in-built unemployment traps. Unlike Continental welfare systems which pay social insurance as a percentage of earnings, and generous children's allowances to everyone whether working or not, the Irish welfare system consists of family based payments which automatically generates high replacement rates for larger families. Whereas wage rates are unrelated to family size, someone on unemployment benefit or assistance receives an extra £13.20 a week per child (1998 rates). Without special adjustment, the Irish system means that people of moderate earning power are likely to face an unemployment trap once they have a dependent family. 1996 figures show that 40% of families with four or more children are on welfare; 60% of those with six or more children are on welfare (*Statistical Information on Social Welfare Services*). While 55% of the unemployed are single without dependants (1996) and larger families are only a minority of the unemployed, the family-based structure of the Irish welfare system creates unemployment traps which grow with family size.

Other factors keeping replacement rates high are secondary benefits such as the medical card, fuel allowances, and Health Board rent allowances (paid to 42,200 unwaged households in 1998). Single people have hit the tax net on very low incomes. For example, in 1998–9 a single person earning £120 a week would pay tax and PRSI totalling £19.60. From April 1999, people earning under £100 per week will move out of the tax net.

SOCIAL POLICIES TO TACKLE UNEMPLOYMENT

Social Factors and Unemployment

As in other countries, Ireland's unemployed are disproportionately drawn from those with poor education or skills levels. There is a significant degree of geographical concentration in unemployment blackspots. There is a high share of long-term unemployment, from which it is significantly more difficult to escape.

Education and Unemployment

Rising average education levels have been an important engine driving Ireland's economic growth. However, unemployed people and in particular the long-term unemployed come disproportionately from those who left school early with no or minimal qualifications. There is a direct relationship between the standard of education achieved, and the probability of unemployment. Poor education levels or limited skills lower earning potential, and those with least qualifications are more likely to experience a real or perceived unemployment trap when incomes on welfare and in work are compared.

Unemployed people who have been six months out of work may opt for a second chance at education while retaining their welfare payments, under the Vocational Training Opportunities Programme (VTOS) or

Table 4. Unemployment and Educational Qualifications, 1996

Education	At work %	Unemployed %	Short-term unemployed	Long-term unemployed
No qualifications	15.2	28.6	18.8	35.2
Junior Cert*	23.2	35.9	34.2	37.2
Leaving Cert	32.3	24.3	29.5	21.0
3rd level	29.3	11.1	17.5	6.7
Total	100.0	100.0	100.0	100.0

* Including Group or Intermediate Certficate
Source: White Paper on Human Resource Development, 1997, Table 3.9 from Labour Force Survey 1996

Back to Education Allowance schemes. The number of participants is low relative to the totals out of work. The Department of Education's dedicated scheme for adults returning to education, VTOS, had 500 out of 5,000 places unfilled in 1998. There has been rapid expansion in numbers in the parallel Back to Education scheme run by the Department of Social, Community and Family Affairs. Of the 4,500 participants in 1998, 85% were on third-level courses.

Early School Leaving and Unemployment

As average education levels have increased, the gap between the unemployment rate for young people with no qualifications and those with a better education has widened. In 1980, the unemployment rate one year later for school leavers with no qualifications was 14% higher than for those who had a Leaving Certificate. By 1995, the gap had widened to 40%, with 53% of those with no qualifications unemployed a year after leaving school (McCoy and Whelan, 1996: Table 2).

About 1000 young people drop out at primary school level, and a further 3,200 before reaching Junior Certificate (NESF, 1997a). As today's early school leavers are at high risk of being tomorrow's long-term unemployed, policies to tackle early school leaving have an important role to play. The rate of long-term unemployment among young people is higher than the average.

The lifetime cost to the Exchequer of the higher unemployment associated with early school leaving means that investment in effective measures to prevent early school leaving offers a high economic return. The Economic and Social Research Institute (1993) estimated the excess lifetime unemployment experienced by those who leave school without qualifications as distinct from with a Junior Certificate costs at a minimum an extra £28m (at 1988 prices) for a given year's cohort of early leavers.

Poor school attendance is a strong indicator of early drop out. A recent survey in Clondalkin (McSorley, 1997) showed only two-thirds of local primary school children were regular school attenders. There is little incentive for schools to follow up non-attendance or drop out, when the teacher complement is calculated on declared enrolments. In rural and outer suburban areas, responsibility for monitoring school attendance has lain with the Gardaí, effectively meaning no service. Pre-school programmes now being developed, such as Early Start, the Home-School Liaison programme, and the Breaking the Cycle initiative in certain primary schools, are all designed to improve education chances and reduce the risk of drop out from mainstream schooling in areas of high disadvantage. It makes much more financial sense to try and keep children in mainstream education than to have to find extra places on programmes for those who have already dropped out. The demographic dividend in education, as rapidly falling birth rates from 1980 on translate into fewer pupil numbers, offers a unique opportunity to target resources at prevention of early drop out.

The Youthreach education and training programme caters for 3300 young people aged 15–18 who have dropped out of school. Successive evaluations of this scheme have noted the acute shortage of places relative to need, and the poor links and progression rates to further job-related education and training from Youthreach's foundation-level programme.

Geographical Concentration of Unemployment

Traditionally, public housing in Ireland in the major urban areas has been provided in fairly large socially segregated estates. The £5000 surrender grant scheme which operated in the 1980s, at a time of accelerating unemployment, led to a significant exodus of those with jobs from these estates, and their replacement largely by tenants without work (Threshold, 1987). With 80% of those renting from a local authority living on social welfare, there are concentrations of unemployment in particular estates and flat complexes, particularly in the major urban centre. Nolan et al. (1998) found that overall, poverty and unemployment are relatively dispersed. They found, however, significant concentrations in local authority rented housing, with local authority tenants in urban areas over six times more likely to be below than above the poverty line (1998: 44). The CSO have identified 110 unemployment blackspots from the small area data of the 1996 Census, with unemployment rates averaging almost 40%, of which 47 are in Dublin, 12 in Cork City, and 11 in Limerick.

Among the policies being developed to respond to the geographical concentration of unemployment and disadvantage are the funding of community development projects in disadvantaged areas, moves to delegate power and responsibility to tenants through estate-based tenant management, the targeting of funds to tackle educational disadvantage to such neighbourhoods, and the development of Area-based Partnerships in unemployment blackspots.

Area Partnerships

The 1991 national pay deal, the Programme for Economic and Social Progress (PESP), provided for twelve Area Partnerships in key unemployment blackspots, to develop innovative approaches to tackling long-term unemployment.

The Partnerships involve local representative of statutory agencies such as FÁS, IDA, local authorities, VECs; local social partners including business and trade unions; and representatives of local community groups. They were initially funded under the European Union's Global Grant scheme. In 1994, the programme was extended to 38 areas of high unemployment and disadvantage (20 in urban areas, covering 24% of the urban population) and incorporated in the Operational Programme for Local Urban and Rural Development (OPLURD).

Each partnership area draws up an Area Action Plan and develops initiatives based on its assessment of priority local needs, so there is no single Partnership 'solution' to long-term unemployment. Some partnerships have concentrated more on local economic development, the development of self-employment opportunities, or starting small businesses to employ long-term unemployed people. Others have built on the links with local employers to develop active programmes of placement. Craig (1994) outlines how relatively small is the scale of Partnership activities. Sabel (1996) points to the strength of these Partnerships in terms of piloting innovative approaches, and warns of weaknesses in terms of potential local tensions, poor sharing of experience between Partnerships themselves and with central Government agencies. Initiatives undertaken by the Partnerships in Ballymun and Coolock were very influential in shaping subsequent policy for a Local Employment Service.

Welfare to Work Schemes

To soften the impact of unemployment traps, a complex array of schemes have been developed to make it worthwhile for unemployed people to take up employment. Some of these allow participants to keep their secondary benefits, including rent allowance and the medical card, if earnings are below a certain threshold, as recommended by the Tax and Welfare Integration Group (Ireland: 1996).

The schemes are complex and there is a major information gap among unemployed people themselves. The Irish National Organisation of Unemployed (INOU) (1997a) concluded that where people claim their entitlements under such schemes, it pays to return to work certainly for an initial period. However, the view that it does not pay to take a job has been widely broadcast by some employer interests and can be widely believed by unemployed people themselves, as it is a far simpler message to communicate than the complex web of welfare to work options. Whatever the underlying reality, if *perceived* replacement rates are high, they will have an impact on the supply of labour.

Table 5. Selected 'Welfare to Work' Schemes

Scheme	Eligible	Conditions	Secondary benefits	Nos (1998)
Family Income Supplement	Low paid with children	60% of gap between pay and prescribed income	No	12,000
Back to Work Allowance	Unemployed over 12 months	Yr 1– 75% of dole Yr 2– 50% of dole Yr 3– 25% of dole	Yes	22,000
Job Assist	Unemployed over 12 months	£3,000 extra tax allowance plus £1,000 per child	Yes	n.a.
Unemployment assistance for part-time workers	Part-time workers	Concessions on means test	No	16,000
Community employment	Unemployed over 12 months	Part-time work in social projects	Yes	40,000

Active Labour Market Programmes

Active labour market programmes, to provide education, training or work experience for unemployed people began to develop in Ireland in the 1970s and the scale of provision and the variety of schemes have particularly accelerated in the 1980s and 1990s as unemployment lifted off. Such policies have long been a feature of Scandinavian approaches to unemployment which emphasize the importance of active measures to assist unemployed people to get work rather than passive income support. A switch from passive to active measures forms a common theme of the Delors White Paper on *Growth Competitiveness and Employment* (EU, 1993), the OECD Jobs Study (1994), and the EU's five point programme on unemployment adopted at the 1994 Essen summit. By 1994, about 90,000 people a year in Ireland participated in some kind of active programme, accounting for 6.5% of the work force (O'Connell and McGinnity, 1997). The variety of such schemes in Ireland stems partly from a wish to try out different approaches, and partly because different agencies (FÁS, and several separate Government departments) each developed their own proposals on unemployment independently of each other. Increased numbers on employment schemes were facilitated by EU structural funds, and in response to rapidly accelerating Live Register figures. These programmes are in a number of categories

- training programmes, in general or specific skills
- wage subsidies to employers
- wage subsidies for employees or self-employment
- work experience and direct employment schemes

O'Connell and McGinnity (1997: 142), on the basis of their 1994 survey of 1992 participants, strongly criticize the current mix of active labour market programmes:

> The category of labour market programmes which has expanded most in recent years – direct employment schemes – is the programme type we have found least effective in improving the employment prospects of their participants . . . Accordingly we believe that the recent expansion of direct employment schemes is a policy choice which favours high volume programmes at the expense of quality and effectiveness . . . While many of those most marginalized in the labour market may need work experience programmes (or, indeed, basic training), our analysis shows that unless participation in such a programme facilitates subsequent progression to programmes with strong market linkages in an individually tailored reintegration path, they are unlikely to convey durable benefits on their participants.

Perverse Incentives

While full-time training may provide a more effective route into main-stream employment than employment on a community employment programme with a limited training element, from the point of view of the unemployed person, participation in Community Employment has been the financially more attractive option, paying more money, and for a half-time rather than full-time commitment. The 1999 Budget proposed measures to ease this disincentive.

Training the Unemployed

FÁS has been the main training provider for the unemployed, with a range of programmes offering general training, and more market-driven specific skills training.

- FÁS training for the unemployed has had little success in reaching the most disadvantaged of the unemployed. Trainees are predominantly under 25, with better education than the average unemployed. In 1996, only 15% of long-term unemployed got specific skills training. McCann and Ronayne (1992), however, report a clear preference among older unemployed for work rather than training

- the system is provider-centred not client-centred

- O'Connell and McGinnity (1997) conclude that general training programmes have had little or no impact on future employment chances, but that specific skill training programmes are worthwhile

- severely disadvantaged people may need personal development, confidence building, and basic skills before they can benefit from specific skills training. Such general programmes and specific skills training are poorly linked

In contrast to the supplier-centred approach, Ballymun Job Centre (Davitt 1998) has developed an interesting approach to training long-term unemployed people, linked to identified job opportunities and training needs as identified by employers. For example, an eight week forklift/warehouse course led to 100% employment for those participating who were all in their 40s. The *Tramlines* programme provides IT training to unemployed people whose aptitude has been identified, with employment guaranteed in a leading computer company for the successful graduates.

Wage Subsidies

Generalized wage subsidies have a high risk of *displacement* – where A's subsidized job undercuts B, and puts B out of work, and *deadweight* – where the jobs attributed to the subsidy would have been created in any case. Breen's (1991) study of the Employment Incentive Scheme found that 90% of expenditure was accounted for by displacement or deadweight, and the scheme was abolished.

More recently, targeted wage subsidies for long-term unemployed have been introduced with the aim not of increasing overall employment but of increasing the share of long-term unemployed taking up job vacancies. (Department of Enterprise and Employment, 1997). The Jobstart £80 a week subsidy to employers had limited initial success, with about 1100 employed in April 1998, eighteen months after its introduction. For employees, it is far less attractive than the Back to Work Allowance discussed below. A new subsidy scheme, Revenue Job Assist introduced from April 1998, offers increased tax allowances to employees as well as new incentives to employers. Burtless (1985) reports on a randomized experiment in Dayton, Ohio which showed that subsidy vouchers actually had a detrimental effect on the employment probability of recipients. One possible explanation is that rather than countering employer prejudice, the subsidy may be taken by employers to signal a potentially difficult or unproductive worker.

Employee and Self-employment Subsidies

The Back to Work Allowance introduced in 1994 provides for phased withdrawal of welfare payments over a three-year period for employees and a four-year period for self-employed when someone returns to work after a year or more unemployed. By June 1998, there were almost 22,000 participants. While initially a majority of participants were self-employed, by 1998 employees were about two-thirds of the total.

An initial evaluation based on a survey in 1995 of two years of the scheme's operation (Department of Social, Community and Family Affairs, 1997a) showed that participants tended to be older, to be men, to be better educated than the average unemployed (although less well educated than the work force as a whole). This may reflect to some extent the early initial bias in take up among self-employed. Overall in the first two years, there was an 81% survival rate on the scheme, although initial earnings figures were low, averaging £90 a week for self-employed and £106 a week for employees. Participants had net gains, including retained social welfare payments, of £50–£70 a week.

Such relatively low earnings suggest poor prospects of long-term survival once the welfare subsidy would be fully withdrawn, although the relatively buoyant job market in the late 1990s appears to have had a cushioning effect. The estimates of deadweight for employees is 27%, and 48% for the self-employed, while 15% of participants were regularizing participation in the black economy.

Work Experience and Direct Employment Programmes

Community Employment

The largest single programme aimed at the unemployed is Community Employment, with 40,000 participants on average (1998), equivalent to 3% of the total workforce. Sponsors, mainly voluntary or community organizations, are offered staff resources and some materials funding which they could not otherwise afford, so it was conceived as mutually beneficial for sponsors and participants. It began as the Social Employment Scheme in 1984, and initially participants were paid half the average industrial wage for half a week's work. This programme has remained one of half-time jobs, although since 1987 pay has been on a 'benefits-plus' basis. By 1998, a quarter of participants were lone parents, to whom the part-time nature of the work is attractive as it minimizes childcare problems. In theory, workers can top up their earnings from Community Employment through additional part-time work. In rural areas, participation is often combined with part-time farming. A 1992 survey in Limerick City (Ronayne and Devereux, 1993) showed only one in seven had a supplementary job. However, the part-time nature of the job may diminish its value as work experience, both for participants themselves and in the eyes of an employer.

To prevent displacement, placements are exclusively in social projects, which may be seen as less relevant by employers than work experience in the open job market. While designed for mutual benefit, there is an inherent conflict between the objectives of the scheme as a labour-market programme and the objectives of sponsors. Sponsors are interested in attracting the most qualified and job-ready participants, and in keeping them as long as possible to recoup investment in on-the-job training. On the other hand, any 'creaming-off' or recycling of the more qualified participants means fewer openings for the hard-core long-term unemployed persons who are the least likely to get a job on the open market. Given the source of funding, the scheme's ultimate intention is not primarily to provide free labour for Tidy Towns committees or welfare rights centres, but to offer a progression route for long-term unemployed people from unemployment to a job on the open labour market.

Following changes in the scheme and improved job prospects generally, the placement rate into employment has risen, from 22% in 1994, to 34% in 1997, and into employment and further training combined, from 40% to 67%. However, fewer than one-quarter of those with the lowest levels of education have moved off the scheme into work. There is also significant recycling of participants who can requalify for CE after six months back on the Live Register (Deloitte and Touche, 1998). The open job market provides few opportunities offering family-friendly working hours at comparable wages, making it less attractive for lone parents than a return to CE. Given the severe labour market disadvantage of many participants and the limited training on offer under the scheme, progression to open-market employment will not always be a realistic outcome. In recognition of the problems for progression on the one hand, and the needs of sponsoring voluntary agencies for staff, on the other, proposals were made in 1998 to designate a proportion of Community Employment places as dedicated social economy jobs, rather than ones geared primarily to participant progression (Deloitte and Touche, 1998; Partnership 2000 Working Group, 1998).

The numbers on CE expanded very rapidly between 1994 and 1995, virtually doubling in twelve months, at a time of rapidly growing Live Register figures. That pace of expansion ran the risk that lower-quality job placements were offered in terms of value as work experience to participants in order to get the numbers up fast. Average project size increased from 8 to 14.5 participants between 1994 to 1997, enabling more projects to hire a supervisor, and facilitating economies of scale in providing training. The criticism that the largest numbers are to be found on the labour-market programme, with one of the lowest success rates in terms of progression to open employment has already been noted. As labour shortages have begun to emerge in the tighter labour market of the late 1990s, the current scale of the CE programme has been queried by Deloitte and Touche (1998), who have recommended a significant scaling-down by 6,000–8,000 participants. That reflects concern that programmes like CE may be competing with employers for low-skilled labour, in offering a more attractive financial package, particularly to lone parents, as well as a concern that part-time work experience is less appropriate than full-time training in making up deficits in education and skills levels (Deloitte and Touche, 1998). For people with poor experience of the education system, work experience pro-grammes can give the confidence to go on to further training. However, while Community Employment has been markedly more successful than FÁS training or other labour market programmes in reaching long-term employed people with poor educational qualifications, its training content has been very limited, and links into mainstream training have been very poor (European Social Fund Evaluation Unit, 1998).

Part-time Job Initiative (CORI)

In 1995, on a proposal from the Conference of Religious of Ireland, a pilot Part-time Job Initiative (PTJI) was introduced, with 1,000 places on three-year contracts. Unlike Community Employment, this was seen by its proposers as providing permanent social economy employment rather than a staging post into mainstream work, and an intrinsic part of the proposal was that the going rate for the job would be paid. Given that total weekly remuneration was set at the equivalent Community Employment rate, a 'benefits plus' rate related to family size, this led to the anomaly that PTJI participants would work different lengths of week depending on family size, with single people earning their weekly income in fewer hours than a married man with three children; and with different length of working week for PTJI and CE participants working in identical projects in adjoining towns. Only 20% of participants in 1995 worked the same 19-hour week as CE workers, while 30% worked less than 13 hours a week. The rate for the job element is understandably popular with participants, and it is planned to progressively switch the one-year CE placements on to this basis. Unlike CE, eligibility was not limited to long-term unemployed, and a significant share of short-term unemployed people participate on this programme.

Long-term Unemployment

As unemployment in Ireland grew during the 1980s, the share of long-term unemployed (those out of work for a year or more) in the total grew sharply, from under 40% of the unemployed in 1983, to peak at over two-thirds by 1987. Ireland's share of long-term unemployment is high by EU standards, and in the early 1990s Ireland's long-term unemployment rate was higher than the total unemployment rate in most of our EU partners.

Table 6. Long-term Unemployment, 1996, Ireland and EU

	Unemployed over 1 year	Unemployed over 2 years
Ireland	59.5%	41.1%
EU Average	48.2%	30.0%

Source: EUROSTAT 1997

While movements in long-term unemployment (over a year) have closely tracked the changes in total unemployment (see chart), given the 'revolving door' nature of schemes like Community Employment for some of the unemployed, people who have little recent experience in the open job market may be reclassified as short-term unemployed when their period on a scheme is over. Other evidence suggests that the longer the period out of the workforce, the higher the chances of becoming locked into long-term unemployment, or dropping out of the workforce altogether. Half of the long-term unemployed have been unemployed for over three years (*Labour Force Survey*, 1997).

Chart 1: Unemployment and Long-Term Unemployment (ILO) 1983–97

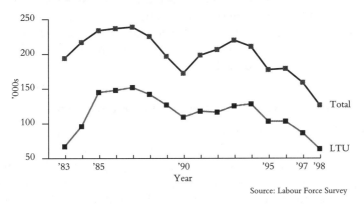

Source: Labour Force Survey

While the Live Register figures are an imperfect guide to the labour market, they show clearly how the chances of moving off welfare are consistently less likely the longer someone is signing on. Throughout the 1990s, between 25–30% of newly unemployed were still signing on six months later. 50–60% of those signing on between one and two years were still signing on a year later. From 1990–96, over 70% of those signing on for 2–3 years were still signing on a year later. Exit figures from the Live Register tell a similar story. In April 1998, while long-term unemployed constituted 47% of the Live Register, they accounted for only 10% of those leaving the Live Register because of finding work in the open job market.

Employer preconceptions about long-term unemployed workers, and lack of skills and self-belief among people who have been out of work for a long period can together place formidable obstacles to accessing a job on the open labour market. ESRI research conducted in 1991 (Whelan et al., 1992) showed that only 16% of vacancies were filled by short-term unemployed and only 6% by long-term unemployed.

Unemployed Organizations and the Framing of Policy

The Irish National Organisation of the Unemployed (INOU) has become an increasingly influential voice in articulating policy on unemployment and focusing attention on long-term unemployment, together with the Irish Congress of Trade Unions (ICTU), which has a network of Unemployed Centres and has built on their experience in lobbying for change. The involvement of unemployed representatives from both the INOU and the ICTU centres for the unemployed in the National Economic and Social Forum (NESF) was a key influence in shaping the analysis of long-term unemployment which now underpins public policy. Involvement in the NESF has also been a stepping stone for unemployed organizations into a wider consultative role and into fuller social partnership. The INOU was involved, along with others from the Community Platform, in negotiating the social elements of the Partnership 2000 national pay agreement, and is also now represented on the National Economic and Social Council.

Developing a Strategy on Long-term Unemployment

Economic and social policy traditionally dealt with unemployment as a homogeneous problem, and only in the 1990s did strategies evolve which specifically focused on long-term unemployment. The first major strategic policy on long-term unemployment was enunciated by the National Economic and Social Forum (1994) and further developed by the Task Force on Long-Term Unemployment (Office of the Tánaiste, 1995). These reports not only led to specific policy changes such as the setting-up of the Local Employment Service, the recasting of Community Employment to provide a more effective pathway back to work for the long-term unemployed, and the Whole-time Jobs Initiative; they also fundamentally changed official thinking on the need to address long-term unemployment as a specific policy issue and not merely rely on economic growth.

The strategy developed by the NESF and the Task Force had four planks:

• sound macroeconomic policies for sustainable jobs growth

• early intervention in education to minimize the numbers leaving school without qualifications

• targeted measures to bring the long-term unemployed into jobs

• preventing the drift from short-term into long-term unemployment

Reintegrating the Long-term Unemployed

The Task Force (Office of the Tánaiste, 1995) targeted not only those already long-term unemployed but also their spouses, those out of work for six months or more and the poorly qualified young unemployed, considered at risk of becoming long-term unemployed, and lone parents. Of these, they felt young people, the 6–12 months group, and the better educated of the long-term unemployed would have good prospects of getting work with initial support. More intensive help would be required with the poorly qualified long-term unemployed, particularly those who were older and had been out of work a number of years.

Given limits on the capacity of the open labour market to absorb long-term unemployed people into jobs, and the difficulty for people who had been out of the labour market for a long time or whose skills were limited or obsolete to obtain work in the open job market, the Task Force (Office of the Tánaiste, 1995) recommended provision of sponsored employment through a recasting of the Community Employment scheme to

- reserve 25% of places for people over 35, over three years out of work (including lone parents and spouses of long-term unemployed) as three-year part-time jobs
- provide one-year part-time jobs for unemployed people aged over 21 and out of work for at least a year
- provide a meaningful training component and support for progression to mainstream employment

These changes were implemented from April 1996. The share of short-term unemployed on CE has fallen from 33% in 1995, to 4% by 1998; those over three years out of work have risen from 13% of participants to 37%, a major success in rebalancing the scheme to favour long-term unemployed. Up to 24 days for training (including job-related training, and training for progression to future employment) can now be given.

For those profoundly disadvantaged on the job market, the Task Force (Office of the Tánaiste, 1995) recommended a pilot three-year programme of 1,000 full-time contract jobs. These are for people five years out of work and aged over 35 from target unemployment blackspots, and the numbers on the scheme are doubled from 1998.

Local Employment Service

The National Economic and Social Forum (1994) saw a new Local Employment Service (LES) as having a key role both in preventing the drift into long-term unemployment and reintegrating the long-term unemployed back into the work force. Modelled on successful initiatives like Contactpoint in Coolock and the Ballymun Jobcentre, the service was intended to offer a gateway for individuals back to the world of work through individual counselling, guidance, training, job placement and employment support. In the first place, an unemployed individual would be assessed, their potential identified, their education and training needs assessed, including pre-labour market support with confidence building or literacy. The LES would be able to buy appropriate training services and arrange work experience placements. The LES would also offer local employers a professional placement service, matching job-ready individuals to identified vacancies. Pilot initiatives on these lines had proved highly successful, with employer involvement, in placing hitherto long-term unemployed people in vacancies, and participating employers were very satisfied with the outcome. The Task Force estimated there were 150,000 vacancies occurring annually in the economy, up to half of which could be suitably filled by long-term unemployed, so that an increase in placement rates could play a significant role.

The LES was set up on an initial basis in 1996 in 14 Partnership areas, and by 1998 covered 18 areas. The intention is to progressively extend the LES to other unemployment blackspots. Coverage relative to the target groups is still low, but the service by 1998 was reaching about one in eleven of long-term unemployed on the Live Register, and one in eight of ILO long-term unemployed. Some evidence of catering for the easier to place is suggested by the fact that 50% of those reached had Junior Certificate or lower education, compared to 72% of all long-term unemployed while a fifth of those catered for are outside the targeted groups.

Table 7. Local Employment Service: Coverage vs Targets

Target group	Task Force target (1994)	With LES May 1998
Long-term unemployed	135,000	10,013
Unemployed 6–12 months	38,000	2,630
Dependent spouses of ltu	70,000	398
Lone parents	44,000	2,888
Young unemployed		2,544
Others		4,389
Total	287,000	22,862

Source: Department of Enterprise, Trade and Employment, *Management Information Report*, May 1998)

The original blueprint for the Local Employment Service envisaged participation would be voluntary, the argument being that it would have to earn clients through delivering a quality service, and that compulsion could devalue the service in the eyes of already marginalized individuals. These are valid arguments. Automatic contact should not, however, be confused with compulsion. The fact that there is not automatic referral of the target clients, who are in weekly contact with the welfare system, to the LES leaves open the possibility that the most disadvantaged of the unemployed who need the service most will fail to be reached by less systematic contact methods.

Table 8. Local Employment Service Placements 1996–March 1998

Status	Number	%
Placed in job	7,835	34.3
On work experience	4,128	18.1
In training/education	4,421	19.3
On active case load	8,660	37.9
Dropped out etc.	4,230	18.5
Total	22,862	100

Source: Department of Enterprise, Trade and Employment, *Management Information Report*, May 1998

The LES has been fairly successful to date in placement of clients in employment, work experience or training. Two years after it began, one third of those with the LES had been placed in employment, with young unemployed slightly over-represented, and long-term unemployed under-represented in those placed.

Stemming the Flow or Reducing the Stock?

The EU Employment Guidelines agreed at the November 1997 Luxembourg Employment Summit call for a refocusing of unemployment policy on preventing the drift into long-term unemployment through interventions aimed at the young unemployed (under 25) who are six months out of work, and other unemployed reaching twelve months out of work. This focus is carried through in Ireland's *Employment Action Plan* (Department of Enterprise, Trade and Employment, 1998a) which contains no additional resources for its implementation. Invariably, any redirection of fixed resources towards preventing the drift into long-term unemployment will mean fewer resources for reducing the existing stock of long-term unemployment through measures to reintegrate the chronically long-term unemployed.

Youth Progression Programme

From 1996, this programme provided that 18–19 year olds who reached six months on the Live Register would be referred to FÁS for intensive guidance, training and job placement. This scheme has been successful in reducing the numbers of young people signing on, by an estimated 14% more than without such contact. It has, however, encountered bottle-necks in providing enough training or work experience places for those who do not get jobs themselves. A further issue FÁS has identified is a significant minority of young people in the target group with drug abuse problems, who will not be in the job market in any real sense without drug treatment. A special Community Employment programme to provide a form of sheltered work experience for recovering drug addicts was planned for late 1998 (FÁS, 1998). It is arguable that a programme of positive help, and positive alternatives to welfare such as training or work experience, should be offered to young unemployed people, particularly those like early school leavers at identifiably high risk of long-term unemployment, when they sign on rather than delaying six months.

The Action Plan on Unemployment provides that from September 1998, young people aged 18–25 over six months out of work must accept an offer of a job or training place, or forfeit their welfare benefits. Older unemployed people face a similar choice after a year out of work. Refusal to work because the going rate for the job is too low can render someone ineligible for unemployment payments (www.dscfa.ie). Experience with the Youth Progression Programme suggests that lack of suitable places to offer is a more substantive obstacle to employment than any refusal to work or take up an offered place.

CONCLUSION

Social as well as economic policies have an important role to play in overcoming unemployment and, in particular, in addressing the multi-faceted problem of long-term unemployment. Ireland's record prosperity heading into the millennium offers a special opportunity to invest in eradicating hard-core unemployment and its causes. The multiplicity of schemes on roughly similar lines and of competing departments and agencies badly require rationalization, in order to offer unemployed people an effective and easily understood path from the world of unemployment back to the world of work. There is over a decade of experimentation with different approaches to long-term unemployment to draw on in reshaping programmes to be more effective in reaching the long-term unemployed, and more effective in terms of quality and outcomes. As the problem of short-term unemployment fades in scale, the primary focus of policy must be on the long-term unemployed, to bring them, their families and communities finally out of the margins.

CHRONOLOGY

1933	Unemployment Assistance
1953	Social Insurance
1968	National Manpower Agency set up, taking job placement out of Labour Exchanges
	AnCo set up (both later subsumed into FÁS)
1973/4	Oil price crisis
1979	Oil price crisis
1975	Live Register goes over 100,000
1983	Social Employment Scheme
1984	Live Register goes over 200,000
	Youth Employment Agency set up (later subsumed into FÁS)
1986	Report of Commission on Social Welfare published
	Equal Treatment Directive adopted giving equal rights to women in the social welfare code
1991	Area-based Partnerships set up in 12 pilot areas under Programme for Economic and Social Progress
1993	National Economic and Social Forum set up with Oireachtas, social partner, and unemployed representatives, and a mandate to address long-term unemployment
	National Development Plan contains Operational Programme for local urban and rural development, extending the Area Partnerships to 38 unemployment blackspots
	Back to Work Allowance introduced
1994	NESF Report no. 4 'Ending Long-term Unemployment published'.
	Task Force on Long-term Unemployment set up to address its detailed recommendations
	Replacement of Social Employment Scheme by Community Employment. Expansion from 17,000 to 34,000 places.

1995   Part-time Job Initiative set up with 1,000 places, on model
       recommended by Conference of Religious of Ireland
       Interim Report of Task Force published.
       Final report of Task Force published.
1996   Local Employment Service set up on pilot basis in 14
       areas
       Recasting of Community Employment on lines
       recommended by Task Force.
       1,000 places on Full-time Job Initiative for very long-term
       unemployed
       Youth Progression programme introduced for 18–19 year
       olds out of work
1997   Luxembourg Summit on unemployment sets targets for
       EU states on reducing inflow into long-term
       unemployment
       Unemployed representatives involved in negotiating
       Partnership 2000
1998   Employment Action Plan published to give effect to EU
       guidelines.
       Amsterdam Treaty ratified, with chapter on EU
       unemployment policy
       Announcement that social welfare will be cut off for
       those refusing offer of a job or training place

RECOMMENDED READING

(a)   Unemployment in Ireland: Economic Perspectives

Leddin, A. and B.M. Walsh (1998) *The Macroeconomy of Ireland*, Ch. 14. Dublin: Gill & Macmillan.
O'Hagan, J. (1995) *The Economy of Ireland: Policy and Performance of a Small European Economy*, Ch. 8. Dublin: IMI.
Tansey, P. (1998) *Ireland at Work: Economic Growth and the Labour Market 1987–97*, Ch. 3. Dublin: Oak Tree Press
Turley, G. and M. Maloney (1997) *Principles of Economics: An Irish Textbook*, pp. 485–507. Dublin: Gill & Macmillan.

(b) Unemployment in Ireland: Development of Social Policies

Allen, M. (1998) *The Bitter Word*. Dublin: Poolbeg.
Office of the Tánaiste (1995a) *Interim Report of the Task Force on Long-term Unemployment*. Dublin: Stationery Office.

National Economic and Social Forum

> (1994) *Ending Long-term Unemployment.* Dublin: NESF Report 4
>
> (1996) *Long-term Unemployment Initiatives.* Dublin: NESF Opinion no. 3
>
> (1997) *Early School Leavers and Long-term Unemployment.* Dublin: NESF Report 11

Office of the Tánaiste (1995b) *Report of the Task Force on Long-term Unemployment.* Dublin: Stationery Office

Report of Partnership 2000 Social Economy Working Group (1998). Dublin: Department of the Taoiseach.

(c)   Replacement Rates

Callan, T., B. Nolan and C.T. Whelan (1996b) *A Review of the Commission on Social Welfare's Minimum Adequate Income.* Dublin: Economic and Social Research Institute, Policy Research Series Paper 29, Ch. 7: 106–203.

Ireland (1996) *Integrating Tax and Social Welfare: Expert Working Group Report* Appendix 5.

(d)   Active Labour Market Policies

Deloitte and Touche (1998) *Review of Community Employment Programme.* Dublin: Stationery Office.

European Social Fund Evaluation Unit (1998) *ESF and the Long-term Unemployed.* Dublin: Department of Enterprise Trade and Employment.

O'Connell, P. and F. McGinnity (1997) *Working Schemes? Active Labour Market Policy in the Republic of Ireland.* Ch 3; Ch.8. Aldershot: Aldgate.

REFERENCES

Area Development Management (1994) *Report on Area-based Responses to Long-term Unemployment.* Dublin: ADM

Barry, F. and J. Bradley (1991) 'On the Causes of Ireland's Unemployment', *Economic and Social Review*, 22 (4): 253–86.

Blanchard, O. (1997) *Macroeconomics.* London: Prentice Hall.

Breen, R. (1991) *Education, Employment and Training in the Youth Labour Market.* Dublin: Economic and Social Research Institute.

Breen, R. and B. Halpin (1988) *Self-employment and the Unemployed.* Dublin: ESRI paper 140.

Breen, R. and B. Halpin (1989) *Subsidised Jobs: An Evaluation of the Employment Incentive Scheme.* Dublin: Economic and Social Research Institute.

Breen, R. and S. Shortall (1992) 'The Exchequer Costs of Unemployment', in J. Bradley, J. FitzGerald and I. Kearney (eds) *The Role of the Structural Funds.* Dublin: Economic and Social Research Institute.

Browne, F. and D. McGettigan (1993) 'The Evolution of Irish Unemployment: Some Explanations and Lessons', *Labour Market Review*, 4 (2):15–49.

Burtless, G. (1985) 'Are Targeted Wage Subsidies Harmful?', *Industrial and Labour Relations Review*, 39 (1): 105–14.

Callan, T., B. Nolan, B.J. Whelan, C.T. Whelan and J. Williams (1996a) *Poverty in the 1990s: Evidence from the 1994 Living in Ireland Survey*. Dublin: Oak Tree Press.

Callan, T., B. Nolan and C.T. Whelan (1996b) *A Review of the Commission on Social Welfare's Minimum Adequate Income*. Dublin: Economic and Social Research Institute, Policy Research Series Paper 29.

Central Statistics Office (annually 1983–1997) *Labour Force Survey*. Dublin: Stationery Office.

Central Statistics Office (1996) *Unemployment Statistics: A Study of the Differences between the Labour Force Survey Estimates of Unemployment and the Live Register*. Cork: CSO.

Central Statistics Office (1997) *Household Budget Survey 1994–5*. Dublin: Stationery Office.

Central Statistics Office (quarterly, from 1998) *Quarterly National Household Survey*). Dublin: Stationery Office.

Commission on Social Welfare (1986) *Report*. Dublin: Stationery Office.

Craig, S. (1994) *Progress through Partnership: A Final Evaluation Report on the PESP Initiative on Long-term Unemployment*. Dublin: Combat Poverty Agency.

Davitt, P. (1998) *Relevant and Quality Training as a Tool for Integration,* Paper for INOU Conference on Active Labour Market Policy, April 1998. Dublin: Ballymun Job Centre.

Deloitte and Touche (1998) *Review of Community Employment Programme*. Dublin: Stationery Office.

Department of Enterprise and Employment (1996) *Growing and Sharing our Employment: Strategy Paper on the Labour Market*. Dublin: Stationery Office.

Department of Enterprise and Employment (1997) *White Paper: Human Resource Development*. Dublin: Stationery Office.

Department of Enterprise, Trade and Employment (1998a) *Ireland: Employment Action Plan*. Dublin: Stationery Office.

Department of Enterprise, Trade and Employment (1998b) *Management Information Report*, May 1998.

Department of Social, Community and Family Affairs (1997a) *Developing Active Welfare Policy – an Evaluation of the Back to Work Allowance Scheme*. Dublin: Stationery Office.

Department of Social, Community and Family Affairs (1997b) *Self-employed and the Long-term Unemployed – an Evaluation of the Area Allowance Enterprise Scheme*. Dublin: Stationery Office.

Department of Social, Community and Family Affairs *Website* www.dscfa.ie

Department of Social Welfare (yearly) *Statistical Information on Social Welfare Services*. Dublin: Stationery Office.

Department of Social Welfare (1997) *Sharing in Progress: National Anti-Poverty Strategy*. Dublin: Stationery Office.

Dublin County Council Community Department (1987) *County Dublin Areas of Need*. Dublin.

Duggan, C. and M. Cosgrave (1994) *Participation Costs on Labour Market Provision for the Long-term Unemployed*. Limerick: PAUL Partnership.

Economic and Social Research Institute (1993) *The Role of the Structural Funds*. Dublin: ESRI.

Economic and Social Research Institute (1997) *Medium-Term Review 1997–2003*. Dublin: ESRI.

EU Commission (1993) *Growth Competitiveness and Employment*. Luxembourg: EU Publications.

EU Council (1996) *Background paper on long-term unemployment presented by Irish Presidency (11938/96)*. Brussels: EU Council Secretariat.

EU Social Fund Programme Evaluation Unit (1996) *Evaluation Report: Early School Leavers Provision*. Dublin: Department of Enterprise and Employment.

EU Social Fund Evaluation Unit (1998) *ESF and the Long-term Unemployed*. Dublin: Department of Enterprise, Trade and Employment.

European Foundation for the Improvement of Living and Working Conditions (1987) *Locally Based Responses to Long-term Unemployment*. Dublin: EU Foundation.

FÁS (1998) *Impact of Youth Progression Measure – Labour Market Data* Update Paper 1/98 (mimeo). Dublin: FÁS.

Finneran, L. and M. Kelly (1996) *Labour Market Networks, Underclasses and Inequalities*. Dublin: UCD, Centre for Economic Research Working Paper 96/21.

Fynes, B., T. Morrissey, W.K. Roche, B.J. Whelan and J. Williams (1997) *Flexible Working Lives: The Changing Nature of Working Time Arrangements in Ireland*. Dublin: Oak Tree Press.

Haase, T. (1996) *Local Development Strategies for Disadvantaged Areas: Evaluation of Global Grants*. Dublin: ADM.

Hannan, D. and S. Ó Riain (1993) *Pathways to Adulthood in Ireland*. Dublin: Economic and Social Research Institute.

Honohan, P. (1992) 'The Link between Irish and UK Unemployment', *Quarterly Economic Commentary*, Spring. Dublin: Economic and Social Research Institute.

Ireland (1991) *Programme for Economic and Social Progress (PESP)*. Dublin: Stationery Office

Ireland (1995) *Operational Programme for Integrated Local Urban and Rural Development* Dublin: Stationery Office.

Ireland (1996) *Integrating Tax and Social Welfare: Expert Working Group Report*

Ireland (1996) *Partnership 2000 for Inclusion, Employment and Competitiveness*. Dublin: Stationery Office.

Irish National Organisation of the Unemployed (1997a) *Welfare to Work*. Dublin: INOU.

Irish National Organisation of the Unemployed (1997b) *Working for Work*. Dublin: INOU.

Keynes, J.M. (1936) *The General Theory of Employment Interest and Money*. London: Macmillan.

Layard, R., S. Nickell and R. Jackman (1994) *The Unemployment Crisis*. Oxford: Oxford University Press.

Leddin, A. and B.M. Walsh (1995) *The Macroeconomy of Ireland*. Dublin: Gill & Macmillan.

McAleese, D. (1997) *Economics for Business*. Englewood Cliffs, New Jersey: Prentice Hall.

McCann, N. and T. Ronayne (1992) *Experiences and Views of Education and Training among Unemployed in Ballymun*. Dublin: Ballymun Partnership/WRC.

McCoy, S. and B. Whelan (1996) *Economic Status of School-leavers 1993–95 – Results of School-leavers' Surveys*. Dublin: Economic and Social Research Institute.

McGettigan, D. (1994) *The Causes of Unemployment: A Review* in ESRI 'Economic Perspectives for the Medium Term'. Dublin: Economic and Social Research Institute.

McSorley, C. (1997) *School Absenteeism in Clondalkin: Causes and Responses*. Dublin: Clondalkin Partnership.

Murphy, A. and B.M. Walsh (1996) 'The Incidence of the male non–employment in Ireland', *Economic and Social Review*, 25: 467–90.

National Economic and Social Council (1993) *The Association between Economic Growth and Employment Growth in Ireland*. Dublin: NESC Report 94.

National Economic and Social Forum (1994) *Ending Long-term Unemployment*. Dublin: NESF Report 4.

National Economic and Social Forum (1996a) *Jobs Potential of Work Sharing*. Dublin: NESF Report 9.

National Economic and Social Forum (1996b) *Long-term Unemployment Initiatives*. Dublin: NESF Opinion, no. 3.

National Economic and Social Forum (1997a) *Early School Leavers and Long-term Unemployment*. Dublin: NESF Report 11.

National Economic and Social Forum (1997b) *Unemployment Statistics*. Dublin: NESF, Report 13.

Nolan, B., T. Callan, C.T. Whelan and J. Williams (1994) *Poverty and Time: Perspectives on the Dynamics of Poverty*. Dublin, Economic and Social Research Institute, General Research Series Paper 166.

Nolan, B., C.T. Whelan and J. Williams (1998) *Where Are Poor Households?* Dublin: Oaktree Press.

Norton, D. (1994) *Economics for an Open Economy: Ireland*. Dublin: Oak Tree Press.

Office of the Tánaiste (1995a) *Interim Report of the Task Force on Long-term Unemployment*. Dublin: Stationery Office.

Office of the Tánaiste (1995b) *Report of the Task Force on Long-term Unemployment*. Dublin: Stationery Office.

O'Connell, P. and F. McGinnity (1997) *Working Schemes? Active Labour Market Policy in the Republic of Ireland*. Aldershot: Aldgate.

OECD (1994) *The OECD Jobs Study*. Paris: OECD.

O'Hagan, J. (1995) *The Economy of Ireland: Policy and Performance of a Small European Country*. Dublin: Gill & Macmillan .

O'Neill, J. (1997) *Tackling Disadvantage in Areas of High Unemployment,* Address to Irish Social Policy Association, 28 Oct 1997. Dublin: Irish Social Policy Association.

Partnership 2000 Social Economy Working Group (1998). Dublin: Department of the Taoiseach.

Ronayne, T. (1991) *Life on the Dole: Experiences and Views of the Long-term Unemployed*. Dublin: Tallaght Centre for the Unemployed.

Ronayne, T. and M. Creedon (1992) *To Whose Benefit?* Dublin: Tallaght Centre for the Unemployed.

Ronayne, T. and E. Devereux (1993) *Labour Market Provision for the Unemployed: The Social Employment Scheme*. Limerick: PAUL Partnership.

Sabel, C. (1996*) Ireland: Local Partnerships and Social Innovation*. Paris: OECD.

Sexton, J. J. and P. O'Connell (1996) *Labour Market Studies: Ireland.* Luxembourg: European Communities.

Tansey, P. (1998) *Ireland at Work: Economic Growth and the Labour Market 1987–97.* Dublin: Oak Tree Press.

Threshold (1987) *Policy Consequences of the £5,000 Surrender Grant.* Dublin: Threshold.

Turley, G. and M. Maloney (1997) *Principles of Economics: An Irish Textbook.* Dublin: Gill & Macmillan.

UCD Services Industry Research Centre (1993) *Urban Development and Employment: Towards an Integrated Strategy.* Dublin: UCD.

Walsh, B. M. and A. Murphy (1997b) *Unemployment, Non-participation and Labour Market Slack among Irish Males.* Dublin: UCD Working Paper Series.

Whelan, B. J., R. Breen, T. Callan and B. Nolan (1992) *A Study of the Employment Possibilities of the Long-term Unemployed.* Dublin: Economic and Social Research Institute (unpublished).

Whelan C., S. Hannan and S. Creighton (1991) *Unemployment, Poverty and Psychological Distress.* Dublin, Economic and Social Research Institute.

7

Moving from Needs to Rights: Social Policy for People with Disability in Ireland

Suzanne Quin
Bairbre Redmond

INTRODUCTION

Within the past twenty years, the growing public awareness of disability has not been matched by a growth in real understanding of people with disabilities and those who provide care for them. This chapter covers some of the major issues relating to disability in present day Irish society. It challenges some of the traditional thinking about the nature of disability, particularly in relation to service provision. The key principles of full participation and consultation are identified as central to new directions in policy making in regard to those with disabilities.

INTELLECTUAL DISABILITY

Defining Intellectual Disability

An individual with an intellectual disability (previously known as mental handicap) has a greater than average difficulty in learning and has a below average intelligence. This results in a delayed or incomplete deve-lopment of a person's mind and presents difficulties for the individual in acquiring adequate social competencies and self-help skills. The terms intellectual disability, learning disability or mental handicap are used to describe a range of people who may have very different needs. On one hand are those with disabilities so severe that they need considerable help in basic living throughout their lives. At the other extreme are individuals who appear no different from any other citizen, whose intellectual abilities while adequate for some tasks may be inadequate for others. Intellectual disability is not an illness: it is a life-long condition which cannot be treated or cured. It can be caused in a number of ways. Some people with intellectual disability have genetic disorders, the most common of which is Down's Syndrome. Other types of intellectual disability are caused by brain damage during pregnancy or at birth, as well as from biological metabolic disease such as severe meningitis or encephalitis or from head injury. In many cases the specific cause of intellectual disability is unknown. Intellectual disability/mental handicap is sometimes confused with mental illness. Mental illness is characterized by inappropriate emotional reactions and emotional disturbance, whereas intellectual disability is marked by lack of understanding and communication.

The words which a society uses to describe someone with an intel-lectual disability can often reveal the attitudes of the society towards that individual. Despite changes in the actual words used, the terminology used to describe intellectual disability has continued to label those with an intellectual disability as being different from and considerably less able than the rest of society. It is perhaps no surprise that words such as moron, idiot, imbecile and retard, which were once simply clinical terms denoting categories of intellectual disability, now exist in the language as expressions of derision. The 1991 *Report of the Review Group on Mental Handicap* recommends that the term mental handicap should cease to be used and should be replaced by terms such as intellectual or developmental disability. The report warns that any new term can be debased over time and a simple change of label in itself will not have a long-lasting positive effect unless a concurrent attempt is made to change professional and public attitudes (*Report of the Review Group on Mental Handicap,* 1991: 14).

Prevalence of Intellectual Disability in Ireland

The National Intellectual Disability Database (1997: 4) shows 26,694 individuals with intellectual disability living in Ireland in 1996 with a prevalence rate of 7.57/1000 total population. Table 1 summarizes the numbers and prevalence rate for each level of intellectual disability. The profile of those with intellectual disability in Ireland in the Database shows an overall decrease in younger people with disability in the last twenty years, but a significant increase in the number of those with intellectual disability aged 35 years and older. This ageing population has major implications for service provision and will create an increased demand on the health services until the population bulge is cleared over the next twenty years (National Intellectual Disability Database, 1997: 7). How Irish society will deal with such demands will be dependent on a number of issues: the policy commitment to provide and design the

Table 1. Number of Individuals in Ireland with Intellectual Disability

Level of Disability	No. of Individuals	%	Rate per 1,000 of total population
Mild	10825	40.6	3.07
Moderate	9592	35.9	2.72
Severe	3953	14.8	1.12
Profound	1188	4.5	.34
No Verified	1136	4.3	.32
Total	26694	100.00	7.57

Source: National Intellectual Disability Database 1996 *Annual Report* (1997: 4)

most appropriate services, the level of funding made available for such service provision and, most importantly, the attitude of society in general towards those who have an intellectual disability. Such attitudes have changed considerably over the past two hundred years, not always for the better, and any examination of major issues surrounding intellectual disability will be illuminated by a brief historical overview of the development of such attitudes.

Development of Services for those with Intellectual Disability

For as long as the human race has existed, some of its members have had intellectual disabilities, but the notion of seeing those with intellectual disability as a separate group needing special treatment is a relatively new phenomenon. In both European and American cultures prior to the mid-nineteenth century, local 'idiots' existed in most small communities, many of them usefully incorporated into the largely manual labour of rural society. Some became the butt of ridicule, while others were prized for their perpetual innocence (Trent, 1994: 9). Wordsworth's poem 'The Idiot Boy', written in 1798, portrays the eponymous boy as being beyond the cares of the material world and at one with nature. Likewise the old Irish term for those with intellectual disability, Duine le Dia [person of God], suggests an innocence which transcends the mortal.

The Industrial Revolution of the mid-nineteenth century saw many societies becoming more technical with an increased value being placed on the abilities to read, write and complete more complex technical tasks. These changes made the assimilation of those with an intellectual disability more problematic. Although this resulted in many suffering the indignity of the workhouse, societies in both Europe and the United

States in the latter half of the nineteenth century also responded with the establishment of institutions or colonies where the 'feeble-minded' could be cared for and be trained in simple tasks (Malin et al., 1980: 39). This is in contrast to the Irish situation where, from the early nineteenth century, most people with an intellectual disability who were not living at home were cared for under the Poor Law, primarily in the workhouse or the insane asylum. It was not until the early twentieth century that any type of special provision for those with intellectual disability in Ireland was made available. Even then, there were still 3,165 people categorized 'mentally handicapped or insane' in Irish workhouses in 1905 (Robins, 1992: 29)

The more progressive European attitude to the educability of those with intellectual disability began to change drastically from the end of the 1880s when the new science of genetics indicated that the incidence of 'feeble-mindedness' was on the increase. This sent out a very clear message that those with feeble minds were a burden to society. Attention was then focused on ways of reducing the opportunities for the feeble-minded to breed, with particular emphasis on controlling the reproductive capabilities of 'feeble-minded women'. In the United States, Catherine Brown had been a previous advocate of education and training for those with intellectual disability (Trent, 1994: 76). However, in her address to the Association of Medical Officers of American Institutions for Idiotic and Feeble-Minded Persons in 1887, she said:

> the feeble-minded woman must be . . . securely hedged in, or she becomes the easy prey of man's lust and the mother of criminals, thus perpetuating the endless chain of human weakness and crime (Brown, 1887: 404, 405)

So began the ideals of eugenics which sought to protect society from the 'mental defective'. Large custodial institutions were established which were less concerned with the education of those with intellectual disability than with wider society's need not to be corrupted by their inmates. Eugenic ideals continued to inform attitudes to those with intellectual disability well into the late 1940s, especially in academic and medical circles, finding their most horrific outlet in the policies of euthanasia for the 'unfit' in Nazi Germany where hundreds of thousands of people with intellectual disability were exterminated to protect the purity of the Aryan race (Ryan and Thomas, 1980: 109; Race, 1995: 51).

Trent (1994: 265) points out that between 1880 and 1950 intellectual disability had largely been seen as a problem of lower-class teenagers and adults, and that 'not infrequently that group were regarded as a threat to the social order'. Certainly the conditions in many of the large institutions for those with intellectual disability both in the United States and in

Europe were wretched in the extreme. However, writers on both sides of the Atlantic were beginning to comment on the major problems created by custodial institutional care for those with intellectual disability. Erving Goffman's seminal work, *Asylums* (Goffman, 1961) argued that the institution robbed patients of their individuality and, in the United Kingdom, writers such as Jack Tizard (1960, 1964) were studying the detrimental effects of institutionalization on children with intellectual disability. It was from Scandinavia that one of the most important influences was to come, when the Swedish psychologist Bengt Nirje (1969) first articulated the principle of normalization, which he defined as:

> Making it possible for the intellectually disabled to experience the normal rhythm of the day, weeks, the seasons and the year, supporting the normal development of the life cycle, encouraging normal personal considerations, giving opportunity for bisexual contacts, confronting them with economic problems and providing them with normal living facilities (Nirje, 1969: 62)

Normalization, Deinstitutionalization and Care in the Community

In examining care for those with intellectual disability from the late 1960s onwards, two factors are of paramount importance: the concept of normalization and the advance towards deinstitutionalization with its movement from institutional care to care within the community. Both deinstitutionalization and normalization are intrinsically linked and it is arguable that they represent two strands of the same argument. Normalization did not *cause* deinstitutionalization, nor the other way round, but each had considerable influence on the development of the other. Normalization and deinstitutionalization can be seen as twin pillars of a philosophy which arose from a growing awareness that the type of care offered to many people with intellectual disability resulted in their lives being socially, emotionally and sexually restricted to a damaging extent.

The term normalization, although initially coined by Nirje, became synonymous with the work of Wolf Wolfensberger. Wolfensberger's normalization model (Wolfensberger, 1972; Wolfensberger and Glenn, 1975) saw the achievement of independence by those with a disability as being possible only when such people acquired social and vocational skills as similar to those of the general population as possible. Wolfensberger further argued that such personal and vocational normalization would only be achieved in social environments which encouraged the development of self-determination, independence and personal dignity: 'Normalization is the utilization of means which are as culturally normative as possible, in order to establish and/or maintain behaviours which are as culturally normative as possible' (Wolfensberger, 1972: 28).

Central to Wolfensberger's model is the creation of environments for those with intellectual disability which maximize interaction and behavioural competence. He wanted to create normal living environments in which people could learn normal behaviour and thus become ordinary and accepted members of society. To this end he developed, with his associate Linda Glenn, a system for measuring the 'normality' of an environment, be it an institution, a hostel, or a school, called the *Program Analysis of Service Systems* or PASS (Wolfensberger and Glenn, 1975). Both Wolfensberger's original work, *The Principle of Normalization in Human Services* (1972), and the PASS system, received widespread interest in the United States and in Western Europe in the early 1980s, and had significant impact on policies for service design in the intellectual disability field.

In the 1970s the conditions of many institutions caring for those with an intellectual disability had begun to come under public scrutiny. In Scandinavia Kugel was comparing the conditions in institutions for those with intellectual disability to those of animals in the zoo (Kugel and Wolfensberger, 1969). In the United States, in 1972, Geraldo Rivera, now better known as a chat-show host, made a TV programme which exposed the appalling conditions of those with intellectual disability in two large institutions in New York State. Mansell and Ericsson (1996: 7) considered Rivera's TV exposé, which attracted over two and a half million viewers, as the single most important event to give impetus to the development away from institutional services. The reader is directed to the work of Joanna Ryan and Frank Thomas, who, in 1980, wrote the first edition of *The Politics of Mental Handicap* (1980, 1987), an arresting and often horrific account of the inhumanity and degradation suffered by many of those with intellectual disability being cared for in old-style 'mental handicap hospitals' in the United Kingdom at around the same time.

Running parallel with the growing public disquiet with conditions of care for those with intellectual disability was political pressure to move services – not only for those with intellectual disability but also for those with mental health problems – out of institutions and into smaller, community settings. Such moves were not only in response to the demands for better quality care, but they were also related to the escalating costs of running large institutions and the belief that services could be provided at less cost within the community (Mansell and Ericsson, 1996; Walker, 1993). In Ireland the Government White Paper *The Problem of the Mentally Handicapped* (1960) and the *Report on the Commission of Enquiry on Mental Handicap* (1965) were tackling growing numbers of those with intellectual disability in need of both better day services and residential care and noting the cost with some alarm. The *Report on the*

Commission of Enquiry on Mental Handicap (1965) specifically favoured the provision of these services through religious orders and voluntary bodies (Robins, 1992: 55), a policy decision which still has a considerable impact on Irish service provision to the present day.

Throughout the 1970s and 1980s in Europe and the United States, the numbers of people with intellectual disability in institutional care have dropped sharply, large institutions have been closed and care in smaller units and houses based in the community has been introduced (Emerson and Hatton, 1994). The cost savings of deinstitutionalization were often being achieved, however, not because care in the community was in itself a cheaper option, but because many of the services needed to support those with intellectual disability adequately in the community were not being fully developed. Doyal (1993) comments that for community care to operate effectively it is necessary for individuals in that community to have access to adequate goods and services which allows them to flourish as persons in their own right and participate as full citizens. He adds, however, that none of the aims of community care will be achieved unless sufficient capital is made available and 'thus far this [finance] has not been forthcoming and there are good arguments for believing that it will not be forthcoming in the future' (Doyal 1993: 283). Gaps in services for those with intellectual disability in the community had to be filled from some other source and, in most cases, meant that the work of caring for those with an intellectual disability was increasingly performed by unpaid family carers.

Family Carers

The ideal of care in community in which those with intellectual disability could live a full, inclusive life nurtured by those around them has never been fully achieved. Community care became a synonym for family care, without the promised support and resources necessary for the system to function properly. Looking at the situation in the United Kingdom, Walker notes that 'despite the rhetoric concerning the needs of carers, there are no proposals designed to ensure that their needs are taken into account' (Walker, 1993: 220).

Most families would say that, given enough appropriate services, they would be able to cope well and it is important to remember that many families would prefer their family member with a disability to live at home in the long term (McConkey, 1989: 37; Redmond, 1996: 38–50). Problems occur when the basic services fail, when mothers become exhausted from heavy burdens of physical care, when families do not get enough time together away from the child with a disability to maintain and enjoy other relationships, or when stress levels become so high that families can no longer maintain their usual problem-solving capabilities. Providing families with well-designed support services must be done so that they do not experience restricted and diminished lives just because they have chosen to care for their family member with disability. Professionals must also remember that families have to be fully included in decision-making processes – not as subordinates, but as full partners in the process. Offering adequate support and recognition to families also has an impact on the quality of life of the person being cared for. Families which are not under great pressure and stress would find it easier to help their family members with disabilities to pursue their own interests and develop their maximum potential.

Sexuality

There are few subjects more likely to engender heated debate between professionals, families and individuals with intellectual disability than that of sexuality. Redmond interviewed 78 parents of teenage girls with an intellectual disability and recorded their fears and anxieties about the future. The largest existing fear the parents had was that their daughter would be sexually exploited or would become pregnant (1996: 11). The writings of Ann Craft (1983, 1987, 1994), a prominent figure in the literature on intellectual disability and sexuality, demonstrate that echoes of eugenic policies still resonate and that many people see any expression of sexuality by those with intellectual disability as highly dangerous. This fear sometimes leads to a debate as to whether any form of sex education should be offered to those with intellectual disability lest it encourages uncontrollable sexual behaviour (Craft, 1987). Craft and Craft (1985: 182) point out that the vast majority of those with intellectual disability develop normal sexual characteristics and need more, not less, help in making sense of their bodily changes and the accompanying strong emotional feelings. More importantly, the Crafts add that knowledge about sexuality will also help to provide protection from exploitation and from unwittingly offending other people.

THE VOLUNTARY AGENCY IN IRISH SERVICE PROVISION

Voluntary organizations have played a major role in the development of services for those with disability and their families. The growth of such organizations is often derived from the work of individuals, concerned groups and religious orders trying to address gaps in state service provision. Some of these organizations have grown very large over time and now employ a range of personnel. These include St Michael's House, Brothers of Charity Services, Daughters of Charity Services, Irish Wheelchair Association, COPE, Central Remedial Clinic and Cerebral Palsy Ireland.

One of the major advantages of the voluntary sector is its ability to develop innovative services in response to identified needs, for example the Personal Assistant scheme, independent living initiatives, the original Breakaway scheme and subsequent nationwide home-based respite schemes such as Take-A-Break and Home Choice. The provision of professional community-based services such as social work, physiotherapy, driving instruction for specially adapted cars, and educational and training services have also been provided in the field of disability by voluntary rather than statutory services.

The development of services provided by such voluntary bodies has been limited by unreliable and often inadequate state funding. Seeking sufficient funding can be very time-consuming for many voluntary agencies and considerable energy may be used up in continual fund-raising. Moreover, the need to raise funds can result in the portrayal of people with disabilities as dependent and needy, rather than promoting a positive image of disability, including the basic right to adequate resources. This lack of funding has also made it difficult for agencies to plan services in the medium to long term; this problem should be addressed by new Health Board arrangements discussed above (pp. 37–8). The widespread use of voluntary organizations to provide services has also resulted in an unequal, or variable, distribution of services geographically, with some families moving to areas with better services.

A further issue regarding voluntary provision is the extent to which people with disability and their family carers have a voice in policy planning. Critics of traditional charities point to a lack of people with disabilities in positions of power in voluntary agencies (Drake, 1996). They argue that there should be a commitment to enabling and encour-aging people with disability and their family carers to become involved in the process of policy making. This does not mean political lobbying alone; it is means ensuring that those with disability and their families have adequate representation at the highest level of decision making at region and national levels. It is suggested that at least 60 per cent of the membership of the proposed National Disability Authority be drawn from those with disability or their families (Commission, 1996: 87).

A unique feature of Irish health policy has been this wide use of voluntary agencies in the provision of services to people with disability. The term voluntary may be confusing. Not only does it refer to individuals offering services for no payment, but also, in this case, to services for those with learning disability run by agencies providing services on behalf of the state. Section 65 of the Irish 1953 Health Act allows health authorities to support voluntary organizations providing services 'similar or ancillary' to their own. As Curry (1998: 173) points out, Section 65 grants 'are, in effect, discretionary and there are no established criteria or guidelines for such grants'.

A major characteristic of these voluntary agencies is that, even after the Irish 1970 Health Act created the community care structures we know today, they retained a great deal of autonomy in the development and delivery of services. This is due in no small part to a number of older and larger voluntary organizations receiving their funding not by means of Section 65 Grants, but instead directly from the Department of Health. Amongst these organizations are Daughters of Charity Services, Brothers of Charity Services, Sunbeam House and COPE. These organizations are significant providers of services a national basis and the direct and centralized funding of them has, arguably, allowed them to maintain a powerful and autonomous status. From a social policy perspective, such funding arrangements have also distanced these agencies from the developing local community care structures, causing not only an uncoordinated approach to service development but also an unevenness in national service provision.

Major policy changes are in train for service providers in the field of learning disability. In July 1997 the *Interim Report of the Task Force on the Eastern Regional Health Authority* signalled the intention of the Minister for Health to replace direct Department of Health funding in the Eastern region with funding from a Regional Health Authority to which the agencies would be accountable (*Interim Report,* 1997: 35). The voluntary organizations would, however, still retain their voluntary autonomy and there would be no change under the new arrangements in the status or operation of any voluntary provider. The Interim Report recommended that both annual and longer-term service plans be implemented with voluntary agencies to foster effectiveness, efficiency, equity and appropriateness of care (*Interim Report,* 1997: 36–73). The report further adds that these new structures should enhance 'responsiveness to the public', but there is no mention of consultation with the public nor of consumer representation at significant levels of the new Health Authority.

ACCOMMODATION AND SERVICE PLANNING

The Department of Health Document, *Services to Persons with a Mental Handicap/Intellectual Disability: An Assessment of Need 1997–2001,* shows that there is a current requirement for 1036 extra places in day services and 1439 extra places in respite/residential care in Ireland (Department of Health, Undated: 13). In many of these cases, it is family carers who are continuing to provide care in the absence of the needed service. The National Intellectual Disability Database 1996 *Annual Report* (1997) notes an increase in the average age of those with intellectual disability. This also implies an increase in the age of parents, with the attendant difficulties of providing care on a long-term basis. Redmond's study of parents of teenagers with intellectual disability showed that one of their greatest concerns was with how their young adult would be cared for after their death (Redmond, 1996: 67). Many parents approached old age without the reassurance of services available when they could no longer take care of their child, resulting in adults with intellectual disability remaining in the family home whether or not their parents were able to cope, or, indeed, whether the individuals themselves liked the arrangement. Most young adults begin to leave the family home from their early twenties onwards, yet those with intellectual disability rarely have the option to do so. Scarcity of appropriate accommodation has meant that many adults with intellectual disability leave home on foot of a crisis, primarily the illness or death of one or both parents. Making available alternative-to-home accommodation at an earlier stage, when families are around to support such a move, would undoubtedly be expensive. It would, however, give the person with intellectual disability the chance to establish their own adult home with dignity and support. Family members would then be able to live out the remaining years of their lives without the nagging worry of what would happen when they died.

Forward Planning and Quality of Life

When services are in short supply, service provision is more likely to be provided on foot of a crisis, rather than as a result of forward planning, which benefits neither the family nor the individual with intellectual disability. Future planning is an essential part of providing appropriate services. In recent years more attention is being paid to the quality of life of those with intellectual disability. Precise 'Quality of Life' measurements (Schalock, 1989) are used to assess all aspects of an individual's life situation. Hogg (1995: 221) argues that such Quality of Life indicators are more effective than those designed by normalization theorists, and Goode (1989: 337) considers that 'Quality of Life' perspectives may soon replace normalization and deinstitutionalization as a guiding principle in the design, delivery and evaluation of services for persons with disability and their families.

Moving Towards the Future

It is vital that individuals with disability and their families play central roles in deciding on a care plan for the short and long term and, to this end, that their opinions are not only heard but also listened to. Finding ways of ensuring that they have a chance to say what services they feel they want is crucial in any effective individual planning system (Simons, 1995: 174). Simons point out, however, that 'the empowerment of people with learning disability will not lead to a quiet life for professionals – sometimes they will tell us things we do not like to hear' (Simons, 1995: 171). Many services have now begun to include those with intellectual disability more in planning and evaluating services, but such inclusion should not be tokenism, and care must be taken in ensuring that the individual's opinions are clearly expressed. This can occur by fostering self-advocacy training among those with intellectual disability or, in the case of those who cannot clearly express themselves, allowing them to have advocates to argue on their behalf.

As we come to the end of the century some heartening trends are emerging. There is a growing realization of the importance of education for those with intellectual disability, even for those with severe and profound impairment. Persons with intellectual disability have more opportunity to work in open employment, some accompanied by job coaches in supported employment schemes (Walsh et al., 1991: 155–61). They are being included in decision-making processes together with their families and more interest is being paid to their quality of life.

DISABILITY IN CONTEXT

'People with disabilities are the neglected citizens of Ireland'. Thus begins the *Report of the Commission on the Status of People with Disabilities: A Strategy for Equality* (Commission, 1996). This was the first major report on the overall situation and service provision for people with disabilities in Ireland since the publication of Department of Health's Green Paper, *Towards a Full Life* in 1984. The contrast in the thrust and approach of these two documents to service delivery is stark and reflects the major changes in thinking about the nature of disability and its consequences that have occurred in the intervening decade. One of the most interesting and critically important features of the Commission Report (1996) was the composition of the Commission, with sixty per cent of its membership consisting of people with a variety of different disabilities, and carers. The consumer voice was clearly represented. The fact that the majority were service users ensured that it was, as Colgan

describes, 'in tune with modern thinking and values concerning parti-
cipatory democracy, equality and self-determination for people with
disabilities' (1997: 122). The result is a document which highlights the
multitude of problems facing those with a disability in Irish society, and
presents a number of policy measures to address them based on the
fundamental concept of rights.

Disability Rights Movement

The concept of rights has been of central importance in switching the
focus from the individual's 'inability' to perform a range of physical tasks
to a society which takes little or no account of such differences,
organizing itself in such a way that those who may need to do things
differently from the norm are hampered. The right to participate equally
in society and to promote conditions which would facilitate this process
are seen as the issues to be promoted. Key players in advocating these
rights have been people with disabilities and families of those with disability, who have been the recipients of inadequate and/or inappropriate
services. The politicizing of disability has been particularly strong in the
United States, where a combination of factors such as lobbying process,
the influence of other rights movements and the number of young men
disabled as a result of the Vietnam War resulted in a groundswell movement towards the recognition of disability as a rights issue. Oliver (1989)
argues that this is the last major rights movement following on from the
civil rights movement in the 1960s, and the women's and gay rights
movements. He identified the three main features of the disability rights
movement as

- offering a critique of existing service provision;
- redefining the problem of disability as social rather than medical;
- encouraging autonomy and the movement away from the dominance
  of professionals as planners and providers of services.

Rights and Citizenship

T.H. Marshall (1952) identified the three key rights of citizenship as
civil, political and social. Oliver (1996) applies Marshall's categorization
to a person with a disability in society. Focusing on civil and political
rights, Oliver points out that those with disability appear to enjoy the
same rights as others, yet closer inspection indicates that this is not so.
While people with disability share the common rights of freedom of
association, thought, speech and ownership of property, in reality their

civil rights are curtailed by such factors as being unable to obtain a mortgage on account of unemployment or temporary work contracts, and the difficulty of meeting together because of inadequate transport facilities. With respect to political rights, although in theory they have the right to exercise their political franchise fully, inaccessible polling stations and infrequent attempts by political parties to involve them means that they have to vote earlier and in a different way from the rest of the electorate.

It is in the third area – of social rights – that the situation of people with disabilities is particularly problematic. The concept of social rights encompasses what is required to be able to participate in social living in its broadest sense, including having a standard of living or lifestyle compatible with current social expectations as well as the use of social facilities similar to everyone else. That this is not so for people with disabilities in Irish society is all too evident, and specific aspects of this problem are discussed on pp. 160–5.

Which rights are most important for social life and service provision can be debated at length. Bruce (1991) suggests they are:

- The right of access, which includes, but goes beyond, the physical accessibility of buildings. It covers such areas as access to communication which takes cognizance of differing physical impairments and access to participation in the social and cultural life of the community.

- The right to self-determination which requires the active participation of people with disabilities in determining the type and range of services suited to their needs. Ultimately, it is about the right to decide one's own lifestyle as an adult including the balancing of risks to health vis à vis achieving life goals.

- The right to resources to cover the extra costs of having a disability. Studies of poverty consistently demonstrate a clear relationship between having a disability and the likelihood of being poor (Oliver and Barnes, 1993; Irish Wheelchair Association, 1994). This is related to the high rates of unemployment amongst people with disability. It is also because having a disability is costly in itself owing to the need for extra/different clothing, special dietary requirements, more than average heating and transport costs, and lack of time, energy and access to a range of shopping giving best value for money.

- The right to be recognized as an individual. Social policy is geared to providing for categories of need, not for individuals. However, each person has a unique set of characteristics of which the disability is but one element. Those involved in service provision must therefore ensure that individual differences and preferences are taken into account and that the assessment of what is possible does not rest solely or primarily with the professional service provider. The focus on consumer rights and consumer input into service planning, which is evident in the health policy document *Shaping a Healthier Future* (Department of Health, 1994), puts the onus on professionals to share decision making power with service recipients. This will help to ensure that individual preferences will be a central consideration to a much greater degree than in the past.

PHYSICAL DISABILITY – SELECTED SOCIAL ISSUES

Vulnerable Categories of People with Disabilities

Before leaving the subject of rights discussed above, it is important to consider some vulnerable categories of people with disabilities, for example women, who have to deal with the double disadvantage of being a woman and having a disability. Morris (1991), already part of the feminist movement when she acquired a disability as a result of an accident, argues that because the disability movement has been dominated by men who have a male perspective on disability issues, the feelings and subjective experiences of the disabled person have tended to be excluded from consideration. In her view the disability movement should adopt the feminist principle that 'the personal is political and, in giving voice to such subjective experiences, assert the value of our lives' (1991: 68).

People with disabilities living in residential care are another group whose rights may be infringed. Basic, everyday decisions about when and what to eat, when to get up and go to bed, have a bath or shower, deciding where and when to go out may be determined by staff rostering rather than the wishes of adult residents. The Commission in its *Report on the Status of People with Disabilities* pointed out that even the right to a basic income for those without resources was limited to discretionary pocket money for those in residential care (Commission, 1996). The restrictions created by living in such a controlled environment which take little account of adult rights led to the creation of the Independent Living Movement in the 1970s in the United States. This movement spread to other countries, including Ireland, and now informs thinking about alternative care facilities for adults with disabilities. Its basic premise is that, as adults, people with disabilities have the right to make decisions, major and minor, about their lifestyle. The purpose of care-giving, therefore, is to enable each person to maximize their choices by having available to them help in the activities of daily living. This help may be specially designed living quarters and/or having someone to carry out tasks such as dressing, cooking, feeding and so on at the behest of the person with the disability. The Report of the Review Group on Health and Personal Social Services for Physically Disabled People (Review Group, 1996) regarded the independent living arrangement as offering the disabled person 'the opportunity to live in a domestic dwelling, supported with the necessary health and social services' (1996: 79). The Review Group supports the development of independent living 'because it promotes independence and respects the service user's right to choose the form of care most appropriate to him or her' (1996: 80). In the independent living approach, the relationship between the person with the disability and his/her helper may be that of employer/employee with reciprocal rights and responsibilities. Increasingly the trend is towards giving resources directly to those not in the paid labour market, who are in need of personal assistance to enable them to purchase the required care.

Problems regarding care also arise where a person with a disability lives with relatives, be they parents, siblings, spouses and/or children. The fundamental issue in the case of a person with physical disability who requires help with activities of daily living is the juxtaposition of adult status with physical dependency. This is where the element of choice is critical for both the cared-for and the carer. Lack of real alternatives and inadequate support services for those with relative carers can put enormous strain on both parties. The National Rehabilitation Board document *Righting the History of Wrongs* (1991) argues that, if the right to adequate services for physical care is not provided, then the rights of family carers are also usurped in that they may feel that they have little or no choice in the matter. Indeed, prevailing ideologies about the family may make them feel guilty if they even wish it to be otherwise. Dalley (1988) uses the term 'compulsory altruism' coined by Land and Rose to describe this. While the policy of community care, which has now been in existence for almost half a century has many positives, its downside has been its tardiness in having sufficient alternatives to family-based care (i.e. independent living) and its failure to provide adequate support service to families providing care. This is not only in respect of direct service provision in relation to community care. In the matter of housing adaptation grants, for example, a grant may be paid to adapt only one accommodation unit which makes economic sense but may effectively prohibit shared care by adult children of a parent with a disability (Owens, 1987).

Experiences of Those with Disabilities

There is now a growing literature on the subjective experience of physical disability (see Nolan, 1987; Doyle, 1988, for example, in relation to Ireland, and Bauby, 1997; Reeves, 1998, for recent and notable accounts based in other countries). Tubridy (1996) provides a qualitative study of 30 young people with different physical disabilities in the Irish context. What is important about this area of literature is that it offers some insight into the experience of disability and illustrates the way in which individual people, professionals and society as a whole respond to the person. They also illustrate the barriers that can impede participation in social life.

A study of its members by the Irish Wheelchair Association (1994) raised particular concerns regarding participation. It found that one-half of respondents identified themselves as not being involved in common/popular activities in Irish social life. Reasons given included: lack of interest (52%); lack of opportunities (40%); inadequate transport (33%); shortage of personal assistance (24%); and absence of encouragement (19%). These findings led the researchers to question whether members 'are so isolated and apathetic that they have just given up or have never had the chance to participate' (Irish Wheelchair Association, 1994: 52). Such lack of participation clearly impedes the opportunity to forge adult relationships. Tubridy (1994), in comparing the lifestyles and views of people who had a disability from birth or early childhood to those who acquire one as an adult, found that only one person in ten of the first group was married. The other nine in this group saw themselves as unlikely to marry because of the social problems associated with the disability. Many in the latter group were married before the onset of the disability which was regarded as posing serious difficulties for the existing relationship. Parker (1993) remarks on the relative dearth of knowledge about marriage and disability generally. She undertook a small, qualitative study of couples where one spouse acquired a disability subsequent to the marriage. Her findings highlight the importance of the pre-existing relationship as well as the effect of the disability on reciprocal roles within marriage.

Physical Access

'One of the greatest forms of discrimination which many people with disabilities face is having lack of access to buildings and functions' (Lonsdale, 1990: 148). 'Access to the built and external environment', states the Commission *Report*, 'is a pre-requisite condition necessary to enable their [people with disabilities] access and participation in any or all of the other aspects of social and civil society' (Commission, 1996: 153). It comments on the 'frustration and anger caused to people with disabilities by the inaccessibility of buildings' as being very evident in the submissions made to it by both individuals and organizations representing people with various disabilities. The Building Regulations (1991), Part M, require all new buildings for public use to be accessible to people with disabilities. However, as the Commission (1996) points out, the approach to access in the Regulations 'is not aimed at establishing an enabling environment for everyone but of making special provision for special cases' (1996: 153). This, it argues, 'generally results in designers and others interpreting the cited minimum requirements as being optimum or even maximum requirements' (1996: 154). Lack of enforcement of Part M by the local authorities is also cited as a problem. The Commission (1996) recommends that the Department of the Environment should require access certificates similar to the existing requirements of fire certificates which confirm that a building is safe and appropriate for use.

Some of the resistance to dealing with access issues stems from the notion that it is for the benefit of a very small minority. Even if this were so, it would not justify creating and maintaining inaccessible buildings since those with disabilities are not a tiny fraction of the population; it is estimated that approximately 10% of the population as a whole has a disability. However, there is a dearth of accurate and detailed knowledge about the numbers of people with physical disability in Ireland. The need for clear information regarding numbers and types of disability in order to be able to plan for and to provide an adequate and appropriate range of services was recommended in the Green Paper on Services for Disabled People, *Towards a Full Life* (Department of Health, 1984). The Report of the Review Body on Health and Personal Social Services for People with Physical and Sensory Disabilities (Review Group, 1996) comments on the absence of a database that would identify service user needs on a regional and national basis for planning services. It points out that the Irish Census does not include a question on disability and that Ireland, unlike a number of our European Union partners, has never carried out a national survey of physical disability (Review Group, 1996: 30). As Colgan (1997) remarks, 'every report on disability and policy that has been produced in the past twenty years in Ireland has expressed concern about the lack of data on disability, for the purpose of planning services' (1997: 121).

Employment

Lack of employment is a major issue for people with physical disability. *The Report of the Commission on the Status of People with Disabilities* (Commission, 1996) states that surveys of organizations for people with disabilities indicate unemployment rates of over 70 per cent. It recommended that there should be further initiatives to create employment for people with disabilities similar to the Pilot Programme on Employment of People with Disabilities. Since 1977, there has been in the public sector a three per cent quota scheme for people with disabilities. Yet the three per cent has not been achieved overall during the past twenty years (Commission, 1996). This quota does not apply to the private sector where efforts to secure jobs for those with disability have concentrated on facilitating and encouraging employers to take them on voluntarily. The Commission's view was that the quota requirement should not be extended immediately to the private sector, but that it should be reviewed after a three-year period. Quota schemes have their advantages and disadvantages as means of creating employment opportunities for a disadvantaged group such as people with disabilities. On the one hand, they force employers to take on such workers who might otherwise never do so, and a positive experience might encourage the reluctant employer to reach or exceed the required numbers. On the other hand, the employers and fellow employees of workers taken on, on this basis, may view them as less than equal/competent for the task or as taking a job that could have been given to someone with better or more suitable qualifications. What does seem to be important is that a quota scheme should be backed by sanctions to ensure that minimum requirements are reached.

Even where a job is secured, through the quota scheme or otherwise, people with disabilities can face problems such as lack of promotional opportunities and restricted facility for moving from one job to another. A particularly significant development for those with physical disabilities is the remarkable advances that have been and continue to be made in the area of information and communication technology, which create the potential to open fields of employment for people with a variety of different disabilities. It is vital that those who could benefit in this way gain access to appropriate technology; it is of little benefit if it exists but is not available. This is where the concept of rights (see pp. 158–60 above) again comes to the fore. Emphasis on the barriers which impede people with disabilities will define technology as a basic requirement 'to open up the employment domain and create an environment in which the chance for expression of abilities to be optimized' (Roulstone, 1993: 247). The Commission acknowledged that the impact of technology and telecommunications have the potential to 'play a major role in helping people with disabilities to secure equal status in most areas of life and society' (Commission, 1996: 209).

CONCLUSION

This chapter has traced the major changes which have occurred in many aspects of the lives of those with a disability. It has demonstrated the similarity of problems experienced by those with intellectual or physical disability, such as social exclusion, paucity of service provision and an overall lack of planning for future service development. The varying practical needs of those with different types of disability, and the lack of wisdom of perceiving all those with disabilities as one homogeneous group, have been identified. Not only must the particular needs of each category of disability be acknowledged but also, within these categories, the unique needs of each individual should be articulated in an individual, person-centred plan.

Traditionally, disability has not been high on the policy agenda, lacking the immediacy of such issues as child abuse. The recent establishment of a permanent Council for the Status of People with Disabilities should help to give the issues of people with disabilities a greater ongoing public profile. How well new initiatives succeed will depend a great deal on how much financial assistance is given to them by government, how current and future policy makers view the importance of those with disabilities in our society, and how the general public support and uphold the rights of their fellow citizens with disability. The creation of the National Disability Authority in July 1998 is of major significance. With the majority of its members having a disability, or having a family member with a disability, it represents a major step in consumer involvement in policy and service development.

TABLE OF POLICY DEVELOPMENTS

1961   Foundation of National Association of Mental Handicap in Ireland, first nationwide association of parents and friends of those with intellectual disability.

1967   Foundation of National Rehabilitation Board (now called NRB) to advise Minster for Health on disability issues and to offer occupational advice to those with disability.

1981   International Year of Disabled People

1984   Publication of Green Paper on Services for People with Disability *Towards a Full Life*.

1991:   Report of the Review Group on Mental Handicap Services, *Needs and Abilities*, recommends changing the term 'mental handicap' to 'intellectual disability'.

1992   Green Paper on Education, *Education for a Changing World*, recommends integrated educational opportunities for children with both physical and intellectual disabilities.

1995   Establishment, by Department of Health, of a National Intellectual Disability Database, to provide accurate information for planning services.

1996   Publication of *A Strategy for Equality*, Report of the Commission on the Status of People with Disabilities.

1997   Marie O'Donoghue wins her case in the Supreme Court which acknowledges the right of her 12-year-old son Paul to have an education provided for him by the state, under Article 42 of the Constitution. Paul has both severe physical and intellectual disability.

1998   Establishment of the National Disability Authority by the Minister for Justice, Equality and Law Reform.

RECOMMENDED READING

Malin, N. (ed.) (1995) *Services for People with Learning Disability*. London: Routledge.

Mittler, P. and H. Mittler (eds) (1994) *Innovations in Family Support for People with Learning Disabilities*. Chorley: Lisieux Hall.

Quinn, P. (1998) *Understanding Disability – A Lifespan Approach*. London: Sage.

Report of the Commission on the Status of People with Disabilities: A Strategy for Equality (1966) Dublin: Stationery Office.

Ryan, J and F. Thomas (1987) *The Politics of Mental Handicap*. London: Free Association Press.

Tubridy, J. (1996) *Pegged Down: Experiences of People in Ireland with Significant Physical Disabilities*. Dublin: Institute of Public Administration.

REFERENCES

Bauby, J-D. (1997) *The Diving Bell and the Butterfly*. London: Fourth Estate.

Brown, C. (1887). 'The Future of the Educated Imbecile', *Proceedings of the Association of Medical Officers of American Institutions for Idiotic and Feeble-Minded Persons*, 1886: 401–6.

Bruce, I. (1991) 'Employment of People with Disabilities', pp. 263–49 in G. Dalley (ed.), *Disability and Social Policy*. London: Policy Studies Institute.

Colgan, A. (1997) 'People with Disabilities and the Health Services', pp. 111–25 in J. Robins (ed.), *Reflections on Health, Commemorating Fifty Years of the Department of Health, 1947–1997*. Dublin: Department of Health.

Commission on the Status of People with Disabilities (1996) *Report of the Commission on the Status of People with Disabilities: A Strategy for Equality*. Dublin: Stationery Office.

Craft, A. (1983) 'Sexuality in Mental Retardation: A Review of the Literature', pp. 1–37 in A. Craft and M. Craft (eds), *Sex Education and Counselling for Mentally Handicapped People*. Tunbridge Wells: Costello.

Craft, A. (1987) 'Mental Handicap and Sexuality: Issues for Individuals with a Mental Handicap, the Parents and Professionals', pp. 13–34 in A. Craft (ed.), *Mental Handicap and Sexuality: Issues and Perspectives*. Tunbridge Wells: Costello.

Craft, A. (1994) *Practical Issues in Sexuality and Learning Disabilities*. London: Routledge.

Craft, A and M. Craft (eds) (1985) *Sex Education and Counselling for Mentally Handicapped People*. Tunbridge Wells: Costello.

Curry, J (1998) *Irish Social Services*, 3rd edition. Dublin: Institute of Public Administration.

Dalley, G. (1988) *Ideologies of Caring: Rethinking Community Collectivism*. London: Macmillan.

Department of Health (undated) *Services to Persons with Mental Handicap/Intellectual Disability: An Assessment of Need, 1997–2001*.

Department of Health (1984) *Towards a Full Life: Green Paper on Services for Disabled People*. Dublin: Stationery Office.

Department of Health (1994) *Shaping a Healthier Future*. Dublin: Stationery Office.

Doyal, L. (1993) 'Human Need and the Moral Right to Optimal Community Care', pp. 276–86 in *Community Care: A Reader*. London: Macmillan/Open University

Doyle, P. (1988) *The God Squad*. Dublin: Raven Arts Press.

Drake, R.F. (1996) 'A Critique of the Role of the Traditional Charities', in L. Barton (ed.), *Disability and Society: Emerging Issues and Insights*. London: Longman.

Emerson, E. and C. Hatton (1994) *Moving Out: Re-location from Hospital to Community*. London: HMSO.

Goffman, E. (1961) *Asylums: Essays on the Social Situation of Mental Patients and Other Inmates*. New York: Doubleday.

Goode, D. A. (1989) 'Quality of Life and Quality of Work Time', pp. 337–49 in W.E. Kiernan and R.L. Schalock (eds), *Economics, Industry and Economy: A Look Ahead*. Baltimore: Paul H. Brookes.

Health Act (1970). Dublin: Department of Health.

Hogg, J. (1995) 'Assessment Methods and Professional Directions', pp. 219–35 in N. Malin (ed.), *Services for People with Learning Disabilities*. London: Routledge.

Interim Report of the Task Force on the Eastern Regional Health Authority (June 1997). Dublin: Department of Health.

Irish Wheelchair Association (1994) *People First*. Dublin: IWA.

Kugel, R.B. and W. Wolfensberger (eds.) (1969) *Changing Patterns in Residential Services for the Mentally Handicapped*. Washington D.C.: President's Committee on Mental Retardation.

Lonsdale, S. (1990) *Women and Disability*. London: Macmillan.

McConkey, R. (1989) 'Our Young Lives: School leavers' Impressions and Those of Their Parents to Life at Home and Their Hopes for the Future', pp. 11–40 in R. McConkey and C. Conliffe (eds), *The Person with Mental Handicap: Preparation for an Adult Life in the Community*. Dublin: St Michael's House.

McConkey, R and C. Conliffe (1989) *The Person with Mental Handicap: Preparation for an Adult Life in the Community*. Dublin: St Michael's House.

Malin, N., D. Race and G. Jones (eds) (1980) *Services for the Mentally Handicapped in Britain*. London: Croom Helm.

Mansell, J and K. Ericsson (eds) (1996) *Deinstitutionalization and Community Living: Intellectual Disability Services in Britain, Scandinavia and the USA*. London: Chapman Hall.

Marshall, T. H. (1952) *Citizenship and Social Class*. Cambridge: Cambridge University Press.

Morris, J. (1991) *Pride against Prejudice: A Personal Politics of Disability*. London: Women's Press.

National Intellectual Disability Database 1996 (1997) *Annual Report of the National Intellectual Disability Database Committee*. Dublin: The Health Research Board.

National Rehabilitation Board (1991) *Righting the History of Wrongs: A Rights Approach to the Issues arising out of Women's Experiences of Disability*. Dublin: Submission to the Commission on the Status of Women.

Nirje, B. (1969) 'The Normalisation Principle and Its Human Management Implications', pp. 231–40 in R.B. Kugel and W. Wolfensberger (eds), *Changing Patterns in Residential Services for the Mentally Handicapped*. Washington D.C.: President's Committee on Mental Retardation.

Nolan, C. (1987) *Under the Eye of the Clock*. London: Weidenfeld & Nicolson.

Oliver, M. (1989) 'The Social Model of Disability: Current Reflections', in T. Jeffs and M. Smith (eds), *Social Work and Social Welfare Year Book One*. Milton Keynes: Open University Press.

Oliver, M. (1996) *Understanding Disability: From Theory to Practice*. London: Macmillan.

Oliver, M. and B. Barnes (1993) 'Discrimination, Disability and Welfare: From Needs to Rights', pp. 267–77 in J. Swain, V. Finkelstein, S. French and M. Oliver (eds), *Disabling Barriers: Enabling Environments*. London: Sage.

Owens, P. (1987) *Community Care and Severe Disability*. Occasional Papers in Social Administration. London: Bedford Square Press.

Parker, G. (1993) 'Disability, Caring and Marriage: The Experiences of Younger Couples when a Partner is Disabled after Marriage', *British Journal of Social Work*, 23: 565–80.

The Problem of the Mentally Handicapped (1960). Government White Paper. Dublin: Stationery Office.

Race, D. (1995) 'Historical Development of Service Provision', pp. 46–78 in N. Malin, D. Race and G. Jones (eds), *Services for People with Learning Disabilities*. London: Routledge.

Redmond, B (1996) *Listening to Parents – The Aspirations, Expectations and Anxieties of Parents about Their Teenagers with Learning Disability*. Dublin: Family Studies Centre, University College Dublin.

Reeves, C. (1998) *Still Me*. London: HarperCollins.

Report of Commission of Inquiry on Mental Handicap (1965). Dublin: Stationery Office.

Review Group on Health and Personal Social Services for People with Physical and Sensory Disabilities (1996) *Towards an Independent Future*. Dublin: Stationery Office.

Review Group on Mental Handicap Services (1991) *Needs and Abilities – A policy for the Intellectually Disabled*. Dublin: Stationery Office.

Robins, J. (1992) *From Rejection to Integration: A Centenary of Service by the Daughters of Charity to Persons with a Mental Handicap*. Dublin: Gill & Macmillan.

Roulstone, A. (1993) 'Access to New Technology in the Employment of Disabled People', pp. 241–8 in J. Swain, V. Finkelstein , S. French and M. Oliver (eds), *Disabling Barriers: Enabling Environments*. London: Sage.

Ryan, J and F. Thomas (1980) *The Politics of Mental Handicap*. London: Penguin.

Ryan, J and F. Thomas (1987) *The Politics of Mental Handicap,* revised and extended edition. London: Free Association Press.

Schalock, R.H. (1989) *Quality of Life: Perspectives and Issues*. Washington D.C.: American Association on Mental Retardation.

Simons, K. (1995) 'Empowerment and Advocacy', in N. Malin, D. Race and G. Jones (eds), *Services for People with Learning Disabilities*. London: Routledge.

Tizard, J. (1960) 'Residential Care of Mentally Handicapped Children', *British Medical Journal,* I: 1041–3.

Tizard, J. (1964) *Community Services for the Mentally Handicapped*. London: Oxford University Press.

Trent, J.W. (1994) *Inventing The Feeble Mind: A History of Mental Retardation in the United States*. California: University of California Press.

Tubridy, J. (1994) 'Social Experiences of Physical Disability in Ireland', *National Rehabilitation Board Report,* Issue 6. Dublin.

Tubridy, J. (1996) *Pegged Down: Experiences of People in Ireland with Significant Physical Disabilities*. Dublin: Institute of Public Administration.

Walker, A. (1993) 'Community Care Policy: From Consensus to Conflict', pp. 204–6 in J. Borna et al. (eds), *Community Care: A Reader*. Basingstoke: Macmillan.

Walsh, P., M. Rafferty and C. Lynch (1991) 'The Open Road Project: Real Jobs for People with Mental Handicap', *International Journal of Rehabilitation Research,* 14: 151–61.

Wolfensberger, W. (1972) *The Principle of Normalisation in Human Services*. Toronto: National Institute on Mental Retardation.

Wolfensberger, W. (1983) 'Social Role Valorisation: A Proposed New Term for the Principle of Normalization', *Mental Retardation,* 21 (6): 234–9.

Wolfensberger, W. and L. Glenn (1975) *Program Analysis of Service Systems,* 3rd edition. Toronto: National Institute for Mental Retardation.

8
Children and Social Policy

Valerie Richardson

The way a society treats children reflects not only its qualities of compassion and protective caring but also its sense of justice, its commitment to the future and its urge to enhance the human condition for coming generations (Perez de Cuellar, UN Secretary General, Lignano, Italy, September 1987)

DEFINITION AND SCOPE OF POLICY AREA

The Child Care Act 1991 (s.2 (1)) defines a child as 'a person under the age of 18 years other than a person who is or has been married'. The 1996 Census of the Population shows that there are 1,071,972 people under the age of 18 years in Ireland. Children therefore make up just under one-third of the total population of 3.6 m and represent a sizeable proportion of the population for whom national policies are needed (Central Statistics Office, 1997). As the Task Force on Child Care Services noted: '. . .children are special in two respects. Firstly, they are persons in the process of formation; secondly they are not independent' (1981: 34). Children, therefore, are dependent on adults to secure their needs and their welfare. Children share with adults the universal human needs for food, shelter, warmth and security. However, children also have specific needs for love and security, new experiences, praise and recognition and responsibility (Kellmer Pringle, 1974), together with the need to be treated as an individual. It is widely accepted that the family, as the basic unit in society, is the primary source of love and individual care for children and provides the setting in which the child's needs can be met. The welfare of children depends on the stability and effectiveness of the family to which they belong. For children who have the benefit of warm, continuous and intimate relationships with their parent or parents throughout their childhood, there is the opportunity to develop a strong sense of identity, self-worth, trust in others and him or herself, the ability to handle stress and frustration and to develop and maintain relationships. The child's experience in a stable and effective family lays the foundation of his future psychological, physical and cognitive development. (see for example, Bowlby (1953); Erikson (1969); Fahlberg (1981)). For some children the opportunity never exists for them to experience family life; some families never exist as a viable unit, some temporarily or permanently break down and some parents are unwilling or unable to care for their children. In these circumstances state intervention in the form of childcare services are needed to ensure that the needs of children are met.

Children, in common with adults, are affected by almost every aspect of social policy and social service provision which are discussed in other chapters in this volume. This chapter addresses social policies which are concerned primarily with the protection and welfare of children in Irish society. It will first present a brief statistical overview in relation to children in need of care and protection, followed by a discussion of the historical development of childcare policy and practice in Ireland before addressing particular issues in contemporary childcare policy.

Statistical Overview

The latest available statistics from the Department of Health and Children show that health boards received 6415 reports of alleged child abuse in 1995 of which approximately one-third (2276) were confirmed cases. This shows an increase of 298 per cent between 1987 and 1995. There were 765 cases of child sexual abuse reported in 1995, which represented an increase of 327 per cent over the previous ten years (Child Care Policy Unit, 1996). However, it is difficult to assess whether the huge increase in cases notified to the health boards is due to a higher incidence of abuse or whether increased public awareness has led to increased reporting. There are no recent national figures available for the number of children who are in residential care or foster-care. Department of Health figures for 1992, the most recent year available, indicate that there were 3090 children in care of whom three-quarters were in foster care and the remainder in residential care (Department of Health, 1993). Statistics for 1996 have been compiled but not yet published by the Department of Health and Children, while figures for the years 1993–95 were not collected. A survey carried out by Focus Ireland (McCarthy, Kennedy and Matthews, 1996: 46) found that there were 669 children in residential care in July 1995. However, they were unable to compile complete figures for children in care as those relating to foster care were not available at the time of the study. According to the 1992 figures, the largest number of children (31 per cent) were admitted because 'parent or parents unable to cope', 'neglect' accounted for 20 per cent, and 'physical or sexual abuse' for 13 per cent of admissions. The independent research studies have also indicated that children of lone parents represent almost one-third of those admitted to care, a percentage which is far higher than that in the total population (Richardson, 1985; O'Higgins, 1993). There is also evidence to suggest that children of the Travelling community (Task Force on the Travelling Community, 1995), children from deprived backgrounds and those from families where drug use is prevalent, are particularly vulnerable to admission to care (McKeown, 1991; Woods, 1994). It is the responsibility of the health boards to supply statistics on children in care. However, the reliability of the statistical information has been questioned. In addition, the failure to analyse the data also raises questions about their usefulness (Children's Rights Alliance, 1997: 29).

The number of children placed for adoption has fallen significantly over the past two decades. In 1976 there were 1104 Adoption Orders made, compared to 405 made in 1996. The majority of the orders made in 1996 were family adoptions made in favour of the child's birth mother and her husband, and adoption orders for foreign children accounted for just over one-third. By 1997 there were only 136 non-family adoption orders made (Reports of An Bord Uchtála, 1976, 1996 and 1997). The drop in the number of children placed for adoption reflects the changing attitudes towards children born outside marriage and the increase in the number of never married women deciding to parent their babies (Flanagan and Richardson, 1992).

HISTORICAL ORIGINS OF CHILDCARE POLICY

The process of the social construction of child abuse as a social problem and the emergence and development of the Irish child protection system have been comprehensively chronicled by Ferguson (1993, 1996) and Buckley (1997). Four distinct periods of development can be identified, these being 1889–1908, 1909–69, 1970–90 and contemporary childcare policy after 1990.

Foundations of Childcare Policy 1889–1908

The first attempts to deal with the protection of children resulted in the passing of the Cruelty to Children Act, 1889, which made child cruelty a criminal act, provided for inspectors to remove children from parental custody and to prosecute parents. The year 1889 also saw the establishment of the National Society for the Prevention of Cruelty to

Children in Ireland (NSPCC). The twin aims of the Society were to investigate cases of suspected cruelty and to work towards changes in the legislation. The NSPCC rapidly developed an inspectorate and by 1908 they were servicing 100 centres throughout the country with annual increases in the number of cases investigated (Ferguson, 1996: 8). In 1908 the Children Act was introduced to provide legislation to protect children against offences and to provide for children who had committed offences (Greene, 1979). It was this Act, regarded as a liberal reform at the time, which became the legislative framework for child protection in Ireland for a further 83 years. Where neglect or abuse was proven, children could be removed from their parents to a 'place of safety' and placed in the care of a 'fit person', either a foster-parent or residential institution (Children Act, 1908 ss. 20,24,58). Children who had committed an offence could be dealt with in a number of ways including being sent to an industrial school or place of detention (Children Act, 1908 s107),

Punishment to Casework Ideology 1909–69

After 1908 there was a shift from the punishment centred ideology involving prosecution of parents to the casework ideology and practice based on the supervision of parent–child relations in their homes (Ferguson, 1996: 9). During this period child protection remained the sole responsibility of voluntary agencies, spearheaded by the NSPCC, with residential facilities provided by the religious in the form of Industrial and Reformatory Schools.

The development of child protection legislation and services was very firmly rooted in the principle of family autonomy, a principle which became enshrined in the 1937 Constitution (*Bunreacht na hÉireann,* 1937, Article 42), recognizing the family as the 'primary and fundamental unit group of society' and ascribing to parents 'inalienable and imprescriptible' rights, that is, rights that cannot be taken away and rights that cannot be given away. Constitutional permission for state intervention was limited under Article 42.5 to 'exceptional cases, where the parents for physical or moral reasons fail in their duty towards their children'. This principle of minimal intervention in family life was endorsed by the social teaching of the Catholic Church which left the family outside the sphere of State intervention (Breen et al., 1990). However, the constitutional support for the rights of parents and families was not matched by similar support for the rights and welfare of children (O'Connor, 1992; Buckley, 1997). During this second period of development of child welfare services there was a growing emphasis on the belief that children could be protected and their welfare promoted through social intervention together with a confidence in professional expertise, which could manage the risk to children at an individual level. In 1956 the Irish Society for the Prevention of Cruelty to Children (ISPCC) broke away from the NSPCC, providing a casework service covering the 26 counties and providing the foundations for development of 'a truly distinctive Irish child protection system' (Ferguson, 1996: 12).

During this period two important pieces of legislation were implemented which changed the nature of childcare policy. The first was the Adoption Act 1952 which regularized the informal nature of the adoption procedures. Until that time adoptions had been arranged on an informal basis between agencies, third parties or directly by the biological parents and the adopting parents. For the first time the State was intervening directly and regulating relationships between parents and children with the permanent and legal transfer of parental rights from biological to adoptive parents, despite strong and prolonged resistance from the Catholic Church (Whyte, 1980). The second piece of legislation was The Guardianship of Infants Act 1964 which marked a significant attitudinal change in childcare policy. This Act was the first piece of legislation to incorporate a definition of 'welfare' as 'the religious, moral, intellectual, physical and social welfare of the infant' (Section 2) and more importantly it enshrined the principle of 'paramountcy', that is, that in any decisions involving a child's welfare the best interests of the child must be the first and paramount consideration (Section 3). This Act, therefore, marked a change in the State's relationship with the family in any dispute over the welfare of a child and raised for the first time the real possibility of conflict between the rights of the parents and the rights of children.

During this period, casework services continued to develop under the auspices of the ISPCC with growing professionalization of the child protection system. Increasing numbers of professionals were obtaining social work training in the UK and USA and social science courses were being developed in the universities in Ireland, eventually leading to the establishment of the first professional social work training course in 1968 in University College Dublin and a course for residential childcare in Kilkenny in 1971. In 1968, following considerable pressure, the Minister for Education, set up the Kennedy Committee, which reported in 1970 on the state of the reformatory and industrial schools. The most important recommendation made by the Committee was that :

> the whole aim of the child care system should be geared towards the prevention of family breakdown and the problems consequent on it. The committal or admission of children to residential care should be considered only when there is no satisfactory alternative. (1970: 6)

The Kennedy Report was to become a watershed in terms of childcare policy since it focused service provision on prevention and the support of families in the community rather than the removal of children where families had failed them.

Child Abuse and Pressure Groups: 1970–90

The publication of the Kennedy Report (1970) coincided with a reorganization of the health and social services. The Health Act 1970 decentralized the delivery of these services to the eight regional health boards and the community care programmes became responsible for the delivery of the personal social services which included those of childcare and protection (Curry, 1998). For those working in the field of childcare it became increasingly obvious that the current legislation was inadequate to deal with the welfare of children. An important feature of the early 1970s was the establishment of CARE – a group of professionals and academics whose aim was to pressurize the government to introduce reforms in line with the recommendations of the Kennedy Report. This group produced an influential document *Children Deprived* (CARE, 1972) which set out best practice in the field of child welfare and made strong recommendations for change. Among the many deficiencies in the system, they highlighted as the most notable the lack of one authority at a national level to coordinate and take responsibility for childcare policy. Such responsibilities were divided between three government ministers causing both overlaps and gaps to occur (CARE, 1972: 28). Under increasing pressure the government established the Task Force on Child Care Services in 1974, whose mandate was to make recommendations for improved services for deprived children and children at risk, to prepare a new Children's Bill to modernize the law and to make recommendations on the administrative reform necessary to implement these. The final report of the Task Force (1981) highlighted the need for one government department to have overall responsibility for children and re-emphasized that, as far as possible, deprived children should be catered for in a family or community setting with support from social services, rather than in residential care. It recommended neighbourhood resource centres whose function would be

> to mobilise community resources on behalf of children and their families and by combining the resources of the community, voluntary organizations [and the relevant statutory authorities] maximise their impact on the well-being of children and families in the area. (Task Force on Child Care Services, 1981: 145).

However, it was the voluntary rather than the statutory services which responded to the recommendations for community services. The ISPCC developed three family centres in Dublin, Cork and Wexford (Nic Giolla Choille, 1983; 1984; 1985), and Barnardos developed a range of community support services for families.

The family-centred philosophy underlying the Kennedy and Task Force reports was, to a certain extent, reflected in changing policies during the 1970s. Many of the large childcare institutions were closed or re-formed as smaller group homes together with an emphasis on placing children in foster homes or with adoptive parents where possible. The health boards developed community care programmes, employing social workers whose primary focus was to offer child-centred family casework with an emphasis on supporting families to provide for the welfare of their children. The need for updated legislation became increasingly obvious as the child protection discourse became more widespread and the inability to provide adequate protection for children and support for families more blatant. During the late 1960s and early 1970s, there was growing awareness internationally about non-accidental injury to children (Kempe and Helfer, 1968). As Buckley (1997: 104) has stated:

> The evolution of the child protection system in Ireland was heavily influenced by international trends and events as well as by its own unique social framework . . . the 'rediscovery' of child abuse in the 1960's in Britain and the USA, with the work of Kempe and Helfer and the repercussions in Britain of the first child abuse 'scandals' started to have an influence on awareness of the problem in Ireland.

In 1975 the Department of Health set up a committee to discuss the issue of non-accidental injury to children which reported in 1976. It received a mixed reception being criticized for its concentration on physical abuse to the exclusion of emotional, psychological and social neglect. In addition there was too great an emphasis on the management of reported abuse and too little on developing prevention and early intervention (Buckley, 1997: 104). The first child abuse guidelines, known as the Memorandum on Non-Accidental Injury to Children, were published in 1977 and subsequently revised in 1980 and 1983. While the first edition concentrated on physical abuse to the exclusion of sexual abuse, later editions extended the definition of abuse to include neglect, emotional abuse and child sexual abuse reflecting the increasing knowledge of the nature of the harm to which children were subjected (Buckley, 1996: 38). The revisions were informed by the work of the Irish Council for Civil Liberties (Cooney and Torode, 1989). This group highlighted the factors affecting the recognition of child sexual abuse in

Ireland as being the patriarchal nature of the Irish family, unresolved moral questions which were too threatening to allow for open debate leading to late disclosure, inadequate legislation, lack of resources and professional awareness. They recommended, inter alia, improved funding to voluntary agencies to provide services, mandatory reporting of child abuse, coordination of childcare services at a national level and a central register of suspected and confirmed cases of child sexual abuse. In response to the growing awareness of child sexual abuse the Department of Health reissued its Child Abuse Guidelines in 1987, the contents of which reflected a change in the conceptualization of child abuse. For the first time abuse was defined as consisting of 'physical injuries, severe neglect and sexual or emotional abuse' and the roles and responsibilities of professionals involved in child protection were spelt out. The Law Reform Commission issued a *Report on Child Sexual Abuse* in 1990 which recommended wide ranging changes in the law in relation to child sexual abuse, including the introduction of mandatory reporting.

The role of pressure groups such as CARE, Children First, the Federation of Services for Unmarried Parents, professional organizations such as the Irish Association of Social Workers and the Residential Care Association, together with groups such as the Irish Foster Parents Association and voluntary agencies working with children, was of considerable importance in the 1980s in putting increasing pressure on governments to update the childcare legislation. Various attempts were made to amend the legislation relating to the protection of children at risk and those in trouble with the law. The first attempt in the form of the Child (Care and Protection) Bill 1985 underwent radical revision to become the Child Care Bill 1988, and finally the Child Care Act 1991. However, the attempts at providing comprehensive legislation to protect children failed to address issues relating to children in trouble with the law. (For a discussion of the Juvenile Justice system see chapter 13, pp. 295–7).

Two pieces of legislation passed during this period were of importance in moving policy towards a recognition of the special needs and rights of particular groups of children. The first, the Status of Children Act 1987, abolished the concept of illegitimacy and was important in its underlying philosophy of equalizing the status of children irrespective of the marital status of their parents. The second Adoption Act 1988 was notable in that, for the first time, it provided for the permanent dissolution of the Constitutional rights of married parents where it could be proved that the parents had failed in their duty towards the child thus allowing for an Adoption Order to be made where appropriate. This Act, therefore, recognized a child's need for a permanent home, guaranteed for the future, rather than a transitory placement in substitute family care.

These two pieces of legislation acted as a prelude to the children's rights movement which was to gain momentum after 1990.

Development of Substitute Care for Children

Until the establishment of workhouses in Ireland after 1838, attempts to provide alternative care for children who were orphaned, abandoned or homeless was on an ad hoc basis operated by individuals and religious organizations mainly concerned with the moral and spiritual welfare of the child. Workhouses provided the majority of the care for children until the early part of the twentieth century when there was a general recognition that they were not the most appropriate institutions for the care of children. The continuing concern of the churches about the religious and moral welfare of children reared in workhouses and the government's recognition of the need to make provisions for young delinquents led to the expansion of the work of voluntary and lay organizations for homeless children and to the introduction of a system of reformatory and industrial schools (Robins, 1980). Reformatory schools for young offenders were set up under the Reformatory Schools Act 1854 and industrial schools for homeless children after 1868. However, local authorities were unwilling to finance these schools and as a result various religious orders were requested to undertake the work (Robins, 1980: 292–302). The Children Act 1908 confirmed the position of the reformatory and industrial schools as the major provision for orphaned, homeless and delinquent children. The first enquiry into the organization of these schools was the Cussen Report published in 1936. This report expressed some reservations about the nature of the education and training, the lack of local authority support and the stigma attached to them but they concluded that the system

> affords the most suitable method of dealing with these children and that schools should remain under the management of the religious orders who have undertaken the work (Committee of Enquiry (Cussen Report), 1936: 49)

In 1966, an independent organization, Tuairim, published a report on residential childcare which was far more critical of the provisions. In response, the government established the Committee of Enquiry into the Industrial and Reformatory Schools in 1967 to make a detailed examination of the existing system. The report of this committee was of enormous significance on the future structure of the residential care system. It recommended that 'residential care should be considered only where there is no satisfactory alternative' and that the institutions should be replaced by group homes which would mirror normal family units (Committee of Enquiry, 1970: 6). Following the publication of the report changes did occur with the closure of many of the large institutions and the rebuilding of smaller family units. The Task Force on Child Care Services (1980: 272–3) pointed to the need for improvement in the training, salaries and career prospects of those wishing to work in the residential sector and to move towards professionalizing the service. This was becoming a matter of concern with the falling numbers of religious vocations and the need to employ skilled lay people to staff the residential homes. The Committee also recommended that residential care should be considered only where there was no satisfactory alternative. Policy began to focus on the development and use of foster care. The Eastern Health Board, for example, operated a specialized Fostering Resource Group from 1977 (O'Sullivan, 1982; Cunniffe, 1983). This change in emphasis was reflected in the changing ratio of children in residential and foster care. In 1968–9 there were 4834 children in care with three-quarters in residential care. By 1988 there were 2614 children in care with just over one quarter in residential care (Gilligan, 1991: 185). Despite the fall in the numbers of children in residential care the sector was by no means obsolete. A research study carried out by the Streetwise National Coalition (1991) highlighted the need to develop more specialized services directed at older and more difficult children who had been omitted from the move towards foster care. In addition they identified a very real gap in the provision for homeless young people. A further independent study on residential care (McCarthy et al., 1996) again highlighted the 'incoherent and unplanned' system which still existed. Despite recommendations dating back to 1970, responsibility for the residential care system remained divided between the Departments of Health, Education and Justice, resulting in uneven resourcing and developments across the sector. The division of responsibility made it impossible to plan for the childcare system as a whole. As the Report states:

> the growing sense of professionalism . . . and the serious attempts to rationalise the service that are evident on the ground need to be matched now by a coherent, openly debated policy on residential child care which integrates and coordinates all the government departments involved and ensures that there are suitable care places for all children in need of care
> (McCarthy et al., 1996: 131)

Once again, two serious gaps in the residential care system were identified: provision for very disturbed children and those categorized as 'homeless'. The use of adult hostels or bed and breakfast establishments to accommodate these children became widespread despite being unsuitable to meet their needs. In 1993, 131 homeless children were placed in bed and breakfast accommodation and 29 in hospitals (Streetwise National Coalition, 1994). Until the Child Care Act 1991 there were no specific statutory provisions for homeless children but the new Act (Section 5) places an obligation on the health boards to provide accommodation for these children. Despite this requirement, the provision of services to meet the needs of these children was very slow and a number of cases were taken in the Courts to ensure that the Eastern Health Board was fulfilling its obligations under the Act (O'Sullivan, 1995: 84; O'Sullivan, 1996: 220).

A study carried out by Focus Ireland in 1998 again highlighted defects in the residential care sector. In particular, major failings were noted as:

- misplacement of a large proportion of young people

- lack of access to services

- lack of appropriate accommodation when young people are being discharged

- lack of a follow-up service for care-leavers

- need to assess the numbers in need of care and the provision available

- need to develop guidelines on a range of issues, such as aftercare, care plans and reviews

- urgent need for a range of care placements for adolescents.

(Focus Ireland, 1998: 99)

Similarly, Craig et al. (1998), in their review of residential care in Ireland, highlighted the importance of listening to and involving children and their families in the decisions affecting their lives in the care system, the need to recognize the central role of the care worker within a multidisciplinary and multiskilled team and the overriding importance of developing a national strategy based on a needs-led approach, rather than an *ad hoc* reactive system.

The development of substitute care for children has been characterized by a movement away from institutional care to the provision of group homes and to foster-care, based on the increasing awareness of a child's need for family life. There has been a long tradition of foster-care in Ireland dating back to the Brehon Laws, although the present system is grounded in The Irish Poor Law Amendment Act 1862 which allowed the boards of guardians to place children with foster parents. The control and regulation of the service was commenced with the appointment of inspectors after the Infant Life Protection Act 1897 (Robins, 1980). The current system is based on the Health Act 1953 and the Boarding Out of Children Regulations, 1983. These regulations not only set down guidelines for the selection and monitoring of foster homes but also required health boards to place children in foster care in preference to residential care (Boarding Out of Children Regulations, 1983: Section 5). As a result of this explicit policy the number of places in residential facilities gradually declined (McCarthy et al., 1996: 32) and health boards put additional resources into recruiting and supporting foster parents (Cunniffe, 1983; Gilligan, 1990). The Irish Foster Parent Association, founded in 1982, played its part in the developing professionalization of the foster care system as a key player in the overall provision of substitute care for children. They emphasized the need for foster parents to be seen as partners with the health boards in meeting the needs of the children for whom they cared resulting in improvements in training and support of the foster parents by the health boards.

CURRENT CHILDCARE POLICY: TOWARDS A CHILDREN'S RIGHTS PERSPECTIVE

The two decades from 1970 laid the foundations for policy developments in the 1990s and the enactment of the Child Care Act 1991. The developing awareness of the extent of child physical and sexual abuse, (Ferguson, 1996: 23–5), the increasing body of research on child abuse, the official reports of child neglect and abuse in the UK (Beckford Report, 1985; Carlile Inquiry, 1987; Butler-Sloss, 1988), the increasing role of voluntary bodies in the support of families, strong pressure group activity, the development of health board structures and the professionalization of social work services all came together to affect policy during this period. The period was characterized by attempts to move towards policies of prevention and support for families in providing for the care and welfare of their children. The overriding responsibility for child welfare became firmly rooted in the health board structures with central government guidelines allowing for regional variations of interpretation (Kenny, 1995: 56). However, Ferguson (1996: 26) has argued that during the late 1980s government policy became much more concerned with influencing what practitioners actually do in relation to suspected cases, putting less emphasis on the prevention and family support aspects. It is this legacy which has carried forward to the present child protection policies.

The current period of development of childcare policy has been characterized by the implementation of new legislation and dominated by increasing public awareness of physical and sexual abuse as a major factor in Irish society. A growing awareness of children's rights has been significant in the development of a philosophy surrounding children and their needs, together with an increasing understanding of the need to institute measures to educate children and the public about child abuse with a concentration on prevention. The passing of the Child Care Act 1991 brought together many of the strands of childcare policy and marked the beginning of the present era.

The Child Care Act 1991

The passing of the Child Care Act 1991 marks a watershed in childcare policy in Ireland. It clarifies and sets out the functions and duties of the health boards and deals with three areas of childcare: child protection, alternative care for children who cannot remain at home, and family support. The Act is based on the principle that it is generally in the best interests of a child to be brought up in his or her own family (S.3.2c) and that it is the function of the health board to promote the welfare of children in its area who are not receiving adequate care and protection (S.3.1). The underlying principle of the Act is that, while having regard to the rights and duties of parents whether under the Constitution or otherwise, the welfare of the child is at the centre of any decision-making process (S.3.1.(b) ii), and that, as far as is practicable, due consideration should be given to the wishes of the child having regard to age and understanding (S.3.2b.ii). This, however, provides for a potential conflict with the constitutional rights of the family as set out in Articles 41 and 42 of the Constitution and the personal rights of the individual members of the family as protected under Article 40.3. Thus attachment to both the autonomy of the family and the paramountcy of the child's welfare creates a difficult tension around the appropriate limits of state intervention into family life. Partly in response to this, the emphasis in the legislation has been on prevention and development of services to promote family welfare. Therefore, the Act places a general duty on health boards to 'provide childcare and family support services' (S.3.3), but does not provide any detail of what is envisaged under this section. In order to monitor such provision the health boards are required to publish an annual report (S.8) setting out their services under this section.

Part III and Part IV of the Act provides measures for the protection of children in emergencies and for care proceedings. It broadens the grounds on which a health board may obtain a Care Order (S. 18) to include both physical and sexual abuse and neglect and under S.18.1.c it allows for a Care Order to be obtained if 'the child's health, development or welfare is likely to be avoidably impaired or neglected'. This anticipatory ground is an important one since it provides protection for a child where he or she is thought to be at risk in the future and may provide an important element of prevention and protection.

In keeping with the principle of support for the family and promoting the welfare of children within the family, the Act provides for a Supervision Order (S.19) which requires the health board to visit a child in his or her own home, on a regular basis, to ensure the child's welfare. This is an important change in policy in relation to children at risk as it allows the child to remain at home while simultaneously receiving protection from the statutory services. (For a detailed discussion of the legal provisions of the Child Care Act 1991, see Ward (1997).)

The Child Care Act 1991 has the potential to promote children's rights in that it provides for a child's wishes to be taken into account and also allows for the appointment of a solicitor to act independently for a child who is a party to any care proceedings (S.25.1 and 2), or the appointment of a Guardian ad Litem (S. 26(1)) where a child is not party to the dispute but is the individual to whom the proceedings relate.

The Child Care Act 1991, despite being signed into law in 1991, was not fully implemented until December 1996. The sections dealing with protection of children in emergencies, taking care proceedings and regulations around the placing of children in care were not implemented until October 1995. O'Sullivan (1995) has argued that the long delay was not only due to lack of staff and resources to work the new system but also had its roots in political inertia. It took three child sexual abuse cases the 'X' case in 1992, the Kilkenny incest case in 1993 and the Kelly Fitzgerald case in 1994 to raise public awareness and to finally motivate the government to fully implement the Child Care Act 1991.

The Kilkenny Incest Inquiry

The Kilkenny Incest Inquiry centred on a case of incest in which a young woman had been abused by her father over a number of years and during which time the health and social services had had continuous contact with the family. The Minister for Health set up a public inquiry under the chairmanship of a circuit court judge. It was the first enquiry of this nature in Ireland. The Report made a number of far reaching recommendations relating to child protection, professional involvement in such cases and the need for greater inter-agency cooperation. It also highlighted the difficulties for professionals working in a system which is based on the principle of family autonomy supported by the constitutional right of parents which may come into conflict with the duty of the State to intervene in situations of abuse. The Report outlined certain principles which, it argued, should inform policy and practice:

- the rights of children
- parental involvement
- multi-disciplinary involvement
- inter-agency collaboration/cooperation
- the need for proper planning and evaluation of services
- the primacy of prevention
- the provision of treatment services
- the need to provide for a balance between child protection and the rights of parents

(Kilkenny Report, 1993: 94)

Among other things the Report recommended changes in the constitution to take account of the rights of children, revision of the child abuse guidelines to include parameters for best practice, a system of mandatory reporting, the introduction of child abuse registers, an emphasis on case conferences as a method of interdisciplinary contact and decision making and the extension of primary prevention programmes and family support services. However, Buckley (1996: 39; 1997: 110) has argued that it is questionable whether or not an inquiry such as this one is a suitable theoretical foundation for the design of a set of general principles aimed at governing professional practice. As she states

> child protection policy making in Ireland has tended to follow high profile happenings in a political, piecemeal fashion and the Report of the Kilkenny Incest Investigation provided the catalyst needed to progress the child care services.

It certainly galvanized the government to address some of the recommendations. It led to the government expediting the implementation of the remaining sections of the Child Care Act 1991, to pledge considerable financial investment in resourcing new services and personnel, to increase the numbers of places for the training of social workers and to open the debate on mandatory reporting. In addition it raised public awareness of the issues and added to the increasing debate on child protection and children's rights.

Regulations Governing Implementation of Childcare Policies

Since the passing of the Child Care Act 1991 there have been increasing attempts to regulate and standardize procedures and practice in the area of childcare services. The Report of the Kilkenny Incest Inquiry (Kilkenny Report, 1993) had highlighted the fact that the Child Abuse Guidelines

(Department of Health, 1987) were not being interpreted in a standardized way and in some instances professionals were unaware of their existence. In addition they particularly noted the lack of coordination between the health boards and the Gardaí. Since that report the government has issued new guidelines on the *Notification of Suspected Cases of Child Abuse between Health Boards and Gardai* (Department of Health, 1995) which lay down standard procedures for the notification of cases between the two agencies. Buckley (1996) offers a valuable critique of child abuse guidelines in Ireland. From her research, she argues that the Gardaí still lack information about services and many of them are unaware of child abuse guidelines. In addition, social workers 'have responded with apprehension to the expectation that they will report all allegations of child abuse to the Gardaí'. (Buckley, 1996: 44). Buckley believes that policies and official guidelines can only form the background to cooperative work between social workers and the Gardaí and that formalizing this in child abuse guidelines does not take account of the fragile nature of the negotiations which go on in families and between family members and the social services. She argues that more effective cooperation and collaboration are achieved in the context of specialized services, referral and liaison systems and training to gain better understanding of each other's tasks and roles.

In 1998 the Department of Health began a review of the 1987 Child Abuse Guidelines with the intention of issuing new procedures and a guide to best practice. Such guidelines can provide a valuable framework for practice and provide a means by which professionals can be made accountable for the work they undertake. In addition they can standardize practice. However, Buckley (1996: 53) makes a cogent argument warning of the dangers of an over-regulated system which can lose the 'individual discretion and therapeutic skill of professionals' in favour of administrative management and regulation. She also suggests that 'the formalizing of procedures with its increased demand for accountability has the potential to re-prioritize protection to cover the worker and agency first and the child and family second (Buckley, 1996: 53).

Following a number of investigations into the abuse of children in residential homes and the publication of the Report on the Inquiry into the Operation of Madonna House (Eastern Health Board, 1996), regulations have been issued in relation to both residential care and foster care. The Child Care (Standards in Children's Residential Centres) Regulations 1996 and *Guide to Good Practice in Children's Residential Centres* (Department of Health, 1997) are the first comprehensive guidelines for this sector. They are based on the principle of respect for a child's dignity and individuality, the need to preserve the child's sense of identity and the child's right to be heard. They are also based on the principle of partnership between the agencies and professionals and both the child and his or her parents. There is, therefore, emphasis on developing a written care plan for each child in residential care which identifies the child's needs and the tasks to be undertaken by named individuals to meet those needs. The plan must be developed with the participation of all parties, including the child and his/her parents and extended family together with the professionals involved. Similarly the principle of partnership underscores the Child Care (Placement of Children in Foster Care) Regulations 1995. They too require a care plan with review meetings to include the child. The Child Care Act 1991 (S.41) specifically makes provision for the placement of children with relatives as foster-parents (Child Care (Placement of Children with Relatives) Regulations 1996). The increase in the formal use of relative foster care is a recent development which adds a further resource which can meet the needs of children. It is in keeping with developing models of child centred practice by maintaining closer links with the family of origin and should help many children currently adrift in the care system (O'Brien, 1998).

Mandatory Reporting of Child Abuse

Both the Law Reform Commission (1990) and the Report of the Kilkenny Incest Investigation (Kilkenny Report, 1993) recommended the introduction of mandatory reporting of child abuse. In their discussions they highlighted the advantages of such a system as empowering professionals to report abuse, securing consistency in the management of the disclosure of child abuse, increasing identification of children who are being abused and providing a better basis for statistical evidence and research. However, these were balanced with some disadvantages: the danger of over-reporting of cases, using scarce resources on unsubstantiated cases, the danger of deterring victims from disclosing abuse and undermining the therapeutic relationship between professionals and their clients. Following extensive discussions with various professional groups the government decided against introducing mandatory reporting on the basis that it would not be in the best interests of children and would not improve the childcare services (Department of Health, 1997). At the Irish Government's meeting with the UN Committee on the Rights of the Child in January 1998, the Junior Minister for Foreign Affairs, who represented the government, indicated that Ireland did intend to introduce mandatory reporting (*The Irish Times*, 13 January 1998). However, it is still unclear whether such measures will be introduced in the near future.

Prevention and Family Support

The concept of family support has been part of childcare provisions since the early 1960s but it was defined mainly in terms of casework with families to prevent children coming into the care of the state. This focus remained during the 1970s with limited discussions on the need to address more fundamental issues of child poverty to prevent child disadvantage. In the 1980s the concept was broadened and neighbourhood resource centres, youth projects and family centres were developed (Murphy, 1996: 75). In general, these were developed by voluntary bodies to incorporate a range of professionals and volunteers widening the concept of family support to include a 'more self-directed and community based approach and one that involves group learning and action' (Murphy, 1996: 76). With the increasing referrals of child abuse in the 1980s the statutory services became primarily child protection agencies providing a system which reacted to events rather than taking a proactive role in prevention. Health boards did begin to develop schemes such as the Community Mothers Programme in the Eastern Health Board and to provide grants to voluntary groups to provide support services. For the first time, the Child Care Act 1991 (S.3) made it a function of the health boards to 'provide childcare and family support services'. Murphy challenges the view inherent in the Act that prevention and family support services are synonymous (1996: 78). She argues that families cannot be seen separately from the existing economic, political and social systems. In addition, family support seems to imply that the family is one unit without conflict of interests among its members. It is necessary, therefore, to disaggregate these concepts and provide policies which touch on each of them separately. Thus policies which develop shared responsibility for childcare between parents, the state and professionals, intergenerational care, and between men and women have the potential to prevent child disadvantage and abuse. Policies which improve levels of low parental incomes, promote employment, provide educational opportunities and improve the community environment may both prevent neglect and abuse and also promote children's welfare (Gilligan, 1995: 60–78; Murphy, 1996: 95). The Interim Report of the Family Commission, *Strengthening Families for Life* (Commission on the Family, 1996: 9) emphasizes the need for health boards to prioritize family support work at the preventive level and to make resources available to do so. In particular they recommend the extension of the Family Support Workers Scheme (Eastern Health Board 1996) and the Community Mothers Programmes (Johnson et al., 1993), together with the introduction of a network of family and community services resource centres throughout the country.

In June 1998 the government indicated that it was allocating £2.4 million per year to provide twelve family support projects aimed at diverting 400 children a year from care or detention. The centres would be 'essentially a social partnership between the statutory and voluntary agencies driven by the communities involved. In addition, the government intended to develop parenting programmes and 'other supports for vulnerable families' (Department of Health Press Release, 22 June 1998). These initiatives indicate a very important policy change in relation to the prevention and support of families, one advocated by voluntary agencies for some years.

A further aspect of prevention has been the development of a national primary school based prevention programme (*Stay Safe Programme*) focusing on educating children to be aware of child abuse issues. (McIntyre, 1993). This programme has been introduced amidst considerable controversy although it appears now to have been accepted as part of national policy (Gilligan, 1996: 64). A similar programme is currently being drawn up for second level schools which will be incorporated into the programme in Relationships and Sexuality Education (First National Report of Ireland, 1996: 53).

'Familialization' and Children's Rights

Much of the development of childcare policy has centred on the conflict between the rights of parents, the rights of children, and the rights of the state to intervene in family life. The concept of 'familialization' is central in the discussion of children's rights and the rights of the state vis à vis the family. The term 'familialization' refers to the fusion of childhood into the institution of the family defining children only as an extension of their parents. Children's social identity is defined only in relation to their parents' social status, set of values and lifestyles. Children then are absorbed into the family and their individual needs are seen to be met through and by the family (Makrinioti, 1994: 268). Thus the fusion of children into the family unit becomes the main frame of reference when dealing with children, both formally and informally.

The essence of the welfare state is to provide minimum standards of income, nutrition, health, housing and education through the provision of social services and state regulation of private activities that alter the conditions of life of individuals or groups (Offe, 1985: 3–4). Such services are designed to supplement the role of the family in meeting the needs of its members. Within the welfare state the family still prevails as the overriding institution expected to meet the needs of the individual members. In particular, policies take for granted that parents will care for their children and will aspire to meet their needs. This conceptualization is based, however, on the assumption that the interests of parents and children are identical and inseparable. In the majority of cases parents do act in the best interests of their children. However, Webb and Wistow (1987: 20) have argued that the welfare state also exercises social control by regulating interpersonal relations in situations in which some individuals, such as children, are weaker than others. Thus the dichotomy between the autonomy of the family and the intervention of the state exists in relation to children. One side of this dichotomy is the state adopting a marginal role in its concern for family privacy and the other side is concerned with intervention in order to promote the welfare of children and maintain their rights as individuals. Policies concerning child protection acknowledge the family's failure to ensure adequate care and protection for their children. Thus the social discourse around child protection widens into a discussion of welfare in terms of children's rights and children as citizens. A change from conceptualizing children in terms of familialization to one of citizenship with individual autonomy, the right to participation and consultation on issues affecting their lives, and the possibility of choosing among alternatives will radically alter welfare policies for children.

The Irish Constitution contains no formal recognition of the rights of children. Their rights have been defined as being subsumed within the rights of the family (Article 41 and 42) In the case of G–v–An Bord Uchtála (1980, IR 32), O'Higgins, J. stated

> The child also has natural rights. Normally these will be safe under the care and protection of its mother. Having been born the child has the right to be fed and to live, to be reared and educated, to have the opportunity of working and of realising his or her full personality and dignity as a human being. These rights . . . must equally be protected and vindicated by the State

The Kilkenny Incest Investigation Report (1993: 31) argued that in taking this view it may well be impossible to regard the welfare of the child as the first and paramount consideration in any dispute as to its upbringing or custody between parents and third parties without first considering the rights of the family. It argued that the emphasis on the rights of the family in the Constitution may be interpreted as giving a higher value to the rights of parents than to the rights of children. The Report therefore recommended amending the Constitution to include a statement of the constitutional rights of children (Kilkenny Report, 1993: 96). The Report of the Constitutional Review Group supported this view. It stated that 'if parental rights and children's rights are both being expressly guaranteed it would be desirable that the Constitution make clear which of these rights should take precedence in the event of a conflict between the rights' (Constitution Review Group, 1996: 330). Thus it recommended that the Constitution should include an Article clearly stating the rights of children and in particular 'the express require-ment that in all actions concerning children, whether by legislative, judicial or administrative authorities, the best interests of the child shall be the paramount consideration' (Constitution Review Group, 1996: 337), which would give a Constitutional guarantee to what already exists in legislation and reduce the potential for a conflict between the rights of parents and the rights of children.

Since September 1992, when Ireland ratified the United Nations Convention on the Rights of the Child, the issue of children's rights has been part of the discourse around child welfare. The UN Convention sets out the rights guaranteed to children and young people under 18 years of age in all areas of their lives and it imposes obligations on parents, the family, the community and the state in this regard (Children's Rights Alliance, 1997: ix; Kilmurray and Richardson, 1994). The Convention is based on three underlying principles: non-discrimination insofar as the articles apply to all children equally, whatever their race, sex, religion, disability, opinion or family background; the child's best interests must govern all decisions affecting the child; the child's view must be taken into consideration in any decisions concerning him or her, in accordance with age and maturity. The Convention covers four broad areas of rights: survival, development, protection and participation rights. However, the Convention merely provides a framework in which governments are required to ensure that children's rights are actualized. It places an onus on them to provide the legislative and administrative structures together with adequate resources to implement them.

How far Ireland fulfils the requirements of the UN Convention has been well documented by *Focus on Children* (Kilmurray and Richardson, 1994), Cousins (1996) and the Children's Rights Alliance (1997) in its submission to the United Nations Committee on the Rights of the Child. In January 1998, the UN Committee published its concerns about Ireland's performance in relation to its obligations under the UN Convention on the Rights of the Child, having heard both the submission of the Irish government (First National Report of Ireland, 1996) and the responses of the Irish non-governmental organizations (Children's Rights Alliance, 1997). The major areas of concern were:

- the need for a comprehensive national policy on children's rights
- the need for greater emphasis on prevention

- improved statistical base for the formulation of policies
- the need to increase awareness of the UN Convention on the Rights of the Child
- concern over the low age limits in the legislation particularly in the area of juvenile justice and the low age of criminal responsibility
- lack of concern for the views of children
- absence of mandatory reporting of child abuse
- lack of a national policy to ensure the rights of children with disabilities, and in the area of mental health of children and families
- concern over children excluded from schools
- the lack of a Right's Commissioner/Ombudsman for children

> (Committee on the Rights of the Child, Geneva,
> 17th Session CRC/C/15/Add.85 23 January 1998)

Cousins (1996) has analysed the existing mechanisms for the promotion and protection of children's rights in Ireland. He concludes that, although the Child Care Act 1991 has the potential to promote the rights of children, there are no overall public mechanisms for the promotion of the rights of children generally and this may make it difficult for public bodies to recognize the special needs of children. He recommends, on the basis of his research, that the office of a statutory Children's Commissioner should be established to promote and protect children's rights (Cousins, 1996: 72). He states that, while such a system would go a long way to promote and protect children's rights, it would be ineffective unless set in the context of coordinated government structures and structures within schools, social services and the legal system which will enable and encourage children to make their voices heard.

Statutory responsibility for the welfare of children remains divided between the Departments of Health and Children, Education and Science, and Justice, Equality and Law Reform, with responsibility for the welfare of children in need of care and protection and children with disabilities lying with the Department of Health and Children. These departments have, in the past, tended to work in an uncoordinated fashion in relation to children's affairs. Every report on childcare policy and practice since 1970 has emphasized the need for rationalization of the administrative systems affecting children. Slow progress has been made since 1974 when the then Department of Health was given the major responsibility for childcare. It was not until 1993 that a Child Care Policy Unit was set up within that Department of Health. The Interim Report of the Commission on the Family (November 1996) once again commented on the inadequate coordination between departments with responsibility for children's affairs. However, some of these criticisms have been accepted and the present Government has created a Department of Health and Children which has a Child Care Policy Unit within it and a junior Minister for Children. It appears that there is now improved coordination between the three departments. This was evidenced during the preparation of the Children Bill 1996. Each health board is required to establish a Child Care Advisory Committee (Child Care Act 1991 S.7) with a membership composed of representatives from both statutory and voluntary agencies whose function is to advise the health board on the provision of child and family support services in its area. In June 1998, it was announced that a new national children's strategy is to be drawn up by the government which will aim to improve the way government departments work together in relation to children, based on children's rights (Department of Health and Children, Press Release, 22 June 1998).

The present administration rejected the concept of a rights commissioner for children, despite criticism from the UN Committee on the Rights of the Child, and has established a social services inspectorate to monitor and promote services for the care and protection of children. The government argues that this body will act as a conduit for the promotion of children's rights and an agency to listen to and process children's concerns. Whether this will be adequate to meet the requirements of the UN Committee on the Rights of the Child remains to be seen.

CONCLUSIONS: CHALLENGES FOR THE FUTURE

Childcare policy in Ireland has developed in an ad hoc and reactive fashion in response to a number of factors including pressure group activity from a range of interest groups, concerned professionals and researchers, voluntary agencies working in the field and a number of significant enquiries and reports some initiated by government and others from independent sources. In addition, policy developments have been circumscribed by the Irish Constitution and the reluctance of the state to interfere in family life. Policies have resulted from attempts to balance the rights of parents, the rights of children and the rights of the state. However, until the early 1990s, the focus was firmly on the rights of parents. The challenge now is for policy developments to change the balance in favour of the rights of the child. The full implementation of the Child Care Act 1991 has laid the foundation for policy to focus far more clearly on the rights and needs of children. Constitutional change is needed now to underpin the legislation. Its emphasis on prevention, on partnership between parents, the state and other social service agencies and cooperation and coordination between all agencies involved with children provides a framework for policy development. However, it is only a framework. Despite the proactive orientation of the Child Care Act, much of the childcare and protection work remains reactive and partnership with families operates at a low level (Buckley, 1997: 120). What is needed in the future is a real commitment by workers and government, to listen to children, involve them and their families in the decision-making process and strive towards a children's rights perspective.

The growing awareness of child abuse in the 1990s has at last brought the issue of child protection firmly into the political arena. Since the passing of the Child Care Act 1991 the amount of money invested in childcare and social work services has risen annually. Since 1993 the Department of Health and Children has financed the creation of 850 new posts within the childcare services. In its submission to the UN Committee on the Rights of the Child (First National Report of Ireland, 1996: 13), the government stated that it has approved a range of developments designed to ensure that:

- child protection services are strengthened and equipped to respond to the needs of children
- intensive counselling and treatment is available for victims of child abuse
- special therapeutic care is provided for those damaged by abuse and neglect
- adequate accommodation is available to help homeless young people
- children in foster-care and residential care are supervised and monitored on a systematic basis
- locally based services are available to assist families in difficulty

The challenge now is for the rhetoric to become a reality and for the resources to be made available for these aspirations to be fulfilled. Policy must now be proactive rather than reactive and driven by a real political commitment to enhancing the position of children in Ireland.

MAIN POLICY DEVELOPMENTS

1889   Cruelty to Children Act
1889   Establishment of the National Society for Prevention of Cruelty to Children in Ireland
1908   Children Act
1936   Report of the Committee of Enquiry into the Reformatory and Industrial Schools System (The Cussen Report)
1937   Irish Constitution
1952   The Adoption Act
1964   Guardianship of Infants Act
1970   Report on Industrial Schools and Reformatories (The Kennedy Report)
1970   Health Act establishing regional health boards
1970   Establishment of the group CARE
1971   Irish Association of Social Workers founded
1972   Publication of the CARE Memorandum
1974   Government sets up the Task Force on Child Care Services
       Children First founded as a pressure group for improvements in adoption and fostering
       Department of Health given the major responsibility for childcare services
1975   Publication of the Interim Report of the Task Force on Child Care Services
1977   Publication of guidelines for professionals dealing with non-accidental injury to children.
1978   Fostering Resource Group established in the Eastern Health Board
1979   Child Care Division established in the Department of Health
1981   Final Report of the Task Force on Child Care Services published
1982   Irish Foster Care Association founded
1983   New Boarding Out of Children Regulations issued
1984   Report of the Review Committee on Adoption published
1985   Child (Care and Protection) Bill published
1987   Department of Health publishes revised Child Abuse Guidelines
       Status of Children Act passed
1988   Child Care Bill replaces the Child (Care and Protection) Bill
       Adoption Act 1988 provides for adoption of children of married parents under particular circumstances

1990	Government commits Ireland to ratifying the UN Convention on the Rights of the Child
1991	Child Care Act signed into law. Its implementation is to be phased in over five years
1992	Ireland ratifies the UN Convention on the Rights of the Child Commencement Order signed under Child Care Act 1991 redefining the age of a child as a person under the age of 18 years other than a person who is or has been married
1993	Report of the Kilkenny Incest Investigation published Child Care Policy Unit established in the Department of Health
1994	Government appointed a Minister of State to the Department of Health, Education and Justice with special responsibility for children and for coordination of the activities of the three departments.
1995	Publication of new guidelines on the Notification of Suspected Cases of Child Abuse between Health Boards and Gardaí Publication of the Child Care (Placement of Children in Foster Care) Regulations Publication of the Child Care (Placement of Children in Residential Care) Regulations Publication of Child Care (Placement of Children with Relatives) Regulations Government establishes the Commission on the Family October 1995 Parts III, IV and V of the Child Care Act 1991 implemented
1996	Report of the Constitutional Review Group published Publication of the First National Report of Ireland under the UN Convention on the Rights of the Child All sections of the Child Care Act 1991 finally implemented Publication of the Report on the Operation of Madonna House
1997	Department of Health and Children established with junior Minister responsible for children Department of Social, Community and Family Affairs established
1998	Final Report of the Family Commission published Ireland appears before the UN Committee on the Rights of the Child in Geneva Government announces that a national children's strategy is to be drawn up

RECOMMENDED READING

Children's Rights Alliance (1997) *Small Voices: Vital Rights*. Dublin: Children's Rights Alliance.

Ferguson, H and P. Kenny (1995) *On Behalf of the Child: Child Welfare, Child Protection and the Child Care Act 1991*. Dublin: Farmar.

First National Report of Ireland (1996) *Ireland: United Nations Convention on the Rights of the Child*. Dublin: Stationery Office.

Gilligan, R. (1991) *Irish Child Care Services: Policy, Practice and Provision*. Dublin: Institute of Public Administration.

Kilmurray, A. and V. Richardson (1994) *Focus on Children: Blueprint for Action*. Dublin/Belfast: Focus on Children.

REFERENCES

Beckford Report (1985) *A Child in Trust*: Report of the Panel of Inquiry into the Death of Jasmine Beckford. London: London Borough of Brent.

An Bord Uchtála. *Reports*. Dublin: Stationery Office.

Bowlby, J. (1953) *Child Care and the Growth of Love*. Harmondsworth: Penguin.

Breen, R., D. Hannan, D. Rottman, and T. Whelan (1990) *Understanding Contemporary Ireland: State, Class and Development in the Republic of Ireland* Dublin: Gill & Macmillan.

Buckley, H. (1996) 'Child Abuse Guidelines in Ireland: For Whose Protection?', in H. Ferguson and T. McNamara (eds), *Protecting Irish Children: Investigation, Protection and Welfare Administration*, 44 (2): 37–56.

Buckley, H. (1997) 'Child Protection in Ireland', pp. 101–26 in M. Harder and K. Pringle (eds), *Protecting Children in Europe: Towards a New Millennium*. Denmark: Aalborg University Press.

Bunreacht na hEireann (1937) *Constitution of Ireland*. Dublin: Stationery Office.

Butler-Sloss, Lord Justice E. (1988) *Report of the Inquiry into Child Abuse in Cleveland in 1987*. London: HMSO.

CARE (1972) *Children Deprived: The CARE Memorandum on Deprived Children and Children's Services in Ireland*. Dublin: CARE.

Carlile Inquiry (1987) *A Child in Mind: Protection of Children in a Responsible Society: Report of the Commission of Inquiry into the Circumstances surrounding the Death of Kimberly Carlile*. London: London Borough of Greenwich.

Central Statistics Office (1997) *Census 96: Planning for the Ireland of Tomorrow* Dublin: Stationery Office.

Child Care Policy Unit (1996). Dublin: Department of Health.

Children's Rights Alliance (1997) *Small Voices: Vital Rights*. Dublin: The Children's Rights Alliance.

Commission on the Family (1996) *Strengthening Families for Life: Interim Report to the Minister for Social Welfare*. Dublin: Stationery Office.

Commission on the Family (1998) *Strengthening Families for Life: Final Report to the Minister for Social, Community and Family Affairs, Executive Summary*. Dublin: Stationery Office.

Committee of Enquiry into the Reformatory and Industrial Schools System (1936) *Report* (The Cussen Report). Dublin: Stationery Office.

Committee of Enquiry into the Reformatory and Industrial Schools System (1970) *Report*. (Kennedy Report). Dublin: Stationery Office.

Constitution Review Group (1996). *Report*. Dublin: Stationery Office.

Cooney, T. and R. Torode (1989) *Report of the Irish Council for Civil Liberties Working Party on Child Sexual Abuse*. Dublin: ICCL.

Cousins, M. (1996) *Seen and Heard: Promoting and Protecting Children's Rights in Ireland*. Dublin: The Children's Rights Alliance.

Craig, S., M. Donnellan, G. Graham and A. Warren (1998) *Learn to Listen: Irish Report of a European Study on Residential Child Care*. Dublin: Centre for Social and Educational Research, Dublin Institute of Technology.

Cunniffe, R. (1983) *Recruiting Foster Parents*. Dublin: Eastern Health Board.

Curry, J. (1998) *Irish Social Services*. 3rd edition. Dublin: IPA.

Department of Health (1977) *Memorandum on Non-Accidental Injury to Children*. Dublin: Stationery Office.

Department of Health (1980) *Non-Accidental Injury to Children. Guidelines on Procedures for the Identification, Investigation and Management of Non-Accidental Injury to Children*. Dublin: Department of Health.

Department of Health (1983) *Non Accidental Injury to Children: Guidelines on Procedures for the Identification, Investigation and Management of Non-Accidental Injury to Children*. Dublin: Department of Health.

Department of Health (1987) *Child Abuse Guidelines: Guidelines on Procedures for the Identification, Investigation and Management of Child Abuse*. Dublin: Department of Health.

Department of Health (1993) *Survey of Children in Care of the Health Boards 1992*. Dublin: Department of Health.

Department of Health (1995) *Notification of Suspected Cases of Child Abuse Between the Health Boards and the Gardaí*. Dublin: Department of Health.

Department of Health (1995) *Child Care (Placement of Children in Foster Care) Regulations 1995*. Dublin: Department of Health.

Department of Health (1996) *Child Care (Placement of Children with Relatives) Regulations 1996*. Dublin: Department of Health.

Department of Health (1996) *Putting Children First Discussion Document on Mandatory Reporting*. Dublin: Stationery Office.

Department of Health (1997) *Putting Children First Promoting and Protecting the Rights of Children*. Dublin:, Stationery Office.

Department of Health (1997) *Child Care (Standards in Children's Residential Centres) Regulations 1996 and Guide to Good Practice in Children's Residential Centres*. Dublin: Department of Health.

Eastern Health Board (1995) *Review of Adequacy of Child Care and Family Support Services 1994*. Dublin: Eastern Health Board.

Eastern Health Board (1996) *Review of Adequacy of Child Care and Family Support Services 1995*. Dublin: Eastern Health Board.

Erikson, E. (1969) *Childhood and Society*. Harmondsworth: Penguin.

Fahlberg, V. (1981) *Helping Children When They Must Move,* Practice Series 6. London: BAAF.

Ferguson, H. (1993) 'Surviving Irish Childhoods: Child Protection and the Deaths of Children in Child Abuse Cases in Ireland since 1884', in H. Ferguson, R. Gilligan, and R. Torode (eds), *Surviving Childhood Adversity: Issues for Policy and Practice*. Dublin: Social Studies Press, Trinity College.

Ferguson, H. (1993/1994) 'Child Abuse Inquiries and the Report of the Kilkenny Incest Investigation: A Critical Analysis', *Administration*, 41: 385–400

Ferguson, H. (1996) 'Protecting Irish Children in Time: Child Abuse as a Social Problem and the Development of the Child Protections System in Ireland', in H. Ferguson and T. McNamara (eds), *Protecting Irish Children: Investigation, Protection and Welfare, Administration*, 44 (2 Summer): 5–36.

First National Report of Ireland (1996) *Ireland: United Nations Convention on the Rights of the Child*. Dublin: Department of Foreign Affairs, Stationery Office.

Flanagan, N. and V. Richardson (1992) *Unmarried Mothers: A Social Profile*. Dublin: National Maternity Hospital/Social Science Research Centre, UCD.

Focus Ireland (1998) *Out on Their Own: Young People Leaving Care in Ireland*. Dublin: Focus Ireland.

Gilligan, R. (1991) *Irish Child Care Services: Policy, Practice and Provision*. Dublin: Institute of Public Administration.

Gilligan, R. (1995) 'Family Support and Child Welfare: Realising the Promise of the Child Care Act 1991', pp. 60–83 in H. Ferguson and P. Kenny (eds), *On Behalf of the Child: Child Welfare, Child Protection and the Child Care Act 1991*. Dublin: Farmar.

Gilligan, R. (1996) 'Irish Child Care Services in the 1990's: The Child Care Act 1991 and Other Developments', pp. 56–74 in M. Hill and J. Aldgate (eds), *Child Welfare Services: Developments in Law, Policy, Practice and Research*. London: Jessica Kingsley.

Greene, R. (1979) 'Legal Aspects of Non-Accidental Injury to Children', *Administration*, 27 (4): 460–74.

Inquiry into the Operation of Madonna House (1996). *Report*. Dublin: Eastern Health Board.

Johnson, Z., F. Howell and B. Molloy (1993) 'Community Mothers Programme: Randomised Controlled Trial of Non-professional Intervention in Parenting', *British Medical Journal* 306: 1449–52.

Kelleher, P. and C. Kelleher (1998) *Out on Their Own: Young People Leaving Care in Ireland*. Dublin: Focus Ireland.

Kellmer Pringle, M. (1974) *The Needs of Children* London: Hutchinson.

Kempe, H, and R. Helfer (1968) *The Battered Child*. Chicago: University of Chicago Press.

Kenny, P. (1995) 'The Child Care Act 1991 and the Social Context of Child Protection', pp. 42–59 in H. Ferguson and P. Kenny (eds), *On Behalf of the Child: Child Welfare, Child Protection and the Child Care Act 1991*. Dublin: Farmar.

Kilkenny Report (1993) *Report of the Kilkenny Incest Investigation*. Dublin: Stationery Office.

Kilmurray, A. and V. Richardson (1994) *Focus on Children: A Blueprint for Action*. Dublin/Belfast: Focus on Children.

Law Reform Commission (1990) *Report on Child Sexual Abuse* (LRC 32–1990). Dublin: Stationery Office.

McCarthy, P., S. Kennedy and C. Matthews (1996) *Focus on Residential Child Care in Ireland: 25 Years Since the Kennedy Report*. Dublin: Focus Ireland.

McIntyre, D. (1993) 'The Stay Safe Programme', *Intercom*, June.

McKeown, K. (1991) *The North Inner City of Dublin – An Overview*. Dublin: Daughters of Charity.

Makrinioti, D. (1994) 'Conceptualization of Childhood in a Welfare State: A Critical Reappraisal', pp. 267–84 in J. Qvortrup, M. Bardy, G. Sgritta, H. Wintersberger (eds), *Childhood Matters: Social Theory, Practice and Politics*. Aldershot: Avebury.

Murphy, M. (1996) 'From Prevention to Family Support and Beyond: Promoting the Welfare of Irish Children', in H. Ferguson and T. McNamara (eds) *Protecting Irish Children, Administration*, 44 (2): 73–101.

Nic Giolla Choille, T. (1983) *Wexford Family Centre*. Dublin: ISPCC.

Nic Giolla Choille, T. (1984) *Cork Family Centre:* Dublin: ISPCC.

Nic Giolla Choille, T. (1985) *Darndale Family Centre*. Dublin: ISPCC.

O'Brien, V. (1998) 'Relative Foster Care: Practice Implications arising from the Relative and Foster Care Regulations 1995'. Unpublished paper, Conference on Relative Foster Care, University College Dublin, 6 June 1998.

O'Connor, P. (1992) 'Child Care Policy: A Provocative Analysis and Research Agenda', *Administration*, 40 (3).

Offe, C (1985) *Contradictions of the Welfare State*. London: Hutchinson.

O'Higgins, K. (1993) *Family Problems – Substitute Care Children in Care and Their Families*. Broadsheet Series Paper No. 28. Dublin: Economic and Social Research Institute.

O'Sullivan, E. (1995) 'Section 5 of the Child Care Act 1991 and Youth Homelessness', pp. 84–104 in H. Ferguson and P. Kenny (eds), *On Behalf of the Child: Child Welfare, Child Protection and the Child Care Act 1991*. Dublin: Farmar.

O'Sullivan, E. (1996) 'Adolescents Leaving Care or Leaving Home and Child Care Provision in Ireland and the UK: A Critical View', in M. Hill and J. Aldgate (eds), *Child Welfare Services: Developments in Law, Policy, Practice and Research*. London: Jessica Kingsley.

O'Sullivan, M. (1982) 'The Fostering Resource Group Five Years On', *Children First*, No. 2

Richardson, V. (1985) *Whose Children?* Dublin: Family Studies Unit, UCD.

Robins, J. (1980) *The Lost Children*. Dublin: Institute of Public Administration.

Streetwise National Coalition (1994) *News Sheet* No. 5. Dublin: Streetwise.

Streetwise National Coalition and Resident Managers Association (1991) *At What Cost?* Dublin: Focus Point.

Task Force on Child Care Services (1980) *Final Report*. Dublin: Stationery Office.

Task Force on the Travelling Community (1995) *Report of the Task Force on the Travelling Community*. Dublin: Stationery Office.

Tuairim (1966) *Some of Our Children – A Report on the Residential Care of the Deprived Child in Ireland*. London: Tuairim.

Ward, P. (1997) *The Child Care Act 1991*. Dublin: Round Hall Sweet & Maxwell.

Webb, A. and G. Wistow (1987) *Social Work, Social Care and Social Planning: The Personal Social Services since Seebohm*. London: Longman.

Whyte, J. (1980) *Church and State in Modern Ireland*. Dublin: Gill & Macmillan.

Woods, M. (1994) 'Drug Using Parents and their Children: The Experience of a Voluntary/Non-statutory Project', *Irish Social Worker*, 12 (2): 10.

9

Irish Youth Policy[1]

Patricia Kennedy

INTRODUCTION

In this chapter youth work is discussed solely in the context of youth policy. There is no simple definition of youth work. It covers a wide range of settings, services and activities but generally it is concerned with enabling young people to improve their own lives through the acquisition of skills and experiences which will facilitate the development of their individual talents and abilities. It is concerned with encouraging and helping young people to participate in and contribute to the society in which they live. The aim of youth work has been defined as to 'offer young people, on the basis of their voluntary involvement, developmental and educational experience which will equip them to play an active part in a democratic society, as well as meeting their own personal development needs' (Department of Labour, 1984: 114). There are many ideas and philosophies as to how this help and encouragement can be given.

The Discovery of Adolescence

The stage of youth is generally seen as synonymous with adolescence. Milson (1970: 2) refers to adolescence as 'a human experience at the meeting place of many changes, physical, psychological, emotional and social' and that 'it is the recognition of the role-change in adolescence which gives "youth service" its universal character'. Both adolescence and youth work are phenomena of modern industrial society. The 'discovery of adolescence' coincided with the industrial revolution in Britain and slowly spread to Ireland, as did the development of youth work services (Springhall, 1977). Sociological and psychological theories of the instability of youth began to appear around the time of industrialization. It was believed that adolescents who were left too much to themselves tended to become disordered (Tobias, 1967; Davies and Gibson, 1967). There was an emphasis on the increase of juvenile mental disorders, misspent leisure and rising crime rates as evidence of increasing delinquency among the young. The origin of youth work was closely related to and depended on broader and deeper processes in nineteenth-century society. In looking at the development of youth work in Ireland, therefore, it is necessary to look to Britain where many of our youth organizations developed in the years 1870–1910. The development of youth work services in both countries runs closely parallel (Kennedy, 1984). Youth policy in Ireland has its roots in nineteenth-century Britain where the earliest youth organizations emerged.

YOUTH ORGANIZATIONS

Voluntarism

Early youth work initiatives were entirely dependent on voluntary endeavour. The first boys' clubs and girls' clubs were established in the 1880s and the early uniformed organizations began to emerge. What took place in the period between 1870 and 1910 tended to shape youth work and give it its most distinguished features which were to a large extent accepted and taken over in later years, given state support and then acted as models for youth centres and clubs.

Uniformed Youth Organizations

Uniformed youth organizations – for example, the Boys Brigade and the Girls Guildry, directed at both boys and girls – grew out of the Victorian age. Almost totally British in origin, most early youth groups were concerned with Christianity, patriotism and militarism. They depended on a spirit of altruism and voluntarism. They emphasized a need for social control and moral education. Youth organizations attempted to develop the model adolescent – the organized youth, secure from temptation – while the independent and precocious youth was stigmatized as delinquent (Gillis, 1975: 97).

The Boys Brigade, established in Glasgow in 1883, was one of the most influential of the early uniformed groups. By 1899 there were 66 companies in Ireland with almost 3000 members. These figures had more than doubled by 1941. In 1900 the Girls Guildry was founded. The Boy Scouts was established in 1907 by Baden-Powell; it was non-denominational, encouraged efficiency and controlled independence (Springhall, 1977). The Scout movement encouraged romantic notions of scoutcraft, resourcefulness, chivalry, trustworthiness and courage rather than the drill of the Boys Brigade. The Girl Guides, founded in Britain in 1909, spread to Ireland in 1911. In writing of the Catholic Girl Guides in France, Marguerite de Perroy (1927: 313) gives an indication of the model of adolescent girl desired by the Girl Guide movement:

> A guide is proud of her faith and subordinates all her life to it . . . the fundamental duties of the guide are within her home . . . the practice of the daily good deed undertaken by the guide combats egotism against which all mothers strive – too often in vain – and which often poisons the peace of the home.

Non-uniformed Youth Organizations

Uniformed organizations, because of geographical and monetary constraints did not reach all of Irish youth. To fill this void, rural and other youth movements of mostly Catholic ethos developed in Ireland. Richardson (1886: 158) refers to 'the necessity of a good religious organization to keep all our youth to the Sacraments and to find them Catholic work to do on Sundays and then wherever they go during the week they will not go far stray and must remain good Catholics'. He recommends a good lending library, and penny banks to encourage 'thrift'. The idea behind such clubs was to offer young people a place to spend their leisure time, which had a strong Catholic ethos and would offer close supervision, and thus keep them out of trouble (Kennedy, 1984).

Revolutionary Nationalism

As nationalism became a more dominant force in nineteenth-century Ireland, it was reflected in the development of youth movements. From 1880 to1890, there was what has been described as a great 'cultural revolution' (Tierney, 1978: 88), which emphasized every characteristic that contributed a unique and distinct quality to Irish life. Many new organizations developed, some of which were directed at young people. One such organization, Inghinidhe na hEireann (Daughters of Ireland), was established in 1900 by Maud Gonne. This was a revolutionary nationalist organization which supported Irish nationalism and the 'Irish Irish' movement (a term which referred to cultural nationalism). It was absorbed into Cumann na mBan in 1913. Under this guise it continued its activities through the troubled years of the 1920s and 1930s. The average age of its members was 20 to 25 years (Ward, 1980), which would be the upper end of the age cohort with which youth services were concerned.

A similar group for boys was Na Fianna Éireann (Sons of Ireland), which was an alternative to the Boy Scouts, formed in 1909 by Bulmer

Hobson (a pioneer of the Sinn Féin Movement) and Countess Markievicz (an active Republican and follower of Sinn Féin). Its objective was to establish the independence of Ireland by training young people, both mentally and physically, by teaching scouting and military exercises, Irish history and Irish language, as indicated in their pledge 'I promise to work for the independence of Ireland, never to join England's armed forces, to obey my superior officers' (*Na Fianna Éireann Handbook*). Na Fianna acted as a recruiting ground for the Irish Republican Brotherhood (IRB) which aimed to overthrow British rule in Ireland and to create an Irish Republic. The organization spread rapidly with a membership of over 20,000 by the early 1920s (O'Driscoll, 1964: 32).

Another important uniformed youth organization of this period was the Young Ireland Association, founded in 1932. It evolved from the Army Comrades Association (the Blueshirts). Members of the organization automatically became members of Fine Gael. The movement was organized in local sections, and its members marched in uniform to meetings. Girls' sections ran dances, while boys' sections were more involved in military-style drill. Thornley (1967: 48) refers to 'proud six-year-olds [who] displayed themselves in uniform'. By 1934 the enthusiasm of members was beginning to decline and this was hastened when the government took steps to ban the wearing of uniforms in public.

Other groups less obviously revolutionary in character, but nevertheless with a strong nationalist ideology, included the Gaelic Athletic Association (GAA). Founded by Michael Cusack in 1884, it was not directed solely at young people but by its very nature it attracted young men as members. It acted as a de-Anglicising force, determined to encourage native Irish games enabling people to assert their Irish identity. It banned two groups from its membership: members of the Royal Irish Constabulary (RIC) and those who played English games. The GAA aimed to build a strong active manhood and its training closely mirrored military drill. As Tierney (1978: 91) indicates: 'In 1891 two thousand hurlers formed a guard of honour at Parnell's funeral, shouldering their hurleys like rifles and marching in military formation through Dublin.'

Political youth movements were thus a particular feature of Irish society in the early decades of this century, originating because of the political climate of the time. They were established by people who had very strong ideals – ideals which they were eager to pass on. They wanted to shape young people, to teach them a specific culture and, most importantly, to use the strength of young people for political reasons, to mould their minds, to instil in them a love of Ireland, a love so great that they were prepared to fight for it. These values were passed on because young people were recognized as a strong force, an asset which could be used to fuel the forces which sought freedom. Thus, there were the revolutionary nationalist movements like Na Fianna Éireann and Inghinidhe na hÉireann, a quieter more conservative movement like the Young Ireland Association and a passive, yet clearly anti-British, Gaelic Athletic Association.

Rural Youth Movements

A distinctive feature of the 1920–50 period was a concern with rural youth. In 1931 Muintir na Tíre (People of the Land), was founded by Father John Hayes. Starting as an economic organization, it later changed its focus to community development. Writing in its 1943 official handbook, O'Barry Walsh (Muintir na Tíre, 1943: 21) remarks that: 'it is remarkable that nothing very significant has yet been done in this country for rural youth clubs or a rural youth movement', which he claimed would lead to laying the 'foundation for better farming and better citizenship'.

In 1943 the Hospital Guild (a regional branch based in County Limerick) inaugurated a youth section which adopted as its model the 4H Movement, a rural club movement in the US which acquired its name from its pledge: 'I pledge my head to clearer thinking, my heart to greater loyalty, my hands to larger service, my health to better living for my club, my community and my country'. Its activities of a practical nature were concerned with training for agriculture, including the construction of beehives and the rearing of calves for sale.

Another rural youth group, Macra na Feirme (Sons of the Farms), was established in 1944, concerned again with social, cultural, personal and community development. It was instrumental in setting up the *Farmers' Journal*, Macra na Tuaithe, the Irish Farmers Association (IFA), the Irish Creamery Milk Suppliers Association (ICMSA), the Agricultural Institute and the Farm Apprenticeship Board. At present its membership is in excess of 10,000 and it provides eight programmes: adult education, travel, young farmers, sports and social, competitions, art and culture and rural development (NYCI, 1996).

STATUTORY INVOLVEMENT

The Beginnings

Looking at statutory involvement in youth policy and youth services, responsibility has tended to shift between two government departments (the Department of Education and the Department of Labour before

1998; since 1998 the Department of Education and Science and the Department of Enterprise and Employment), depending on whatever the social emphasis was at a particular time, which was largely dictated by economic factors. In time of economic depression and stagnation, emphasis has tended to be on labour, concern with unemployment and training for young people, preparing them as workers, as potential members of the labour force. At other times, there has been an emphasis on social education, and on young people as potential social citizens.

The state became involved with youth provision for the first time in 1930. In the wake of a very turbulent period in Irish history which included the 1916 Rising, the establishment of Dáil Éireann, the struggle for Independence, the Civil War, and the economic war with Britain, there was an increasing concern with the perceived decline in moral standards. Church and state were increasingly focused on temperance and sexual morality. Whyte (1980) explains this concern as stemming from an increasing rate of illegitimate births, with an upward trend in the 25 years following independence. Church and state became preoccupied with dance halls, cinemas and literature, as is evident from a 1925 statement issued by the Irish Roman Catholic hierarchy: 'The surroundings of the dance hall, withdrawal from the hall for intervals and the back way home have been the destruction of virtue in every part of Ireland' (quoted in Whyte, 1980: 26). Writing in the *Irish Ecclesiastical Record* of 1930, the Rev. R.S. Devane blamed the state for the perceived increasing immorality: 'This country so backward in youth organizations may have done nothing by way of real scientific study of youth' (1930: 23). Considering these viewpoints, it is no surprise that the state became involved in youth provision during the 1930s.

Continuation Education

In 1930 the Vocational Education Act placed responsibility for 'continuation education' in the hands of the Vocational Education Committee (VEC). By continuation education, it meant:

> Education to continue and supplement education provided in secondary schools and includes general and practical training in preparation for employment in trades, manufacture, agriculture, commerce, and other industrial pursuits and also general and practical training for the improvement of persons in the early stages of such employment.

The 1930 Act empowered the VEC to subscribe to any organization which included among its functions, the collection and communication of information with respect to employment of people under 18 years.

This was the first attempt at state involvement in youth provision. However, no direct action was taken until the 1940s after much pressure had been brought to bear on the state to intervene in youth affairs. In 1939, an article in *Hibernia,* referred to the need for youth services:

> Every village should have its hall, the centre of entertainment for the surrounding district. This should be capable of conversion into a theatre, cinema, ceilidhe or lecture hall with all arrangements entrusted to a representative committee who would procure for the people the enter- tainment they need. Cannot the Vocational Education Committee make a contribution? (*Hibernia*, 1939: 8).

The *Annual Report* of the Department of Education for 1941–42 outlined the beginnings of a statutory youth service. The Dublin VEC in 1942 set up youth training schemes and a statutory committee, known as Comhairle le Leas Óige, was established with wide powers. It made provision for the training of youth leaders who were volunteers from the Society of St Vincent de Paul and the Legion of Mary to receive training in physical education, arts and crafts and international youth movements. By 1942 there were 14 such youth centres established, catering for 200 boys. These had a nationalist and Catholic ideology, with Irish language and ballads featuring as an important part of the curriculum together with trades such as boot repair and woodwork. The importance of the role of the chaplain was emphasized. Boys were taught a trade which would be beneficial both socially and individually. Comhairle le Leas Óige also supported clubs and societies which satisfied certain conditions. By 1943 there were 23 affiliated clubs with 1,400 members.

In looking at youth policy in Ireland from a historical perspective it is useful to refer to Kennedy's classification of the Irish Social Services (1975) where she outlines the objectives of social policy in Ireland from the Second World War until the mid-1970s. Kennedy outlines three distinct phases which were closely linked to the prevailing economic climate. Firstly, the 1947–51 period was an expansionary phase during which public social expenditure doubled. The period 1952–62 was a regressive phase when social expenditure fell from 14.9% to 13.7% of GNP. Thirdly, 1963 to 1974 was a period of social as well as economic growth and development. The first phase coincided with the 1951 Commission on Youth Unemployment.

The Commission on Youth Unemployment

In 1943, the Minister for Industry and Commerce, Seán Lemass, set up the Commission on Youth Unemployment during 'The Emergency' or Second World War, when there was high unemployment in Ireland together with high emigration partly as a response to the demand for Irish labour in Britain. The Report was commissioned in the same year in which *The Youth Service after the War* was commissioned in Britain. The British report promoted integration, stating that 'we do not want to see young people segregated . . . from the community as a whole' (Youth Service, 1943). These views were echoed in the Irish report which viewed young people not as a separate entity but as members of the wider economy and encouraged young people to play a useful part in the economic life of the country (Department of Industry and Commerce, 1951: 1). It saw the problem of youth unemployment as a reflection of general unemployment; its remedies included the expansion of industry, raising of the school leaving age, the retirement of over-age workers, the introduction of special schemes designed to provide employment for young people and special measures to deal with 'unoccupied youth'.

The 1951 Report attempted to look at 'the problem of youth' in a methodical way. This included looking at its extent and causes, with a view to submitting recommendations which were 'designed to afford the boys and girls of this country a better opportunity of becoming useful citizens of a Christian state, adequately instructed in the teaching of religion, healthy in mind and body, willing and able to work for their own benefit and that of their country' (Department of Industry and Commerce, 1951: 1), in the context of a Nationalist and Christian ideology. It touched on many issues other than unemployment, such as the physical development, education, training and welfare of young people, and juvenile delinquency.

The report, referring to the link between youth unemployment and adult unemployment, stressed that the solution of one 'is bound up inextricably with the solution of the other' (Department of Industry and Commerce, 1951: 8). The Government was beginning to adopt a Keynesian approach. It was actively encouraging economic growth by establishing two new semi-state bodies, encouraging agricultural development and entering into a new trade agreement with Britain. The Report claimed that 'the backbone of industry is skilled tradesmen' (Department of Industry and Commerce, 1951: 21). It was very much concerned with developing a skilled and healthy workforce (sentiments which are often echoed in Ireland in the 1990s). Thus it emphasised the importance of good physique, health and intelligence. It called for increased thrift, criticising the individual who 'is turning more and more to the State to look after him in illness, unemployment and old age' (Department of Industry and Commerce, 1951: 19). This fell in line with Catholic social teaching and the principle of subsidiarity. Noteworthy is the fact that

Reverend John Charles McQuaid, Archbishop of Dublin, chaired the Committee. The report indicates: 'we deal first with the question of promoting the religious development of young persons and controlling conditions of employment for the purpose of controlling their spiritual development' (Department of Industry and Commerce, 1951: 14).

A notable aspect of the 1951 Report was its attitude towards sex roles. It spoke of the need to train a girl for her natural vocation – 'the care and management of a home and children', while for boys 'manual instruction is an asset'. Louie Bennett, a committee member and trade union activist, refused to sign the document, claiming:

> I am obliged to assert that the report shows little understanding of the modern girl. Nor does it draw attention to the very serious national problem raised by the exodus of girls to seek employment in other countries. It is futile to cling to domestic occupations as the main employment outlet for girls. The home and family rightly form the basis of woman's life and interests, but in the modern world, industry too demands her aid. (Department of Industry and Commerce, 1951: 51)

Expansion

Returning to Kennedy's classification of the Irish social services (1975), she refers to the period between 1963 and 1974, as a period of social as well as economic growth and development. With the 1960s came a period of growth in education. The publication of *Investment in Education* (Department of Education, 1965) in this period ushered in free post-primary education, the establishment of comprehensive and community schools and Regional Technical Colleges (see pp. 75, 94, 96 above). There was a parallel expansion of the youth service. From 1963 onwards the state became increasingly involved in youth provision, in part due to the increasing youth population, but also the publication in Britain of the Albermarle Report (1960), the first of many influential British reports on youth provision.

The early years of the decade were marked by many negotiations between the National Federation of Youth Clubs (NFYC) and the Departments of Education, Justice and Finance. This led to the payment in 1967–68 of the first state grant of £450, which was increased to £2220 a year later and to £7000 by 1970 (Kennedy, 1984). As the state became increasingly involved in financing youth provision it also became involved in youth policy. In 1967 the National Youth Council (NYC) was established with the objectives of bringing together youth-serving organizations and agencies in Ireland, the promotion and advancement of education and learning of young people, and the encouragement and safeguarding of the common interests of young people. The NYC (now NWCI) is still in existence, and at present it is the coordinating body for voluntary youth organizations and services in Ireland and claims to represent over half a million young people.

A National Youth Policy

In the 1970s, the state became more involved in formulating youth policy. A series of youth policy documents made many recommendations which for the most part were never implemented. In 1974, John Bruton, TD, Parliamentary Secretary to the Minister for Education, initiated a study entitled *The Development of Youth Work Services*, which was the first in a series of such reports to be written over the following twenty years. It encouraged increased VEC involvement, it acknowledged the importance of monitoring and evaluation and called for the grant aid scheme to be expanded and encouraged local agency networking.

In 1977, another report, *A Policy for Youth and Sport*, was published by the Department of Education. It acknowledged that while youth work alone could not remedy the physical and economic causes of social deprivation, it could nevertheless uncover the potential of young people and encourage optimism and ambition, while at the same time providing skills for 'commercial self-help and self-government'. It claimed 'the fulfilment of five objectives of education, recreation, counselling, voluntary service and community development has significance' (Department of Education, 1977: 41) for the development of youth services.

In 1978, a National Youth Council (NYC) report, *A Policy on Youth Work Services*, looked at the educational contribution of youth work, the role of professional youth workers, statutory funding, evaluation and assessment, the role of VECs, and training for full-time workers – issues which are still being addressed twenty years later (Department of Education, 1995). In the following year, a second document entitled *The Development of Youth Work Services* was commissioned by James Tunney, TD, Minister of State at the Department of Education. It dealt with youth work and the needs of young people and addressed such issues as the nature and effectiveness of youth programmes, the voluntary sector, youth unemployment, the statutory sector, particularly, the role of the Department of Education.

The *Task Force Report on Child Care Services* (Department of Health, 1980) claimed there was a lack of coordination of services and recommended that responsibility for young people should be handed to the Department of Health as part of the childcare system. It recommended the establishment of Neighbourhood Youth Projects for the 12–16 year age group. These were set up on a pilot scheme, stressing the importance of family and community relationships and involvement, focusing on young people's needs in the context of their age, friendships, neighbourhood groups and concentrating on their interests and skills. This report recognized the stage of youth as being the last opportunity for constructive education (a view that has since been questioned by the development of adult education and the philosophy of life-long learning). The Task Force also recommended the development of Youth Encounter Projects to provide an alternative educational opportunity for 10–15 year olds who might otherwise face institutionalization.

The National Youth Policy Committee (Costello Committee)

Despite the recommendation that responsibility for youth provision be handed over to the Department of Health, three years later it was in fact handed over to the Department of Labour perhaps reflecting the unemployment crisis of the period. In that year, the Youth Policy Committee was officially launched by Dr Garret FitzGerald and George Bermingham, Minister of State for Youth Affairs, and was chaired by Justice Declan Costello. It was asked to draw up policy recommendations. The launch coincided with the publication of a discussion document which was, in the words of George Bermingham, 'a major stimulant for a major Irish debate on the role of young people in modern Irish Society and on the problems and challenges which they face'(government statement on the launching of the Youth Policy Committee, September 1983). Entitled *Shaping the Future: Towards a National Youth Policy, A Discussion Document* (Department of Labour, 1983), it addressed such issues as participation, transition from school to work, disadvantaged young people and the development of youth organizations.

The Report of the Costello Committee (Department of Labour, 1984) was particularly significant as, in recommending that a National Youth Service be established, it was the first time that a need for such a service was officially recognized in Ireland. It envisaged a Youth Service that would be distinct and independent, while at the same time having links with other services for youth. The target group for the youth service would be 12–21 years, with priority given to the older teenage group and with special services for those with particular needs. It recognized the need for training, including in-service training, and it recommended that a Department of Youth and Community Studies should be developed within a third-level institution. However it also stated that it did not recognize the need for full-time professional training. This would imply that the Committee did not view youth workers as professionals to the same extent as, for example, teachers. It also recommended the establishment of a National Advisory Committee to advise the Minister generally on youth affairs.

In Partnership with Youth was the Government's response published in December 1985. It pledged to make funds available for the establishment of Local Youth Service Boards, which would include funding and staffing. The Costello Committee had made explicit the philosophy which informed its recommendations. In formulating a youth policy the committee sought to address the question of what kind of society was desired, acknowledging that a youth policy would inevitably reflect this vision. It aimed to enable all young people to become 'self-reliant, responsible and active participants in society' (government statement on the launching of the Youth Policy Committee, September 1983). It argued that this would involve a democratic philosophy which it viewed as:

> The best ideal for government . . . it most assuredly promotes the moral, social economic, political, cultural and intellectual development of the people and it permits the maximum freedom consistent with social order. It should also inculcate a spirit of mutual cooperation, informed by a strong sense of social justice. To approach this ideal the concept of the 'active' citizen of participation in social, and political life of the growth of a responsible public spirit, as tending to elevate the life of the community as a whole, is of fundamental importance (Department of Labour, 1984: 15).

At a time when 48 per cent of the country's population was aged under 25 years, it identified the special needs of youth with reference to the transition to adult and working life and the specific needs of disadvantaged youth (Kennedy, 1987).

Jenkinson (1997) indicates how, in 1987, a new Fianna Fáil government recommended a re-examination of youth policy. This was presented as part of the green paper on education, *Education for a Changing World* (Department of Education, 1992), which examined Irish education as a whole (see p. 72 above). In the following year, 1993, a response to the green paper, *Report of the Consultative Groups on the Development of Youth Work,* was prepared by a committee representing youth work agencies. It made recommendations on issues central to future development of a youth policy. These were incorporated two years later into the white paper on education, *Charting our Education Future,* (Department of Education, 1995) which included among its recommendations:

• The establishment of Local Education Boards with statutory responsibility for youth work services and policy.

- The establishment of a single body to represent all voluntary youth organizations.

- The establishment of a National Youth Advisory Committee.

- A system of monitoring and evaluating youth services, as well as research.

- A Youth Service Act.

There was much hope by youth workers that these long-awaited recommendations would be implemented, but once again there was a change of government and the plans were shelved (for a critique of *Charting our Education Future* see National Youth Federation, 1995)

Irish Youth Policy: The Current Situation

Responsibility for youth provision now falls to the Youth Affairs Section of the Department of Education and Science. It is viewed as an educational process, but a less formal one perhaps than the structured school system. The latest developments in Irish youth policy under the Fianna Fáil/ Progressive Democrats coalition government are twofold. First of all, the Youth Act is in preparation. Secondly, on 21 January 1998, the Taoiseach Mr Bertie Ahern announced that the government had decided on a Programme for Young People at Risk. This is an innovative initiative in terms of youth policy as it is a coordinated response to meeting the needs of young people in disadvantaged areas, four of which are to be piloted initially. Of these four, three are in Dublin (the Northeast Inner City, the Canal Communities of St Michael's Estate, St Teresa's Gardens, Dolphin House and Fatima Mansions, and Jobstown) and one in Togher, Cork. There is to be a coordinated approach to meeting the needs of young people in disadvantaged areas. These have been identified by the Cabinet Committee on Social Inclusion as a need for measures to counter early school leaving, and the provision of more intensive support for children at risk and their families. A priority is a more focused and coordinated response by the statutory bodies to the needs of those most at risk. Central to this programme is a Young People's Facilities and Services Fund of £30 million, to be provided over a three-year period to support a variety of capital and non–capital projects. At least £20m will be targeted at those areas particularly affected by the heroin problem. The initial amount of £1.25m which had been allocated in the 1997–98 budget has been increased to £7.5m, in addition to amounts of £10m to implement the plans of the Local Drugs Task Forces and the £10m provided for the Youth Services. The allocations from the Young People's Services and Facilities Fund will be made by the Cabinet Committee on Social Inclusion which is chaired by the Taoiseach. The Cabinet Committee consists of the Tánaiste and the Ministers for Finance, Health and Children, Environment and Local Government, Justice, Equality and Law Reform, Education and Science, Social Community and Family Affairs, Tourism, Sport and Recreation and the Ministers for State, Chris Flood and Frank Fahey, and so is an attempt at a coordinated response to meeting the needs of young people in disadvantaged areas. Adams (1998: 3) describes the evolution of the Young People's Facilities and Services Fund stating: 'Like all things in life, the £30m fund did not come easy'.

Youth policy is not solely involved with young people in disadvantaged areas, therefore when looking at youth policy in the 1990s it is helpful to refer to Staunton's (1997) model of youth work in Ireland. While it might be argued that Staunton's model is itself conservative in that it does not recognise the very important role of youth organisations in political activism, it nevertheless offers some analysis of the shape of youth services in Ireland. According to Staunton there are four strands: the youth club model, youth information services model, special projects for youth at risk model and the partnership model.

The Youth Club Model

Staunton (1997: 59) reminds us that this is perhaps the oldest form of youth provision. It was shown earlier in this chapter how this model of youth work originated in Victorian Britain in an attempt to offer adolescents a place to spend their leisure time in a safe, controlled environment. Staunton suggest this model can be identified as having five elements: social dimension, activities, community involvement, extending horizons and participation. First of all, there is the social dimension which involves the provision of an informal setting where young people can socialize with the support of adult leaders. This could take the form of a youth centre providing such drop-in facilities as a coffee bar, pool table and activities such as sports, cookery or arts and crafts. This again gives the young person the opportunity to socialize while developing and practising new skills. Community involvement is included, extending horizons and participation by means of a diverse range of activities which can include involvement in the running of community activities, summer play-schemes, exchange visits and participating in communities and consultative groups. Staunton concludes that the youth club model caters primarily for younger adolescents who have limited access to other facilities and resources. He argues that these activity-based programmes 'are limited in what the model seeks to achieve in terms of personal and social development. There is a quantum leap from these recreational activities to developmental youth work' (Staunton, 1997: 60).

Youth Information Services Model

Staunton (1997) indicates how this model developed out of extra funding made available as a result of the establishment of the Disadvantaged Youth Work Scheme in the wake of the 1985 *In Partnership with Youth* document. Youth Information Centres, which are nationwide, provide information to young people on a wide range of services and issues. Staunton (1997: 61) recognizes six 'helping strategies' which are part of the practice in these centres. These are giving advice, information, direct action, coaching, systems change and counselling. Looking at some of the difficulties associated with these centres, Staunton indicates there is a lack of funding and staff, with an over-reliance in some centres on volunteers.

Special Projects for Youth at Risk

Almost half of the annual youth work budget is spent on projects targeting disadvantaged youth. Financed from the National Lottery, out-of-school projects are funded for young people who are viewed as particularly disadvantaged. There are approximately 200 such projects in Ireland funded through voluntary organizations, VECs and Health Boards (Staunton, 1997).

The Partnership Model

Historically, development work in Ireland has both an urban and a rural base. In urban areas it evolved through the voluntary endeavours of such groups as tenants' organisations, the labour movement and the women's movement and in rural areas through such groups as Muintir na Tíre. In the 1980s, as unemployment increased in Ireland the state became more involved at local level through the provision of temporary training and employment schemes. In the 1990s development work in Ireland occurs within the context of social partnership at both a national and a local level.

Partnership at National Level

At a national level there has been a series of national agreements in the last decade between the social partners. In the ten-year period between

1987 and 1997, four successive national programmes were developed between government and the social partners: the Programme for National Recovery (PNR), the Programme for Economic and Social Progress (PESP), the Programme for Competitiveness and Work (PCW) and Partnership 2000. These Programmes were based on a belief that there was a need for economic stability, moderate economic growth and structural reform. The traditional social partners were the government, the trade unions, business interests and the farming organisations. Since 1993 the National Economic and Social Forum (NESF) has represented the interests of the Third Strand – those previously marginalized, including the community and voluntary sectors. In the Partnership 2000 talks (1996), the Third Strand participated as a social partner for the first time in the guise of a community platform.

The National Youth Council of Ireland (NYCI) as a Social Partner

The National Youth Council of Ireland (NYCI) is represented as a social partner. In this capacity it has participated in negotiations. The NYCI structure consists of a 'Board' and two standing conferences, consisting of representatives from member organisations. The main decision-making arm is the NYCI Assembly, held annually. The Council Assembly determines and ratifies all policy. It reviews all work of the previous year and plans for the future. There are two standing conferences: one on Youth Services, which provides a forum for youth organisations to discuss issues such as funding, training, programme development and national youth policy, and a second one, the standing conference on Youth Affairs, which addressees issues of concern to young people, for example unemployment. The NYCI represents youth interests at European level through the European Youth Forum. It is represented on the National Economic and Social Council (NESC), the National Economic and Social Forum (NESF) and FÁS. It is concerned with lobbying, information dissemination, the press, and representation on outside organisations and broad areas of concern to young people, unemployment, civil and political rights and education. It receives its core funding from the Department of Education and Science through the Youth Affairs Section. It also receives fees from its 40 members and works in partnership with other agencies on certain projects. These include the Arts Council, the Health Promotion Unit and the National Committee for Development Education. It receives EU funding and private sponsorship.

Partnership at Local Level

At a local level, the development of area-based partnerships has institutionalized the partnership approach. For a critical evaluation of partnership process as it affects youth organisations see Treacy (1998). In some areas youth services are a part of this process. The National Development Plan 1994–99 contains a section on local development which recommends that this model of working be introduced on a wider scale throughout the country. There are now 39 such designated areas. Area Development Management, Ltd (ADM) is responsible for the management of the area-based strategy. The National Youth Federation is one of fifteen organizations selected by ADM to support the local partnership process. A 1997 Report prepared by the NYF, with the support of ADM Ltd, *Partnership and Youth: Report on the Linkages between Partnership Companies and Local Youth Services*, outlines the specifics of what such partnership entails (National Youth Federation, 1997).

The National Anti Poverty Strategy

The National Anti-Poverty Strategy of 1997 (NAPS) is an important part of the Partnership 2000 (1996) agreement between the social partners. The Strategy which has been under preparation since 1995 has involved consultation with those experiencing poverty and social exclusion together with their representative organisations. NAPS argues for a local development programme to bring about social and economic development at local level and to enable communities to be centrally involved in that development. This is to be done through partnership and selected community groups which depending on the ethos of the particular partnership will incorporate youth groups to varying degrees.

CONCLUSION

Looking at the development of youth work services and policy in Ireland, what emerges is a picture of services developing over the last century which were very much shaped by the context from which they emerged. The spirit of voluntarism has always been, and still is, strong. Statutory intervention, since its beginnings in 1930, has tended more towards rhetoric than action with a series of reports stretching from the mid-1970s to the mid-1990s. As the millennium approaches, there would appear to be some commitment by government to a coordinated approach to meeting the needs of those young people who are most at risk in society. Jenkinson (1997: 42) summarizes five factors particularly pertinent to youth work in the Ireland of the 1990s. These are the principle of voluntarism, development in thinking regarding the aims and purposes of youth work, lack of unity between youth organizations, lack of security, and uncertainty in relation to funding. Perhaps some of these issues could be taken up by the body of professional youth workers which has emerged in Ireland in recent years (National Youth Federation, 1998). Treacy, Director of the City of Dublin Youth Services Board, argues 'if we believe in our own rhetoric of empowerment, of providing real alternatives to an educational system that has failed significant numbers of young people then we must engage in a process of critical reflection as a sector. We must begin again to become actively involved in strategic thinking and policy formation at a national level' (1998: 4).

CHRONOLOGY OF DEVELOPMENTS OF YOUTH WORK SERVICES AND POLICY IN IRELAND

1880s to 1910	The early uniformed and non uniformed organizations emerged
1930	Vocational Education Act
1942	Comhairle le Leas Oige was established
1943	Commission on Youth Unemployment established
1951	*Report of Commission on Youth Unemployment*
1967	National Youth Council established
1974	*Development of Youth Work Services*
1977	*A Policy on Youth and Sport*
1978	*A Policy on Youth Work Services*
1980	*The Development of Youth Work Services*
1980	*Task Force Report on Childcare Services*
1984	*Shaping the Future*
1985	Costello Committee
1985	*In Partnership with Youth*
1992	*Education for a Changing World*
1993	*Report of the Consultative Group on the Development of Youth Work*
1995	White Paper on Education *Charting our Education Future*
1997	Youth Work Bill
1998	Programme for Young People at Risk

NOTE

1 The author wishes to thank Elizabeth Kiely, Department of Applied Social Studies, University College Cork, for commenting on an earlier draft of this chapter.

RECOMMENDED READING

Books

Burgess, P. (ed.) (1977) *Youth and Community Work*. Cork: UCC Centre for Adult and Continuing Education.

Evans, K. and I.G. Hasffenden (eds) (1991*) Education for Young Adults, International Perspectives*. London: Routledge.

Forde, W. (1995) *Growing Up in Ireland: The Development of Irish Youth Services*. Wexford: Cara Publications.

National Youth Council of Ireland (1996*) The State of Youth Report: Putting Youth on the Agenda*. Dublin: NYCI.

National Youth Federation (1998) Directory of Youth and Community work Courses 1998/1999. Dublin: NYF.

O'Connor, P. (1998) 'Young Women: Just Other Young People' in *Emerging Voices: Women in Contemporary Irish Society*. Dublin: IPA.

Roche J. and S. Tucker (eds) (1997) *Youth in Society*. London: Sage.

Journals

Irish Youth Work Scene: A Journal for Youth Workers, published by the National Federation of Youth Clubs

Youth and Policy, Journal of Critical Analysis. London: Sage.

REFERENCES

Adams J. (1998) '£30 Million Young People's Facilities and Services Fund – How it was Won/ How it will be Used', *Irish Youth Work Scene*, Dublin: NYF.

Albemarle Report (1960) *The Youth Service in England and Wales*. London: HMSO.

Davies' B. and A. Gibson (1967) *The Social Education of the Adolescent*. London: University of London Press.

De Perroy, M. (1927) 'Catholic Girl Guides in France', *Irish Monthly*, ILV: 313 (translated by Bowers).

Department of Education (1941–42) *Annual Report*. Dublin: Stationery Office.

Department of Education (1943) *Annual Report*. Dublin: Stationery Office.

Department of Education (1965) *Investment in Education*. Dublin: Stationery Office.

Department of Education (1974), *The Development of Youth Work Services*. Dublin: Stationery Office.

Department of Education (1977) *A Policy for Youth and Sport*. Dublin: Stationery Office.

Department of Education (1978) *The Development of Youth Work Services*. Dublin: Stationery Office.

Department of Education (1992) *Education for a Changing World*, Green Paper on Education. Dublin: Stationery Office.

Department of Education (1995) *Charting Our Education Future*, White Paper on Education (April). Dublin: Stationery Office.

Department of Education (1996) *Information Note on Youth Services Bill*, Youth Affairs Section.

Department of Education Consultative Group (1993*) Report of the Consultative Group on the Development of Youth Work*. Dublin: SNSL.

Department of Health (1980), *Task Force Report on Child Care Services*, Dublin.

Department of Industry and Commerce (1951), *Commission on Youth Unemployment*, Dublin.

Department of Labour (1983) *Shaping the Future – Towards a National Youth Policy*, Dublin.

Department of Labour (1984) *National Youth Policy Committee Final Report*

Devane, R.S. (1930) *Irish Ecclesiastical Record*, 36 (5th Series, July–December).

Dublin Stationery Office (1985) *In Partnership with Youth: The National Youth Policy* laid before the House of the Oireachtas, December.

Gillis, J.R. (1975)'The Evolution of Juvenile Delinquency in England 1890–1914', *Past and Present,* 67: 97.

Government Renewal (1994) Policy Document (Dublin: Stationery Office:) Stationery Office.

Hibernia (1939) III (7).

Hurley, L. (1992) *The Historical Development of Irish Youth Work*, Youth Work Research Series: No.1. Dublin: Irish Youth Work Centre.

In Partnership with Youth: The National Youth Policy, (1985) Dublin: Stationery Office.

Jenkinson, H. (1997) 'History of Youth Work', pp. 35–43 in P. Burgess (ed.), *Youth and Community Work*, Cork: UCC Centre for Adult and Continuing Education.

Kennedy, F. (1975) *Public Social Expenditure in Ireland,* Dublin: Economic and Social Research Institute.

Kennedy, P. (1984) 'The Development of Youth Work Services and Policy in Ireland', Unpublished MSocSc thesis, University College Cork.

Kennedy, P. (1987) 'The Historical Development of Irish Youth Policy', *Youth and Policy: The Journal of Critical Analysis*, 21: 7–12.

Kiely, E. (1997) 'Theory and Values of Youth Work', pp. 44–54 in P. Burgess (ed.), *Youth and Community Work.* Cork: UCC Centre for Adult and Continuing Education.

Milson, F. (1970) *Youth Work in the 1970s*. London: Routledge & Kegan Paul.

Muintir na Tíre. (1943) *Official Handbook.*

Na Fianna Handbook. Date and publisher unknown.

National Youth Council (1978) *A Policy on Youth Work Services.* Dublin: National Youth Council.

National Youth Council (1980) *The Development of Youth Work Services,* Dublin: National Youth Council.

National Youth Council of Ireland (NYCI) (1996) *Youth in Focus, a Comprehensive Overview of the National Youth Council of Ireland,* Dublin: National Youth Council of Ireland.

National Youth Federation (1995) *Irish Youth Work Scene*, NYF, Issue 13.

National Youth Federation (1997) *Partnership and Youth ;Report on the linkages between partnership companies and local Youth Services*, Dublin: National Youth Federation.

O'Driscoll R. (1964) *The Young Guard of Eireann*. Poblacht na hEireann.

Partnership 2000 for Inclusion, Employment and Competitiveness (1996) Dublin: Stationery Office.

Report of the Consultative Group on the Development of Youth Work (November 1993) Dublin: Stationery Office.

Richardson, R. (1886) 'On the Best Means of Saving Youth When They Leave School Especially in Large Towns', *Irish Ecclesiastical Record*: 158–60.

Springhall, J (1977) *Youth, Empire and Society*. London: Croom Helm.

Staunton, D. (1997) 'Models of Youth Work', pp. 55–65 in P. Burgess (ed.), *Youth and Community Work*. Cork: UCC Centre for Adult and Continuing Education.

Thornley, D. (1967) 'The Blueshirts, from the Years of the Great Test 1926–1939', in F. MacManus (ed.), *The Thomas Davis Lectures*. Cork: Mercier Press.

Tierney, M (1978) *Modern Ireland Since 1850*. Dublin: Gill & Macmillan.

Tobias, J.J. (1967) *Crime and Industrial Society in the Nineteenth Century*. London: Batesford.

Treacy, D. (1998) 'Time to Choose Between Partitionism and Partnership', *Irish Youth Work Scene: A Journal for Youth Workers*, 22: 3–4.

Vocational Education Act, (1930). Dublin.

Ward, M. (1980) 'Marginality and Militancy, Cumann na mBan', in A. Morgan and B. Purdie (eds), *Ireland, Divided Nation, Divided Class*. London: Ink Links.

Whyte, J (1980) *Church and State in Modern Ireland, 1923–1979*. Dublin: Gill & Macmillan.

Youth Service after the War (1943) London: HMSO.

10

Social Policy and Older People in Ireland

Anne O'Loughlin

INTRODUCTION

Directing policy towards older people carries with it the risk of perceiving them as a single population. Elderly people have always been an important group in relation to social policy. Current ideas about ageing and old age have a long history. The conception and measurement of age and old age in the past have a close connection to the form of social oppression we now know as ageism (Bytheway, 1995). Social policy making is often based, at least in part, on a set of assumptions and attitudes, which can influence and shape older people's lives. A more critical appreciation of the role of the social policies in this chapter requires consideration of the significance of old age in the past, the social and personal process of ageing and the potential power of ageism.

Old Age in History

A degree of scepticism is necessary when looking at historical accounts of old age, as they are coloured by the authors' experiences of the ageism of their own society, and an uncritical adoption of popular assumptions (Bytheway, 1995: 17). De Beauvoir (1977: 44–99) reviewed the ethnological data and found that few made any organized synthesis of their observations on the subject of old age. While urging caution against oversimplification, the survey highlighted the link between the condition of the aged and their social context in primitive societies. The picture of the condition of old people in history is 'blurred, uncertain and contradictory' (De Beauvoir, 1977: 99). In particular, the history of the aged poor is passed over. In so far as old age is revealed, it refers to the privileged classes and to the personal experiences of men. The attitudes and images of historical societies towards older people give little support to the images of a 'golden age' of ageing, whether the focus is classical

Rome (Haynes, 1963), pre-industrial Britain (Thomas, 1976) or the United States (Haber, 1983).

AGEISM

Bytheway (1995) reviews the complex phenomenon of ageism. This concept was introduced in the 1960s through Butler (1975) and gradually became established in the popular consciousness with a number of other publications (Hendricks and Hendricks, 1977; Comfort, 1977). The 'working definition' of Bytheway and Johnson (1990, cited in Bytheway, 1995: 14) is a useful framework for this chapter:

- Ageism is a set of beliefs originating in the biological variation between people and relating to the ageing process.

- It is in the actions of corporate bodies, what is said and done by their representatives, and the resulting views that are held by ordinary ageing people, that ageism is made manifest.

In consequence of this, it follows that:

- Ageism generates and reinforces a fear and denigration of the ageing process and stereotyping assumptions regarding competence and the need for protection.

- In particular, ageism legitimates the use of chronological age to mark out classes of people who are systematically denied resources and opportunities that others enjoy, and who suffer the consequences of such denigration, ranging from well-meaning patronage to unambiguous vilification.

In this definition the emphasis is on expanding the popular conception of ageism as discrimination against older people to include the fact that young people can also suffer from ageist prejudice. It also highlights that ageism puts forward a biological basis for discrimination with the dangers of the ultimate oppression of euthanasia and 'chronological cleansing' (Bytheway, 1995: 27). Ageism is more than individual prejudice. The idea of old age is a powerful element in making distinctions and imposing expectations upon individuals in those categories. Ageism can be manifest in individual actions but organizations and institutions can also be intrinsically ageist.

A focus on social policy and older people must also take into account the role of images. Featherstone and Hepworth (1990: 250–75) highlight the tension between the ways of seeing and defining ageing which are in public circulation and 'the private and unspoken thoughts of individuals'.

Images of ageing help to simplify and categorize but they do not do justice to the highly individual process of ageing. The tension between social categories and the actual experience of ageing is an increasingly important issue for policy makers.

> Ageing, then, is not reducible to biological processes of physical decline which take place in some vacuum sealed off from social life, but is shaped or constructed in terms of the symbolic imagery available to us at any given time (Featherstone and Hepworth, 1990: 253).

There are many ways in which ageism is evident and how 'important and pervasive age has become in the relationship between the individual and society' should be recognized (Bytheway, 1995: 8). There is a certain lack of understanding about the status of older people in Irish society. Some recent insights into the concept of ageism have implications for policy making. Progress may be achieved by a broader conception of age discrimination, which considers its harmful consequences for older people, for children and young people. The characterization of childhood as a time of 'innocence' and old age as a time of 'serenity' are both manifestations of an ageist ideology (Bytheway, 1995; Thompson, 1997: 59–65). Acknowledging the commonalities across forms of age discrimination and developing links between those who are attempting to combat it are possible ways forward.

HISTORICAL OVERVIEW

Historically there are records of a form of hospital service in Ireland dating as far back as 300 BC with the foundation of *Broin Berg* or the 'house of sorrow' near Armagh. Under Brehon Law the ruler of every territory had to provide hospital facilities known as briugu. A fragmentary text in early Irish law, *Do brethaib gaire* (appendix 1, Nr 28) deals with the kin's obligation to care for its members who were insane, aged or suffering from physical disability (Kelly, 1988; O'Connor 1995). The advent of Christianity in the late fourth and early fifth centuries led to the development and expansion of the monasteries, which provided care for the sick, the poor and the aged. The suppression of the monasteries which began with the Reformation in 1535 'meant that the poor, the sick and the elderly had now no avenue of escape from the harsh reality of deprivation' (O'Connor, 1995: 25). The Poor Relief Act of 1601 instituted England's first statutory social service. It did not extend to Ireland. The rapidly growing population in Ireland compounded the widespread poverty. In 1703 the Irish Parliament enacted legislation for the building of a 'House of Industry' in Dublin. The old and infirm were among those provided for but the record of provision was very limited. The care of older people who were mentally ill was not considered before the eighteenth century. The Dublin House of Industry, set up in 1773 for the shelter of the poor, found that it soon had to contend also with the mentally ill. The conditions of overcrowding, with the ill treatment of patients and the lack of segregation have been graphically described (Reynolds, 1992: 9–14). A separate institution named the Richmond Lunatic Asylum was officially opened in 1815. However the care of the aged and infirm continued at the House of Industry, with their numbers reaching 610 out of 2,900 in 1817 (Reynolds, 1992: 32). Squalid conditions endured by old and incontinent patients in the Richmond Asylum were also evident in 1830 (Reynolds 1992: 44).

The existence of the lunatic asylums, voluntary and state aided hospitals, workhouses and houses of industry, voluntary dispensaries and relief-giving charities and public works schemes provided the background into which the Irish Poor Law of 1838 was introduced. These services 'made no real impression on Ireland's vast social problems in the early nineteenth century' (Burke, 1987: 14). O'Connor describes older people as being totally reliant on charity in the absence of legal provision (1995: 47). After numerous Royal Commissions and special Committees of Enquiry set up to report on conditions of the poor in Ireland between 1800 and 1840, the Act of 1838 for the more Effectual Relief of the Destitute Poor in Ireland, passed into law. The workhouse was a central feature of poor law relief and included among its inmates 'such destitute poor persons as by reason of old age, infirmity or defect may be unable to support themselves' (O'Connor, 1995: 69). They were accommodated in segregated quarters; workhouse plans show wards for aged women and aged men on opposite sides of the entrance block. The Great Famine in 1845 resulted in the system of workhouses being completely overwhelmed leading to appalling conditions and high mortality. From the end of the Famine, conditions began to improve. The Poor Relief (Ireland) Act 1862 led to the appointment of the Sisters of Mercy as qualified nurses and the improvement of the care of the sick. The workhouse became more and more an institution for the old and sick. However, for many older people the stigma still remains, the memory of the workhouse deep in folk consciousness (O'Connor, 1995: 181).

The formation of the Irish Workhouse Association in 1896 was a sign of increasing public awareness of the need for reform. The Commissions on Poor Law Reform of 1903 and 1909 recommended that the infirm and the aged be removed from workhouses and placed in separate institutions. These recommendations were not implemented, and in 1921 there were still 127 workhouses in Ireland. A Commission on Poor

Relief in 1927 recommended that the County Homes, which were converted workhouses, be reserved for the aged and infirm poor and chronic invalids. In 1949 an Inter-Departmental Committee recommended the reconstruction of the County Homes to house the aged and chronic sick (*Report of Inter-Departmental Committee*, 1949). A White Paper issued in 1951 accepted these recommendations and grant-aided the work. This continued until the *Report of an Inter-Departmental Committee on the Care of the Aged* reported to the Minister for Health in 1968. This report has been described as 'a major catalyst for change' (Ruddle et al., 1997: 38).

Before moving on to the 1968 Report, a number of significant developments will be discussed. The establishment of a structured system of social welfare payments began in 1847 when 'outdoor' relief was authorized for Ireland. This scheme was abolished by the establishment of a national means-tested supplementary welfare allowance scheme in 1975, which was generally applied to older people for additional payments for rent, heating, diet etc. The non-contributory old age pension was introduced in 1908 and it established 'for the first time in the British Isles the important principle of regular cash payments being made available to a specified group of citizens from monies provided by parliament' (Carney, 1985: 486). This was a highly controversial scheme initially that gradually became a central component of government income maintenance strategies. In the early years of the Irish social welfare system, means-tested payments dominated. The establishment of the Department of Social Welfare in 1947 and the passing of the Social Welfare Act 1952 led to expansion of the social insurance scheme. A contributory old age pension was introduced in 1961 and pension age was reduced from 70 to 66 by 1977. A retirement pension at age 65 began in 1970. The structure and development of social welfare payments for care in Ireland will be addressed later in this chapter (pp. 231–2). These payments developed in the context of a growing emphasis on community care in the 1960s which is made evident by the Inter-Departmental Report on the Care of the Aged (*Report of an Inter-Departmental Committee*, 1968).

The Care of the Aged Report

An Inter-Departmental Committee was appointed in 1965 by the Minister for Health in consultation with the Ministers for Local Government and Social Welfare to 'examine and report on the general problem of the care of the aged and to make recommendations regarding the improvement and extension of services' (*Report of an Inter-Departmental*

Committee, 1968: 22). The major shift in policy evident in this report is outlined in the recommendations of the committee 'based on the belief that it is better, and probably much cheaper, to help the aged to live in the community than to provide for them in hospitals or other institutions' (*Report of an Inter-Departmental Committee*, 1968: 13). The policy is outlined in the aims of services as follows:

(*a*) to enable the aged who can do so to continue to live in their own homes;

(*b*) to enable the aged who cannot live in their own homes to live in other similar accommodation;

(*c*) to provide substitutes for normal homes for those who cannot be dealt with as at (*a*) and (*b*);

(*d*) to provide hospital services for those who cannot be dealt with as at (*a*), (*b*) or (*c*)

(*Report of an Inter-Departmental Committee*, 1968: 49)

To achieve these aims, the Committee recommended planning, coordination and the integration of housing services, schemes of financial assistance and health services. Emphasis was placed on the concept of 'partnership', between the family and public and voluntary organizations. In total, the Care of the Aged Report made 94 recommendations. The Report has been described as having 'dominated policy towards services for the elderly' for twenty years after its publication (*Working Party*, 1988: 15). Improvements in income maintenance schemes resulted in a general improvement in the income position of older people with a minority of older people still remaining economically vulnerable – those dependent on social welfare pensions and those living alone (Blackwell, 1984). Some significant developments took place in housing policy. The majority of sheltered housing schemes dated from the mid-1970s. A later research study on the role of sheltered housing identified wide regional variation and inadequacy of provision (O'Connor et al., 1989). Housing policy for the elderly also focused on home improvement schemes for the adaptation and repair of existing dwellings. The recommendations of the Care of the Aged Report (*Report*, 1968) in relation to community services covered a broad range including the provision of domiciliary nursing, medical care, specialist advice, provision of appliances, ophthalmic services, dental services, paramedical and social work services, home helps, home visiting and meals. In reviewing the progress of imple- menting these recommendations, the Working Party on Services for the Elderly established in 1986 noted 'substantial progress' and 'a rapid expansion in health services' (Working Party, 1988: 21). However 'shortcomings in services' and 'many gaps in service provision' were also documented. Direct quotation from this Report provides a sobering reflection on social policy in relation to older people up to 1988.

> It is clear to us that housing, health and welfare services are not sufficiently targeted at assisting the most vulnerable elderly people. Existing domiciliary health and welfare services are inadequate in most parts of the country to maintain the elderly at home when ill or infirm. Persons caring for their elderly relatives at home receive insufficient support from statutory bodies. The shortcomings in domiciliary support services lead to a continuing bias towards long term institutional care. This is aggravated by the absence of adequate assessment and rehabilitation facilities. There is a major gap in the provision of facilities for the demented elderly, a need to which little attention has been given up to now. Where the administration of services is concerned, there is a lack of coordination. The care of the elderly in the professional training courses is accorded a low priority.
>
> (Working Party, 1988: 28)

CURRENT POLICY

The Working Party on Services for the Elderly was appointed by the Minister for Health in 1986. Acknowledging that they were standing 'on the shoulders of the Care of the Aged Report' of twenty years earlier (Working Party, 1988: 26), the committee published *The Years Ahead – A Policy for the Elderly*. This Report is the basis of official policy for older people in Ireland. Its terms of reference, clearly related to the policy of the Care of the Aged Report, accepted that the aims of services for the elderly were:

(*a*) to enable the elderly person to live at home, where possible, at an optimum level of health and independence;

(*b*) to enable those who cannot live at home to receive treatment, rehabilitation and care in accommodation and in an environment as near as possible to home.

(Working Party, 1988: ix)

Detailed recommendations were made in relation to proposals for an appropriate framework for coordination of services: the development and expansion of community care services; the provision of support, information and advice for carers; improving care of older people in general hospitals; the development of community hospitals; care of elderly mentally infirm; development of the psychiatry of old age; housing policy; health promotion and education.

The Care of the Aged Report (*Report*, 1968) emphasized the encouragement of voluntary activity in the provision of services, viewing their role as 'complementary' to the health authorities (Par. 6.24). The voluntary nature of the work was heavily emphasized and seen to represent a considerable saving to the public authorities (Par. 6.24). The setting up of Social Service Councils and a National Council for the Aged was proposed to coordinate activities at local and national level, motivated by the view that 'the field of voluntary effort is almost unlimited' (Par 6.24). The stimulation provided by the Care of the Aged Report was further enhanced by the Health Act, 1970, which established health boards and a structure for community care (Department of Health, 1970). The Health Act, 1953, contributed to the current operation of voluntary bodies by the power given in Section 65 to 'give assistance' to any organization 'which provides or proposes to provide a service similar or ancillary to a service which the health authority may provide' (Department of Health, 1953). *The Years Ahead* (1988) proposed that voluntary organizations are 'major partners' along with 'families' and 'professionals working for statutory agencies'. The recommendations in *The Years Ahead* (Working Party, 1988) in relation to voluntary organizations were as follows: 'encouragement by all possible means the involvement of voluntary organisations in caring for the elderly' (Par. 11.17); formal contract setting out services to be provided for a period of two or three years (Par. 11.17); establishment of a development fund (Par 11.18); development of a mechanism of to coordinate voluntary activity locally (Par. 11.18); a formal review of the relationship of statutory and voluntary sectors; development of national guidelines (Par. 11.19).

The Years Ahead (Working Party, 1988) outlined the objectives of public policy. Services were to be guided by these underlying principles: comprehensiveness, equity, accessibility, responsiveness, flexibility, coordination, planning and cost effectiveness. The objectives proposed in *The Years Ahead* and those of the Care of the Aged Report (*Report*, 1968) are very similar. The later document adds an emphasis on rehabilitation and on the values of 'dignity and independence' (Working Party, 1988: 38). The objectives of public policy were put forward as: to maintain elderly people in dignity and independence in their own home; to restore those elderly people who become ill or dependent to independence at home; to encourage and support the care of the elderly in their own community by family neighbours and voluntary bodies in every way possible; to provide a high quality of hospital and residential care for the elderly people when they can no longer be maintained in dignity and independence at home (1988: 38).

The main advances in the recommendations between the Care of the Aged Report (*Report*, 1968) and *The Years Ahead* (Working Party, 1988) were in the area of coordination of services, the development of the community hospital to provide a wide range of services in each district and the making of specific recommendations on the financial implications of implementation. *The Years Ahead* focused most of its recommendations on a normative approach to service provision based on projected changes in the demographic situation up to the early years of the twenty-first century. Some of the underlying assumptions have been questioned (Ruddle et al., 1997: 43–8). In particular the estimation of the demand for services and the actual growth in population aged over 75 were underestimated. The assumption that there would be an opportunity to redeploy resources from child care have been offset by the urgency of implementing the Child Care Act 1990. *The Years Ahead* also tended towards a service delivery model that relied on service providers and administrators rather than user involvement in planning and evaluation.

Policy for Health Services : The Health Strategy 1994

Shaping a Healthier Future: A Strategy for Effective Healthcare in the 1990s (Department of Health, 1994) (hereafter referred to as *Shaping a Healthier Future*) outlined a comprehensive health strategy, whose main theme was 'the reorientation or reshaping of our health services' (1994: 3). The dimensions of this reorientation were in the following areas:

- *service provision* – an increased emphasis on the provision of the most appropriate care;

- *management and organisational structures* – more decision making and accountability allied to better methods of performance measurement;

- *the participants* – greater sensitivity to the right of the consumer to a service which responds to his or her needs in an equitable and quality driven manner and greater recognition to service providers (Department of Health, 1994: 8).

The key principles underpinning the Health Strategy are equity, quality of service and accountability. A four-year Action Plan for the implementation of the Health Strategy was set out. One aspect of this plan focused on 'ill and dependent elderly'. While acknowledging that 'much remains to be done' before the objectives of *The Years Ahead* (Working Party, 1988) are achieved, the plan reiterates the objectives of the 1988 report and prioritizes: promoting healthy ageing; increasing specialist departments of medicine of old age; funding the Health (Nursing Homes) Act, 1990; providing additional convalescent care and small scale nursing units. The support of older people who live at home is designed 'to ensure that not less than 90 per cent of those over 75 years of age continue to live at home' (Department of Health, 1994: 67). Enhancement of services for the care of people with mental illness or infirmity is also included in the Action Plan (1994: 70).

Policy Development in Mental Health

In 1992 a Green Paper on Mental Health was published to review progress in the development of a new psychiatric service as recommended in the report *Planning for the Future* (Department of Health, 1984). It was also concerned with new legislation to replace the Mental Treatment Act 1945. Public comment on the proposals in the Green Paper led to the publication in 1995 of the White Paper, *A New Mental Health Act* (Department of Health, 1995). The White Paper proposals remain stated policy of the Department of Health and Children but, so far, they have not been implemented. Significant issues for older people, which were addressed in the White Paper serve to emphasize the unacceptable delay in the policy-making process.

The most significant proposals of the White Paper relevant to older people are as follows: changing criteria for involuntary admission to an approved centre; defining 'mental disorder' to include the term 'severe dementia' associated with severe behavioural disturbance; broadening the category of centres where involuntary admission is possible e.g. a centre specializing in the care of persons with dementia; setting up Mental Health Review Board to review decisions to detain patients in psychiatric hospitals and developing the Inspectorate of Mental Hospitals; introduction of an adult care order which could be used to protect mentally disordered persons (including those with mental infirmity) from abuse; considerably narrowing the grounds for detention of a person with dementia (currently classified as a person of unsound mind, who may be detained for an indefinite period); and the development of specialized centres for the care of those with severe dementia.

As these proposals have not been implemented, the current statutory framework for the psychiatric services is the Mental Treatment Act, 1945 (Department of Health, 1945) whose provisions 'do not fully comply with the country's obligations under international law' (Department of Health, 1995: 13). The situation is further outlined by the shocking revelation in the *Green Paper on Mental Health* (Department of Health, 1992) which states:

> There are over 3,000 persons aged 65 years and over in psychiatric hospitals, the majority of whom have been there for a long time. . . . Few of these elderly patients have an active psychiatric component to their illness but they remain heavily institutionalised (Department of Health, 1992: 33).

There is also this solemn warning for policy makers:

> There is a danger that as the focus of the psychiatric services moves from the hospital to the community that the elderly could be left behind in deteriorating accommodation and that standards of care could fall (Department of Health, 1992: 34).

Development of Social Welfare Payment for Care

The development of payments for care must be seen in the context of the policy of 'community care' outlined in this chapter. The first payment for care in Ireland was introduced in 1968, and was known as the Prescribed Relative's Allowance. It was payable to older people aged over seventy years, who required full-time care and attention. The payment, a supplement to the pension, was paid in return for the provision of full time care by a co-residing female relative (initially only daughter or step-daughter). Gradually the restrictiveness of the payment lessened. The rules on social insurance contributions of the prescribed relative were abolished and the range of female relatives extended in 1969. By 1972 the scheme extended to male relatives and social welfare contributions were credited to those who gave up employment to provide care. The Social Welfare Act 1989 paid the Prescribed Relative's Allowance directly to the carer. The Prescribed Relative's Allowance was restrictive and very small financially. The Social Welfare Act 1990 introduced a means-tested Carer's Allowance. The Carer's Allowance is a social assistance payment payable to someone providing care to a person in receipt of a range of social welfare payments and needing 'full-time care and attention'. The payment is very much constructed as an earnings substitution, prohibiting the carer from engaging in employment. The means-testing procedure has been changed gradually. In the case of married carers, disregard of spouse's income was introduced in 1994 (£100) and 1995 (£150). However, spouses or partners who receive a social welfare payment must forfeit the adult dependent allowance if the claim is successful, thus greatly reducing the net gain to the household. This has led to a situation where, in 1996, '36 per cent of applicants were not transferred to the Carer's Allowance, even though they were eligible because they would actually have been worse off' (Yeates, 1997: 35). Recent developments in criteria of eligibility include the possibility for the carer to attend a course of education or training, take up voluntary or community work for up to ten hours per week or work part-time as a home help for a health board for around ten hours per week, or engage in limited self-employment within the home for up to ten hours (from which income will be assessed). This is subject to 'adequate care being arranged for the care recipient'. This change represents an alteration of the conditions for the allowance which up to now focused on the dependence of the care-recipient. Introducing some 'monitoring' in the caring situation may change the payment from an allowance to 'quasi-wage payment' with conditions attached to evidence that the caring has been carried out.

Health (Nursing Homes) Act 1990

The policy planning report *The Years Ahead* (Report of the Working Party, 1988) points the way towards the objective of 'community care' for older people but also the provision of 'high quality hospital and residential care'. Prior to *The Years Ahead,* nursing homes were regulated under the Health (Homes for Incapacitated Persons) Act 1964. The Health (Nursing Homes) Act 1990 introduced regulation in relation to subvention arrangements, regulation and inspection of private and voluntary homes and stricter enforcement of care and welfare regulations. The legislation, which became operational in 1993, has led to debate on policy issues such as the under provision of resources for community care, the large increase in spending on private nursing home care by the Department of Health and Children, inspection and regulation, and financing options. The rising cost of institutional care is a major issue and the existing division between public and private provision requires a more integrated approach. One of the most controversial aspects of the Health (Nursing Homes) Act 1990 has been that of family responsibility for financing long-term care. This is enshrined in the legislation in the process of assessment of applicants for the subvention. The subvention regulations (Statutory Instrument 227 of 1993) require an assessment of 'means' and 'circumstances' of applicants. 'Means' are defined as income and imputed value of assets. 'Circumstances' are defined as 'the capacity of a son and/or daughter aged 21 years and over residing in the jurisdiction of a person who has qualified for a subvention to contribute towards to cost of nursing home care of his or her parent'. This definition of 'circumstances' and the ensuing de facto obligation of support between children and parents is a glaring example of the use of delegated or secondary legislation to introduce restrictions not specifically provided for in primary legislation, i.e. the Act itself. As a public policy measure, the regulation introduces very difficult issues, which will be addressed in the final section of this chapter.

The National Council of Ageing and Older People

The Care of the Aged Report in 1968 first suggested the formation of a National Council for the Aged 'to promote in every way possible the general welfare of the aged' (*Report*, 1968: 122). The National Council for the Aged was set up in 1981. Its terms of reference were to advise the Minister for Health on all aspects of the welfare of the aged, on methods of ensuring coordination in planning and provision of services, on ways of meeting the needs of the most vulnerable elderly, on ways of encouraging positive attitudes to ageing, on encouraging greater participation by elderly people, on models of good practice and on research. It was set up for a three-year term, followed by a second council's five-year term of office. It was succeeded by the National Council for the Elderly in January 1990, which added to the terms of reference the responsibility to advise the Minister for Health on 'the implementation of the recommendations of the report, *The Years Ahead – A Policy for the Elderly*' (Working Party, 1988). In March 1997 the National Council on Ageing and Older People succeeded the National Council for the Elderly, adding to the terms of reference 'measures to promote the social inclusion of older people' and 'to assist in the development of national and regional policies and strategies designed to produce health and social gain for older people'. The National Council on Ageing and Older People (and its forerunners) has, through analysis and research conducted on its behalf, identified for policy makers the emerging issues which require policy change, e.g. the home-help service, mental disorders in older people, financing long term care. In each study, the Council makes detailed recommendations for changes in policy and practice and has held consultative seminars on the subject of each study. While the implementation of policy changes can be very slow, there is no doubt that the Council is very influential as a specialist advisory body.

Implementation of Current Policy

The National Council on Ageing and Older People, in accordance with its terms of reference, commissioned the Policy Research Centre of the National College of Industrial Relations to carry out a review of the implementation of *The Years Ahead* Report (Working Party, 1988). The reader is referred to the detailed and painstaking research for a complete evaluation of the current situation (Ruddle et al., 1997). However, a summary of some key findings will point the way forward to the final section of this chapter on challenges for the future. The review found: 'significant gaps in the care options for older people' (1997: 306);

significant steps in health promotion in the development of a Healthy Ageing Programme by the National Council on Ageing and Older People but 'little evidence of interdepartmental cooperation' (1997: 306); a number of deficits in the provision of effective support services in the community (1997: 300); slow development of community hospitals, assessment and rehabilitation facilities (1997: 310); poorly developed services for psychiatry of old age (1997: 311); 'major needs of carers are not being adequately addressed' (1997: 312); no legislation underpinning the provision of services (1997: 313); coordination of services 'requires a much greater commitment of personnel and financial resources' (1997: 318). It is now over ten years since the publication of *The Years Ahead*. The policy document on the overall health services, *Shaping a Healthier Future* (Department of Health, 1994) added some changes in policy orientation and emphasis, notably the importance of evaluation, greater consumer orientation and user responsiveness. The obstacles to policy implementation such as ambivalence at management level, lack of information on the part of some agencies outside the health boards about recommendations, the absence of a legislative framework and failure to provide funding, highlight the challenges ahead in responding to key issues for future policy. Many of the issues involved radical questioning about the assumptions on which current policy is based.

CHALLENGES FOR THE FUTURE

In this section some of the major issues that confront policy makers will be addressed. Space allows merely the highlighting of issues, with references for further reading rather than detailed analysis.

Ageism

The challenge for policy makers is the need to rethink the concept of ageism. Bytheway (1995), in the concluding chapter of his study of ageism, proposes that the assumption that old people exist as a group must be questioned and that the us/them question must be resolved. He argues that we must critically examine the creation of a category of people called the elderly.

> Where ageism comes in is, in our pathetic attempts to be certain about the changes that come with age, in the assumptions that they are all universal, in our efforts to distance ourselves from those who appear different, in our negative interpretations and in the consequential regulations of the social order (Bytheway, 1995: 125).

Challenging the power of ageism will require facing the reality that it is a shared experience and seeing ourselves in terms of the broader context of the whole of our lives.

Demography

There are many academic controversies concerning the relationships between mortality, morbidity and disability and how to make projections which will define the demand for medical care and social services. In Ireland, the trend towards population ageing, which will intensify after 2001 'is not exceptional by the standards of the last 20 to 30 years' (Fahey, 1995: 37). In absolute terms the increase among the old elderly occurs more among women than men. The growth in the population aged eighty years and over is the largest both in absolute and relative terms and represents the most dramatic change (Fahey, 1995: 43). A full discussion of demography as an influence on health and social care provision is undertaken in Fahey's (1995) report for the National Council on Ageing and Older People. While the report outlines the reasons for 'the puzzling absence of a relationship between population ageing and health expenditure', it makes a very significant point in relation to 'social care'. The role of demographic factors could be very significant on the size of the population pool in need of social care services such as personal care, home help, and surveillance. This must be incorporated into policy analysis. A theory that is particularly appealing to policy makers was put forward by Fries (1980: 130–5). Referred to as 'the compression of morbidity', the theory suggests that '. . . illness and death will be progressively confined to a few months and occupy a smaller proportion of the typical lifespan. Evidence however shows that increased longevity may be accompanied by an extension of the period of dependency' (Guralnik, 1990; Kaplan, 1991). In the light of these findings lies one of the most difficult challenges – that of 'constructing a positive image of deep old age which will help us detach ourselves from the emotional response of aversion and disgust' (Featherstone and Hepworth, 1990: 273).

Family Responsibility

The Years Ahead (Working Party, 1988) identified the family as making by far the greatest contribution to the care of dependent older people. The review of its implementation in relation to support states that 'several substantial studies have demonstrated clearly that little has been done' (Ruddle et al., 1997: 291). Policy makers hold many assumptions about family obligations, which may or may not be accurate. There is a need for a greater understanding of patterns of support for older people and the kind of factors that bring this about. The assumption that elderly people would prefer family care also needs a more detailed understanding. Qureshi (1996: 100–19) discusses the issue of obligations and support within families, highlighting the need for nationally representative data about who provides care. Important questions face policy makers – what networks of care can respond to high levels of dependency? On what basis is care provided? Is there agreement about the responsibility of kin? The complex negotiations about caring for kin in the context of social and demographic changes will continue to be a major challenge for services (Finch, 1989; Finch and Mason, 1993). The issue of family obligation and its treatment in law and social policy is an important one and may be different in many societies for historical and cultural reasons. The contrasting conceptions of family obligation in France and England are explored by Twigg and Grand (1998). In a detailed discussion of the laws on family obligation and inheritance in both countries, the conclusion that the financial contribution of relatives comes into play mainly in the context of means-tested benefits at the point of transition into institutional care is similar to the controversial aspects of the Irish Health (Nursing Homes) Act 1990 as discussed earlier.[1] The provision of care is an area in which the issue of family obligation is not legally 'enforced'. How much it is enforced through 'an absence of alternatives' is a key question (Twigg and Grand, 1998: 146). The problem of financial responsibility of spouses and children to support older people requires consideration of the moral and administrative issues involved and 'entails finding solutions to agonisingly difficult legal issues in embarrassing, sometimes even tragic, factual contexts' (Levy, 1989: 257).

Concepts of Care

Much Irish research on caring has involved studies focusing on the 'costs' of caring (O'Connor and Ruddle, 1988; Blackwell et al., 1992; Ruddle and O'Connor, 1993). An analytical framework, which introduces a broader picture of caring has been developed by Thomas (1993: 649–69). She identified seven dimensions that are common to all concepts of care. These dimensions are: the social identity of the carer; the social identity of the care recipient; the interpersonal relationship between the carer and the care-recipient; the nature of the care; the social domain within which the caring relationship is located; the economic character of the care relationship; the institutional setting in which the care is delivered. O'Donovan (1997) uses this framework to explore the concept of care used by the health boards in relation to the home-help service. The home-help service was established under Section 61 of the Health Act, 1970 (Department of Health, 1970) and has greatly expanded since its establishment. It consists predominantly of female workers employed on a part-time basis with low rates of pay and a lack of investment in training. The service is mainly provided by the health boards with some voluntary sector involvement. Its development has been constrained by the absence of an adequate legal basis. If the service is to have an impact on the more dependent elderly person at home, considerable additional resources are required. The concept of care identified – one which focuses on care provided by women, whose primary motivation is philanthropic, whose work is a form of paid volunteering – exposes the policy agenda of the health boards' as 'promoting care of older people in the 'community', but not resourcing this care' and 'the gender ideology that informs this policy' (O'Donovan, 1997: 153).

Payments for Care

Payments for care systems are likely to be developed further and this poses many dilemmas in the current social and economic climate. The Carer's Allowance is a payment, made directly to carers, which is relatively rare and occurs only in Britain and Ireland. Other forms of payment are those paid directly to the person who is disabled and 'symbolic payments' made to volunteers. (The term 'symbolic payments' is used by O'Donovan (1997) to describe payment to home helps in Ireland.) It is increasingly important to understand the classification of payments for care as 'quasi-wages payments' (those made to 'volunteers' or to caregivers by care recipients using benefits) or 'carer-allowance payments for care' (benefits paid to carers). These are leading to 'a politics of payments and allowances for care' (Ungerson, 1995: 31–52). The ways in which such payments impact on the public/private dichotomy, the gender issues involved in the disproportionate number of women receiving such payments and the threat of an informal labour market of 'unregulated caring labour' are issues that need to be seriously considered. The challenge is summarized by Yeates (1997).

> Any attempt to overhaul the Carer's Allowance to more effectively support care giving across the population must explicitly address the relationship between the state and the family on the one hand and the expectation of women as providers of care on the other (1997: 22).

It is clear that the challenge is not confined to the Carer's Allowance nor to gender alone, but may also broaden to issues of race and nationality (Ungerson, 1995: 48).

Elder Abuse

The abuse of older people in Ireland – both in the domestic and the institutional setting – is slowly making its way onto the political agenda. Raising awareness about the reality of elder abuse and the dissemination of information are important activities for members of the public and for professionals. From the early attention to the phenomenon in the United Kingdom in the early 1970s (Burston, 1975: 592), elder abuse has become an issue in many countries with much debate about definition, causation, appropriate forms of legislation, intervention and a growing research base. In Ireland, the recognition of elder abuse is taking place in the context of the 'discovery' of many other forms of abuse, both in the domestic and institutional setting. The possibility of addressing elder abuse within a clear and satisfactory social policy framework will hopefully come about with the publication by the National Council on Ageing and Older People of a report on the issue with recommendations for a way forward (O'Loughlin and Duggan, 1998).

CONCLUSION

This chapter has offered an overview of some of the social policy developments in relation to older people in Ireland. A future strategy outlined by Ruddle et al. (1997: 325) addresses the importance of the perspective of older people themselves. The language pertaining to the old is an example of a categorization used to 'bring a sense of order to an otherwise unfathomable experience' (Hazan, 1994: 1). So much knowledge about older people and the professional literature relies on professional expertise and is interested in the state of the elderly as objects. Perhaps the most demanding task for social policy development is that of deciphering the world of older people as subjects and understanding the ways in which knowledge about ageing is produced.

CHRONOLOGY OF LEADING POLICY DEVELOPMENTS

1703	Act providing for the erection of a 'House of Industry' in Dublin
1773	Dublin House of Industry set up
1815	Richmond Lunatic Asylum officially opened

1838	Act 'for the more effectual relief of the Destitute Poor in Ireland'
1847	'Outdoor relief' authorized
1862	Poor Relief (Ireland) Act (qualified nursing in workhouses)
1896	Irish Workhouse Association formed
1903, 1909	Commission on Poor Law Reform
1908	Old Age Pension Act (non-contributory old age pension)
1927	Commission of Poor Relief (development of County Homes for Aged
1953	Health Act (grants to voluntary bodies)
1961	Contributory Old Age Pension
1965	Interdepartmental Committee on Care of the Aged appointed
1968	Report of an Interdepartmental Committee Care of the Aged
1968	Prescribed Relatives' Allowance
1970	Health Act (community care structures)
1970	Retirement Pension
1975	Supplementary Welfare Allowance Scheme (remnants of Poor Law abolished)
1977	Pension age reduced to 66 years
1981	National Council for the Aged appointed
1986	Appointment of Working Party on Services for the Elderly
1988	Report of Working Party on Services for the Elderly – *The Years Ahead – A Policy for the Elderly*
1990	Carer's Allowance introduced
1990	Health (Nursing Homes) Act passed
1990	National Council for the Elderly established
1992	Green Paper on Mental Health
1993	Health (Nursing Homes) Act implemented
1994	*Shaping a Healthier Future – A Strategy for Effective Healthcare in the 1990s*
1995	White Paper – A New Mental Health Act
1996	Domestic Violence Act
1997	National Council on Ageing and Older People appointed
1997	Report of the Task Force on Violence Against Women
1997	Review of the Implementation of *The Years Ahead*

NOTE

1 On 1 January 1999, regulations came into operation removing the provisions which allowed for the assessment of the capacity of sons and/or daughters over 21 years of age to contribute towards the cost of nursing home care of their parent (S.I. no. 498, 1998). This means that all relevant sections of the Health (Nursing Homes) Act, 1990, were revoked or amended. The change followed years of controversy, notably involving the intervention of the office of the Ombudsman.

RECOMMENDED READING

Bytheway, B. (1995) *Ageism*. Buckingham: Open University Press.

Report of an Inter-Departmental Committee on the Care of the Aged (1968). Dublin: Stationery Office.

Ruddle, H., F. Donoghue and R. Mulvihill (1997) *The Years Ahead Report: A Review of the Implementation of Its Recommendations*. Dublin: National Council on Aging and Older People.

Working Party on Services for the Elderly (1988) *The Years Ahead: A Policy for the Elderly*. Dublin: Stationery Office.

The National Council on Ageing and Older People has published a number of studies on older people in Ireland.

REFERENCES

Blackwell, J. (1984) *Incomes of the Elderly in Ireland: An Analysis of the State's Contribution*. Dublin: National Council for the Aged.

Blackwell, J., G. Moane, P. Murray and E. O'Shea (1992) *Care Provision and Cost Management: Dependent Elderly People at Home and in Geriatric Hospitals*. Dublin: the Economic and Social Research Institute.

Burke, H. (1987) *The People and the Poor Law in 19th Century Ireland*. Littlehampton: WEB.

Burston, G. (1975) 'Granny Battering', *British Medical Journal*, 6 September, p. 592

Butler, R.N. (1975) *Why Survive? Being Old in America*. New York: Harper & Row.

Bytheway, B. (1995) *Ageism*. Buckingham: Open University Press.

Bytheway, B. and J. Johnson (1990) 'On Defining Ageism', *Critical Social Policy*, 27: 27–39.

Carney, C. (1985) 'A Case Study in Social Policy: the Non-Contributory Old Age Pension', *Administration*, 33 (4): 483–525.

Comfort, A. (1977) *A Good Age*. London: Mitchell Beazley.

De Beauvoir, S. (1977) *Old Age*. Harmondsworth: Penguin.

Department of Health (1945) *Mental Treatment Act 1945*. Dublin: Stationery Office.

Department of Health (1953) *Health Act 1953*. Dublin: Stationery Office.

Department of Health (1964) *Health (Homes for Incapacitated Persons) Act 1964*. Dublin: Stationery Office.

Department of Health (1970) Health Act 1970. Dublin: Stationery Office.

Department of Health (1984) *Planning for the Future*. Dublin: Stationery Office.

Department of Health (1990) *Health (Nursing Homes) Act 1990*. Dublin: Stationery Office.

Department of Health (1992) *Green Paper on Mental Health*. Dublin: Stationery Office.

Department of Health (1994) *Shaping a Healthier Future: A Strategy for Effective Healthcare in the 1990s*. Dublin: Stationery Office.

Department of Health (1995) *White Paper: A New Mental Health Act*. Dublin: Stationery Office.

Fahey, T. (1995) *Health and Social Care Implications of Population Aging in Ireland 1991–2011*. Dublin: National Council for the Elderly.

Featherstone, M. and M. Hepworth (1990) 'Images of Aging', in J. Bond and P. Coleman (eds), *Aging and Society*. London: Sage.

Finch, J. (1989) *Family Obligations and Social Change*. London: Polity Press.

Finch, J. and J. Mason (1993) *Negotiating Family Responsibilities*. London: Routledge.

Fries, J.F. (1980) 'Aging, Natural Death and the Compression of Morbidity', *New England Journal of Medicine*, 303 (3): 130–5.

Guralnik, J.M. (1990) 'Prospects for the Compression of Morbidity', *Journal of Aging and Health*, 3: 138–54.

Haber, C. (1983) *Beyond 60 – Five: The Dilemma of Old Age in America's Past*. Cambridge: University Press.

Haynes, M.S. (1963) 'The Supposedly Golden Age for the Aged', *The Gerontologist*, 3 (26): 26–35.

Hazan, H. (1994) *Old Age: Constructions and Deconstructions*. Cambridge: University Press.

Hendricks, J. and C.D. Hendricks (1977) *Aging in a Mass Society*. Cambridge: Winthrop.

Kaplan, G.A. (1991) 'Epidemiologic Observations on the Compression of Morbidity', *Journal of Aging and Health*, 3: 155–71.

Kelly, F. (1988) *A Guide to Early Irish Law*. Dublin: Dublin Institute for Advanced Studies.

Levy, R.J. (1989) 'Supporting the Aged: The Problem of Family Responsibility', in J. Eckelaar and D. Pearl (eds), *An Aging World: Dilemmas and Challenges for Law and Social Policy*. Oxford: Clarendon Press.

O'Connor, J. (1995) *The Workhouses of Ireland*. Dublin: Anvil Books.

O'Connor, J. and H. Ruddle (1988) *Caring for the Elderly Part 2: The Caring Process: A Study of Carers at Home and in the Community*. Dublin: National Council for the Aged.

O'Connor, J., H. Ruddle and M. O'Gallagher (1989) *Sheltered Housing in Ireland: Its Role and Contribution in the Care of the Elderly*. Dublin: National Council for the Aged.

O'Donovan, O. (1997) 'Contesting Concepts of Care: The Case of the Home Help Service in Ireland', pp. 69–84 in A. Cleary and M.P. Treacy (eds), *The Sociology of Health and Illness in Ireland*. Dublin: University College Dublin Press.

O'Loughlin, A. and J. Duggan (1998) *Abuse, Mistreatment and Neglect of Older People in Ireland: An Exploratory Study*. Dublin: National Council on Aging and Older People.

Qureshi, H. (1996) 'Obligations and Support within Families', in A. Walker (ed.), *The New Generational Contract*. London: UCL Press.

Report of the Inter-Department Committee on the Reconstruction and Replacement of County Homes (1949). Dublin: Stationery Office.

Report of an Inter-Departmental Committee on the Care of the Aged (1968). Dublin: Stationery Office.

Reynolds, J. (1992). *Grangegorman: Psychiatric Care in Dublin since 1915*. Dublin: Institute of Public Administration.

Ruddle, H. and J. O'Connor (1993) *Caring without Limits: Sufferers of Dementia/Alzheimer's Disease*. Dublin: The Alzheimer Society of Ireland.

Ruddle, H., F. Donoghue and R. Mulvihill (1997) *The Years Ahead Report: A Review of the Implementation of Its Recommendations*. Dublin: National Council on Aging and Older People.

Thomas, C. (1993) 'De-Constructing Concepts of Care', *Sociology*, 27 (4): 649–69.

Thomas, K. (1976) 'Age and Authority in Early Modern England', *Proceedings of the British Academy*, 62: 205–48.

Thompson, N. (1997) 'Children, Death and Ageism', *Child and Family Social Work*, 2 (1): 59–65.

Twigg, J. and A. Grand (1998) 'Contrasting Legal Conceptions of Family Obligation and Financial Reciprocity in the Support of Older People: France and England', *Aging and Society*, 18: 132–46.

Ungerson, C. (1995) 'Gender, Cash and Informal Care: European Perspectives and Dilemmas', *Journal of Social Policy*, 24 (1): 31–52.

Working Party on Services for the Elderly (1988) *The Years Ahead: A Policy for the Elderly*. Dublin: Stationery Office.

Yeates, N. (1997) 'Gender, Informal Care and Social Welfare: The Case of the Carer's Allowance', *Administration*, 45 (2): 21–43.

11
Travellers and Social Policy

Niall Crowley

INTRODUCTION

In 1960, the then Parliamentary Secretary to the Minister for Justice, Charles Haughey, addressed the inaugural meeting of the Commission on Itinerancy. Referring to their terms of reference, he stated that these 'acknowledge the fact that there can be no final solution to the problems created by itinerants until they are absorbed into the general community' (Report of the Commission on Itinerancy, 1963: 111). In 1991, the then Taoiseach, Charles Haughey, stated in his address to the Fianna Fáil Ard Fheis that

> Local authorities throughout the country will be called upon to take special urgent action in this anniversary year to meet the needs of all Travellers within their area. And we should respect the culture of our Travelling community and develop a better public understanding of their time-honoured way of life.

The contrast between the two quotations illustrates the distance travelled by policy and policy makers in seeking to address the situation of Travellers, yet social policy in relation to Travellers is very much an unfinished business.

The two quotations above also illustrate the importance of a broad focus in relation to social policy that encompasses the thinking which informs policy, policy making and implementation. That 'urgent action' was still considered necessary 28 years after the Commission Report of 1963 raises questions as to the quality of thinking informing policy and to the ability of public sector systems to implement policy.

The National Economic and Social Forum (NESF), in their review of social partnership (*A Framework for Partnership*, 1997), addressed the need for this broad focus in highlighting the frustration of the social partners in translating agreed policy into real change. A need to focus on the concept of 'policy design' was suggested, which was defined as the 'fusion of policy making, implementation and monitoring' (NESF, 1997: 47). Reform of the public sector system through the Strategic Management Initiative was recommended, and also a more active engagement by the social partners with policy implementation and monitoring if the challenges of 'policy design' were to be met.

This chapter explores how social policy is addressing the situation of Travellers in Ireland. It sets out current policy and the influences that have contributed to it and concludes by identifying issues in relation to policy implementation and monitoring.

THE TRAVELLERS

Travellers are a minority ethnic group with a nomadic tradition. They identify themselves as a distinct community and are seen by others as such. They share common cultural characteristics, traditions and values which are evident in their organization of family, social and economic life. Nomadism, in a range of forms, has been central to the development and expression of these characteristics, traditions and values. Travellers have a long shared history which, though undocumented, can be traced back before the twelfth century through mention of Travellers in the law and through analysis of their language, the Cant. They have a distinct oral tradition and largely marry within their own community. These elements have all been identified as defining an ethnic group. Ethnicity focuses on the importance of identity and cultural difference. It is defined as 'a symbolic meaning system, a way of a "people" to organise social reality in terms of their cultural similarities and differences' (Tovey, 1989: 8).

Traveller ethnicity has been contested by the majority settled community. It has been a focus for struggle by Travellers and Traveller organizations. Travellers have been defined as deviants or misfits. This definition perceives Travellers as failed settled people in need of rehabilitation and assimilation. It denies Travellers their history, their language and their cultural contribution. Travellers have been defined as a subculture of poverty. This definition perceives Travellers' economic circumstances as defining their identity and culture. Welfare, education and anti-poverty strategies would therefore aim to remove their differences and secure their reintegration. However, this definition incorrectly suggests that Travellers are economically homogeneous and ignores the fact that the wealthiest Travellers tend to be the more nomadic, with the least interest in integration.

The contest over Traveller ethnicity highlights their minority status in relation to a dominant settled community. Tovey (1989) has described these power relations:

> Dominant ethnicity contrasts sharply with subordinate ethnicity. The one
> enjoys both political and economic power, as well as cultural presumption,
> while the other, in extreme cases, may be so marginal as to be at the centre
> of nothing in the larger system but its own ethnic world. (Tovey, 1989: 8)

This process and relationship pose the Traveller situation in terms of
racism. Racism involves discrimination against groups on the basis of
physical or cultural difference. It occurs at both the level of the
individual and of a society's institutions. Racism at the individual level
tends to be more overt, often involving verbal and physical abuse.
However, it is racism at the level of the institution which creates the
conditions for individual-level racism and which perpetuates this from
one generation to another. At this institutional level, racism can be
invisible and is all too often ignored. Yet it is at this level that the outcomes of inequitable power relations are at their most damaging.

Racism at the institutional level is most visible in the outcomes of
policy and provision for minority ethnic groups, where these outcomes
are significantly worse than those for the dominant group. Institutional
racism rarely involves intent. Institutions where people pursue routine
practices, often with the best of intentions, produce these outcomes.
Specific account is not taken of the particular needs and aspirations of
minority ethnic groups.

The outcomes for Travellers provide very graphic evidence of
institutional racism. The most disturbing figures come from *The Travellers
Health Status Study* (Barry et al., 1989). This found that 'the infant mortality rate for Travellers in 1987 was 18.1 per 1000 live births compared
to the national figure of 7.4' (1989: 14). It also found that 'male
Travellers have over twice the risk of dying in a given year than settled
males, whereas for female Travellers the risk is increased more than
threefold' (Barry et al., 1989: 15).

The educational status of Travellers provides further evidence of
racism. *The Report of the Special Education Review Committee* (Special
Education Review Committee, 1993) estimated that there were about
5000 Traveller children of primary school age, with 4200 attending
primary schools. A substantial number do not attend, while the
outcomes for those who do are generally regarded as disappointing. A
Department of Education Working Group on Post Primary Education
for Travellers (1992) estimated that 80 per cent of Traveller children in
the 12 to 15 age group did not attend any school in the 1989–90 school
year. Of those who did, many were still in primary school, while most
left within the first two years of second-level school.

It should be noted that accurate up-to-date data on Travellers are not
available. Data gathering systems do not include a focus on Travellers.

The last census did have a 'Traveller' question; however it was for the enumerator to fill in, rather than the census recipient. No preparation was given to the enumerators and no criteria established for Traveller identification. This resulted in a significant under-counting of Travellers. However, the data available indicate significant disadvantage experienced by the Traveller community in comparison with the settled community. The outcomes do evidence institutional racism as a core issue. The most recent count of Traveller families provides yet further evidence. It identified 1127 families as living on the side of the road without basic facilities and subject to the constant threat of eviction. This figure is out of a total of 4521 families identified in the count, which took place in 1997.

In this brief description of the situation of Travellers, it is important to acknowledge the specific experience of Traveller women and Travellers with a disability. While Traveller women experience discrimination as Travellers together with the rest of their community, they also experience discrimination as women within the Traveller community and the wider society. While there has been significant work done by Traveller organizations with Traveller women, there remains a lack of information about the specificity of Traveller women's experience of racism. Travellers with a disability also live out of a twofold identity. They have been a particularly invisible subgroup within the Traveller community. In care, Travellers with a disability have been isolated from their community and their Traveller identity has not been recognized and resourced. Within their own community, services specific to Travellers have not addressed the need to be accessible to Travellers with a disability.

POLICY THINKING

The ideas and analysis that have informed policy making are neatly encapsulated in the three major reports on Travellers:

- Report of the Commission on Itinerancy (1963)
- Report of the Travelling People Review Body (1983)
- Report of the Task Force on the Travelling Community (1995).

The Commission on Itinerancy (1963)

The policy thinking encapsulated in the Report of the Commission on Itinerancy (Commission on Itinerancy, 1963) was set out in the central objective identified by the Commission:

> While it is appreciated that difficulties and objections will be met in the early years from many members of the settled population, it is not

considered that there is any alternative to a positive drive for housing itinerants if a permanent solution of the problem of itinerancy, based on absorption and integration is to be achieved (1963: 62).

Housing and education were seen as key to addressing the problem, which was defined as itinerancy or nomadism. The Commission stated that:

> The immediate objective should be to provide dwellings as soon as possible for all itinerant families who desire to settle. Eventually, the example given by those who successfully settle should encourage the remainder to leave the road. (1963: 61)

The Commission stated the purpose of education:

> It is urgently necessary, both as a means of providing opportunities for a better way of life and of promoting their absorption into the settled community, to make such arrangements which, in the light of the following paragraphs (14–21), may be practicable to ensure that as many itinerant children as possible may from now on receive an adequate elementary education. (1963: 67)

The objectives and strategies for policy that flowed from this thinking focused on rehabilitation and assimilation. What was defined as Travellers' failure to live according to the norms of the dominant groups was to be corrected.

Report of the Travelling People Review Body (1983)

The Review Body (Travelling People Review Body, 1983), although flawed, was a major advance on the policy thinking encapsulated in the Report of the Commission on Itinerancy (1963). The significant evolution of this thinking over 20 years can be seen by exploring the policy thinking encapsulated by the Review Body (1983) in comparison with that of the Commission on Itinerancy (1963).

The Review Body put forward a valuable definition of Travellers:

> They are an identifiable group of people, identified both by themselves and by other members of the community (referred to for convenience as the 'settled community') as people with their own distinctive lifestyle, traditionally of a nomadic nature but not now habitual wanderers. They have needs, wants and values which are different in some ways from those of the settled community (1983: 6).

This would suggest an ethnic status for Travellers. However, the Review Body failed to develop this, partly because they saw cultural difference as a focus for individual choice rather than collective rights. It suggested that 'as far as Travellers are concerned the extent to which they will integrate with the settled community will depend on individual decisions by them and not on decisions by Travellers as a whole or of any grouping of them' (1983: 6).

The Review Body also limited their focus on culture as being about what people do. This approach is evident in the recommendation that 'the traditional self-employed occupations of Travellers should be encouraged. Even though many of the skills involved belong to another era, consideration should be given to the adaptation of such skills for use in modern light industrial employment' (1963: 82). By focusing on the tangible – the economic activity – the Review Body missed the point of how that activity is organized. While the skills used might have suggested a future in modern light industry, the manner in which they were deployed do not. As such, despite significant investment, few Travellers are found employed in 'modern light industrial employment'.

The thinking encapsulated by the Review Body encompassed a range of perspectives. The dominant view, however, was one of a community in need of reintegration whose difference was a product of disadvantage and poverty. This was neatly suggested in the recommendation: 'Newly wed couples who have to occupy caravans following their marriage should be considered extra sympathetically for housing to lessen the risks of regression to a Travelling way of life' (1983: 45). The objectives and strategies suggested were focused on integration, with policy designed to support Travellers adapting to the settled 'norm' and provision included for targeting Travellers for this purpose. No particular provision was identified as necessary to resource nomadism.

Task Force on the Travelling Community 1995

The Report of the Task Force on the Travelling Community (Task Force, 1995) established current policy thinking in its chapter on culture which was central to the whole report. It recommended that the distinct culture and identity of Travellers should be taken into account. It defined culture in the following terms:

> Everybody has a culture. It is the package of customs, traditions, symbols, values, phrases and other forms of communication by which we can belong to a community. The belonging is in understanding the meanings of these culture forms and in sharing values and identity. Culture is the way we learn to think, behave and do things (Task Force, 1995: 71).

This definition is valuable in its acknowledgement of culture as both tangible and intangible. The understanding of culture is often limited to doing or making or behaving in a particular way. However, at its most profound, culture is about thinking, about how the world is seen and understood, about values and what is defined as important. The Report of the Task Force applied its own recommendation and understanding to the fields of discrimination, accommodation, health, education and training, and the Traveller economy.

This thinking has been further consolidated. The National Economic and Social Forum, in their report *Equality Proofing Issues* (1996), recommended that 'the proposed Equal Status Legislation will provide an unique opportunity to validate and accept the ethnic identity of the Travellers'. The Irish National Coordinating Committee for the European Year against Racism (1997), set up by the then Department of Equality and Law Reform to develop a programme of action, found that 'one of the more visible forms of racism is that experienced by the Traveller community, based on their distinct culture and identity which is rooted in a tradition of nomadism' (1997: 5). It has been a considerable achievement for a small minority to overcome the challenge to its ethnic status made by the dominant group. It provides a new basis for policy making with significant potential to change the current situation of Travellers. The policy focus that flows from this is one of mainstreaming. 'Mainstreaming' involves making special provision, targeting the distinct needs and aspirations of Travellers as well as adapting standard provision to ensure that it is accessible and relevant to Travellers. Nomadism has become a central concern within policy.

While policy making is currently informed by the Task Force Report (1995), evidence would suggest that policy implementation continues to be informed by the thinking encapsulated by the Travelling People Review Body Report (1983), and even by the Report of the Commission on Itinerancy (Commission on Itinerancy, 1963).

POLICY MAKING

National-level policy making in relation to Travellers is in a state of flux, as government departments seek to respond to the recommendations of the Task Force on the Travelling Community (1995). New policy reflects the new thinking encapsulated in the *Task Force Report*. This is a 'mainstreaming approach' to policy making which involves:

- Naming Travellers within mainstream legislation and policy documentation

- Developing Traveller-specific approaches within policy where these are required by distinct aspirations, values and cultural characteristics or by the need to address a history of discrimination.

- Changing policy delivery systems to secure an equality of outcomes for Travellers.
- Setting targets and timescales to address a backlog of inequitable outcomes for Travellers.

Accommodation

The Dáil has enacted the Housing (Traveller Accommodation) Act 1998, which was published by the Department of the Environment and Local Government. This is the first piece of legislation specifically dedicated to addressing the Traveller situation and will change local authority provision, by requiring local authorities to:

- Make an assessment of the need for halting sites in their functional area.
- Prepare and adopt an accommodation programme specifying the accommodation needs of Travellers and the provision of accommodation to be made to meet those needs over a five-year period. This will be a reserved function, but where councillors fail to adopt such a programme in the specified timescale, the manager will be required to adopt it by order.
- Take any necessary reasonable steps to implement the programme and to report annually on progress.

The legislation will put increased pressure on local authorities to address Traveller accommodation needs – a responsibility they have failed to live up to in the past. The legislation acknowledges Traveller nomadism. This breaks important new ground. Local accommodation programmes must now have regard to 'the provision of sites to address the accommodation needs of Travellers other than as their normal place of residence and having regard to the annual patterns of movement by Travellers' (Housing (Traveller Accommodation) Act, 1998: 10). The new Act amends the 1988 Housing Act which itself broke new ground as the first piece of legislation to specifically name Travellers. Section 13 of that Act is applied to 'persons belonging to the class of persons who traditionally pursue or have pursued a nomadic way of life'. This section enabled local authorities to 'provide, improve, manage and control' halting sites.

To date, Traveller accommodation provision has included a mix of standard houses, group housing schemes for Travellers, Traveller halting sites and temporary sites. This provision has been criticized for:

- Inadequate provision with one-quarter of families living on the side of the road without access to basic facilities.

- Inappropriate provision with accommodation provided not allowing for Traveller economic activities traditionally organized about a home and family basis.

- The absence of provision for Travellers transient through or within a local authority area.

- The appalling conditions on overcrowded and under-serviced temporary sites over long time periods.

Education

The Department of Education published a White Paper on education in 1995. This set important targets and timescales for Traveller participation in education. It stated that:

> The policy objective is that all Traveller children in primary school age be enrolled and participate fully in primary education, according to their individual abilities and potential within five years (*Charting Our Education Future: White Paper on Education* (1995: 26)).

> The overall policy object is that, within ten years, all Traveller children of second level, school-going age will complete junior cycle education and 50 per cent will complete the senior cycle (1995: 58).

The White Paper highlighted that progress will be made only if Traveller children 'are encouraged to enjoy a full and integrated education within the schools system' (1995: 26), and if this participation involves 'retaining respect and value for their individual culture' (1995: 57). A number of actions to be taken are specified, including:

- Work by the National Council for Curriculum and Assessment to develop appropriate curriculum and assessment procedures to meet special needs of Traveller children.

- Provision of modules on Traveller culture in teacher pre-service and in-service training.

- Developing the visiting teacher service.

- Induction programmes to support transfer from primary to second level.

The challenge remains to develop a detailed strategy to achieve these important targets within the proposed timescales.

Policy within the Department has witnessed a valuable shift towards inter-cultural education. Inter-cultural education has been described by the Irish Traveller Movement as involving 'an education that promotes interaction and understanding among and between different cultures and ethnic groups on the assumption that ethnic diversity can enrich society

(Irish Traveller Movement, 1993: 19). The Report of the Task Force on the Travelling Community proposed a number of principles to be reflected in an inter-cultural curriculum: the experiences of minority groups such as Travellers should be presented accurately and sensitively; texts should be monitored to avoid ethnocentric and racist interpretations; information about Travellers and other minority groups should be integrated into the total curriculum; and a focus should be introduced on broader equality and human rights issues, including anti-racism, rather than on exotic customs and practices of Travellers. The Report also considered that a study of minority and majority ethnic groups was needed to help students acquire the knowledge, values and skills to contribute to social change in a multi-cultural context.

Current, Traveller-specific provision includes:

- Traveller pre-schools with an estimated enrolment of 660 children in 1994.

- Four special schools catering for about 260 Traveller children at primary level, two in Dublin, and one in Wicklow and Galway.

- Two hundred special classes attached to standard national schools, catering for about 2400 pupils (estimated in 1995), which operate as segregated classrooms or on a withdrawal basis with a special class teacher provided. Current policy is to avoid segregated classroom settings.

- Junior Training Centres catering for about 300 children in the 12 to 15 age group.

- A Visiting Teacher Service (established in 1980) to identify the educational needs of Traveller children in their region, assist in planning and establishment of education provision and ensure optimal use of existing educational facilities by Travellers. Visiting teachers provide an important liaison between schools and Traveller families.

- Twenty-eight Senior Traveller Training Centres which cater for about 600 Traveller trainees over the age of 15.

Current provision has been criticized for several reasons. High levels of early school leaving among Travellers have not been prevented. An inter-cultural curriculum to affirm the Traveller identity and to challenge racism is lacking. The absence of guidelines and support hinders a common quality standard across pre-school provision. Access to education remains a major problem for many Traveller children, owing to discrimination or a failure to facilitate constantly nomadic families. A support infrastructure to sustain Travellers in second-level education is not in place. The Visiting Teacher Service needs a wider geographical spread. Junior Training Centres should be phased out as the Task Force recommended.

There is a danger that Senior Traveller Training Centres serve as an alternative system drawing Travellers out of the mainstream second-level provision. Segregation remains inherent in separate classroom settings.

Health

In April 1994, the Department of Health published a national health strategy, which established equity as one of three underlying principles: 'the pursuit of equity must extend beyond the question of access to treatment and care, and must examine variations in the health status of different groups in society and how these might be addressed' (Department of Health, 1994: 10). This was of a particular relevance to Travellers. The National Health Strategy focused on Traveller health and promised to publish a policy on Travellers' health on the basis of the Task Force recommendations. It highlighted the importance of targeted health education programmes and models of Traveller participation in health promotion, the need for special arrangements to encourage and permit Traveller access to primary healthcare services, and proposed simplifying services under the GMS scheme.

The Report of the Task Force on the Travelling Community (Task Force, 1995) focused on strategies to enhance Traveller access to the health system and to improve channels of communication between Travellers and service providers. The Task Force highlighted the need for change in:

- The gathering of data on Traveller take-up of health services and improved systems to transfer medical records within and between health board regions.
- Developing systems of personal communication between Traveller patients and the health service.
- Developing a range of Traveller-specific services which should be designed to complement mainstream services and to improve Traveller access to them.
- Simplifying the renewal of medical cards and extending their validity.
- Providing health education to Travellers.
- Providing training to all health professionals on the circumstances and culture of Travellers, and the discrimination practised against them.

A Plan for Women's Health (1997) lists Traveller women among those particularly disadvantaged in relation to health care. It pointed to the significant difference in life expectancy between Traveller women and those from the settled community.

Economic Development

The naming of Travellers in economic development policy is both recent and rare, but it is central to the achievement of equality for them. Social policy objectives and strategies need to be integrated with economic policy objectives and strategies, if the Traveller community is to secure its future as an independent ethnic group in Irish society. *Partnership 2000* contains an important commitment in this regard:

> Action will be taken to endorse labour force participation by the Traveller community and the viability of the Traveller economy on foot of the recommendations of the Task Force and in the context of the National Anti-Poverty Strategy (1997: 35).

This action is still awaited. The Task Force set out a two-pronged strategy:

- To support the Traveller economy. This refers to those economic activities engaged in by Travellers and organized in a manner traditional to that community. The Task Force explored recycling, trading and horse dealing as key activities pursued within the Traveller economy and identified obstacles to be removed and supports to be provided so that the activity, and the manner in which it is organized, could be protected and used as a foundation for further development.

- To support Traveller access to the mainstream labour market. Two strategies of potential are identified. The first is through providing support to Travellers and Traveller organizations in setting up Traveller enterprises, particularly within the social economy. The second is through positive-action measures to secure employment, particularly within the public sector, for Travellers in providing services to their own community.

Two important policy developments in this regard have been the identification of special access criteria for Travellers to Community Employment and the naming of Travellers as a target group in the EU-funded Operational Programme for Local Urban and Rural Development. Community Employment is the largest labour market scheme in operation in Ireland. Traveller take-up has been poor but has improved since criteria for access to it were relaxed for Travellers. The Operational Programme for Local Urban and Rural Development targets structural funds at designated areas of disadvantage. The funds support locally defined area-based action plans of integrated socio-economic development. Pavee Point, a national Traveller organization, is funded as a positive action flanking measure to support and advocate appropriate inclusion of Travellers in local plans.

Discrimination

Equality policy to date in Ireland has principally focused on gender equality. This is currently changing to embrace other groups, including Travellers. Employment Equality Legislation was passed by both Houses of the Oireachtas on 26 March 1997. Equal Status legislation, covering discrimination in non-employment areas, was passed by both Houses of the Oireachtas on 29 April 1997. Both pieces of legislation identified discrimination based upon membership of the Traveller community as being unlawful. Unfortunately, elements of the Employment Equality Bill were found by the Supreme Court to be unconstitutional, and the Equal Status Bill suffered from being inextricably linked to the Employment Equality Bill. The Employment Equality Act was eventually amended and passed in 1998. It is planned to enact the Equal Status legislation in 1999.

This legislation represents an important policy advance for Travellers. Discrimination and racism are a root cause of their current precarious situation. The new legislation should have the potential to reach into all areas of Traveller life. Unfortunately, the proposed legislation is weakened in that it does not specifically identify Travellers as an ethnic group and it does not, as recommended by the Task Force, 'specifically identify its intention to protect cultural identity' (Task Force, 1995: 85).

In earlier legislation, Travellers had been named in the 1993 Unfair Dismissals Act and the 1989 Prohibition of Incitement to Hatred Act. This 1989 Act has been found to be ineffective, owing to the difficulty of proving that actual hatred was incited. The commitment to equality legislation also found expression in the 'Agreement reached in the Multi-Party Negotiations' on the future of Northern Ireland. The Agreement introduces a new focus on human rights that should have a particular relevance to Travellers, with commitments to establish a Human Rights Commission and to ratify the Council of Europe Framework Convention on National Minorities.

Previous Legislation

The naming of Travellers as a specific concern for social policy is a relatively recent and still emerging phenomenon. Formerly, legislation and policy were undifferentiated and were assumed to cover all citizens equally, which often resulted in unintended consequences for Travellers. At the same time, undifferentiated legislation and policies have failed to have an impact on Travellers even where it appeared that it would have the potential to do so.

A body of legislation emerged prior to the 1990s that served as a basis for Traveller evictions and for action to block the construction of Traveller-specific accommodation. This included:

- Local Government (Sanitary Services) Act 1948 gave powers to local authorities to regulate and control land used for camping and temporary dwellings and to use prohibition orders to this end.

- Road Safety Act 1961 regulated the distance from the roadside that a tent or caravan might be placed.

- The third section of the Local Government (Planning and Development) Act 1963 sets out certain categories of objectives to be catered for in the development plan. None of these categories relate specifically to the Traveller community. Planning legislation has been used by residents' associations to legally challenge the construction of Travellers' accommodation.

POLICY IMPLEMENTATION AND MONITORING

Participation

The participation of Travellers and Traveller organizations is emerging as a key element of policy making, implementation and monitoring. The following important developments can be identified:

- The three national Traveller organizations (Irish Traveller Movement, National Traveller Women's Forum, and Pavee Point) are represented on the National Traveller Consultative Committee set up to advise the Minister for the Environment and Local Government in relation to any general matter concerning accommodation for Travellers. This committee was given a legislative basis in the Housing (Travellers Accommodation) Act 1998.

- The same representation has been invited to participate in the Travellers' Health Advisory Committee which is advising the Minister for Health and Children on the design and implementation of the Travellers' Health Policy Statement.

- The Department of Education has convened a liaison committee for Traveller organizations and an internal committee established to develop the national policy framework for Traveller education.

- Local authorities are to be required to set up Traveller Accommodation Consultative Committees, with Traveller organizations, councillors and officials as members, to advise on the preparation of local accommodation programmes.

- Health boards are setting up Traveller health units with representation from Traveller organizations to provide a regional focus on Traveller health status and service provision to Travellers.

- Travellers are among the interests represented on the Equality Authority created to support and promote the implementation of new equality legislation.

These developments enhance the fusion of policy making and policy implementation and also the possibility of national policy being transformed into local action. However, one area of concern that has been identified is the advisory and consultative nature of these bodies. The resistance at local level to securing change in the situation of Travellers has proved durable and effective. It is this resistance that the new structures have to overcome and their status and powers need to be adequate to this challenge.

Strategic Management Initiative

Policy implementation could be significantly enhanced by the Strategic Management Initiative. This initiative is focused on modernizing the public sector. It aims to deliver better government through improved service delivery, better quality regulation and more effective management of major national issues, and to give improved performance and a clear focus on achieving objectives.

Six working groups have been established to progress key areas of the Initiative. The Irish National Coordinating Committee for the European Year against Racism identified quality service and human resources as being of particular relevance: 'quality of service requires an anti-racist dimension. Such a dimension in turn, requires appropriate human resource management strategies' (Irish National Coordinating Committee for the European Year against Racism, 1997: 6).

An important advance was achieved when the Department of the Taoiseach launched a set of principles for quality customer service, which included the need to 'respect the rights of minorities at all times in the delivery of services'. Government departments were required to reflect these principles in the preparation of customer action plans. This particular principle was not taken up to any significant extent in the plans, although they are subject to review and revision. Overall, the equality dimension to the Strategic Management Initiative remains unproven. This was emphasized when the National Economic and Social Forum found it necessary to recommend that 'equality should be an explicit principle underlying the Strategic Management Initiative as a whole' (NESF, 1997: 29).

National Anti-Poverty Strategy

Another key policy initiative with the potential to impact on policy implementation is the National Anti-Poverty Strategy (NAPS) which was launched in 1997. It has been described as 'a major cross-departmental policy initiative by the government designed to place the needs of the poor and the socially excluded among the issues at the top of the national agenda in terms of government policy development and action' (*Sharing in Progress: National Anti-Poverty Strategy*, 1997: 2). The Strategy requires government departments, state agencies, local and regional bodies to address the question of poverty in their statements of strategy under the Strategic Management Initiative. They are also required to report annually on progress.

Five theme areas were identified to be progressed under the NAPS – educational disadvantage, unemployment (particularly long-term unemployment), income adequacy, disadvantaged urban areas, and rural poverty. Travellers are identified as a target group for the NAPS and receive specific mention in relation to educational disadvantage, where the commitments of the White Paper are reiterated, and to unemployment where there is a commitment to address the 'double discrimination' experienced by Travellers in accessing employment (NAPS, 1997: 12).

The NAPS also identified a number of over-arching principles which have a relevance to Traveller inclusion. They include 'ensuring equal access and encouraging participation for all', and 'guaranteeing the rights of minorities especially through anti-discrimination measures' (NAPS, 1997: 7).

The NAPS has the potential to secure an enhanced targeting of provision and resources on Travellers. To achieve this, it will have to prove itself to be an effective mechanism to achieve re-prioritizing within existing resources. This is a major and vital challenge that has yet to be met. In this regard, the following commitment in the NAPS is of central importance:

> The question of the impact of poverty will also be a key consideration when decisions are being made about spending priorities in the context of the national budgetary process and the allocation of EU Structural Funds (NAPS, 1997: 21)

The NAPS also has the potential to 'mainstream', with all policy making and programme design having a focus on the impact on Travellers. In this connection the commitment to poverty and equality-proofing is of central importance. Guidelines have been developed to assist government departments, state agencies and local authorities to assess the impact of substantive policy initiatives on a range of groups, including Travellers, experiencing poverty and inequality. These guidelines are currently being piloted and, after review, should be extended to state agencies and local authorities.

The NAPS is being implemented very slowly. The Irish National Coordinating Committee for the European Year against Racism recommended that as part of the strategy, government departments, state agencies, semi-state bodies and local authorities should commit themselves to:

- Collecting data on the outcomes for black and minority ethnic groups from their provision.

- Preparing an equal status policy statement to support the elimination of any discrimination within their policies and practices, the provision of services in an inter-cultural manner and the implementation of positive action programmes.

- Providing a specific anti-racist dimension and a focus on outcomes for black and minority ethnic groups in their annual progress statements to the inter-departmental committee responsible for the NAPS.

Monitoring

The Department of Justice, Equality and Law Reform has established a committee to monitor the implementation of the recommendations of the Task Force on the Travelling Community. This is made up of government departments, Travellers and Traveller organizations and representatives of the social partners. Previous experience of monitoring committees would suggest that they have little to offer in terms of promoting and supporting progress. A monitoring committee established after the Report of the Review Body (Travelling People Review Body, 1983) was widely criticized for its powerlessness to have an impact on government policy and provision and for being reduced to presenting annual lists of actions taken by government departments, with little analysis or critique.

Yet monitoring should be a key element in a process of policy design, providing space for review and reflection that would serve where necessary to reformulate policy and provision. The National Economic and Social Forum sought the realization of this potential in recommending that:

A more active role for the monitoring committees be encouraged. This would mean going beyond monitoring to evaluating the implementation process and identifying inaction and constraints as well as good practice. It would also involve the committees in taking a more proactive role in addressing issues relating to inaction and constraints as well as identifying new priorities for action (NESF, 1997: 34).

Such a role requires adequate terms of reference for, provision of resources to, and attribution of status to the monitoring committee. It remains to be seen if this challenge will be met in a manner that will allow monitoring to make its full contribution to the policy design process.

POLICY INFLUENCING

Traveller Organizations

Traveller organizations have played a key role in creating the conditions for, establishing the need for, and informing the content of new policy making. The Task Force on the Travelling Community usefully established three identifying features of Traveller organizations: they are non-governmental; they involve effective Traveller participation; they are in solidarity with Traveller interests. The Task Force also highlighted the growth in number and the changing nature and role of Traveller organizations over the previous decade. It described a shift in focus 'from a welfare approach inspired by charity to a more rights-based approach', an increase in Traveller participation, a redefinition 'of the Traveller situation in terms of cultural rights, as opposed to simply being a poverty issue', and

> The emergence of a range of more conflictual relationships with statutory bodies is evident. These relationships were preceded by earlier consensus around a welfare agenda. The present thrust is now towards a new partnership based on a common understanding of the cultural rights of Travellers and of the urgent need to respond to the situation of Travellers (Task Force, 1995: 63).

The strategies pursued by Traveller organizations evolved over the decade. A number of central elements can be identified:

- Securing national and European funding to develop new responses in education, training, capacity building, youth and community work, health and economic development to the situation of Travellers.
- Linking analysis and policy development to this local action to create a body of knowledge and a political agenda to inform change.
- Generating a new and extensive media coverage of Travellers focusing on issues of ethnicity and racism over those of poverty and deprivation.
- Targeting Travellers and settled people within their work programmes.
- Extensive networking between Traveller organizations, particularly within the Irish Traveller Movement and the National Traveller

Women's Forum, and between Traveller organizations and the wider community sector.

- Engaging in negotiations within the statutory sector on the basis of partnership.

Social Partnership Arenas

This period of change has coincided with the achievement of social partnership status by the community sector. This was realized in the Partnership 2000 national agreement, 1996, where the sector was identified as one of the four pillars to the partnership process. Traveller groups, such as the Irish Traveller Movement and Pavee Point, made a contribution to the development of the Community Platform as a mechanism for the sector to organize its representation in the arenas of social partnership.

This involvement of the sector has provided an enhanced focus within social partnership arenas for Traveller issues. This is evident in:

- *Partnership 2000 for Inclusion, Employment and Competitiveness* (1996), which identified Travellers as a particular focus in its equality agenda. A section on Travellers made important commitments to Traveller accommodation, education, health, employment, participation and anti-discrimination measures.

- The National Economic and Social Council report *Strategy into the 21st Century* (1996), which preceded and informed *Partnership 2000*, includes Travellers within what they refer to as 'The Modern Equality Focus'. A section on Travellers contains important endorsements of a range of strategies recommended by the Task Force.

- The National Economic and Social Forum has included a Traveller dimension across the full body of its broad-ranging work. There are Traveller dimensions to equality provisions, rural renewal, delivery of social services, job creation and unemployment, among other topics.

The Courts

Travellers and Traveller organizations have used the courts for advancing policy making and the interpretation of policy. A number of key cases can be identified:

- *McDonald vs Feeley and Dublin County Council (1980)*. This case established that Traveller evictions by local authorities from areas deemed unsuitable required the local authority to provide reasonable alternative accommodation.

- *O'Reilly and Others vs. Limerick Corporation (1989)*. This case established that if a need for halting sites was established, then the local authority had to include proposals to meet those needs in their building programme. It also established that services could be provided to Travellers on unofficial sites.

- *University of Limerick vs. Ryan, McCarthy and Limerick County Council Third Party High Court (1991)*. This case established that Section 13 of the 1988 Housing Act imposed a duty on the local authority to provide halting sites for Travellers living permanently in an area.

The European Union

The European Union is only currently developing a coherent policy position on racism and minority ethnic groups. One early initiative, the EC Resolution (89K/53/02) on School Provision for Travellers, has been influential in establishing a focus on inter-cultural approaches within the education system. The European Commission published *An Action Plan against Racism* (1998) which consisted of four strands:

- Introducing legislation to combat racism
- Mainstreaming a focus on racism into Community policies
- Piloting new initiatives
- Information work

This action plan would inevitably have an impact on Irish policy and provision. The Irish Government has already responded to the work of the Irish National Coordinating Committee for the European Year against Racism by forming a longer-term National Consultative Committee on Racism and Interculturalism. This has representation from Traveller organizations and will seek to mainstream a focus on anti-racism within Irish policy making.

The European Commission has also established a European Monitoring Centre on Racism and Xenophobia which is based in Vienna. 'The main remit of the Centre is to study the extent of and trends in racism, xenophobia and anti-Semitism in the European Union and to analyse underlying causes, consequences and effects.' (European Commission, 1998: 7)

International Agreements

A range of international agreements in the human rights field have begun to exert an influence on Irish policy making in a manner that has the potential to benefit Travellers, including:

- The International Covenant on Economic, Social and Cultural Rights: The Irish Government has to report on its performance in relation to these rights to the UN Human Rights Committee.

- The International Covenant on Civil and Political Rights: The Irish Government reported in 1992 to the UN Human Rights Committee. The Committee's published response included a focus on the need to improve the situation for Travellers.

- International Covenant on the Elimination of All Forms of Racial Discrimination: The European Parliament has criticized the Irish government for its failure to ratify this covenant. There is a commitment to ratify once the Irish Government has passed equality legislation. At that point a report on performance will have to be prepared for the Committee on the Elimination of Racial Discrimination.

CONCLUSION

The study of Travellers and social policy indicates the present period as one of significant change and potential. Emerging policy at national level reflects new thinking in terms of its understanding and response to the Traveller community. A significant gap between policy making and policy implementation remains to be bridged before the potential of this new policy context can be realized in a definitive improvement in the status and situation of the Traveller community.

POLICY DEVELOPMENTS

1948   Local Government (Sanitary Services) Act
1961   Road Safety Act
1963   Report of the Commission on Itinerancy
1963   Local Government (Planning and Development) Act
1966   Housing Act
1983   Report of the Travelling People Review Body
1988   Housing Act
1989   Prohibition of Incitement to Hatred Act
1990   Unfair Dismissals Act
1994   National Health Strategy *Shaping a Healthier Future*
1995   Report of the Task Force on the Travelling Community
1995   White Paper on Education *Charting Our Education Future*
1996   *Partnership 2000 for Inclusion, Employment and Competitiveness*
1997   *Sharing in Progress*, National Anti-Poverty Strategy
1998   Employment Equality Bill
1998   Housing (Traveller Accommodation) Bill

RECOMMENDED READING

DTEDG File: Irish Travellers: New Analysis and New Initiatives (1992) Dublin: Pavee
    Point Publications.
McCann, M., S. Ó Siocháin and J. Ruane (1994) *Irish Travellers: Culture and Ethnicity*.
    Belfast: Queen's University, Institute of Irish Studies.
Task Force on the Travelling Community. (1995) *Report*. Dublin: Stationery Office.

REFERENCES

Barry, J., B. Herity and J. Solan (1989) *The Travellers' Health Status Study: Vital
    Statistics of Travelling People*. Dublin: Health Research Board.
Commission on Itinerancy (1963) *Report of the Commission on Itinerancy*. Dublin:
    Stationery Office.
Department of Education (1995) *Charting Our Education Future: White Paper on
    Education*. Dublin: Stationery Office.
Department of Education Working Group on Post-Primary Education for Traveller
    Children (1992) *Report of the Department of Education Working Group on Post-
    Primary Education for Traveller Children*. Dublin: Department of Education.
Department of Health (1994) *Shaping a Healthier Future: A Strategy for Effective Care
    in the 1990s*. Dublin: Stationery Office.
Department of Health (1997) *A Plan for Women's Health*. Dublin: Stationery Office.

DTEDG File: Irish Travellers: New Analysis and New Initiatives (1992) Dublin: Pavee Point Publications.

European Commission (1998) *An Action Plan Against Racism*. Brussels: European Commission.

A Heritage Ahead: Cultural Action and Travellers (1995) Dublin: Pavee Point Publications.

Irish National Coordinating Committee for the European Year against Racism (1997) *The Framework Programme for the European Year against Racism 1997*. Dublin.

Irish National Coordinating Committee for the European Year against Racism (1998) *Equality Proofing and Racism: Proofing Government Policy, Provision and Procedures against Racism*. Dublin.

Irish Traveller Movement (1991) *Traveller Accommodation and the Law*. Dublin: Irish Traveller Movement.

Irish Traveller Movement (1993) *Education and Travellers*. Dublin: Irish Traveller Movement

Liegeois, J.P. (1987) *Gypsies and Travellers*. Council of Europe, Council for Cultural Cooperation.

McCann, M., S. Ó Siocháin and J. Ruane (1994) *Irish Travellers: Culture and Ethnicity*. Belfast: Queen's University, Institute of Irish Studies.

McCarthy, P. (1998) *Market Economies: Trading in the Traveller Economy*. Dublin: Pavee Point Publications.

Molloy, S. (1998) *Accommodating Nomadism*. Belfast: Traveller Movement Northern Ireland.

National Economic and Social Council (1996) *Stategy into the 21st Century: Conclusions and Recommendations*. Dublin: NESC.

National Economic and Social Forum (1996) *Equality Proofing Issues*. Forum Report. No.10. Dublin: NESF.

National Economic and Social Forum (1997) *A Framework for Partnership: Enriching Strategic Consensus through Participation*. Dublin: NESF.

Partnership 2000 for Inclusion, Employment and Competitiveness (1996) Dublin: Stationery Office.

Primary Health Care for Travellers Project Report (1996) Dublin: Pavee Point Publications.

Sharing in Progress: National Anti-Poverty Strategy (1997) Dublin: Stationery Office.

Special Education Review Committee (1993) *Report of the Special Education Review Committee*. Dublin: Stationery Office.

Task Force on the Travelling Community. (1995) *Report*. Dublin: Stationery Office.

Tovey, H. (1989) *Why Irish? Irish Identity and the Irish Language*. Dublin: Bord na Gaeilge.

Travelling People Review Body (1983) *Report of the Travelling People Review Body*. Dublin: Stationery Office.

12
Refugees and Social Policy

Joe Moran

. . . [A refugee is any person] who owing to a well-founded fear of being persecuted for reasons of race, religion, nationality, membership of a particular social group or political opinion, is outside the country of his nationality and is unable, or owing to such fear, is unwilling to avail himself of the protection of that country; or who, not having nationality and being outside the country of his former habitual residence, is unable, or owing to such fear, is unwilling to return to it.

(Definition of a refugee in Article 1 of the Geneva Convention of 1951 Relating to the Status of Refugees cited in Schedule 3, Refugee Act 1996: 30).

INTRODUCTION

Refugees and social policy are not usually spoken of in the same breath. When we think of refugees and public policy we normally think in terms of political and legal policies around the issue of asylum determination and associated procedures. Even on these terms, the discourse on refugees and public policy is relatively new in Ireland. The reason for this has been the comparatively few refugees and asylum seekers who have sought protection in Ireland in the past. As a result it is possible to claim that of all the policy areas discussed in this volume, social policy for refugees is the least developed.

To understand the policy context and the developments which have taken place it is important to distinguish between the different categories of refugees. These are described in Figure 1. These distinctions are very important, as each confers a different status upon those to whom it refers, especially in legal terms. Furthermore, the nature of the status permits or limits access to the services normally discussed under social policy. Thus the policy objectives are different for those on one side – those with a status (Convention refugee/leave to remain/programme refugee)

Figure 1. Categories of Refugee

Programme Refugee – A person who has been invited to Ireland on foot of a Government decision in response to humanitarian requests from bodies such as the United Nations High Commission on Refugees (UNHCR).

Asylum Seeker – A person who seeks to be recognized as a refugee in accordance with the terms of the 1951 Convention relating to the Status of Refugees.

Refugee/Convention Refugee – A person who fulfils the requirements of the definition of a refugee under the 1951 Convention and is granted refugee status.

Leave to Remain – Permission granted to a person to remain in the State. This is granted at the discretion of the Minister for Justice, Equality and Law Reform and may be granted, for example, to a person who does not fully meet the requirements of the definition of a refugee under the 1951 Convention, but whom the Minister decides should be allowed to remain in the State for humanitarian reasons.

Source: Refugee Agency Annual Report 1996

as against asylum seekers on the other hand. For ease of usage throughout this chapter the generic term refugee will be applied to all groups of refugees and asylum seekers except where clarification is needed; then the more specific terms will be used.

CURRENT POLICY

Those with a refugee status can avail of all public services which fall within the social policy arena on the same terms as Irish citizens. In other words, those with status can avail of housing, health and social services, social welfare, education, and vocational training. They may also take up employment. Asylum seekers are more restricted in their access to these services. They are entitled to health care, accommodation, and basic income maintenance payments. What this means in practice is that asylum seekers may use the health services on the same basis as Irish nationals, and are entitled to a medical card. They are provided with accommodation, and the relevant health board through the community welfare service assists with arranging this accommodation on an emergency basis in the first instance, paying for it according to local practice. This practice may vary from one health board area to another. In Dublin, where the overwhelming majority of refugees and asylum seekers live, the Eastern Health Board established the Refugee Unit at St James's Hospital in 1997 to deal with all of these welfare matters for asylum seekers. If and when the asylum seeker obtains private rented accommodation, his or her rent is supplemented under the Supplementary Welfare Allowance Scheme. It is also under this scheme that basic income maintenance is paid. The crucial difference between asylum seekers and those with a status is that asylum seekers are not permitted to work or to engage in vocational training or formal education.

Although those with a status may avail of the services provided on the same basis as Irish nationals, not all of those with a status are treated on equal terms. Programme refugees are more favourably treated than the other refugees who have achieved a status and this is evident in a number of different ways. Programme refugees have a government agency (The Refugee Agency) to assist them with their resettlement in Ireland. They have available to them special English language support at primary and post-primary school levels. Mother tongue and culture classes are funded by the Department of Education and Science. A special psychological service has been set up to meet their needs, as have special dental and health services. Programme refugees have also had the facility of a reception centre until recently. And, finally, they have the facility of a translation service to assist them in their communications with service providers. Programme refugees and others with a status have access to English language training funded by the Department of Education and Science. This is the only 'extra' service which others with a status currently share with programme refugees. The services for programme refugees were developed in response to their specific needs at a time when the numbers of other refugees entering the state were very small.

Given the centrality of English for those living in Ireland, one of the most important social policy developments has been a proposal to establish a Refugee Language Support Unit (RLSU). The RLSU, as it is proposed, will be funded by the Department of Education and Science, when necessary financial approval is granted, but administratively located and managed through Trinity College and to be based in Dublin. This Unit will play the central role in the development and monitoring of all aspects of the education services for refugees across all age cohorts amongst those with a status. Furthermore, it will mean the development of educational services to take account of the needs of the different groups who have a status, and no longer will one group be provided for more favourably than another.

A related development is in the area of vocational training. Vocational training through State agencies such as FÁS and CERT are available to those with a status. However, appropriate and sufficient level of language skills are often not to be found in those who have spent time in English language training, thus restricting access to these vocational training opportunities. An initiative to develop the next step – the link between English language and vocational training which has received European Union funding – is also acknowledged and included in the planned Refugee Language Support Unit.

Within the health area there are also some developments which are noteworthy. In December 1997, a special health unit was added to the Eastern Health Board's Refugee Unit to deal with the health needs of asylum seekers on their arrival. This service, which includes a general practitioner service and a health screening service, provides immediate health care to newly arrived asylum seekers until their medical card claim is processed. The Eastern Health Board has also been asked by the Department of Health and Children to provide a psychological service for refugees and asylum seekers. It is expected that this service will be in place before the end of 1998.

Housing is provided for refugees with a status on the same basis as Irish nationals. Those who can afford it buy their own homes or rent in the private rented sector. Those who are on low income – the majority of refugees – are provided with temporary accommodation until they can locate an apartment or house to rent. They can go on local authority housing lists where their access to housing is decided on the same criteria and through the same allocation system as apply to the rest of the population. The main difference between housing for asylum seekers and other refugees is that the former are not normally allowed on to local authority housing lists, although O'Sullivan (1997: 45) suggests that the entitlement of asylum seekers to apply for local authority housing is unclear. Those living in private rented accommodation may receive rent supplement if they fulfil the criteria. Initial accommodation organized through the community welfare service is usually hostel or bed and breakfast accommodation. A new initiative established in 1998 by the Refugee Agency is a refugee housing association which will provide accommodation and related services for the most vulnerable refugees with a status. O'Sullivan (1997: 45) claims that voluntary social housing 'offers substantial potential to contribute to meeting the housing needs of low income households'.

HISTORICAL ORIGINS

Social policy development for refugees has only recent historical origins in Ireland. However, it is worth examining the historical context of Irish refugee policy to allow the observer an overview and an understanding of some of the internal circumstances which have led to the present situation. It must be pointed out that the limited literature available on this subject is almost entirely critical of Ireland's attitude and response to refugees since the foundation of the state.

At the foundation of the state and for many years afterwards, Ireland was not an attractive location for those fleeing from persecution, given its own impoverishment and its geographical position, a monocultural island on the fringe of Europe (McGovern, 1990: 126). It was not solely a problem of place or of poverty, however; it was also, according to Ward (1996), due to a reluctance by the Irish state to offer protection to those from beyond its shores who needed it. Ward, in her publication on Ireland's response to the Hungarian refugee crisis in 1956, documents how this reluctance manifested itself. She describes how 'from the early years of the state, it was clear that Ireland never saw itself as offering a protective mantle to stateless persons' (Ward, 1996: 132). She also shows how certain groups were specifically discouraged and discriminated against, such as Jews and refugees from the Spanish Civil War, and quotes a secretary of the Department of External Affairs saying about the latter group '. . . that Ireland's unemployment problems excluded extending the hand of mercy to non-nationals in need – most particularly to "Spanish reds"' (Ward, 1996: 133). On the former, Ward quotes from a 1945 Department of Justice Memorandum:

> . . . it was said that because Jews 'do not become assimilated with the native population like other immigrants, there is a danger that any big increase in their numbers might create a social problem' (1996: 133).

Ireland acceded to the 1951 Geneva Convention Relating to the Status of Refugees in 1956 and announced in its maiden speech to the United Nations in that same year its intention to participate in the international response to the Hungarian refugee crisis. An Interdepartmental Conference on Hungarian Refugees was set up to prepare the way for the arrival of a group of 539 refugees, the first group of 'programme' refugees accepted by the state for resettlement. The agreed criteria for the acceptance of the refugees had a resonance in the attitude towards other groups who might have sought asylum in Ireland in the 1930s and 1940s. The criteria required amongst other things that 'they would be suitable on grounds of race and religion, to ensure assimilation' (Ward, 1996: 136). McGovern (1990: 127) describes how no resettlement strategy was put in place for the Hungarian refugees. Instead they were 'literally dumped in disused army huts' in the middle of the Irish countryside. Ward recounts in some detail the experience of the Hungarian refugees in Ireland, which turned out to be a very unhappy one for them and for the Irish authorities. She observes that:

> [t]he key problem that emerged during the Hungarian situation . . . was the absence of domestic legislation and the unwillingness of the state to provide adequate housing, accommodation, work and schooling for the refugees (Ward, 1996: 140).

Some have argued that the next two large groups of refugees accepted for resettlement by the Irish government, the 120 Chileans who arrived in 1973 and 1974, and the 212 Vietnamese who arrived in 1979, fared little better. The difficulties the Chileans encountered have been said to be due to the absence of any resettlement strategy by the government (McGovern, 1990: 119; Collins, 1993: 38). Regarding the Vietnamese, McGovern (1990: 185) has argued that the state decided to maintain a 'peripheral' involvement and 'devolved' its responsibilities for the resettlement of the Vietnamese on to church organizations and non-governmental organizations. She concludes that

> the reason for the Irish Government's failure to respond positively to the challenge of resettling the Vietnamese can be attributed to a fear that the Government would not be able to accomplish their resettlement successfully in a society which was predominantly monocultural (McGovern, 1990: 244).

Moran (1998a) suggests that three important trends have emerged during the 1990s which have had an impact on the state's policy towards refugees. These are, firstly in the state's own policy towards programme refugees; secondly in its response to its obligation under the 1951 UN Convention and the related 1967 Protocol and as a Member State of the European Union to legislate for refugees; and thirdly, the increase in the number who have sought asylum in the state. Of its policy towards programme refugees Moran says, '[t]he Government has been a more willing participant, and has provided more resources to a Government agency to develop a strategy and integrated response for resettlement' (1998a: 9). Ward (1998: 18) also acknowledges the improvements which came with the Bosnian resettlement programme and suggests that it 'provides a good model for how future programmes might look'.

The second development in the 1990s has been the debate on refugee issues, the deliberations of interdepartmental committees, and three Bills which went before the Oireachtas, culminating in the Refugee Act 1996, passed with all party support and welcomed by the non-governmental organizations who had campaigned for the introduction of such legislation. Only five sections of the Act have been implemented thus far, leaving those who campaigned for the legislation, to believe that the legislation as it exists will not be implemented at all (Moran, 1998b).

The third and crucial trend to arise in this decade has been the upward increase in asylum seekers arriving in Ireland over the past four years. Table 1 shows the growth in these numbers.

Table 1. Number of People Seeking Asylum in Ireland 1991–98

Year	1991	1992	1993	1994	1995	1996	1997	1998 Jan-May*
No.	31	39	91	355	424	1,179	3,883	2,175

Source: Department of Justice and *The Irish Times* 18 June 1998

Although in line with the number of asylum seekers arriving in other European countries of the same population size as Ireland, these figures are large in an Irish context, and the state was ill-prepared to deal with them (see comparative figures in UNHCR, 1997: 290–2). These increased numbers have been given as the main reason by both the current and former Ministers for Justice for the non-implementation of the Refugee Act (*Prime Time*, RTÉ, 9 December 1997). On the same programme a leading academic in the area of refugee law, Rosemary Byrne, said that the problem was not in the numbers themselves. Instead, she claimed, the 'actual problem lies with the government's inability to respond effectively to these arrivals . . . the real crisis lies with government inertia'.

The policy and legislative approach to asylum seekers and refugees has not yet been resolved to the satisfaction of all the interested parties and undoubtedly this debate will continue for some time. From a social policy perspective a potentially very important beginning has taken place for those who have achieved status. The government, through the Minister for Justice, Equality and Law Reform, has accepted that not enough has been done to facilitate the integration of recognized refugees into Irish society and a commitment to doing more in this regard has been given (O'Donoghue, 1998).

The development of specific social policy for refugees is a relatively new departure in Ireland. In the early years of refugee arrivals, which were mainly through government programmes, the apparent reluctance by the state to accept people for resettlement was reflected in an assimilationist approach, where people were expected to avail of the services provided generally for the native population. The more recent approach to the resettlement and integration of Bosnian programme refugees has shown a shift in this policy where services specifically aimed at assisting refugees have been introduced. These policies are likely to be extended to the wider refugee community with a status – a process which will be given a greater impetus over the coming months and years. For asylum seekers, on the other hand, social policy developments are restricted to basic income maintenance, accommodation, and health, and there are no obvious indications that this will alter in the near future.

PRINCIPAL ACTORS IN THE DEVELOPMENT OF POLICY

As with any social policy area there is a number of actors and interested parties involved. The main ones in this sphere consist of the government itself, the various government departments within whose remit lies a particular aspect of policy, government agencies which have direct dealings with refugees through the provision of general public services, or more specifically – as in the case of the Refugee Agency – a government body with responsibility for resettling programme refugees, political parties, individual politicians, and non-governmental organizations – both Irish-led and refugee-led. It is relatively easy to identify the main protagonists in this area as the numbers are small, but it is more difficult to assess the relative importance of each.

The government's decisions on matters of public policy are supported and informed by the civil service. It is stated frequently that it is within this combination that the power over matters of policy remains; that the Oireachtas, political parties and interest groups have limited say in the development of public policy (Chubb, 1992: 12). In the area of immigration where refugee issues reside, the Minister for Justice has enormous powers (Costello, 1994: 358). It is therefore true to say that the most important and most powerful influence on refugee policy comes from the Minister for Justice and the Department of Justice, Equality and Law Reform (DJELR). However, the Minister for Foreign Affairs and his department plays the lead role in government policy towards programme refugees. Furthermore, once a policy area is outside the remit of the DJELR and does not lead to a breach of immigration law and procedures, other ministers and departments can respond to the needs of refugees and asylum seekers as they see fit within the normal guidelines and restrictions which operate in the government decision-making process. Any new policy developments for refugees are sought and promoted in the way all other public policy developments are progressed. It was through this decision-making process that the basis for the current policies on programme refugees was established in government decisions of the early 1990s.

State agencies are also developers of social policy in their role as providers of services. The Eastern Health Board provides an example of this with the setting up of the Refugee Unit to meet the basic income maintenance, accommodation and health needs of asylum seekers. A second example of state agency involvement is that of FÁS Dublin North Region which, in partnership with other interested groups, set up a special vocational training project for refugees with a status.

The most influential government agency in the development of social policy for refugees since its establishment in 1991 has been the Refugee Agency. In this period a number of initiatives have been undertaken with the Refugee Agency as the leading promoter. The Refugee Agency has commissioned research on the language needs of refugees, which has been carried out by the Centre for Language and Communication Studies, at Trinity College Dublin, and funded by the Department of Education and Science (Little & Lazenby Simpson, 1996). Based on the findings of this research and the expressed needs of the Bosnian community, the special vocational training project referred to above with FÁS Dublin North Region was promoted by the Refugee Agency. Furthermore, the findings of the research, completed in 1996, have led to the Department of Education and Science supporting the proposed establishment of the Refugee Language Support Unit. The Refugee Agency, as the lead partner, established the Bosnian Community Development Project in 1995, which in turn has received recognition by the Department of Social, Community and Family Affairs as a disadvantaged community through its inclusion for funding from the Department's Community Development Programme. The Refugee Agency, as lead agency, is currently establishing an independent refugee housing association to respond to the housing needs of refugees with a status.

Political parties and individual politicians have contributed to the policy debate on refugees. The 1993 commitment by the newly formed Fianna Fáil-Labour coalition government introduced the commitment to the highest international standards for dealing with refugees. In 1996 a White Paper on Foreign Policy contained within it a commitment to best international practice in resettling refugees (Government of Ireland, 1996: 237). The Oireachtas debates in the lead up to the passing of the Refugee Act 1996 were in general well-informed, with the eventual coming together of opinion across both houses over the years of the debate providing all-party support for the final passing of the legislation. This process was begun by an individual politician, when Alan Shatter, an opposition deputy, introduced the 1993 Refugee Protection Bill. Whilst the Bill was defeated by the government side, the thrust of the Bill was accepted by the then Minister for Justice, who set up an inter-departmental committee to examine the issues involved, and pledged to introduce legislation when the findings of the committee became known. The Refugee Act 1996 was the final outcome of this process which had begun its legislative journey three years earlier.

Within the non-governmental organization (NGO) sector the biggest contribution to policy development was without doubt the development and passing of the Refugee Act 1996. Two NGOs in particular were to the forefront in making this contribution – Amnesty International and the Irish Refugee Council. Moran (1998b) argues that these two organizations contributed substantially to getting this legislation passed after five years of campaigning. It is a fundamental part of Amnesty International's human rights brief to influence public policy to protect those at risk of persecution, including refugees. Social policy issues which do not directly fall within this very specific domain are not pursued. The Irish Refugee Council on the other hand has a broader brief which spans issues such as legislation on asylum determination and the welfare of refugees, both those awaiting a decision and those who receive status. The Irish Refugee Council is involved in many of the service developments which have taken place, in a consultative capacity, as a promoter of services, as a partner in new developments or as an initiator of new projects. The Ennis office has successfully influenced local service providers to make increasing provision for refugees and asylum seekers living there. Next to Dublin, Ennis is the biggest centre of refugee residence. However, the Council's own very limited financial and human resources have restricted its capacity to respond to the needs of refugees to the extent that it envisaged at its foundation (Irish Refugee Council, 1990).

The Irish Red Cross Society, Comhlamh, Irish Council for Civil Liberties, and Trócaire, are all involved in refugee issues in Ireland, either as campaigning organizations and/or providers of some services to refugees and asylum seekers. One of the smallest NGOs is Rescue Trust which has campaigned for nine years to have an independent centre for the treatment of victims of torture and trauma established in Ireland. Whilst this objective has yet to be achieved, there is little doubt that the campaigning of Rescue Trust has influenced the decision by the Department of Health and Children to provide the Eastern Health Board with funding to establish a psychological service for refugees in Dublin.

There are a number of organizations and groups becoming involved in the provision of services to refugees and asylum seekers. Some are newly established and others are already providers of services to the Irish population who, seeing the need, expand or develop their operations to provide for refugees. These organizations include Refugee Information Service (an advice and information service) and Focus Ireland (a flat-finding service). It is too early to say what impact if any they are making on social policy in this field.

Apart from Irish NGOs working with and on behalf of refugees, there are developing refugee associations which are offering services and supports for refugees, either specifically for members of their own national communities, such as the Bosnian Community Development Project (BCDP), or responding to a wider target group, such as the Association of Refugees and Asylum Seekers in Ireland. At a social policy level these groups have not made as yet any significant inroads, although the BCDP has been a partner in the development of the special vocational training project referred to above.

EVALUATION OF CURRENT POLICY

The basis of all refugee policy, including social policy for refugees, is protection. Protection at its most fundamental is immediate physical safety and security. In terms of social policy this is reflected in the state's response to these basic needs by making policy decisions on the provision of shelter and food (see UNHCR, 1993: 5). Social policy development is determined by the priorities and attitudes of the host country towards refugees and asylum seekers. Priorities and attitudes inform decisions which are inevitably political decisions. In Ireland in the past there have been three distinct approaches in evidence: one towards asylum seekers, the second towards those given convention status and humanitarian leave to remain, and the third towards programme refugees. Those given priority in terms of what the state has to offer have been programme refugees, those with convention status and humanitarian leave to remain come next, and asylum seekers in third place. More recently there has been a significant move in the state's thinking towards those given convention status and humanitarian leave to remain, with the issue of supporting 'integration' of those who fit into this group moving up the policy agenda. Both the Minister for Justice and the Junior Minister at the Department of Foreign Affairs with Responsibility for Human Rights in statements to the Dáil and Seanad respectively have indicated this shift in policy. The Minister for Justice, John O'Donoghue, said on integration, 'I believe that more can be done more quickly to help recognised refugees . . . I will be pursuing this matter with appropriate colleagues' (O'Donoghue, 1998). Minister Liz O'Donnell told the Seanad, '[m]y own view is that it would make sense from a number of perspectives to bring under one organization, the co-ordination of state services for programme refugees and those asylum seekers recognized as refugees under the Geneva Convention' (O'Donnell, 1998). Such a move towards an integration strategy and the actions taken in support of this development should lead to this group receiving the same attention as programme refugees. In turn this should introduce two rather than three distinctions in policy towards refugees.

Social policy objectives are determined by political objectives, which in the case of asylum seekers mean that they should be assisted only so far as it maintains their basic need for accommodation, health care, and basic income maintenance. The Department of Justice, in a 1996 information leaflet, outlines the state's policy in relation to asylum seekers:

> As asylum seekers are allowed to stay in the state only on a temporary basis while their claim is being processed it would be inappropriate for the state to give aid to non-nationals to assist integration into the state (Department of Justice 1996: 6).

Furthermore, in June 1998, the Minister for Justice reiterated this position when he addressed the Oireachtas Committee on Justice, Equality and Women's Rights. In response to opposition requests to allow asylum seekers to work after a six month stay in the state he said that 'to grant work permits to people who might eventually be "found to be illegal immigrants" would "surely confer a legitimacy on their status in the state they would not merit"' (*The Irish Times*, 18 June 1998).

It is necessary to lay down some guiding principles on which an assessment of policy can be made. Although some principles overlap, I propose to address each of the two groups separately – asylum seekers and those with a status. Social policy objectives for asylum seekers even within the context of existing political priorities should meet basic needs. The achievement of these objectives should be underlined by the principle of protection, the fundamental concept which underpins all refugee policy. As Moran (1998a) points out, protection is not only about access to a country of asylum, and the opportunity provided on reaching such a country to apply for asylum. It is also about the quality of life available to the asylum seeker awaiting a decision and to the refugee who has received a positive decision. As already outlined, basic needs are being met – using the provision of accommodation, health care, and basic income maintenance as the guide. There are issues around the supply of these services, however, which must also be considered, such as the accessibility and quality of the accommodation in the first instance, and once in the accommodation the lack of security of tenure which is prevalent in the private rented sector (O'Sullivan, 1997: 44). Secondly, a health service must be accessible, and while it may seem so by permitting asylum seekers to avail of free health care as holders of medical cards, the lack of a proper translation service restricts access. Thirdly, Supplementary Welfare Allowance and the various other payments which are made through this scheme are discretionary, and therefore, even if most generously applied, as is often the case, the scheme is less than transparent. In theory the state meets the basic needs of asylum seekers but in practice individuals may be confronted with a host of difficulties trying to ensure that these needs are met. In each of these three areas of provision there are weaknesses in the application of social policy to the particular group.

The increased number of staff appointed by the Department of Justice, Equality and Law Reform in early 1998 to reduce the backlog of asylum cases and speed up the asylum process is an important step in improving the quality of lives of asylum seekers by reducing the waiting period for decisions. The development of a psychological and other services to help to meet the basic needs of asylum seekers is also a positive move. Notwithstanding the state's current policy of not allowing asylum seekers to work or avail of any services beyond those currently open to them there is an alternative approach practised in other European states. In Sweden, for example, asylum seekers are obliged to attend organized activities provided by the municipalities in which they live (Swedish Ministry for Foreign Affairs, 1997: 33). Organized activities for asylum seekers would at the very least assist with the prevention of further psychological distress and might help reduce the level of public antipathy towards the refugee population, thereby adding to the quality of life asylum seekers can enjoy. Depending on the political objectives of the state's refugee policy, the range of activities could go from recreational at one end of the scale, through to orientation, language training, education, vocational training, up to and including employment at the other end.

For those with a status, the objectives of social policy should be to meet basic needs in the first instance leading to resettlement and finally integration. The principles on which these objectives should be built are protection, the prevention of marginalization and isolation, the promotion of meaningful lives, and the promotion of equal opportunity. The protection principle has already been discussed, but it is worth noting its inclusion for this group of refugees. It is included because protection does not end when the individual gains status. There is a need for the state to continue to protect the refugee for as long as such protection is required.

The second principle is to prevent refugees from becoming marginalized and isolated within Irish society. Social policies for refugees in the spheres of education, housing, income support, health, and vocational training must meet this basic principle and thus require considerable thought, application and finance. Refugees are one of the most marginalized groups in Europe according to a report commissioned by the European Union on the Integra strand of the Social Fund:

> Both labour immigrants and the growing number of settled refugees occupy the bottom rungs of our societies, individual exceptions notwithstanding. They constitute disadvantaged populations, or more precisely, populations at risk. They are constantly at the risk of unemployment, of having to accept the worst housing, of encountering disproportionate difficulties at school and in formal training situations. In short, of being down-and-out and remaining so (*Braun Report*, cited in Rojas, 1997: 27).

Successful integration is fundamental if the third principle of living meaningful lives is to be achieved. O'Regan (1998: 127) describes successful integration as follows:

> Successful integration means that the refugee is able to participate to the extent that he/she needs and wishes in all of the major components of the new society, without having to relinquish his or her own identity.

The promotion of equal opportunity is the final principle which should inform social policy for refugees. The lack of a translation service in the health setting is an example of the lack of equal opportunity. It prevents someone who does not have sufficient skills in the language of the host society from gaining access to a service on an equal basis with the native language speaker. This principle is not only relevant to health services but across all public services. Equal opportunity does not of course just refer to having translation services available. It refers to the removal of any barrier in society which prevents refugees from gaining access to goods or services which as a participant in that society they might reasonably be expected to have.

The strength of current social policy for refugees is probably best described in its potential for future development. It is possible to be more optimistic in this regard for those with a status, as the commitment by government to promote the integration of refugees with a status should impact on social policy in this area. When such policy developments take place there is a need to ensure an integrated and comprehensive strategy at local and national levels. At this juncture there is no evidence to suggest that any improvement will be offered to enhance the current situation of asylum seekers. There is currently much confusion and lack of clarity about who is entitled to what services. Such difficulties arise most frequently in the areas of local authority housing, FÁS training, and entitlement to unemployment assistance, causing much distress for individual refugees and adding to the workloads of public service staff.

CHALLENGES FOR THE FUTURE

There are many challenges which confront policy makers and not all of them relate to the future. Some of the more profound challenges are currently before us. There are two particularly difficult issues which need urgent attention: racism is the first, and the second is the impact in poorer areas of Dublin of large numbers of refugees. The issue of racism has entered the public arena and public discourse like no other in the past twelve months. Certain sections of the media have been accused of inflaming a racist and xenophobic atmosphere (Pollak, 1998). Such has been the impact of this development that an all-party motion on the issue of racism was proposed and passed in the Dáil in December 1997. There continues to be a great deal of unease about this matter. While legislation will not in itself change attitudes, the introduction of legislation to outlaw racism in all its forms and manifestations is crucial as it shows that as a society Ireland does not accept such discrimination. It would also provide some recourse to those at the receiving end of racism and discrimination. Social policy development as a matter of course must be proofed against discrimination.

The second challenge which needs urgent attention is the impact of large numbers of refugees on the poorer, marginalized areas of Dublin. Despite growing economic prosperity in Ireland over recent years there are sections of the population who have not benefited and these communities remain as disadvantaged now as they were prior to this period of sustained economic growth. The areas of Dublin where disadvantage is most prevalent are the same areas where refugees on rent supplements locate their accommodation, as it is in these areas that accommodation is most affordable. While in overall terms the number of refugees in Ireland may not be as high as in other European countries the concentration of those who are here, in the most marginalized communities of the capital, is a cause for concern. Moran states that people in these communities feel under threat by the arrival of the refugees in their neighbourhoods and suggests that 'any plans for the integration of refugees must also contain a component directed at helping the local Irish populations' (1998a: 13).

This particular challenge would be something less if accommodation were more widely and more readily available for refugees. However, this particular problem is not just one for refugees. It has also become a critical problem for society as a whole. The scarcity of accommodation leads to another challenge inextricably linked with it. How long can the current reception policy survive? The current reception policy is to accommodate refugees and asylum seekers in the housing market on the same basis as homeless Irish people. Where private rented accommodation at the appropriate rent levels can be found by the refugees themselves that is the preferred option; but often people are having to use bed and breakfast or hostel accommodation, a situation which may continue for several months (O'Sullivan, 1997: 41–2). Due to the shortage of accommodation in the Dublin region other alternatives are being looked at. This problem brings to the fore the appropriateness of reception centres and dispersion as responses to this need. There are no easy answers to these difficult questions but both have received much criticism when used in other countries (Carey-Wood et al., 1995; Dutch Refugee Council, 1997). Yet O'Regan's (1998) research points to very positive outcomes for Vietnamese and Bosnian programme refugees who spent periods of time in reception centres where their stay was relatively short and purposeful. It is also a fact that the majority of the Vietnamese who were dispersed in Ireland returned to Dublin as soon as they could. The main criticism of reception centres is that asylum seekers invariably remain there too long and as a result become more susceptible to mental health problems (Dutch Refugee Council, 1997: 11).

A challenge for the future that also needs to receive early attention is the development of social policies directed at ethnic minorities. The current practice in Ireland is to regard those who come here as refugees, as refugees for life. People who come to Ireland or indeed to any other country and remain there for a period of time rebuilding their lives do not remain as refugees. The status of refugee is rightfully only a temporary one. There is no recognition in Ireland of this fact nor of the fact that ethnic minorities exist, apart from the Travelling Community, and that services, irrespective of whether or not someone is a refugee, should be able to meet their needs. Social policy or any other aspect of public policy in Ireland has never recognized this fact. The needs of refugees are important and must be met, but many of these needs and the problems faced are common to those of all racial and ethnic minority groups.

A further challenge in all of this is the unknown, the future itself. An argument which one would have expected to hear against refugees being in the state is that 'they are taking our jobs'. Thankfully due to sustained economic growth this is not an argument which one hears or one which could be justified. However, when the economy begins to slow down and less work is available, one wonders how the public will react to refugees and other foreigners then. This is a major challenge and one which is closely related to the fight against racism and xenophobia. If anti-racist and anti-discriminatory legislation is not in place and an effort has not been made to develop public awareness of the needs and rights of refugees in our society and our obligations to them, then our policies will be confronted with enormous difficulties.

European integration in this policy area will also provide a challenge for the state's policy towards refugees. It is expected that within five years of the implementation of the Treaty of Amsterdam there will be a uniform policy in Europe on refugee reception and burden sharing (Government of Ireland, 1998: 43–4). The effects of such policies, as yet unknown, will impact on the development of Irish refugee policy as the state will no longer be able to act on its own in these matters. There are some who fear that a future European policy on refugees will be based on the lowest common standards (Amnesty International, 1995).

CONCLUSION

Irish social policy for refugees has been to date ad hoc and lacking in strategic management or planning. However, there are developments taking place which suggest that the prevailing approach is changing. It is also evident that asylum seekers will remain in a much less advantageous situation than those with a status. It is likely too that the disparities between programme refugees and those with convention status and humanitarian leave to remain will end as there is a policy commitment at government level to assist the integration of the latter.

Without doubt there have been many failures in this policy area but there have also been some successes. Over the years the state appeared to bury its head in the sand when it came to refugee issues. That is changing and efforts are being made at many levels to respond to the needs of refugees. However, therein lies a potential problem. Many levels, if not properly coordinated, can add to the already widespread confusion which exists about refugees in the public mind and amongst service providers. Furthermore, social policy for refugees should not be developed in isolation from general social policy. In fact the opposite should prevail, that social policy for refugees should be developed within the same framework as for society generally but taking into account that what is appropriate for society as a whole may not always be appropriate for refugees. In such circumstances it may then be necessary for the state and its agencies to develop refugee-specific responses or services based on the yardstick that all social policies for refugees respect the human rights and human dignity of those who have sought protection from the Irish state.

MAIN POLICY DEVELOPMENTS

Nov. 1956	Ireland signs 1951 UN Convention on Status Relating to Refugees and agrees to accept a quota of Hungarian refugees.
May 1979	Government Decision: to accept a quota of Vietnamese refugees; to request Irish Red Cross to set up and manage reception centre; and, to establish ad hoc group under Department of Defence to formulate and administer a refugee resettlement programme.
Nov. 1985	Government Decision to establish a policy Advisory Committee and Refugee Resettlement Committee under the Department of Foreign Affairs.
Dec. 1985	Letter from Department of Justice to UNHCR setting out procedure for the determination of refugee status in Ireland.
April 1991	Government Decision to merge the Policy Advisory Committee and Refugee Resettlement Committee to establish the Refugee Agency under the Department of Foreign Affairs.
July 1992	First of a number of Government Decisions about the admittance of refugees from the former Yugoslavia.
March 1993	High Court found that December 1985 letter on determination of status was binding against the Government.
March 1993	Alan Shatter TD introduced Refugee Protection Bill.
May 1993	Interdepartmental Committee on Non-Irish Nationals established, published report in November 1993.
June 1996	Refugee Act passed.
March 1997	Refugee Language and Training Project established.
April 1997	Eastern Health Board established Refugee Unit for asylum seekers.
Sept. 1997	Five Sections of Refugee Act 1996 implemented.
March 1998	Minister for Justice, Equality and Law Reform announces Government commitment to integration of refugees with a status.
June 1998	Refugee housing association established
1998	Establishment of 'one-stop-shop' in October 1998 for asylum seekers; Proposed establishment of Refugee Language Support Unit by the Department of Education in second half of 1998; Proposed establishment of specialist psychological service for refugees in second half of 1998.

RECOMMENDED READING

For an overview of the development of both general refugee policy and social policy issues related to refugees in Ireland, the following five sources are recommended. Both of Eilis Ward's (1996; 1998) publications provide an historical review of Ireland's refugee policy. Two other studies look at particular policy areas: Freda McGovern's (1990) on education and resettlement of the Vietnamese community, and Eoin O'Sullivan's (1997) on housing issues for asylum seekers. Finally, I would recommend Cathal O'Regan's (1998) study on the resettlement of the Bosnian and Vietnamese communities in Ireland.

REFERENCES

Amnesty International (1995) 'Asylum Procedures in the European Union: Towards A Lowest Common Denominator?' Brussels: Amnesty International.

Carey-Wood, J., K. Duke, V. Karn and T. Marshall (1995) *The Settlement of Refugees in Britain*. Home Office Research Study No. 141. London: HMSO.

Chubb, B. (1992) *The Government and Politics of Ireland*. 3rd edition, London: Longman.

Collins, A. (1993) 'Inequality in Treatment of Asylum Seekers in Ireland'. MA thesis, National University of Ireland, Dublin: unpublished.

Costello, K. (1994) 'Some Issues in the Control of Immigration in Irish Law', pp. 354–65 in L. Heffernan (ed.), *Human Rights: A European Perspective*. Dublin: Round Hall Press.

Department of Justice, Equality and Law Reform (1996) 'Guidelines on the Procedures for the Reception of Asylum Applicants', Dublin: unpublished.

Dutch Refugee Council (1997) 'Asylum Seekers – Don't Let Them Sit and Wait', Amsterdam: Dutch Refugee Council.

Government of Ireland (1996) *Challenge and Opportunities Abroad*. White Paper on Foreign Policy. Dublin: The Stationery Office.

Government of Ireland, *Refugee Act 1996*. Dublin: The Stationary Office.

Government of Ireland (1998) *Treaty of Amsterdam White Paper*. Dublin: Stationery Office.

Irish Refugee Council (1990) 'Statute of the Irish Refugee Council'. Dublin: unpublished.

The Irish Times, 18 June 1998.

Little, D. and B.C. Lazenby Simpson (1996) *Meeting the Language Needs of Refugees*. Dublin: Centre for Language and Communication Studies, Trinity College Dublin.

McGovern, F. (1990) 'Vietnamese Refugees in Ireland 1979–1989: A Case Study in Resettlement and Education'. Unpublished MEd thesis, Trinity College, Dublin.

Moran, J. (1998a) 'An Overview of the Current Refugee Situation in Ireland and an Examination of Practice Issues'. Paper presented at the Annual Conference of the Irish Association of Social Workers, held in Kilkenny, 7 May, unpublished.

Refugees and Social Policy   285

Moran, J. (1998b) 'Interest Groups and the Making of Public Policy: The Role of
    Non-Governmental Organisations in the Development of the Refugee Act
    1996'. MA Thesis, Institute of Public Administration, Dublin: unpublished.
O'Donnell, L., TD, Minister of State at the Department of Foreign Affairs,
    Adjournment Debate, Seanad Éireann, 10 June 1998.
O'Donoghue, J., TD, Minister for Justice, Equality and Law Reform, Speech on
    Second Stage of the Asylum Seekers (Regularisation of Status) (No. 2) Bill
    1998, 10 March 1998.
O'Regan, C. (1998) *Report of a Survey of the Vietnamese and Bosnian Refugee
    Communities in Ireland*. Dublin: Refugee Agency/Department of Psychology,
    Eastern Health Board.
O'Sullivan, E. (1997) *Homelessness, Housing Needs and Asylum Seekers in Ireland*.
    Dublin: Homeless Initiative.
Pollak, A. (1998) 'Address to Cleraun Media Conference'. 21 February 1998,
    unpublished.
Prime Time, 'The Politics of Asylum'. Roisin Boyd, Reporter, and Tamsin Fontes,
    Producer, RTÉ, 9 December 1997.
Refugee Agency (1996) *Annual Report*. Dublin: Refugee Agency.
Rojas, M. (1997) 'The Fight Against Social Exclusion in the European Union'.
    Lund Sweden: Department of Economic History, Lund University.
Swedish Ministry for Foreign Affairs (1997) *Immigration and Refugee Policy*.
    Stockholm: Ministry for Foreign Affairs.
UNHCR (1993) *The State of the World's Refugees: The Challenge of Protection*.
    Harmondsworth: Penguin.
UNHCR, (1997) *The State of the World's Refugees: A Humanitarian Agenda*. Oxford:
    Oxford University Press.
Ward, E. (1996) 'Ireland's Refugee Policies and the Case of the Hungarians', *Irish
    Studies in International Affairs*, 7: 131–41.
Ward, E. (1998) 'Ireland's Refugee Policies: A Critical Overview', forthcoming in
    Irish Human Rights Review.

13

The Criminal Justice System in Ireland: Towards Change and Transformation

Anthony Cotter

Public Debate on crime is not something to be avoided but actively encouraged; it is essential to the longer term viability and success of any crime strategy

Tackling Crime (Department of Justice, 1997)

INTRODUCTION

In 1998 the Government published its three-year strategy document on crime and related matters, *Community, Security and Equality*, confirming that crime and 'the crime problem' are a central political and social issue in Ireland in the 1990s. In Ireland, the prison population increased from 963 inmates in 1973, to 2171 in 1993. In response to this increase, all political parties competed to convince the electorate that their particular policies would deal with criminal activity in a tough and uncompromising manner. The concept of 'zero tolerance' towards crime has become part of the public discourse on crime.

THE CRIMINAL JUSTICE SYSTEM

The criminal justice system is a complex and multilayered structure which provides the framework for the operation of many distinct but interrelated agencies and institutions, including the Garda, the Courts, Probation service and Prisons, all coordinated by the Department of Justice, Equality and Law Reform which is the central government agency responsible for all issues relating to law and order. Other State agencies which play a pivotal role in the operation of the system are the offices of the Director of Public Prosecutions (DPP), Attorney-General

(AG) and the Chief State Solicitor. The Department of Justice, Equality and Law Reform has a very powerful role in relation to the security of the State, social order and legislative provisions. It has published policy documents in relation to a number of aspects of criminal justice in recent years, such as: *Tackling Crime: Discussion Paper* (1997), *The Law on Sexual Offences: Discussion Paper* (1998a), and *The Strategy Statement 1998–2000* (1998b). This section examines the operations of the key agencies of this department.

The Garda Siochána

With the establishment of the Irish Free State in 1922, the new government adopted the British policing system already in place, merely changing personnel and leaving the structures and administration largely in place. Subsequent developments in the police reflected what was happening throughout Europe, where 'police organisations tended to be structured militarily, and to be nationally organized and centrally controlled' (O'Reilly, 1986: 34). Such a development has meant that the Gardaí are very much a centralized organization, controlled, apart from operational matters, by the Department of Justice, Equality and Law Reform and, as a consequence, directly answerable to the Minister of this Department. A further unique inheritance has been the maintenance of the force as an unarmed one, with the exception of particular units which account for approximately fifteen per cent of the total (Garda Review, 1991). In his article on policing in Ireland, O'Reilly (1986: 38) states that the Gardaí have two central areas of operation: the detection and prevention of crime. While these may be primary functions of the Gardaí, research has indicated that a considerable amount of time is devoted to what might be called service works, whereby Gardaí respond to people seeking assistance and advice not directly associated with criminal or illegal activity. The five key areas of Gardaí work in contemporary Ireland are crime prevention and detection; traffic control and related matters; community relations and dealing with community problems; answering and responding to calls for assistance; public reassurance; and public order maintenance.

The role of the Gardaí has expanded considerably over the past twenty years. This has increased the complexity of their work, necessitating new skills of operation and demanding an increased sophistication in their relations with the public. Because of the diversity of tasks now demanded of the Gardaí, policing has become so laden with expectations that the reality it can deliver in terms of detection, prosecution and the reduction of crime levels is an ongoing source of debate, argument and ideological conflict. When a crime is reported, it is the job of the Gardaí to detect and successfully prosecute the offender. As the number of crimes has increased, the rate of detection has continually declined, from 66 per cent in 1966, to 36 per cent in 1993 (Garda Siochána, 1995). In an effort to combat this imbalance between crime rate and crime detection and to reduce the level of juvenile crime, the Gardaí have developed a variety of ways in which they not only detect crime but also prevent it.

The Neighbourhood Watch and Community Alert (rural) strategies were instituted to involve the community in preventing and reporting criminal activity. The most radical development in the Gardaí, however, has been the scheme for diverting juvenile offenders, wherever possible, from entry into the formal criminal justice system. Established in 1963 as the Juvenile Liaison Scheme, it now operates as the Juvenile Diversion Programme. Since the inception of the programme, 77,000 offenders from a total of 86,195 reached their eighteenth year without being prosecuted for a criminal offence (National Juvenile Office, 1991). Instead of being charged with a usually minor offence, the juvenile is cautioned and placed under the supervision of a special Garda Juvenile Liaison Officer (JLO) if considered necessary. This policy has a number of benefits not only for the offender but also for the Gardaí and the community. These include the diversion of juveniles from the formal criminal justice system – 1555 during 1996 (Garda Siochána, 1996), and the reduction of the workload of juvenile courts. The cooperation between parents, communities and the Garda has improved as a result of this scheme.

The Courts

The Courts are the pivotal institution in the criminal justice system. It is here that the determination of guilt or innocence is decided, circumscribing the defendant's future contact with the system. There are a number of different courts, with different jurisdictions, different and disparate powers, and different sentencing capacities. Rothman (1984) highlights the main sequential decisions involved in court proceedings as being arrest and summons; initiation of court proceedings, which will involve the Director of Public Prosecutions (DPP) in serious cases; determination of charges and court jurisdiction; verdict; and sentencing.

The defendant appears before the District Court, which is the Court of first hearing, where a preliminary examination of the facts of the case is conducted, unless the defendant waives his or her right and opts to have the case heard before the Court without a jury. If the Court decides there is a prima facie case to answer, the case goes forward to the Circuit

Criminal Court, or to the Central Criminal Court in cases of rape, murder, and treason. The prosecution must put together, in written form, all the evidence to be used against the accused. This is presented in what is called a Book of Evidence. The accused and his or her legal representatives are legally entitled to a copy of the evidence to allow them to prepare their defence strategy. The case is then heard by a judge and jury to determine guilt or innocence.

The Court system functions on the basis of a due process philosophy whereby justice is administered within a framework of legal rules and procedures which are generally known, totally fair, and perceived as being just. Over the centuries the court system has been perceived to be distant, uncaring, out of touch – even when it functions competently within the context of due process. The court system has itself not helped this viewpoint by communicating in archaic language, by moving slowly and in apparently mysterious ways. The Constitution (1937) guarantees 'due process' under section 38.1, which states that 'no person shall be tried on any criminal charge save in due course of law'. The term 'due process' means that a defendant in the courts is entitled to a decision-making process subject to, and open to, public scrutiny, an unalienable right to defend his or her position, and an independence and impartiality on the part of the decision makers.

The Law Reform Commission was established in 1975 to provide a constant review of procedures and legislation. The Commission, comprised of six members, is presided over by a Senior Judge of the High or Supreme Court. Its task is to discuss and evaluate aspects of the law before submitting detailed proposals to Government. These proposals frequently form the basis for subsequent legislative changes which have had considerable implications for the operation of the criminal justice system. Since its inception, the Commission has published 54 reports on various legal topics including sexual abuse, family courts, contempt of court and sentencing.

Probably the most revolutionary change in the administration of the Irish Court system was proposed by a Working Group on a Courts Commission established by the Minister. Its Report (1996) reviewed the operation of the courts system and made recommendations in relation to its future development. The primary recommendation of the Report was the establishment of an independent body to manage a unified court system, to be known as the Court Service. A secondary recommendation was the need for an enhanced form of communication between the courts and the public. The government has accepted the recommendations in the Report, creating the basis for radical reform which will undoubtedly make its mark on the entire Irish legal system.

The Probation and Welfare Service

The Probation and Welfare Service originated in the nineteenth century as an alternative to custody. It is the social work service attached to the courts, prisons, places of detention, special schools, hostels, workshops and various ancillary community inter-agency projects. However, its primary role is that of providing an advisory service to the courts; writing pre-sentence reports; supervising offenders in the community; organizing and administering Community Service Orders; and, under the direction of the Probation of Offenders Act (1907), advising and befriending all those entrusted to its care and supervision by the courts. In 1969, after a review of the work of the Service, three senior officers and 27 probation officers were appointed. This expansion marked the beginning of the modern Probation Service. The voluntary sector was involved until the 1970s, and the Service still maintains and develops, on a formal basis, links with voluntary and community groups.

The Probation and Welfare Service is organized on a national basis, with offices in all major centres of population. It is a professional agency attached to the Department of Justice, Equality and Law Reform. Like the Gardaí, it has a centralized and hierarchical bureaucratic structure similar to that pertaining in all civil service departments. Since its development into a formal professional organization, it has expanded not only in size but also in terms of the variety of services it provides to the courts and other organizations. In 1980, the first year an Annual Report was produced, there were 777 Pre-Sentence Reports presented to the courts and a total of 1712 new cases were placed under supervision. In 1994 there were a total of 3587 Pre-Sentence Reports and 2060 Community Service Reports presented to the Courts. The total number placed under supervision was 2633 (Probation and Welfare Service, 1980, 1994).

The Probation and Welfare Service has three principal community-based sanctions available to it:

1. Probation Order – a statutory period of supervision, from 1 to 3 years, imposed by the District Court, under which the offender must enter into a recognisance. Conditions may be attached to the order (Probation of Offenders Act 1907).

2. Community Service Order – this order is in lieu of a prison sentence after a verdict of guilty. The order can last from 60 hours to 240 hours. An offender cannot be assigned to the Community Service Scheme unless a Probation Officer's report deems him or her suitable and the offender is in agreement. Examples of such orders are renovating school premises and creating raised gardens for the disabled.

3. Supervision during deferment of sentence – this order has no formal legislative basis. It is used by all courts, but especially the higher ones, i.e. Circuit and Central Criminal Courts. During the deferred period the offender is supervised by a Probation Officer. On completion of the order, the offender returns to court where an assessment report presented to the judge outlines progress made and other relevant information.

The considerable increase in the number of community-based sanctions would seem to indicate a major move by the courts in the direction of imposing non-prison sentences. However, according to O'Mahony, there is no definitive evidence that these cases 'represent the substitution of a non-custodial sentence for what would otherwise have been a custodial sentence' (1993: 81).

In 1983, with the enactment of the Criminal Justice (Community Service) Act, the first major policy change in the Probation and Welfare Service's dealings with offenders was implemented. Under the Act, offenders do community work in lieu of a prison sentence, the underlying philosophy being that the offenders should make restitution to society for their wrongdoing. It has proved to be a very successful development, having the confidence of both the judiciary and the public.

In the early 1990s the Probation and Welfare Service, following another policy decision, provided structured community-based programmes to the courts which addressed the needs of more serious offenders. One such programme is the Bridge Project in Dublin which is a community-based intensive supervision initiative for young offenders between the ages of seventeen and 26 years. The project is managed by a board composed of representatives of many diverse interests, i.e. business community, trade unions and the Department of Justice, Equality and Law Reform. The programmes offered are group-based and, while they primarily address in a systematic way the offending and thinking of the participants (Ross and Fabiano, 1985), issues such as substance abuse, anger control and social skills are also addressed. A similar programme is run by the Probation and Welfare Service in Cork. Target, a community-based project, was begun in Dublin in 1998. It is based on a holistic approach emphasizing the person, the community and both owning and accepting the integration of the former. It may, if successful, become a central feature of all work with offenders.

As part of the ongoing development, the Probation and Welfare Service will be establishing a community-based programme for convicted sex offenders in 1999. This will be an integral part of a proactive strategy towards sex offenders which includes the Sex Offender Programme run in Arbour Hill Prison by the Service in collaboration with the Psychology Unit in the Department of Justice, Equality and Law Reform.

In November 1997 a group was appointed to examine the Probation and Welfare Service and to make recommendations. In particular the role, needs and organization of the Service are to be examined within the context of current developments in the criminal justice system. Their first report has been published as this publication goes to press.

The Prisons

Imprisonment is clearly central to the Criminal Justice System in Ireland. Its primary function is exclusion. It is the most severe sanction that society, through the courts, can impose on those who fail to comply with the criminal law. When a person's behaviour is seen as being so detrimental to the functioning of society, exclusion – sometimes for life – is regarded as the only option. When somebody knowingly transgresses the law then the possibility of incarceration is always in the background. The philosophy of imprisonment is elucidated by Beccaria when he says 'Anyone who disturbs the public peace, who does not obey the laws, that is, the conditions under which men agree to support one another, must be excluded from society – he must be banished from it' (1764: 11).

In the prison system, exclusion from the mainstream of society is reinforced by a structured and regimented organization whereby control and independence of movement is totally removed from the prisoner. The smooth running of the prison is based on compliance with the prevailing rules and regulations. Prisoners are categorized as either compliant or non-compliant, the latter being perceived as doubly deviant and appropriate subjects for further correction. The philosophical and political motivation for the establishment, maintenance and expansion of imprisonment is beyond the scope of this chapter. However, it is important to mention that many theorists see the prison not solely as a means of punishing transgressors of the criminal law, but as part of a wider strategy of social control which seeks to develop a new kind of 'individual, subject to habits, rules, orders, an authority that is exercised continually around him and upon him and which he must allow to function automatically in him' (Foucault, 1977: 198).

Since the establishment of the prison system in the thirteenth century, the purpose of imprisonment has changed depending on the prevailing criminal philosophy. During the nineteenth century, two distinct approaches to crime and imprisonment developed. The classical school viewed crime to be the result of a person freely choosing to offend, with prison being the best means of achieving reformation. Compliance within the prison ensured reward; disobedience resulted in harsh and continuous repression. With the rise of positivism severe punishment was rejected in favour of a rehabilitative ethos which acknowledged the circumstances of individual prisoners and had as its central purpose the humanization of the individual.

While the concept of rehabilitation remained a central aspect of the prison system until the 1980s, the exponential increase in the level of crime brought about a change of attitude. Three of the most common defensible reasons for increasing the severity of punishments are retribution, denunciation and deterrence. McCullagh's view that 'the increase in the numbers of committals to prison under sentence and the size of the remand population suggests that Irish society is becoming a more punitive one' (1996: 193) indicates a hardening of public attitude towards crime and its perpetrators.

The Irish prison system has expanded enormously over the last twenty years, in terms of prisoner numbers, prison personnel and the numbers of prisons. The daily average number of prisoners in custody has increased dramatically during that period from 963 in 1973, to 2171 in 1993 (Department of Justice, 1993). Since 1973, eight new prisons have been opened. The most recently opened prison (1997) is in Castlerea, Co. Roscommon, housed in a converted mental institution. Nevertheless, the increase in prisons has not kept pace with the increasing number of prisoners and this has resulted in a huge prison building programme which, when finished, will provide approximately 4000 prison places. The programme includes the building of a purpose-built secure women's prison in the grounds of Mountjoy.

The Department of Justice, Equality and Law Reform in its Strategy Statement (1998–2000) has as its objective 2000 extra prison places and the establishment of a custodial detention centre for convicted addicts and addicted remand prisoners, with all other prisons to be drug free. The aim of such a policy is to provide sufficient space to accommodate prisoners without overcrowding, and to reduce and eliminate the crisis in a chaotic temporary release system. The background to this policy has been an overcrowded prison system, with many prisoners housed in Victorian and ill-designed converted buildings. This position has been compounded by an increase in the number of prisoners serving longer sentences, thus reducing the number of cells available for new committals. The numbers serving sentences of two years to life increased from 30 in 1970 to 550 in 1995. In many of our prisons the physical environment is totally inadequate and unhygienic, psychologically and socially detrimental to the well-being of both prisoners and staff. As the Whitaker Report (Committee of Inquiry, 1985) states 'the possible rehabilitative effect of education, training, welfare and guidance are offset by the triple depressant of overcrowding, idleness and squalor which dominates most Irish prisons'. On a humane level Irish prisons tend to be more relaxed, less regimented and repressive than those in other western countries. The ill-treatment of prisoners in any form is not a widespread problem and evidence for institutional physical ill-treatment is small and periodic, a fact confirmed by an EU Committee Report. (CPT, 1995). The Prison authorities have, however, instituted a number of changes in the system, such as an ongoing programme of improvement to the physical and especially sanitary conditions in prison; the establishment of advisory committees on communicable diseases; the establishment of a Director of Prison Medical Services; the establishment of a 'positive custody' approach, whereby the new extension to Portlaoise Prison will be virtually self-sufficient, containing five factory units operating as full industrial units. However, the biggest policy change in the prison system has been the proposal to remove the organization, administration, and operational functions away from the Department of Justice, Equality and Law Reform to a new, as yet to be established, Prisons Agency. In 1996 an expert group was established to make recommendations on the structure of the new agency. Its report, published in 1997, made a number of recommendations:

- The Prisons Agency should be answerable to an independent Board appointed by the Minister.
- An Inspector of Prisons should be appointed.
- A Parole Board should be established.
- The management ethos should be inclusive rather than hierarchical.
- A Director General and a Deputy should be appointed to carry out the executive functions of the Agency.

The prison system, after a long period of inertia and crisis, now has the opportunity to begin a new chapter of positive and organized change. This will only be achieved, however, when a clarity of purpose about prisons is elucidated and when 'society itself takes a more understanding attitude to the imprisoned' (Lonergan, 1986: 32).

SOCIAL POLICY AND CRIME

As has been stated, crime is a complex and contested issue. It is inevitable therefore that social policy directed at the problem will also be both complex and contested. Rynn (1992), addressing the Safety for Women Conference in Dublin Castle, summarized the difficulty when she stated 'we are not dealing with a simple problem which is easily described with catch-all phrases, but with a serious and complex series of problems which will not be solved by any government department, or professional body, or treatment programme or Garda force'. According to her analysis it can only be adequately addressed 'with these bodies co-operating and with the involvement of concerned and responsible people in communities' (1992: 31). Progress in pursuit of such a coordinated and focused strategy will determine the success of any social policy.

Since 1985 the basis of virtually all discussion on the Criminal Justice System has been *the Report of the Committee of Inquiry into the Penal System* known as the Whitaker Report (Committee of Inquiry, 1985). This was the first independent government-sponsored investigation into the penal system in the history of the State. Its contents have provoked controversy, argument and opposition since its publication. It was effectively shelved for many years and occasionally dusted down and reintroduced in support of arguments deemed opportune at the time. It was, and remains, a humane, enlightened and progressive analysis of the Irish Penal system. While the report is not beyond criticism, it provides a basis for a rational and proactive criminal justice strategy.

While much lip service and laudatory comment from both commentators and politicians followed the publication of the Whitaker Report, for many years there was no strategy to implement its recommendations as part of any overall plan to change and reform a system already strained by the increased number of offenders. Some recommendations of the Report have been implemented piecemeal. Many reasons have been proposed for this apparent inertia. One definite reason is that the criminal justice system is a large bureaucracy essentially conservative in its thinking and its operation. In addition, the different bodies and institutions working within the system frequently have different functions, motivations and agendas which can make any coordinated policy and strategy difficult to implement. A much more critical analysis has been proposed by O'Mahony (1996) in his discourse on the crisis facing the system. Accepting the difficulties in achieving change in a bureaucracy, he firmly lays the blame on what he calls 'the culture of non-accountability'. Accordingly, he highlights the defensive attitudes, the demarcation disputes, the jealous protection of areas of power and influence, and the continuous hiding behind the rules as a malign influence on the vibrancy of the system.

Juvenile Crime

In 1996 juvenile crime rose by six per cent over the previous year (An Garda Siochána: 1996). However while the incidence of some offences decreased, there was a worrying increase in drink-related offences (21%)

and, alarmingly, serious assaults rose by 65%. Overall there were 14,285 offences committed during 1996 involving juveniles (An Garda Síochána, 1996). Evidently much work needs to be done in this area. Juvenile justice policy is a 'political hot potato' which has resulted in a rather disjointed strategy operated, often in an uncoordinated manner, by the Department of Justice, Equality and Law Reform, the Department of Education and the Department of Health and Children.

In an effort to bring the law on juvenile justice, which dates from the Probation of Offenders Act 1907, into the late twentieth century, the most comprehensive proposed piece of legislation in the history of the state was introduced in the form of the Children's Bill 1996. It shifts the emphasis away from punishment and detention and proposes a comprehensive range of community-based sanctions. Commenting on all the provisions of the Bill is beyond the scope of this section, but a number of central provisions need to be outlined:

• Eighteen years to be the upper age limit to be regarded as a child

• The age of criminal responsibility to be raised from seven years to ten years

• The Garda Diversionary Scheme (JLO) to be placed on a statutory footing. The Scheme will aim to divert children who accept responsibility for acts or omissions that form the basis of offences that they are alleged to have committed from committing offences (Section 9)

• The health boards to have responsibility for under-age children where parental/adult care is not present. The status of children is not defined but they would probably be those not receiving adequate care and attention (Section 3.1. Child Care Act 1991)

• The Bill provides for the abolition of reformatory and industrial schools, renaming them Children's Detention Schools

• Sections 216–18 provide for increased powers to be given to health boards to allow them to provide special care for non-offending, out-of-control children.

The Bill received a very positive reception from all professionals working in the area of child protection and in juvenile criminal justice. As Tutt states 'The proposals in the Children's Bill for diverting young people from crime are a serious attempt to implement the principles of restorative justice, which invites and enables victims, offenders and the community to repair some of the injustices resulting from crime' (1996: 8). There are, however, other perspectives on the objectives of juvenile justice. O'Sullivan sees the move from industrialized schools to community sanctions as being underlined by the same ideology. For him the 'new technologies of regulation' have the same purpose as the institutional confinement of old, 'to contain the risk that these children exhibit through technologies of normalization, socialization, and prevention. For those that fail to adapt or conform to the new technologies of prevention, the carceral archipelagos of Lusk, Clonmel and the North Circular Road retain their central role in the disciplining of the poor' (1998: 91).

Women and Crime

Criminal behaviour is largely perceived as being male dominated, with women contributing to a relatively insignificant percentage of crimes. As a consequence, women tend to be disadvantaged by comparison with their male counterparts when it comes to facilities and resources. James shows that the institutions of the Irish Criminal Justice System are predominantly patriarchal in nature and that there is a dearth of research on the subject of female offending and appropriate services (1998). In the prison system, in July 1998, a young girl, sentenced to seven years' imprisonment for murder in the Central Criminal Court at the age of sixteen, was subsequently released by the Supreme Court because there was no appropriate place of detention for young women after the age of seventeen. Although the Irish prison system is broadly a humane regime, women have been confined in what were, until recently refurbished, shameful conditions. Indeed even the refurbished prison in the Mountjoy complex, which caters for a maximum of forty women, has come in for harsh criticism. 'A proliferation of new metal cage-like barriers and steel meshing in the passageways and landings of the women's prison fails to disguise the gloomy Victorian penitentiary, but rather adds dramatically to the brutal and demoralising spirit of the place' (O'Mahony, 1996: 101).

A study of Irish female prisoners by Carmody and McEvoy (1996) makes grim reading. One hundred women committed to prison over a six-week period were interviewed. The general conclusion to be drawn from the study is that women prisoners are a very vulnerable and disadvantaged group in our community. Most were in their mid-twenties and came from Dublin's inner city. Many had drug or alcohol problems, a sizeable minority were HIV-positive, and half the sample had previous psychiatric treatment. Most had a previous history of being in prison. Offence categories tended to be minor, with larceny and robbery being the most usual categories.

In its *Strategy Statement 1998–2000* the Department of Justice, Equality and Law Reform (1998b) is committed to building a new female prison for 80 prisoners. While the building will undoubtedly be a

qualitative improvement on present conditions it will be a closed institution. Considering the problems associated with female offenders, an open,
more 'therapeutic community' style prison would appear much more
appropriate and provide a greater possibility of reducing re-offending.
The Whitaker Report (1985) realized this, when it proposed an open
centre to accommodate most women offenders, and a secure probation
hostel as an alternative to prison for some juvenile (female) offenders.

Sex Offending

Sexual assaults against adults and children are now recognized as a major
social and criminal problem in Ireland. In 1993 there were 159 sex
offenders in our prisons (Department of Justice, Prisons Annual Report,
1993). In 1997 there were 279 such offenders serving prison sentences.
This number comprised 12% of all adult male prisoners in Irish prisons
(Murphy, 1998). There has also been an increase of 80% in the number
of sexual assaults reported to the Gardaí between 1991 and 1996 (Garda
Siochána, 1991, 1996). In April 1997, in the greater Dublin area, there
were 36 sex offenders on statutory supervision by the Probation and
Welfare Service from the Courts. The vast majority of these offenders
would have been convicted of less serious assaults. As our knowledge of
the aetiology of sexual abuse has increased so has the body of legislation
governing it. The legislation recognizes fundamental and philosophical
distinctions between rape and other lesser assaults on the one hand and
incest on the other. *The Law Reform Commission Report on Rape* (1988)
was very influential in the extended definitions of rape in the Criminal
Law Rape (Amendment) Act 1990 which underlie most cases tried in
the courts. The most recent legislation has been the Sexual Offences
(Jurisdiction) Act 1996 making it a criminal offence for a citizen of
the state to commit a sexual assault on a child (under 15 years) outside
the jurisdiction.

At present the policy of the Department of Justice, Equality and Law
Reform is clear and unequivocal. No sex offenders are released from jail
prior to the expiry of their sentence. They are not considered for
temporary release, supervised or otherwise, under the Criminal Justice
Act (1960). On their release they are not statutorily supervised by the
Probation and Welfare Service.

Contrary to the stereotype frequently portrayed in the media, the
perpetrators of sexual assault are not insane, sex-starved and readily
identifiable as different. 'No overall or easy attribution of deviant sexual
arousal to single factors will probably be forthcoming, at least in the near
future' (Maletzky, 1991: 224). The complexity of sexual abuse demands

a sophisticated programme of intervention aimed at reducing the rate of recidivism. An example of this is the Arbour Hill Sex Offender Programme which was established in 1994. It has the expressed aim of addressing offenders who sexually assault thereby enhancing victim safety.

A number of developments are relevant in addressing the problem of sexual offending. These include mandatory reporting, longer sentences, registering of known offenders, electronic monitoring, and structured intervention programmes. The Department's publication of its *Discussion Document on Sexual Offences* (1998a) represents a new departure in stimulating discussion on the complex problem that is sexual offending.

Hidden Crime

The trend in criminal behaviour and the strategies, policies and interventions to deal with it are primarily determined by the statistics recorded by the courts, prisons and particularly the Gardaí. However, while such official statistics are generally accepted as being the 'true facts' of crime, it is increasingly recognized by researchers that they are only a true measure of the level of reported and recorded crime. Even here there can be anomalies: not all crimes committed are reported; crimes reported may not be recorded as such; some crimes such as assaults in the home, although reported, may be largely ignored. (Domestic assault was not criminalized until 1996.) In England and Wales, British Crime Surveys, while not definitive, indicate a continuous discrepancy between the level of recorded and unrecorded crime. In addition, the reliability of statistical information for different crimes can be subject to dispute. While the figures on burglary (necessary for insurance claims), murder and manslaughter can be taken as 'hard facts', sexual assault, domestic assault, and 'trivial' offences are notoriously under-reported (Dublin Rape Crisis Centre Annual Report, 1997). 'The deeper we delve into the processes of criminal justice and the more we rely on Court and prison statistics, the more we reduce our chances of saying anything straightforward about the nature and extent of crime' (Muncie and McLaughlin, 1996: 25).

Criminal Discourse and Voluntary Organizations

Until recently much of the discussion on crime, analysis of trends and proposals for change have come not from state bodies and institutions but from concerned individuals, academics and various voluntary organizations who, because of their work, see the need for the framework of the Criminal Justice System to be reformed and sometimes transformed.

These include Rape Crisis Centres and Women's Aid. The Irish Penal Reform Trust is a new and welcome development in the discursive arena of crime and criminal justice. An independent non-governmental agency, it has four clear objectives: to promote the constructive treatment of all offenders; to increase public knowledge of the Irish penal system; to generate rational debate on the penal system; and to provide objective research and analysis of Irish penal policy which should add to the limited body of knowledge already available.

Victim Support, founded in 1985, has been instrumental in promoting the primacy of the victims of crime in a system where traditionally they were forgotten. Initially treated with caution and suspicion by the establishment, it is now fully supported by government, receiving £280,000 in 1997 from the Department of Justice, Equality and Law Reform. Primarily the organization makes arrangements for trained volunteers to contact victims of crime, mostly through Garda referrals, in order to provide support and practical help wherever required. As it developed its contacts with victims it became clear that victims of serious crime needed more long-term support. As a result it has expanded its activities to include a Court Project, Tourist Victim Support, a Hospital Project and, in 1996, it established a Families of Murder Victims Programme.

CONCLUSION

This examination of the Criminal Justice System highlights the complexity of crime, criminal behaviour and society's inadequate response to an escalating level of offending. Solutions to the problem have been strongly influenced by the ideology prevailing at any particular time. As we move into the new millennium, however, a new pragmatism is evident in the strategy being implemented. This strategy includes high-profile Garda operations against 'hard core' criminals, i.e. Operation Dochas (1997) and Operation Cleanstreet (1998), with a parallel increase in the severity of penalties (The Criminal Justice Bill 1997 provides for mandatory minimum sentences for certain drug offences.); an expanded prison system to accommodate the increase in number of prisoners and the development and expansion of community penalties which would specifically target particular offending behaviour. In this context it is important to remember the argument put forward in the National Economic and Social Council's report, *The Criminal Justice System: Policy and Performance* (1984): 'there is, and will remain, a core of law breaking activity that cannot be reduced by any policy option available, either the most severe crime control measures or the most extensive programme to combat inequality'. The celebrated sociologist Emile Durkheim

(1895) goes even further, making the point that crime is present in all societies. Accepting that crime is an ephemeral concept and that the criminality of particular acts changes over time (with society periodically re-examining what constitutes criminal behaviour), he states that 'crime is necessary, it is bound up with the fundamental conditions of all social life and by that very fact it is useful, because these conditions of which it is a part are themselves indispensable to the normal evaluation of morality and law' (Durkheim, 1895: 70).

It is now generally accepted that, in itself, prison is an ineffective means of rehabilitating those incarcerated. This is not to say that particular focused rehabilitative programmes within prison cannot have an effect on the behaviour of some offenders, such as violence and sexual assault. However, imprisonment is going to remain a central factor in our efforts to control crime. If it is to serve its purpose adequately, i.e. a combination of incapacitation, deterrence and rehabilitation, then it is going to have to be used more judiciously and more selectively. The present building programme is aimed at providing more prison places and at reducing the present chaotic state of temporary release. Unless imprisonment is increasingly focused on the more serious offenders, and unless diversionary programmes are adequately financed and resourced, then, notwithstanding present developments, the chaos which now characterizes our prison system will continue unabated.

Custody dominates all discussion about the penal system and acts as a reference point for everything else. As we grapple intellectually and emotionally with the concepts surrounding the crime problem, it is clear that the importance of what could be termed community-based sanctions/penalties are gaining ground, particularly as the financial cost of imprisonment soars. However, progress in expanding community sanctions has been slow. The use of the term 'alternatives to custody' has contributed to this. This term suggests the centrality of custody as the norm, with alternatives competing with it rather than being part of a range of sentencing options (Pratt, 1987). While there has been a reasonably clear conceptualization in successive governments in Ireland about the objectives of reducing the use of custody, there has not been a parallel emphasis on how community-based penalties might be promoted or on outlining the circumstances in which such penalties might be applied. In Ireland, probation, intensive supervision and community service have been the central pillars of the community approach. Latterly, multi-agency community strategies are being implemented, i.e. Target and the Bridge project. As part of this developing strategy the following issues should be examined: fines (with failure to pay being dealt with through community sanctions rather than prison); suspended sentences with a supervisory condition, as advocated by Whitaker (Committee of Inquiry, 1985); electronic monitoring when combined with mandatory supervision could be used with great effect for particular offenders (Mair and Nee, 1990).

In its submission to the Review Group of the Probation and Welfare Service, the Probation Officers' branch of Impact accepted Henderson's (1987) four aims in the development of a community-based approach: crime prevention; reconciliation of offenders with their communities; work with victims; and inter-agency cooperation. This strategy has the benefit of being flexible, clear and integrative.

A major hindrance to the development of a cohesive and comprehensive analysis of crime in Ireland, and to the implementation of the most appropriate intervention strategies, is the absence of a single unified source of research data. There is an urgent need for a proactive coordinated plan to be developed, with adequate resources, by which research and data analysis become an integral part of the overall strategic management of the Department of Justice, Equality and Law Reform. In 1974, the Henchy Committee recommended that the Minister for Justice establish a 'suitably staffed research and statistics unit as a matter of urgency'. If the present Secretary General of the Department wishes to leave a lasting legacy, he could do no better than to create a research unit to enhance the knowledge base from which long term strategies and future planning could be developed.

Bacik and O'Connell state that 'Crime is best understood primarily as a social problem arising from particular economic conditions' (1998: vi). In *Crime and Poverty in Ireland* (1998), O'Donnell, discussing begging, a crime under the Vagrancy Act 1847, for which the only penalty available is imprisonment, states that 'it is a cause of some concern that the criminal law is used in this way to penalise poverty and social inadequacy. This is hardly the hallmark of an enlightened society' (1998: 36). In the same publication, O'Mahony exhorts us to stop believing in the comfortable certitude that the offender is the only one responsible for criminal behaviour. We need to look at the influence of the functioning of society on the existence and persistence of crime. Such an analysis might lead to the uncomfortable conclusion that the changes needed are broader than that of the Criminal Justice system itself, raising 'fundamental issues of social justice which cannot be solved simply by ensuring that the penal system is run in a just and decent manner' (O'Mahony, 1998: 65). A complex problem needs and demands complex solutions. Our current concept of crime implies a unity to what is essentially a vast array of diverse behaviours, events and legal sanctions. Crime, while being a major problem, is also one of the most enduring factors in modern society. A significant proportion of crime is avoidable if, through policies in areas like education and unemployment, all individuals, particularly the young, are enabled to participate fully in their community and society. If such a commitment is unforthcoming, it is foolish to expect the Criminal Justice System by itself to limit crime to an irreducible minimum.

CHRONOLOGY OF DEVELOPMENTS IN THE CRIMINAL JUSTICE SYSTEM IN IRELAND

1847	Vagrancy Act
1907	Probation of Offenders Act
1937	Bunreacht na hÉireann
1939	Office of Attorney General
1960	Criminal Justice (Temporary Release) Act
1963	Garda Juvenile Liaison Scheme
1974	Director of Public Prosecutions
1974	Henchy Committee
1975	Law Reform Commission
1983	Criminal Justice (Community Service) Act
1985	Report of the Committee of Inquiry into the Penal System (Whitaker Report)
1985	Victim Support established
1994	Irish Penal Reform Trust established
1994	Sex Offender Treatment Programme
1995	Committee (EU) for the Prevention of Torture and Inhuman or Degrading Treatment or Punishment
1996	Working Group on a Courts Commission
1996	Sexual Offences (Jurisdiction) Act
1996	Law Reform Commission Report
1997	Criminal Justice Bill
1997	Department of Justice, Equality and Law Reform Annual Report
1997	Towards an Independent Prisons Agency Report of Expert Group
1998	Department of Justice, Equality and Law Reform Strategy Statement
1998	Expert Group on the Probation and Welfare Service – First Report

RECOMMENDED READING

Bacik, I. and M. O'Connell (eds) (1998) *Crime and Poverty in Ireland*. Dublin: Round Hall Sweet & Maxwell.

Cook, G. and V. Richardson (1981) *Juvenile Justice at the Crossroads*. Dublin: Department Social Administration, University College Dublin.

Department of Justice. (1997) *Tackling Crime–Discussion Paper*. Dublin: Stationery Office.

McCullagh, C. (1996) *Crime in Ireland–A Sociological Introduction*. Cork: Cork University Press.

O'Mahony, P. (1993) *Crime and Punishment in Ireland*. Dublin: Round Hall Press.

Rothman, D. (1984) *The Criminal Justice System: Policy and Performance no. 77*. Dublin: NESC.

REFERENCES

Assessment Services for the Courts in Respect of Juveniles (Hency Committee) (1974) First Interim Report. Dublin: Stationery Office.

Bacik, I. and M. O'Connell, M. (eds) (1998) *Crime and Poverty in Ireland*. Dublin: Round Hall Sweet & Maxwell

Beccaria, C. (1764) 'On Crimes and Punishments', in J. Muncie et al. (eds) (1996) *Criminological Perspectives*. London: Open University Press.

Carmody, P and M. McEvoy (1996) *A Study of Irish Female Prisoners*. Dublin: Stationery Office.

Committee of Inquiry into the Penal System. *Report* (Whitaker Report) (1985). Dublin: Stationery Office.

Constitution of Ireland (1937) Dublin: Stationery Office.

CPT–Committee for the Prevention of Torture and Inhuman or Degrading Treatment or Punishment (1995), Report on 'Irish Places of Detention' (Strasbourg: Council of Europe).

Department of Justice (1993) *Annual Report on Prisons and Places of Detention*. Dublin: Stationery Office.

Department of Justice. (1997) *Tackling Crime*. Dublin: Stationery Office.

Department of Justice, Equality and Law Reform (1998a) *The Law on Sexual Offences*. Dublin: Stationery Office.

Department of Justice, Equality and Law Reform (1998b) *Strategy Statement 1998–2000: Community, Security and Equality*. Dublin: Stationery Office.

Dublin Rape Crisis Centre (1996, 1997) *Annual Report*.

Durkheim, E. (1964, orig. 1895) *The Rules of Sociological Method*. New York: Free Press.

Foucault, M. (1977) *Discipline and Punish*. London: Penguin.

An Garda Siochána (1991, 1995, 1996) *Annual Reports*. Dublin: Stationery Office.

An Garda Siochána National Juvenile Office (1991) Police of and Garda Siochána in Respect of Juvenile Offenders and Guidelines for the Implementation of Procedures in Dealing with Juvenile Offenders. Dublin: An Garda Siochana.

Henderson, (1987) *Community Work and the Probation Service*. London: National Institute of Social Work.

Impact (1998) *Submission to the Review Group of the Probation and Welfare Service.* Dublin: Impact.

James, C. (1998) 'Women in Prison: The Irish Experience', PhD thesis in progress, NUI, Galway.

Law Reform Commission (1988) *Report: Rape and Allied Offences.* Dublin: Stationery Office.

Lonergan, J. (1986) 'Prisons and Irish Society', *Studies*, Spring.

McCullagh, C. (1996) *Crime in Ireland.* Cork: Cork University Press.

Mair, G. and C. Nee (1990) *Electronic Monitoring: The Trials and Their Results.* London: HMSO.

Maletzky, B.M. (1991) *Treating the Sexual Offender.* California: Sage.

Muncie, J. and E. McLaughlin (eds) (1996) *Controlling Crime.* London: Open University.

Murphy, P. (1998) 'A Therapeutic Programme for Imprisoned Sex Offenders: Progress to Date and issues for the Future', *The Irish Journal of Psychology*, 190–207.

National Economic and Social Council (1984) *The Criminal Justice System: Policy and Performance.* Dublin: NESC.

O'Donnell, I. (1998) 'Crime, Punishment and Poverty', in I. Bacik and M. O'Connell (eds), *Crime and Poverty in Ireland.* Dublin: Round Hall, Sweet & Maxwell.

O'Mahony, P. (1993) *Crime and Punishment in Ireland.* Dublin: Round Hall Press.

O'Mahony, P. (1996) *Criminal Chaos.* Dublin: Round Hall Press.

O'Mahony, P. (1998) 'Punishing Poverty and Personal Adversity', in I. Bacik and M. O'Connell (eds.), *Crime and Poverty in Ireland.* Dublin: Round Hall, Sweet & Maxwell.

O'Reilly, T. (1986) 'The Practice of Policing in Ireland', *Studies* (Spring).

O'Sullivan, E. (1998) 'Juvenile Justice and the Regulation of the Poor: Restored to Virtue, Society and to God', in I. Bacik and M. O'Connell (eds), *Crime and Poverty in Ireland.* Dublin: Round Hall, Sweet & Maxwell.

Pratt, J. (1987) 'Dilemmas of the Alternative to Custody Concept: Implications for New Zealand Penal Policy in the Light of International Evidence and Experience', *Australia and New Zealand Journal of Criminology*, 20.

Probation and Welfare Service. (1980 and 1994). *Annual Reports.* Dublin: Stationery Office.

Review Group of the Probation and Welfare Service (1998) *First Report.*

Ross, R. and E. Fabiano (1985) *Time to Think: A Cognitive Model of Delinquency Prevention and Rehabilitation.* Canada: Institute of Social Sciences and Arts.

Rothman, D. (1984) *The Criminal Justice System: Policy and Performance.* Dublin: National Economic and Social Council.

Rynn, A. (1992) 'Working with Perpetrators: What Are the Issues?', *Conference Papers: Safety for Women Conference*, Dublin.

Towards an Independent Prisons Agency (1997) Report of Expert Group. Dublin: Stationery Office.

Tutt, N. (1996) 'The Search for Justice: Home and Away', in *The Children's Bill 1996: Issues and Perspectives.* Dublin: The Children's Legal Centre.

Vagrancy Act 1847.

Working Group on a Courts Commission (1996) *Report.*

14

Drugs Policy in Ireland in the 1990s

Hilda Loughran

INTRODUCTION

Drug use is a major concern in Ireland in the 1990s. The problems related to drug use impacts not just on those who actually take drugs but also on the general population. The scope of the drugs issue spans several areas relevant to social policy studies. Perhaps the most widely discussed of these is that of crime. Criminal activity is associated with drug users attempting to finance their habit, and with organized crime which is so central to the expansion of the drugs problem. The drugs problem has medical aspects as well, of course, which have perhaps been highlighted by the emergence of HIV and AIDS in the 1980s. However, the medical questions go beyond transmission of HIV and AIDS to the broader definition of health care which incorporates the immediate and long-term effects of drug use on the user's general health status and the need for health promotion as an integral part of drugs policy. Other areas linked to the drugs issue are social welfare, local development and housing, education and youth services. This chapter will explore and evaluate the complex nature of the drugs problem in Ireland as it has developed in the 1990s. The various government initiatives to address the problem will be outlined and the sometimes conflicting needs of drug users and the communities they live in will also be discussed.

Definition and Scope of this Policy Area

A discussion about drugs policy must first define the parameters of the term drug. In most countries, as in Ireland, a distinction is made between drugs which are legal and those which have been designated as illegal. The distinction may, in fact, be unhelpful in that it may offer some air of safety to legal drugs and focus attention almost exclusively on illegal drugs. In reality, the health, social and economic costs of both legal and illegal drugs are a major cause for concern in our society today. The term legal drugs is generally used in relation to alcohol, tobacco and prescription drugs. In the present context, the term illegal drugs refers to 'street drugs'; this includes opiates (predominantly heroin), stimulants (including cocaine, crack and ecstasy), cannabis, LSD and various tranquillizers (which can be acquired both legally and illegally). For the purposes of policy formulation and treatment provision in Ireland, the legal and illegal substances are treated completely separately. This situation is currently under review in relation to treatment services. With regard to policy developments, however, the two areas remain relatively segregated. The main policy document dealing with policy developments for alcohol is the *National Alcohol Policy* of 1996; the equivalent for illegal substances is the *Government Strategy to Prevent Drug Misuse*, 1996 and the two Task Force Reports of 1996 and 1997. While the separation of the two aspects of the drugs issue is a fact of life in the Irish scene, it may be misleading in that this separation might suggest that the problems with legal drugs are somehow less significant. In fact problems relating to alcohol accounted in 1992 for up to 23 per cent of admissions to psychiatric hospitals, 22,482 prosecutions for all types of offences involving alcohol, as well as road traffic accidents (Corrigan, 1994: 22–3). Alcohol policy and other drug policy have developed in quite a diverse manner. This chapter focuses on policy strategies that relate to illegal drugs.

Several questions emerge in a discussion of illegal drugs. What constitutes a problem in relation to the use of drugs? Is use alone definitive of a problem, or is it necessary that some medical, social or economic damage is incurred because of the drug use? What level or nature of problem is evidence of abuse or addiction? In Irish policy the use of illegal drugs is, in and of itself, considered problematic. This, of course, is inevitable in a situation where the very possession of such drugs constitutes an illegal activity – hence the possessor is already 'in trouble'. While all drug use is therefore covered in the ambit of drug policy, it is fair to say that the central focus of concern is on those who could be classified as problem drug users,

> A problem drug taker would be any person who experiences social, psychological, physical or legal problems related to intoxication and/or regular excessive consumption and/or dependence as a consequence of his own use of drugs or other chemical substances (excluding alcohol and tobacco). (*Report of the Advisory Council on the Misuse of Drugs*, 1982: 34)

HISTORICAL OVERVIEW OF DRUGS POLICY IN IRELAND

Government drugs policy in Ireland has been greatly influenced by the historical temperance movement in the USA and the UK. The movement, initiated by Rush in 1784, identified addiction as a disease and clearly recommended that the only course of action to resolve the addiction problem was total abstinence. While this model for dealing with addiction problems clearly fitted with a view that combined the medical concerns about the disease with the moral concern about the evils of addiction, it did little to assist in the development of inclusive and tolerant policy strategies. Rather, the history of both legislation and social policy in Ireland in relation to drug use would be typified by its exclusionist nature. The result of this construction of drug addiction as primarily an issue of medical concern, was to deny the socio-cultural and socio-economic nature of the predominance of drug problems in economically deprived communities. The dual concerns of tackling the supply and the demand for drugs formed the central rationale for policy in the 1990s. It is also from these early influences that the emphasis on the individual as the target of policy and treatment has its roots. The supply-and-demand reduction factors, along with the individual focus, will form the basis of a paradigm for understanding drug policy presented later in this chapter.

The history of the development of Irish drugs policy is comprehensively analysed by Butler (1991). He points out that, as far back as 1983, there was clear evidence of the connection between developing drug problems, poverty and the powerlessness of a small number of working-class neighbourhoods (Butler, 1991: 19). However, recommendations of the 1983 Task Force were never endorsed in policy and it was not until the 1990s that any attempt was made to follow through on this earlier suggestion to identify 'Community Priority Areas'. The failure to identify and acknowledge the marginalizing effects of the drug problem itself and governmental attempts to control that problem are evident in activities in the drugs arena today. In Ireland, evidence confirms that the problems relating to drug use are concentrated in the Greater Dublin area (Task Force, 1996). This is especially so in relation to opiate use. Cork, for example, has a serious cannabis problem, twice the rate of other areas for lifetime use (Jackson, 1998: 31). Dublin has both a cannabis and an opiate problem (Task Force, 1996).

The 1990s have seen more activity in the area of policy development than previously witnessed. Of course, the presence of policy documents does not ensure the resolution of the drugs problem. One has to examine the rash of policy initiatives in the light of past experiences. In particular, it is important to question whether traditional interpretations of what 'addiction' actually means and the subsequent legislative avenues for addressing the problem have in fact altered at all since the early days of the drug problem in the 1960s.

It could be argued that in spite of a pressure to act on the drug problem because of growing social concern, fuelled by increased drug related crime and the establishment of ecstasy-use as a young middle class activity, successive governments have been unable to transcend the strictures of what Murphy (1996) refers to as a deterrence perspective. Perhaps current policy is yet another attempt to condemn drug users to the margins of society while attempting to safeguard the rest of society from the evils of drug use. This concern was echoed in an article by Loughran (1996), in which McCabe, a member of the Inner City Organisations Network (ICON), suggests that

> we either address the major economic and social issues that underpin the problems of crime and drug abuse or we go the route of other countries and attempt to build a ring of steel around areas – keep a lid on it – contain it (Loughran, 1996: 13).

The 1990s have been one of the most active phases in the Irish government's attempts to tackle the drugs issue. This is in contrast to the early years where political responses to the problem were at best reactive and at worst restrictive. The struggle to understand the drugs issue in Ireland has been hampered by the importation of ideas about the nature of drug addiction and the political and, indeed, philosophical commitment to prohibitions perspectives (predominantly from the USA). These perspectives propound the view that drugs are bad and that they must be stamped out. The goal is to remove the problem of drug abuse from society. This viewpoint has its merits, although many in the treatment and policy field would probably support the view that, from a social policy perspective, it is not enough to consider ideals. Social policy must address the reality of the situation and in doing so recognize that previous attempts at prohibition have failed (Murphy, 1996). Social policy must address the needs of the socially excluded, in this case drug users and often their families. Policy must also concern itself with effectiveness and fairness. Forder (1974), in his classic work on need, drew attention not only to need as defined by society at large, but also to the validity of the felt needs of service users and marginalized groups.

Murphy(1996) contends that prohibitionist policies promoted the war-on-drugs paradigm. The central tenets of such a policy are the implementation of legislation which criminalizes drug use and the manufacturing, distribution and supply of drugs. They also support the promotion of abstinence as *the* treatment response. These approaches have proved unsuccessful (Murphy, 1996). This lack of success needs no further evidence than the combined escalation of the drug problem as documented by O'Hare and O'Brien (1993), O'Higgins (1996), and Moran et al. (1997).

The most comprehensive review of Irish drugs policy is presented by Butler (1991). He identifies three phases in the development of the drugs problem and government responses to them over a 25-year period from 1966–90. The first stage was from 1966–79, which he refers to as 'The early years'(Butler, 1991: 212–18). Drugs issues were considered within the ambit of mental health policy. This era witnessed the establishment of the Drugs Squad, the publication of a *Report of the Working Party on Drug Abuse* (1971), and the establishment of the first treatment facilities in the form of Coolmine Therapeutic Community and the National Drug Treatment Centre. The second stage Butler refers to was from 1980–85, which he calls 'The Opiate Epidemic' (1991: 218–25). He documents the escalating heroin problems in Dublin and various attempts to address the 'epidemic'.

> No effort was made to establish clear conceptual and practical distinctions between drug control policies, which are the responsibility of the criminal justice system, and health and welfare policies which operate on a radically different value system and are the responsibility of the health and welfare institutions. (Butler, 1991: 224)

The third stage discussed is 1986–91 – The AIDS Connection (Butler, 1991: 225–9). The impact of the emergence of HIV and AIDS is outlined and government reaction is critically analysed. In concluding his review of 25 years of drugs policy, Butler suggests that

> the consensus which has been a feature of Irish drug policy making has been superficial, that it has been achieved and maintained by ignoring many real policy dilemmas, and that such consensus-seeking may in the long run be of less societal value than an open acknowledgement of institutional and cultural ambivalence. (1991: 230)

Table 2 (p. 327) gives details of developments since the late 1960s. Prior to that time, legislation regarding drugs was predominately vested in Customs legislation, including the Dangerous Drugs Act 1934, the Customs Act 1956, and the Customs Consolidation Act 1976.

Before looking more critically at policy developments in the 1990s, it might be useful to summarize policy-led activities prior to that time (see Table 2, p. 327), which reflect a policy commitment to control drug problems by tackling supply and criminalizing drug use and were the underlying reason for the development of the generally one-dimensional services to drug users; that is the emphasis was on assisting those drug users who were prepared to attempt total withdrawal from drug use. The biggest shift in policy was inevitably the need to address the broader public health issues which emanated from the emergence of HIV and AIDS. At this time, the task of attracting all drug users to services, even if they had no interest in total abstinence, was clearly of paramount importance. This is because it is only by attracting such users to services that there is any hope, first, of estimating the extent of drug use and second of reducing the risk of harm to both users and the non-using population. The phase identified in Butler as 'AIDS and HIV' inevitably set the context for a change of direction in policy. This phase clearly marked the transition of the drugs problem from the confines of the 'marginalized' in society to the centre of general public health concerns. Crossing this boundary has highlighted both concern and commitment to tackling the drug problem in a meaningful and effective manner. However, one might pessimistically suggest that the shift away from abstinence models to harm reduction models may also reflect a further attempt to cordon off the drug problem and protect the general public by keeping drug users under control, if not by criminalizing their activity, then more subtly endorsing their drug use by choosing to offer a substitute drug to diminish if not eliminate criminal behaviour associated with drug use.

DRUGS POLICY FROM 1990 TO 1998

The 1990s represent another phase in the ongoing story of drugs in Ireland. During the 1990s attempts have been made to move on from the early restrictive responses to drug policy and to allow more creative and inclusive initiatives to develop.

By the time the *Government Strategy for the Prevention of Drug Misuse* arrived in 1991, it was clear that 'all evidence here points to a concentration of the problem in specific areas of Dublin with poor housing and high levels of employment (Department of Health, 1991: 8). The social marginalization of sectors of society, of communities and neighbourhoods was acknowledged but unchallenged by the strategy document.

1991: Government Strategy for the Prevention of Drug Misuse

The main thrust of the Strategy was to establish and formalize cooperation between various interested parties. Specifically mentioned were the links between voluntary and statutory services, education, treatment services, local communities, prison services and customs and international drug agencies. The overall goal of the new policy was to 'set out to implement realistic and achievable objectives in the areas of supply reduction, demand reduction and increased access to treatment and methadone programmes coupled with a comprehensive structure geared toward their effective implementation' (Department of Health, 1991: 2).

Perhaps the most innovative moves at this time were the attempt to develop community-based services and the official backing for harm reduction approaches to treatment. The community-based services were envisaged as being community drug teams which incorporated a major role for General Practitioners (GPs). Paradoxically, the strategy document specifically highlighted a plan to deal with GPs who might be engaged in 'irresponsible prescribing' (1991: 2).

Apart from GPs, one of the other features of this strategy was the recommendation for legislation to enable the confiscation of the proceeds of drug trafficking. This strategy, perhaps more than the others, offered a new approach to dealing with the supply of drugs as it was directed at the rewards accruing to dealers from their illegal activities. As with many other recommendations of this Strategy, it would take the further impetus of the 1996 Task Force to have its potiental realized. Details of the drug situation in Ireland were clearly laid out in the Strategy document (1991). The report confirmed that the main focus of the problem was in the Greater Dublin area. The prevalence of drug problems in Limerick, Cork and Galway appeared to refer specifically to use of cannabis, not heroin.

In reading the strategy document, the attention given to the soft drug cannabis is striking (1991: 6–7). For example, the report notes that in 1989, 70 per cent of charges for drug offences related to cannabis, and the increase in seizures related mainly to cannabis (1991: 7). As already suggested, the definition of what a drug problem is has been influenced by the prohibitionist philosophy of total abstinence from all drugs classified as illegal. The debate about where cannabis should be situated in this drug problem paradigm is strongly debated. It could be argued that the resources used to police the use of cannabis might be better directed to dealing with harder drugs, specifically heroin. However, such a position has never been clearly stated in government policy. (Of course, by the mid-1990s, the extent of concern for the heroin problem far outweighed that of the cannabis issue.) Murphy (1996) suggests a continuum of illegality where cannabis would be situated at one end, with fewer resources being used to police its use, and resources being diverted to a more exclusive pursuit of hard drugs.

The concern that 'soft drugs' act as 'gateway drugs' (Department of Health, 1991: 26) to the use of hard drugs has contributed to the evolution of drug responses that bind the two categories of drugs inextricably together. Yet there is growing evidence that the use of heroin as the initial drug of choice is on the increase. A report by Keogh (1997: ix) confirms that 30 per cent of known drug users started on heroin. This raises the concern that heroin is becoming more acceptable and accessible as a 'start-up' drug. The implication of this development is that there will be more younger users who potentially will engage in risky behaviour through inexperience and immaturity. Health and safety issues about safe injecting, understanding the strength and the quality of the drug used, and taking precautions in relation to HIV and AIDS may be neglected by this group of users. This aspect of the problem is still not discussed in the Government Strategy document of 1991. Because of the problem of compiling accurate statistics on the prevalence of drug use, particularly heroin use and specifically intravenous heroin use, it is difficult to develop strategies to effectively plan services or monitor progress. Some of the most fruitful sources of information are the Health Research Board reports which relate to treated drug misuse only (O'Hare and O'Brien, 1992, 1993; O'Higgins and O'Brien, 1994; O'Higgins, 1996; Moran et al., 1997).

Plans for a more coordinated and structured cooperation between all parties involved in working with the drugs issue were of course welcomed, as were the suggestions regarding the development of community-based structures. Disappointing however, was the failure to address the concerns identified by the 1983 Committee regarding the real nature of the drug problems, as established and nurtured by social deprivation. This was in spite of the recognition that specific areas of the city of Dublin were clearly 'drug black spots'. The fact that these correlated with areas of social and economic disadvantage could not really be misinterpreted, but perhaps it was again side-stepped. Policy commitments to decentralize services, specifically in developing the role of the GP, were a major step toward developing services which would be more easily accessible to potential clients. The community-based aspects of this strategy did not meet with universal acclaim. Issues such as the stigmatizing of specific communities and labelling of areas as 'drug areas', while attempting to focus services where required, had the effect of alienating those communities and escalating fears that communities with special services would in fact attract more drug misusers. This unforeseen response had ongoing implications for the implementation of some aspects of the 1991 Government Strategy.

The supply reduction approach, combined with a greater emphasis on demand reduction measures, was established as the central framework for future policy developments. This happened in a climate where a core aspect of such a framework, in the form of education for prevention, was being seriously criticized by researchers (Cripps, 1997: 18). The development of community-based responses appeared to hold more promise.

Tracking the drugs problem through a series of Health Research Board reports from 1991 to 1996 does nothing to instil confidence that the 1991 Strategy worked. There was evidence that the percentage treated for heroin had doubled from 1990 to 1996. This indicates that services are more successful in reaching drug users, but it does not support the theory that the drugs problem is under control, as the figures for those receiving treatment can be regarded only as a percentage of those currently using drugs. The proliferation of services in community-based settings is documented in Moran et al.'s report (1996: Appendix D). The move towards providing community-based, not centralized, services seems to be supported by these results. The concept of outreach intrinsic to the 1991 Strategy demonstrated some success. The fact that in 1996 policy making was still dependent on data derived only from those already in contact with services was disappointing. If one looks at how those drug users gain access to the services, it is of further concern, in that the 1991 Strategy seeking to engage a broad range of professionals in the task of working with drug users had shown only a limited success. According to O'Higgins (1996: 43), almost 55 per cent of those treated were self- or family-referred, while only 15.5 per cent came through a combination of GPs, hospital, medical settings and social services, with a further 11.3 per cent arriving through the court/probation system.

In its five-year review (O'Higgins, 1996: 8), the Health Research Board noted the decreasing age of users attending for treatment. The Report stated that 'evidence was found of the increase, both proportionate and numerical, in the specific citing of heroin as their drug of misuse by clients who were in treatment' (1996: 11). Again, since data sources are limited to those in treatment, it is difficult to interpret these facts. Perhaps it is a good thing that the age of users in treatment is down, if it indicates that users are getting to services earlier. However, it may also indicate younger people getting into more serious difficulties earlier in their drug use. The information about the levels of heroin as primary drug of choice is again open to interpretation. One possibility is that services are viewed as predominantly services for heroin users and are seen as unacceptable by other drug users. Alternatively the facts might reflect the relative social acceptability of other drug use, specifically cannabis, and therefore use of the drug is less likely to lead to admission to treatment.

The push towards harm reduction strategies such as needle exchange and methadone maintenance would clearly indicate concern for heroin

users rather than cannabis users. Some positive effects on the treatment/
outreach front can be indicated by O'Higgins (1996) and Moran et
al. (1997).

There is no evidence, however, that the strategy instigated in 1991
has had any impact on the major social issues underlying the drugs
problem in Dublin. Eighty to ninety per cent (O'Higgins, 1996: 26) of
those counted in the statistics are still unemployed and the same socially
and economically deprived areas are over-represented in the statistics
(O'Higgins and O'Brien, 1994: 25; Moran et al., 1997: 34). School-
leaving age has levelled-off (O'Higgins and O'Brien, 1994: 4), but it still
shows 35 per cent leaving before the age of fifteen. The good news was
that the HIV and AIDS education programme as a harm reduction
strategy in relation to needle-sharing and needle-use seems in general to
be having an effect. This is apparent in the reduction in numbers of
those injecting and sharing (Moran et al., 1997: 2–25). The fact that this
is part of a greater health promotion strategy should not be overlooked.
The total numbers receiving treatment for drug misuse in 1996 were
4,865. Most were resident in the Eastern Health Board region (Moran et
al., 1997: 5); 2,821 of these were in contact with treatment prior to
1996. This means that over 50 per cent of those included in the statistics
of the Report had been in contact with services for some time.

Any analysis of the data indicates reasons for concern. The 1991
Strategy had not reaped the hoped-for results. The 1991 Strategy, which
placed confidence in the drug supply and demand reduction tactics, had
overestimated the possibilities of curtailing supply and ignored at least
some of the factors contributing to demand.

Ministerial Committee

In the mid-1990s, Pat Rabbitte chaired a Ministerial Committee to
review drug policy. The committee produced two reports, in 1996 and
1997. Once again, policy development was designed along the dual axes
of supply-and-demand reduction. The Rabbitte Reports dealt with
demand reduction and refer to complementary efforts when outlining
the issues relating to supply reduction. Did these efforts so clearly based
on a long-established formulation offer anything new for drugs policy
initiatives? Concepts such as 'war on drugs' (Murphy, 1996) and 'zero
tolerance' continue to underpin Irish drugs policy. This supply/demand
dichotomy will be further analysed later in this chapter.

Table 3 (see p. 327) presents a brief summary of developments in
policy and service relevant to the drugs field since 1991. The legislative
changes are summarized in Table 5 (p. 328). There was no comprehensive

evaluation of the 1991 Strategy; hopefully this lack of evaluation will be redressed in relation to the Task Force. The Eastern Health Board commissioned an evaluation of their services in 1995 (Farrell and Buning, 1996).

The first Task Force report again contextualized the drug problem, looking at underlying causes, and the nature and extent of the problem. The report presents a summary of current and proposed services in a variety of areas. A major effect of the First Task Force was to validate earlier concerns about the relationship between drug use and social and economic deprivation. The earlier call for the identification of priority areas, where issues of drug use and social deprivation clearly coincide, may have been controversial. However, it did allow for the targeting of those areas as areas of special need. Eleven areas were so identified – ten in the greater Dublin Area and one in Cork (Task Force, 1996: 59–61). Interestingly, the designation of the area in Cork was later criticized, following the publication of a report on drug use in the Southern region (Jackson, 1998).

The second major development from the First Task Force Report (1996) was the setting-up of structures to encourage a more integrated approach across government departments. The membership of the Task Force was comprised of: the Minister of State to the Government, the Minister of State to the Departments of Education, the Environment, Health, Justice, Social Welfare, and the Minister of State to the Taoiseach and Foreign Affairs (Task Force, 1996: 23). These departments were to devise a structure for interdepartmental cooperation (Table 4, p. 328) and work in conjunction with community partnerships.

The First Task Force Report was mainly concerned with the heroin problem. Issues such as misuse of non-opiates (ecstasy and cannabis), prevention and development of youth services, drug use in prisons and the role of therapeutic communities are examined in the Second Task Force Report (1997). A research project is currently being commissioned to evaluate the effectiveness of these Task Force policies. This is a critical aspect of policy development, perhaps more crucial since £10 million was allocated to the Task Force since their inception and a further £20 million has been assigned to Youth Services developments.

PRINCIPAL ACTORS INVOLVED IN POLICY DEVELOPMENT IN THE AREA

Political

Interests in the area of drug policy are diverse and often conflicting. The main actors in the field, by virtue of their power and authority, are perhaps inevitably the relevant government departments. However this central group is strongly influenced, on the one hand, by the medical profession and, on the other, by law enforcement agencies. These two parties have managed to bring to bear their respective concerns and beliefs to shape current political responses to drug policy as designed and supported through government departments.

In the government at the time of writing in early 1999, the department with special responsibility for drugs issues is the Department of Tourism, Sport and Recreation. This seems somewhat misplaced, in particular since this is not a high-status department. One of the core functions of the department with responsibility for drugs is to provide an integrative structure for the other departments with interests in the drugs problem. According to the Task Force 1996, these departments include the Departments of Education and Science, Environment, Health and Children, Justice, Foreign Affairs, Social Welfare, and, more directly, Employment and Enterprise.

From a political perspective, however, a difficult balance must be struck between responding to the demands of voters at large to control the drugs problem, while attempting to respond in a responsible way to the needs of drug users and their families. This balance has at times given rise to intense controversy. The interests of political parties are apparently united in attempts to tackle the drugs problem. This is perhaps evident in the continuity of policy across rival political parties, as they succeed to government.

Community

Apart from the key government departments and the influence of political parties, various interest groups attempt to have a voice in policy. The most significant of these has been the various attempts by local communities – specifically Community Action against Drugs, and inner-city organizations – to draw attention to the plight of their communities. Communities are now finally being recognized as having a key role both in the provision of services at community level, and also in the development of policies and anti-drug strategies. This is reflected in the partnership and Task Force response to drugs issues that was adopted from 1996, and still supported despite the change in government.

Service Providers

Other significant players are the service providers, particularly the Eastern Health Board. As the health board with the biggest problem in relation to drugs, the Eastern Health Board must inevitably be at the forefront of responses to the drugs problem. Their policy development strategy has been referred to earlier in this chapter (Eastern Health Board, 1996). Decisions about funding from direct government funds or through the Health Board are critical in shaping responses to the drug issues at all levels, from prevention initiatives through direct service provisions to rehabilitation and support.

The Eastern Health Board, while responsible for the majority of services, does not have an exclusive role. Since the early days of the drugs problem, voluntary bodies have been a very important aspect of the service choices for drug users, their families and communities. Some of the voluntary services were established by religious organizations (for example, Merchants Quay Project, Mater Dei), while others were initially developed by a variety of organizations having independent funds, e.g. Anna Liffey, Talbot Day Centre. Many of the services initiated by voluntary bodies have since become partly or solely state-funded. The presence of voluntary service providers offers a flexible and wider range of services for those with drug-related problems. Their philosophical influences on services are therefore diverse and this is more likely to be a positive feature of services as it ensures real choice for service users.

Consumers

Like many of those who utilize government services, the consumers of drug services are not in general either well organized or articulate in voicing their demands. It could be said that the consumer must fit the service, rather than the service being made to fit the clients. This is not a condemnation of services, but more accurately a reflection of the major gap in our knowledge about drug users. This is an inevitable result of the criminalization of drug use which sends those affected under cover, giving a clear indication that they have no right to service, or to making demands on the system. Consumers must rely on the relationships they develop with professional helpers and on their community organizations to provide a voice on their behalf, where it can make a difference. Families of consumers are equally marginalized in the process. At times the more strident, well-organized voice of communities who are concerned about the macro picture can drown out the voices of those focused on the more personal micro experiences. An attempt is being made to organize drug users in the form of a Drug Users Forum. This idea is being developed in conjunction with one of the service providers, Merchants Quay (Merchants Quay, 1998: 8–9).

Since the two Task Force Reports in 1996 and 1997, there has been a growing emphasis on the need for youth and sports services to develop preventative initiatives at community level. The allocation of £20m in 1998 for this purpose emphasizes the investment in this area and at least for the moment gives these sectors some say in how to respond to the needs of young people in general.

The Media

No discussion of the players that affect this area of policy development would be complete without some comment on the role of the media. Media coverage of issues relating to drugs has been an important aspect of keeping the public informed. They can also serve as a catalyst for marshalling public opinion and creating pressure for particular action. Reports on the arrival of ecstasy and subsequent fatalities were influential in formulating public opinion on the potential problems of ecstasy use. Of potential difficulty in this regard is, of course, the power of the media to sensationalize specific events and create an environment where there is pressure for policy to respond to specific cases, rather than to overall patterns. Media coverage in relation to criminal activities has also been very important in Ireland. This covers both the reporting of drug-related crime on a smaller scale and large-scale drug-dealing activities and organized crime. The murder of Veronica Guerin in June 1996, an Irish investigative journalist who had been persistently reporting on various elements of the 'drugs Mafia', might indeed be considered a turning point. Her reports and the public outcry following her death resulted in a palpable increase in the determination to deal with the criminal activities of major drug-barons. For example, the introduction of powerful legislation to allow the confiscation of assets from drug-dealers coincided with the backlash from Ms Guerin's death. From 1996 onwards the legal back up for law enforcement was strengthened and extended. Eleven pieces of legislation were introduced.

It is perhaps interesting to note that in attempting to create, rationalize and effect policy and political responses, the outcome of research and the experiences of other countries have had little impact in Ireland. Some examples of this lack of integrating research with policy are shown in the delay in formulating policy strategy to target socioeconomic factors which had long been identified as central to the development of the drugs problem. Further examples relate to the awareness of the usefulness of harm-reduction strategies as part of a comprehensive drugs service. The concept of harm reduction, for example, was developed in the late 1970s (Buning and van Brussel, 1995: 93), yet it did not become part of Irish policy for another decade. Indeed, education as a preventative measure – strongly endorsed by government policy – is not strongly supported in research findings (Cripps, 1997).

Delays in incorporating new ideas and an apparent determination to learn by our own mistakes hamper the development of the most effective policies and limit the flexibility and creativity required to tackle the problem which is clearly still a major concern.

EVALUATING CURRENT POLICY

As already discussed, drug policy can be epitomized by reference to two main categories of activity: demand reduction and supply reduction. (See Table 1, p. 323, for an analysis of the demand/supply reduction and individual/community focused policy paradigm.)

Supply Reduction

Taking a look at supply reduction, the aspects of policy directed at achieving this goal fall principally into the domain of the criminal justice and customs and excise systems. Murphy (1996), in an excellent review of prohibitionist policies, concludes that such measures have failed to have a substantial impact on overall drugs-supply. Murphy cites information relating to the relative profitability of drug-dealing, vis à vis the costs of detection and confiscation by law-enforcement agencies, as a factor in the failure of prohibition (Murphy, 1996: 51). He also quotes Superintendent John McGroarty, former Garda Drugs Liaison Officer, who suggested that, while 'cannabis seizures in Europe in 1993 amounted to £170 million, . . . a mere 10% of the quantities available were seized.' (Murphy: 1996: 51). He therefore concludes that 'the occasional drug seizures which are sensationalized by the media, in other words, are merely the tip of an iceberg.' (Murphy, 1996: 50)

The Garda report of 1997 (Keogh) gives a profile of the drug-related crime situation. It suggests that, of the indictable crimes detected during that year, 91 per cent were larceny-type crimes. A reasonable estimate is offered that 43 per cent of these crimes are committed by drug users (Keogh, 1997: xi).

In detailing the profile of known drug users, it becomes evident that strategies which have attempted to address demand reduction have been ineffective in reaching the drug-user population indicted for crimes; 91 per cent were identified as using heroin, with two per cent using methadone. This figure suggests that those drug users who are accessing methadone services are less likely to appear in criminal justice statistics, a finding confirmed in many reports on the effectiveness of methadone maintenance programmes (Ball and Ross, 1991: 1). This research may indicate a need to redress the balance away from the punishment of drug users who commit crimes to feed their habits, and to the expansion of methadone programmes which are consistently proving successful in reducing criminal activity among drug users (Ball and Ross, 1991) Increasing methadone programmes could only be viable with the introduction of clearly defined guidelines and protocols. A protocol is scheduled for circulation in late 1998.

While this is a logical conclusion to draw, a cautionary note must be struck. If policy becomes exclusively concerned with minimizing the negative effect of drug problems on the general public, i.e. crimes against the public committed by drug users, their unrestricted access to methadone is clearly an option. However, there is a danger that this could distract attention away from the structural inequalities that underpin the drugs problem and therefore further ostracize and marginalize those with drug-related difficulties.

The imprisonment of drug users has also been a cause for concern. Anecdotal evidence indicates that a prison sentence, in fact, may mark the beginning of a drug career for some offenders. The continued development of alternatives to custodial sentences is clearly indicated. Projects such as intensive supervision by the probation service, in conjunction with the Bridge Project, appear to offer a more effective response.

In summary, the emphasis on supply reduction has not yet proven itself as a cost-effective tenet of an effective drugs policy. Attention needs to be paid to what aspects of supply-reduction strategies are legitimate and efficient use of resources.

Demand Reduction

Like its related axis of supply reduction, demand reduction comprises a multidimensional set of activities. These include prevention and education, treatment and rehabilitation and also a variety of community based initiatives. The framework is outlined in Table 1 (p. 323).

The current policy strategies are dependent on the successful development of inter-departmental structural initiatives and an extensive partnership model. The primary statutory service provider is the Eastern Health Board. The EHB has restructured its areas of administrative responsibilities in the late 1990s. Initially, the health board introduced a special programme to deal with the drugs issue. In a subsequent reorganization, the current programme was established. The programme manager with responsibility for drugs services holds the position of Manager of the Social Inclusion Programme. This programme, as well as dealing with drugs services, also covers mental health, mental handicap, social inclusion, refugees and health promotion.

The current trend to incorporate drugs issues under the broad umbrella of social inclusion or social development is a welcome advance. Certainly recognition of the social nature, as distinct from the individual pathology, of drug addiction is significant. However, given the struggle to get drugs usage a higher profile in policy formulation, it is important that the issues relating to it do not get sidelined by other social inclusion concerns.

As discussed earlier, most activity until the 1990s centred in the community/supply reduction quadrant and the individual/demand reduction quadrant. In the 1990s, and specifically since 1996, the need to expand on the community/demand reduction dimension has been emphasized. While this paradigm is in fact too restrictive to depict clearly the need for overlap in these areas, it is important to note that all strategies and policy developments must be of an integrated and coordinated nature. This analysis poses some important questions which will serve to stimulate responses which it is hoped will transcend the confines of these limited parameters.

The paradigm in Table 1 raises the question of where individual and supply/demand reduction strategies fit into the policy equation. In fact the paradigm challenges us to review the function of such measures as methadone maintenance and harm reduction, which may be misrepresented if they are viewed only as targeting individual demand reduction. Perhaps they should be viewed as offering an alternative supply to individual drug users. If this move is analysed within the more complex nature of the drugs market, then the presence of alternative sources of supply would serve to undermine the dominant suppliers and therefore might be considered a legitimate supply-reduction approach. This alternative interpretation of methadone maintenance and harm reduction measures provides a clearer rationale for the expansion of such services, than does an attempt simply to reduce demand. This analysis also raises the question of the desirability of offering a more attractive option than methadone. Experiments of heroin programmes in the UK should be monitored with interest. One suggestion is that drugs should be viewed not only as a social, legal and medical concern but also as a business problem. Moving beyond the confines of the four quadrant paradigm, it may be useful to explore the incentives, motivation and rewards that pertain to drug dealing as a business, albeit an illegal business. Some organizational analysis for the field of business and marketing might help to establish a more informed picture of what, in essence, we are attempting to dismantle when we tackle the issue of supply reduction. It seems

Table 1. A Paradigm for Analysis of Drug Policy (Demand-reduction/supply-reduction forming one axis, and an individual/communities focus forming the second.)

INDIVIDUAL	
education and prevention	(offer of alternative supply)
abstinence treatment	methadone maintenance
harm reduction treatment	needle exchange
rehabilitation	targetting of individual dealers
deterrents (prison/probation)	
DEMAND REDUCTION	**SUPPLY REDUCTION**
Education and Prevention	Drugs Squad
Youth Services and Employment	Europol
Diversionary Strategies (e.g. Sport)	Increased number of judges and gardaí
Community-Based Services	Improved Legislation
Development of Community Awareness	Supported Community Action
Estate Management	
Structural Change*	
COMMUNITIES	

*Structural Change is currently aspirational rather than evident in policy.

evident that although drug dealing is a high risk enterprise, the potential rewards encourage involvement. If not the financial reward, then the need to access a personal supply may be the greatest incentive to expand the market-base and encourage new purchasers. The familiar marketing strategy of offering free samples is also a widespread practice in engaging new customers in the illegal drugs market. The employment of a highly motivated sales force in the form of user/dealers is perhaps not unique to the illegal drugs market. This perspective suggests that the drugs policy field must look beyond the confines of already tried strategies to find more effective ways to tackle the problem.

The complexities inherent in dealing with the Irish drug problem can best be illustrated by a case example. Since the early days of community responses to drugs in the 1970s, concern was voiced about the impact on specific areas of the city of a developing concentration of drug-related problems. Communities began to feel abandoned by the law enforcement agencies. The resultant frustration and anger culminated in the Community Action against Drugs Movement (CADs). The initial intent of this movement, to mobilize communities to respond more effectively to the drugs problems in their own communities was commendable. However, over time, a vigilante element grew and was involved in such acts as compulsory evictions and the apparent harassment of persons considered to be users or dealers. Following promises to police these areas and develop community responses, the CADs disbanded. In the 1990s no real progress had been made in these vulnerable communities. Their continued erosion led to the re-emergence of the perceived needs for Community Action against Drugs (Loughran: 1996: 12–13). This revival of community initiatives was supported by organizations such as Inner City Organisations Network which sympathized with their plight.

The Task Force concept was conceived in concert with the partnership movement as developed in other policy measures. The Task Force ideal was designed to formalize relationships and organize voluntary agencies, community action groups and local partnerships with statutory interests. This recognition of the contribution of local communities to their own welfare represented a shift in government drugs strategies. Collaboration and integration became key features of policy.

In the midst of these developments, one issue continued to highlight the inherent difficulties in attempts to address conflicting needs. This was the question of how housing policy could complement and support the work of the Task Forces and enhance community development. The Task Force Reports of 1996 and 1997 affirm the need for estate management. Inevitably, communities had identified that the presence of drug users and, more particularly, drug dealers in their areas was aggravating the situation. Any move to 'clear up' this anti-social behaviour would be welcome. The Task Forces' recommendations regarding estate management incorporated plans to empower local communities in 'greater control of their environment' (Task Force, 1996: 685). The initiatives introduced included:

• Tenant development and information to tenants on the duties and responsibilities of both local authorities and tenants.

• Various steps to ensure improvements in housing management, remedial work schemes and projects to improve run down estates and their immediate environment.

• Legislative proposals to combat anti-social behaviours in local authority housing.

(Task Force, 1996: 85–6)

These initiatives culminated in the Housing (Miscellaneous Provision) Act 1997, which provides for an excluding-order procedure against individual occupants of a local authority house who are involved in anti-social behaviour, including drug dealing. The Act also supports attempts to promote estate management, particularly in the area of partnership and the authority of tenants (Department of Justice correspondence, 1998).

These moves to empower communities to deal with anti-social behaviour and drug dealing, in cooperation with the local housing authority, are certainly progressive. However, the impact of these developments on some drug users should be considered. In a conference held in June 1998, professionals working in the field of drug use claimed that the most difficult problem now being experienced by drug users attempting to come off drugs or to stabilize their lifestyles was home-lessness (Conference on Pilot Drug Project, Community Care Area 5, Dublin, 1998). This escalation in their housing problems was reiterated at the launch of the Merchants Quay Annual Report in July 1998. Removing drug users from communities is an attractive measure, but in the overall resolution of the problem it will in fact create serious difficulties for users attempting to address their problems and also for services trying to attract current users. If users become homeless it exacerbates the chaos in their lives and at a fundamental level makes it even more difficult to keep track of, or to estimate, the numbers involved.

DRUGS POLICY QUESTIONS FOR THE TWENTY-FIRST CENTURY

While the 1990s have witnessed some major progress in the attitude towards and commitment to the dilemmas of drug users, many concerns remain. There is little evidence to support an optimistic view that the drugs problem is abating. Indeed there is reason to be concerned that the problem continues to gain ground. There are then many issues facing policy makers and service providers in the last years of this century. These include:

- The continued development of community responses to the drugs problem is likely to be a central tenet of future policy. However a cautionary note must be struck. Focus on local community task forces may distract from the need to address structural inequalities which must be tackled at national level. Community empowerment is helpful only if it is viewed in the context of overall change and not as a mechanism for dispersing responsibility from central government.

- Task force effectiveness has yet to be reviewed. The question of whether the funding available has been spent disproportionately on the more acceptable aspects of drug prevention and education and not on more contentious areas such as locally based harm minimization services must be examined.

- The continued confidence in the effectiveness of increased legislation as a policy strategy in the area of supply reduction must be a cause for concern. A recent World Health Report tentatively suggests reconsideration of the illegal status of cannabis in the light of the more serious problems being posed by heroin and cocaine use. The climate in Ireland is a long way away from radical legal reforms in relation to drug offences. With limited resources and competing demands for services from all areas, the question of the cost effectiveness of legal sanctions and law enforcement strategies will have to be closely scrutinized. The question is whether or not we can afford to continue to create legal sanctions and whether this will ultimately undermine the whole judicial system. Another concern is the impact of legal sanctions and 'drug-busting' operations on to the availability of hard drugs on the streets.

- There is a need to target clearly specific categories of the population in relation to the drugs issue. The various levels of drug-related problems demand specifically designed approaches. While the demand and supply reduction paradigm may serve as an appropriate overriding ideal, there may be a case for compartmentalizing the problem. This may demand the provision of more flexible and liberal policies for those already caught up in drugs in order to undermine the fabric of the 'drugs industry' per se.

- More comprehensive information is needed about the structure and organization of the drugs 'industry'. The appeal of the high gain for high-risk incentives continues to encourage involvement in this illegal activity. This is not just at the level of 'drugs barons' but, just as importantly, at street level with small-time deals and dealers/users. This aspect must be clearly acknowledged before it can be tackled. The financial gains, whether to feed a habit or simply to make a profit, are incredibly motivating factors in the continued survival and expansion of the drugs market.

For the first time in the history of the drugs problem in Ireland, substantial resources have been channelled into resolving the problem. This coincides with one of the most active phases in the field of drugs policy initiatives. There is a united political will to tackle the problem and the development of a partnership approach holds great promise. The anticipated evaluation of the Task Force activities will be crucial in discovering if apportioning money to the problem is enough or if a radical rethinking of the philosophical, political, social, economic and commercial underpinning of the problem will, in fact, be required.

DEVELOPMENTS IN DRUG-POLICY STRATEGY IN IRELAND

Table 2. SUMMARY OF POLICY INITIATIVES, 1968–85

1968   Establishment of Garda Drug Squad.
1968   Establishment of Working Party on Drug Abuse.
1969   Establishment of National Drug Treatment Centre.
1971   *Report of Working Party on Drug Abuse*
1977   Misuse of Drugs Act.
1983   Special Governmental Task Force on Drug Abuse.
        (Report not published, aspects of it were leaked)
1984   Misuse of Drugs Act.
1984   Criminal Justice Act.
1985   National Coordinating Committee on Drug Abuse.

Table 3. SUMMARY OF GOVERNMENT REPORTS, 1991–98

1991   Government Strategy for the Prevention of Drug Use.
1994   Shaping a Healthier Future
1994   Criminal Justice Act.
1995   A Health Promotion Strategy
1996   EHB Drug Services Review of 1995 and Development
        Plans for 1996 Treated Drug Misuse in the Greater Dublin
        Area a Review of Five Years, 1990–94.
1996   First Report of the Ministerial Task Force on Measures to
        Reduce the Demand for Drugs
1997   Second Report of the Ministerial Task Force on Measures
        to Reduce the Demand for Drugs
1997   Report on Illicit Drug Use and Related Criminal Activity
        in the Dublin Metropolitan Area (Keogh)
1997   Smoking, Alcohol and Drug Use in Cork and Kerry.
1998   Department of Justice and Law Reform Strategy Statement
        1998–2000 *Community Security and Equality.*

Table 4. CURRENT FRAMEWORK FOR DRUGS POLICY MONITORING AND DEVELOPMENT

Cabinet Committee on Social Inclusion
(expanded from Drugs Committee in original Task Force
Report 1996)
chaired by An Taoiseach

|

National Drugs Strategy Team
Coordinated through Department of Tourism, Sports and Recreation
and reporting to Cabinet Committee

|

Eleven Drugs Task Forces
Including members from relevant health board, gardaí, probation service,
welfare, relevant local authority, local youth services, voluntary drug
agencies, community representatives and chairperson proposed by local
Partnership Board and coordination provided by the relevant health board

(Adapted from Task Force, 1996, to include 1998 structures)

Table 5. SUMMARY OF DRUG-RELATED LEGISLATION, 1996–98

The Criminal Assets Bureau Act 1996
The Proceeds of Crime Act 1996
The Criminal Justice (Drug Trafficking) Act 1996
The Disclosure of Certain Information for Taxation and Other
    Purposes Act 1996
Housing (Miscellaneous Provisions) Act 1997
The Criminal Justice (Miscellaneous Provisions) Act 1997
Licensing (Combating Drug Abuse) Act 1997
Bail Act 1997
The Non-Fatal Offences against the Person Act 1997
The Europol Act 1997
Criminal Justice Bill 1997

(Compiled from Department of Justice, Equality and Law Reform Memo, 1998)

RECOMMENDED READING

Butler, S. (1991) 'Drug Problems and Drug Policies in Ireland: A Quarter of a Century Reviewed', *Administration,* 39 (3): 210–33.

First Report of the Ministerial Task Force on Measures and Reduce the Demand for Drugs. (1996). Dublin: Stationery Office.

*Government Strategy to Prevent Drug Misuse (*1991). Dublin: Department of Health.

Murphy, T. (1996) *Rethinking the War on Drugs in Ireland.* Cork: Cork University Press.

O'Higgins, K. (1996) *Treated Drug Misuse in the Greater Dublin Area: A Review of Five Years, 1990–1994.* Dublin: Health Research Board.

Second Report of the Ministerial Task Force on Measures and Reduce the Demand for Drugs (1997). Dublin: Stationery Office.

REFERENCES

Ball, J. and A. Ross (1991) *The Effectiveness of Methadone Maintenance Treatment, Patients, Programs, Services and Outcome.* New York: Springer-Verlag.

Buning, E. and E. van Brussel (1995) 'The Effects of Harm Reduction in Amsterdam', *European Addiction Research,* 1: 92–8

Butler, S. (1991) 'Drug Problems and Drug Policies in Ireland: A Quarter of a Century Reviewed', *Administration,* 39 (3): 210–33.

Butler, S (1994) 'Alcohol and Drug Education in Ireland: Aims, Methods and Difficulties', *Oideas,* Samhradh: 137

Corrigan, D. (1994) *Facts about Drug Abuse in Ireland.* Dublin: Health Promotion Unit, Department of Health.

Cripps, C. (1997) *Drugs: Losing the War.* Cheltenham: New Clarion Press.

Department of Health (1984) *The Psychiatric Services: Planning for the Future* (1984) Report on a Study Group on the Development of the Psychiatric Services. Dublin: Stationery Office.

Department of Health (1991) *Government Strategy to Prevent Drug Misuse.* Dublin: Stationery Office.

Department of Health (1992) *Green Paper on Mental Health.* Dublin: Stationery Office.

Department of Health (1994) *Shaping a Healthier Future: A Strategy for Effective Healthcare in the 1990s* (1994) Dublin: Stationery Office.

Department of Health (1995) *A Health Promotion Strategy, Making the Healthier Choice the Easier Choice.* Dublin: Stationery Office.

Drug Abuse: A Report to the Churches of Ireland (1972) Dublin: Irish Council of Churches.

Eastern Health Board (1996) *Drug Services Review of 1995 and Development Plans for 1996.* Special Board Meeting. Dublin: Eastern Health Board.

Farrell, M and E. Buning (1996) *Review of Drug Services in the Eastern Health Board Area.* Dublin: Eastern Health Board.

Forder, A. (1974) *Concepts in Social Administration: A Framework for Analysis.* London: Routledge & Kegan Paul.

Grasping the Future: An Action Plan for Dublin's North–East Inner City (1994). Dublin: Inner City Organisations Network.

Jackson, A. (1998) *Smoking, Alcohol and Drug Use in Cork and Kerry,* Southern Health Board. Cork: Department of Public Health.

Keogh, F. (1997) *Illicit Drug Use and Related Criminal Activity in the Dublin Metropolitan Area*, Report No. 10/97. Dublin: Garda Research Unit.

Loughran, H (1996), 'Interview with Fergus McCabe', *Irish Social Worker*, 14 (3/4).

McKeown, K., G. Fitzgerald and A. Deehan (1993) *The Merchants Quay Project: A Drug/H.I.V. Service in the Inner City of Dublin 1989–1992*. Dublin: Franciscan Friary, Merchants Quay.

Merchants Quay Project (1998) *Annual Report 1997*. Dublin: Merchants Quay Project.

Moran, R., M. O'Brien and P. Duff (1997) *Treated Drug Misuse in Ireland, National Report 1996*. Dublin: Health Research Board.

Murphy, T. (1996) *Rethinking the War on Drugs in Ireland*. Cork: Cork University Press.

National Alcohol Policy Ireland (1996) Dublin: Department of Health.

O'Hare, A and M. O'Brien (1992) *Treated Drug Misuse in the Greater Dublin Area,1990*. Dublin: Health Research Board.

O'Hare, A. and M. O'Brien (1993) *Treated Drug Misuse in the Greater Dublin Area*. Dublin: Health Research Board.

O'Higgins, K. (1996) *Treated Drug Misuse in the Greater Dublin Area. A Review of Five Years 1990–1994*. Dublin: Health Research Board.

O'Higgins, K. and M. O'Brien (1994) *Treated Drug Misuse in the Greater Dublin Area: Report for 1992 and 1993*. Dublin: Health Research Board.

Report of the Advisory Council on the Misuse of Drugs (1982) London: HMSO.

Report of the Working Party of Drug Abuse (1971) Dublin: Stationary Office.

Task Force (1996) *First Report of the Ministerial Task Force on Measures to Reduce the Demand for Drugs*. Dublin: Stationery Office.

Task Force (1997) *Second Report of the Ministerial Task Force on Measures to Reduce the Demand for Drugs*. Dublin: Stationery Office.

Biographical Details of Authors

Patrick Clancy is an Associate Professor of Sociology and Dean of the Faculty of Philosophy and Sociology at University College Dublin. Before joining UCD, he worked for a number of years as a primary school teacher. His main areas of research and publication are higher education, sociology of education and demographic and social change in Ireland. He was a member of the Secretariat of the National Education Convention and served on a variety of advisory boards and education policy committees. He is a graduate of St Patrick's College, Drumcondra, University College Dublin, and the University of Toronto.

Anthony Cotter is a Senior Probation and Welfare Officer and is presently Co-Director of the Sex Offenders' Treatment Programme in Arbour Hill Prison. He has wide experience in all areas of probation and in the criminal justice system. A member of the accreditation panel of the National Social Work Qualifications Board, he holds a Master's Degree in Social Science from UCD and is a member of the Board of Advisors to the Masters of Social Science (Social Work) Course. He is an Associate Lecturer on the Crime, Order and Social Control Course in the Open University.

Niall Crowley is a Director of Pavee Point Travellers' Centre. He has been working on Travellers' rights issues over the past decade. His is currently Chairperson of the Community Workers' Cooperative and serves as their representative on the National Economic and Social Council.

Eithne Fitzgerald is a Lecturer in Social Policy in the Department of Social Policy and Social Work, University College Dublin. As Minister of State from 1993 to 1997, she drew up Ireland's National Development Plan, set up the National Economic and Social Forum, chaired the Task Force on Violence against Women, and enacted the Ethics in Public

Office Act, the Freedom of Information Act and the Organization of Working Time Act. She has written several social policy reports for the National Economic and Social Council and Combat Poverty Agency. She was Research Officer with Threshold, and is former secretary of the National Campaign for the Homeless.

Patricia Kennedy is a Lecturer in Social Policy in the Department of Social Policy and Social Work, University College Dublin. She also lectures in the area of feminist social policy in the Women's Research and Resource Centre in UCD. She has worked in the voluntary and community sectors as well as in the Department of Justice, Equality and Law Reform. A graduate of University College Cork, she was awarded her PhD by the National University of Ireland.

Hilda Loughran is a Lecturer in the Department of Social Policy and Social Work in UCD. She lectures on a range of topics relating to social work interventions, group work as well as on alcohol and drug policy and treatment. She worked with the Eastern Health Board in Stanhope Alcohol Treatment Centre and spent many years as a housing welfare officer in Dublin County Council. A graduate of UCD, she is currently working on a PhD thesis in alternative alcohol treatment responses.

Frank Mills is a social policy analyst, currently employed as a Superintendent Community Welfare Officer in the Eastern Health Board. He lectures part-time on social policy both in UCD and the Institute of Public Administration. His area of research and practice is income maintenance.

Joe Moran is Senior Resettlement Officer at the Refugee Agency which is under the aegis of the Department of Foreign Affairs. He has worked as a social worker in Beaumont Hospital, the Galway Association for Mentally Handicapped Children, Sunderland Social Services Department and the Eastern Health Board. He studied at University College Cork, Trinity College Dublin, University of Liverpool and the Institute of Public Administration.

Anne O'Loughlin is Senior Social Worker in St Mary's Hospital, Phoenix Park, Dublin. Her social work career has been in the geriatric medicine service of North Dublin City and County. She is a graduate of Social Science from UCD, from where she also holds a Diploma in Applied Social Studies and a Masters Degree in Social Science. She was formerly President of the Irish Association of Social Workers.

Suzanne Quin is a Senior Lecturer in Social Policy and Social Work and Director of postgraduate training in social work in University College Dublin. She has worked as a social worker in St Vincent's Hospital, the Eastern Health Board and as Head of the Social Work Department in the National Rehabilitation Hospital. She has also lectured in social policy in Trinity College Dublin and in the Institute of Public Administration. Her area of research is the psychosocial effects of illness on individuals and families. She is a graduate of Trinity College Dublin, University of Wales and was awarded her PhD by the National University of Ireland.

Bairbre Redmond is a Lecturer in Social Policy and Social Work in University College Dublin. She has worked for over ten years in services for those with intellectual disability and their families. Her areas of research and teaching are disability issues and the development of innovative teaching techniques. A graduate of UCD, she is currently completing her PhD on new ways to develop equitable and productive relationships between parents who have children with disability and the professionals they encounter.

Valerie Richardson is a Senior Lecturer in the Department of Social Policy and Social Work, University College Dublin. Her research interests are childcare policy and children's rights, European and Irish family policy, in particular lone parenthood, the integration of work and family roles, and social work and the law. She is a graduate of the University of Wales, undertook her postgraduate professional training in social work in the University of Edinburgh, and was awarded her PhD by the National University of Ireland.

David Silke works in the Combat Poverty Agency as a research officer. He also teaches social policy in the Department of Social Policy and Social Work, and the Equality Studies Centre, University College Dublin, the Institute of Public Administration and the Open University in Ireland. His particular areas of interest are taxation and social welfare policy, educational disadvantage and issues regarding older people. He worked as a Senior Research Officer in the Analytical Services Division of the Department of Social Security (UK). He is a graduate of University College Dublin and of the London School of Economics.

Index